The TK!Solver® Book

A Guide to Problem-Solving In Science, Engineering, Business, and Education

Milos Konopasek
Sundaresan Jayaraman

Osborne/McGraw-Hill
Berkeley, California

Published by
Osborne/McGraw-Hill
2600 Tenth Street
Berkeley, California 94710
U.S.A.

For information on translations and book distributors outside of the U.S.A., please write to Osborne/McGraw-Hill at the above address.

The TK!Solver® Book

1234567890 DODO 8987654

ISBN 0-88134-115-0

Judy Ziajka, Acquisitions Editor
Gail Todd, Technical Editor
Ralph Baumgartner, Technical Reviewer
Ted Gartner, Copy Editor
Judy Wohlfrom, Text Design
Yaski Okita, Cover Design

To my family.
M.K.

To my parents.
S.J.

CONTENTS

PREFACE

TK!Solver is an innovative software product conceived and designed to help people who are experts in their fields but who have no specialized knowledge of computers to gain direct access to the information processing power of a personal computer. First-time users may be overwhelmed by TK!Solver's enormous problem-solving potential. They may ask, "How can I possibly control all this power?" Our first objective in writing this book was to answer this question. The book explains in detail, and illustrates by example, the concept of equation processing as embodied in the Direct and Iterative Solvers, the TK!Solver information sheets, the command structure, the functions, and other features.

Our second objective was to share the benefits of our 15 years combined experience with the concept of computer-assisted problem-solving that permits the user to communicate with the computer at the level of mathematical models and relationships rather than by writing and running computer programs.

In this era of making things obvious and effortless we do take a risk by telling readers of this book and users of TK!Solver, "TK! is a great amplifier of your knowledge and skill; accordingly, in order to take advantage of it, you should command a certain critical mass of mathematical and subject-specific knowledge." Our final objectives were to show how a TK!Solver user can learn applied math through hands-on experience with computers, and how human skills and the capabilities of TK!Solver can be combined and applied to quantitative problem-solving in the broad areas of mathematics, science, engineering, finance, and management.

We wish to express our profound thanks to the many individuals at Software Arts and Osborne/McGraw-Hill without whose efforts neither TK!Solver nor this book would have become a reality. We also would like to acknowledge the encouragement and support we received from our families during the course of this project.

January 1984
Milos Konopasek
Sundaresan Jayaraman

1

Introduction

The statement "Now you don't have to think like a computer to use one!" is a trademark-protected motto under which Software Arts, Inc. introduced its new product TK!Solver to the personal computer market. These few words highlight the fact that traditionally the computer user or programmer had to think in terms of a sequence of elementary operations that the computer had to perform in order to produce the desired results. TK!Solver relieves the computer user of the task of setting up this sequence and of writing a program. It redistributes the burden of the problem-solving process by shifting a substantial portion of it onto the computer.

The first product of Software Arts, VisiCalc, made history by a similar redistribution of chores between humans and computers. VisiCalc is well suited to perform calculations that follow predetermined sequences of operations, and it provides for generating, manipulating, and accessing tables of data. VisiCalc proved to be a timely match between people's needs and the rising affordability and power of personal computers. VisiCalc and other spreadsheet programs that followed in VisiCalc's footsteps have since become indispensable components of personal computer software for business and other applications. Apart from spreadsheets, there are other categories of applications software for personal computers such as word processing, data base management, presentation graphics, and communications.

TK!Solver differs from other software (including spreadsheets) in its philosophy, design, and purpose. It is a trendsetter for an entirely new category of computer software, the category of "Equation Processors" or "Equation Solvers."

The "TK" in TK!Solver stands for Tool Kit, implying that there are several problem-solving tools in the kit and more to be expected. The exclamation mark refers to the Action key, which is pressed to solve a problem or to make other things happen. TK!Solver solves problems for professionals working with numbers and formulas. It does this by processing equations entered in their natural form.

PROBLEMS, COMPUTERS, AND TK!SOLVER

Computer-assisted problem-solving typically goes through the following steps:

Problem → Model → Algorithm → Program → Results

The first step, based on the analysis of the problem, is to set up a mathematical model expressing the relationships between the variables. Then an algorithm must be developed for solving specific problems. Next a program implementing the algorithm is written in a conventional programming language. A considerable amount of time is spent in these two stages, especially in the programming stage when the computer must be instructed in a step-by-step manner. Finally, of course, the program has to be debugged and run. All this means that a user has to "think like a computer" to solve a problem. This siphons a lot of time into mundane tasks like fixing an unmatched parenthesis or formatting the output correctly. Solving a slightly different problem often means modifying the program and sometimes even reworking the algorithm. And changes in the model invariably mean that the user has to modify the algorithm first and then the program.

TK!Solver shortcuts this problem-solving process by eliminating two steps—developing an algorithm and writing a program. Instead, the user inputs the mathematical model directly using standard algebraic notation. The model is now ready to solve a variety of problems without requiring reformulation of its rules each time it is used. Asking "what happens if" and "how to" questions becomes a simple matter of changing the variable values and pressing the Action key. Thus, the problem-solving process with TK!Solver can be represented as follows:

Problem → Model → Results

can be considered a non-procedural, very high-level computer language: "non-procedural" because its user doesn't need to define particular computation procedures and "very high-level" because the user communicates with the computer at the level of rules or relationships, that is, without the tedium of setting up the sequences of instructions or program statements required in high-level languages like BASIC, FORTRAN, or Pascal.

TK!Solver models usually reflect certain segments of subject-specific knowledge represented by the mathematical relationships, associated data, and comments. The fact that knowledge in the model format is readily available to the user for solving relevant problems makes TK!Solver an ideal framework for developing simple versions of so-called expert systems.

THE SCOPE OF THIS BOOK

The book follows TK!Solver's structure and logic. Since TK!Solver is intended for a diverse audience, this book will try to accommodate readers with vastly differing backgrounds, interests, and needs. Some parts may be hard to follow for some people and elementary for others. If you find a section difficult, don't despair; skip or just browse through it on the first reading. Most of the chapters can be read independently of each other.

Chapter 2, however, should be considered a prerequisite for all of the chapters that follow. In this chapter, the authors conduct a "guided tour through the world of TK!Solver"; the skills acquired during this tour should equip you to use TK!Solver at once. You should participate by trying everything on your computer.

Chapters 3, 4, and 5 complement, systematize, and in some instances, extend the information given in the *TK!Solver Instruction* and *Reference Manuals*. Chapter 3 deals with the organization and composition of the sheets and subsheets. Chapter 4 discusses the entire command structure. Chapter 5 summarizes the syntax and semantics of the rule language used for building TK!Solver models. You may skip this fairly technical chapter or parts of it at first and return to it later. You can also use it for reference and arbitration if you have problems with the model design or resolution.

Chapters 6, 7, and 11 will help you design models for more complex applications. Chapter 6 explains and illustrates the use of special and TK-specific functions. Chapter 7 covers thoroughly the basics of model design. It introduces a few helpful concepts, such as the Relationship graph (the TK!Solver equivalent of flowcharts used in sequential programming). Chapter 11 takes the subject of model design still further; it shows how to build conditional rules and how to do a few other things that you might not expect to be feasible in TK!Solver (logical inferences, building a random number generator, creating drill exercises to quiz a student on a particular subject, interspersing the numerical problem-solving process with English, and so on).

Chapters 8 and 9 give you a thorough insight into the workings of the Direct Solver and the Iterative Solver—the two main TK!Solver problem-solving tools. These chapters demystify the seemingly magic powers of TK!Solver, show its limitations, and advise you how to get the most out of TK!Solver, how to formulate problems to avoid errors, and how to interpret and remedy the error conditions.

The ability to solve sets of non-linear equations iteratively is the most coveted of TK!Solver's features. Chapter 9 discusses in detail the principles of the Newton-Raphson procedure used in the Iterative Solver and also the art and science of formulating the problems and choosing the guess variables and their values.

Chapter 10 deals with the concepts of lists and List Solving. A special treatment is given to the somewhat perplexing relationship between List Solving and List functions. Chapter 12 discusses the relative merits of TK!Solver, BASIC, and spreadsheet programs for problem-solving. The chapter shows how a single short TK!Solver model can substitute for eight different BASIC programs. Chapter 12 also shows you how to interface TK!Solver with spreadsheets, sequential programs, and word-processing programs.

The last five chapters discuss specific applications of TK!Solver in a variety of fields. You will be able to find a selection of models pertaining to specific disciplines (such as mechanical engineering, financial management, introductory science, and building design and construction) in the TK!SolverPacks published by Software Arts. Each of these SolverPacks covers topics pertaining to a particular discipline. The SolverPacks may help you appreciate the breadth and depth of the role of TK!Solver as a depository of subject-specific knowledge and a problem-solving tool combined.

The last five chapters are intended to convey the same message, although with fewer models per application area. Another distinction between SolverPacks and the models in these chapters is that on many occasions the authors could not resist going into more details of TK!Solver methodology than were warranted by a particular topic.

Though a knowledge of the subject area is not absolutely essential for understanding the examples presented in these chapters, it definitely will enhance your understanding of what TK!Solver can do. These case studies show how knowledge from reference literature and other sources can be directly translated into TK models which, in turn, can be used not only for problem-solving in the subject-matter domain, but also as an educational tool and launching pad for further exploration.

Chapter 13, "Case Studies: Mathematics," starts by turning a quadratic equation formula upside down (that is, solving for unknown coefficients from known roots) and shows how to extend the mathematical capabilities of TK!Solver to evaluate definite integrals or to get solutions of differential equations. Chapters 14 and 15 (applications in science, engineering, finance, and management) deal with areas in which TK!Solver is most popular.

Chapters 16 and 17 discuss home applications and word problems and demonstrate some less technical but equally enlightening examples of TK!Solver use. You will see how TK!Solver clears the way for the mathematical interpretation of mind-boggling word problems and yields their solutions on the spot. A simple "dui" model shows the essence of using TK!Solver for decision-making under constraints: just one formula and one law, and you can find out either how much you can safely drink if you want to leave a party at a particular time, or how long you have to stay if you drink a specified amount!

The TK!Solver package comes with thorough documentation that explains what to do in the process of using the program. In contrast, this book not only explains what to do, but how the program works and how to use its different features to the utmost advantage. TK!Solver brings about a radical change in the use of personal computers for problem-solving. This book should give you the necessary guidance and encouragement to explore these new avenues.

TECHNICAL NOTES

The exercises and examples in this book were developed on the IBM Personal Computer. The operation and response of other personal computers running TK!Solver may differ slightly. In general, TK!Solver behaves the same regardless of the computer make. As a result, the material in the book is generic, that is, applicable to different versions of TK!Solver running on different machines.

The TK!Solver program itself may change slightly from one version to another. The authors have had a chance to try several released and prerelease versions and found that the responses were identical in all respects except for such minor details as scaling of graphs or, in a few instances, error pointing. Don't let these minor differences distract or confuse you; the correct results returned by different versions are obviously identical.

Most of the figures in the book reflect the state of the sheets as they appear on the screen at different points in the problem-solving process. As a space-saving and highlighting measure, the irrelevant portions of the screen image have been cut off in both column-wise and row-wise directions. The position of the cursor and the corresponding information in the Status line on the top of the screen have also been ignored unless they are relevant to the discussion. Variable names are set in italics and anything that is to be typed into the computer is printed in boldface.

2

A Guided Tour Through The World of TK!Solver

In this chapter we introduce some of the commands of TK!Solver and take you through a guided tour of its features. As you proceed through the chapter, you may want to try the examples on your personal computer. First, of course, you must load TK!Solver into the computer and have available one or more formatted disks for saving files created during the exercises. The *TK!Solver Instruction Manual* explains how to format disks and how to load the program.

When you initially load TK!Solver you will see the Variable and Rule Sheets displayed in two different windows—top and bottom respectively—as shown in Figure 2-1. The cursor is in the first row in the Rule Sheet. Interaction with TK!Solver is primarily through these sheets, six other sheets, and three subsheets discussed in detail in Chapter 3.

This interaction is carried out through a well-structured set of commands which is easy to master. In addition, an excellent map of the TK!Solver world—the poster with the summary of the commands and sheets—is supplied with the software package. This map will be a big help during our guided tour as well as during subsequent use of the program. We now describe some of the basic commands necessary for accessing the different sheets and for entering information in them.

```
(1r) Rule:                                                          196/
For Help, type ?
==================== VARIABLE SHEET =================================
St Input      Name    Output     Unit       Comment
-- -----      ----    ------     ----       -------


=================== RULE SHEET =======================================
S Rule
- ----
```

Figure 2-1.
The Variable and Rule Sheets

BASIC ACCESS AND MOVEMENT COMMANDS

Information is entered in specific locations called *fields.* You move the cursor to the desired field using the Arrow keys. The direction of cursor movement depends on the particular Arrow key pressed. In order to let TK!Solver accept the typed-in information, press either the Enter key or one of the Arrow keys. When you press an Arrow key, the entry, if valid, is accepted and the cursor moves in the direction designated by the Arrow key. The Break key can be used to interrupt any action, for example, entering or editing information or solving.

You move the cursor from one window to the other with the Switch command, that is, pressing the ; key. The Dive command is used to access a sheet's dependent subsheet. Typing > executes the Dive command. The Return command, which is the opposite of the Dive command, is executed by typing <. Executing this command returns you to the sheet or subsheet from which you dived.

BAILING OUT WHEN LOST

During the course of the following tour, you may inadvertently make some typing mistakes that prevent you from moving farther with us. If you spot your mistake before pressing the Enter or Arrow keys, you may use either the Backspace key, which will erase the character and move the cue to the left, or the Break key, which will produce a beep and restore the previous contents of the field.

When you type in something blatantly incorrect, TK!Solver will beep, will not accept the entry, and will wait for you to correct it. Sometimes, however, your entry may be valid but not what you wanted. In that case it is accepted by TK!Solver. If you have entered a wrong value, correct it simply by entering the right one. If you have entered a value in the wrong field, remove it by typing **/B** and pressing the Enter key. If an incorrect entry is followed by a computer action (for example, getting into the wrong sheet, solving an incorrectly formulated problem, and so on), you could become really lost. But depending on your level of acquired TK!Solver competence, you can either pick up the trail by simple remedial action (you will soon see that this is not hard at all), or you can wipe the slate clean by typing **/RAY** and start again.

CALCULATOR MODE

We begin the tour with the illustration of a simple and very useful feature of TK!Solver—Calculator mode. Consider the example of finding the area of one face of a quarter. The quarter is circular in shape, so the area of one face can be expressed as π r^2. Its radius r is 1.24 cm.

Load TK!Solver into the computer. Then move the cursor to the Input field of the Variable Sheet by pressing the ; key. This executes the Switch command. Type **pi()*1.24^2** and press the Enter key. Note TK!Solver's way of representing π by pi(). The solution to the problem in cm^2, 4.8305129, is displayed immediately. The value displayed in the Status line, 4.8305128642 (see Figure 2-2), is the complete internal representation of the calculated value up to 11 or 12 digits. The value in the Input field, however, is rounded up to fit the field width.

This example illustrates the use of TK!Solver in the simplest possible way—as a calculator. You can experiment with other examples, such as finding the monthly pay if the annual income is $30,000 (type **30000/12**

```
(1i) Input: 4.8305128642

==================== VARIABLE SHEET ===============...
St Input      Name     Output     Unit       Comment
-- -----      ----     ------     ----       -------
   4.8305129
```

Figure 2-2.
Partial screen with area of a quarter

and press the Enter key), or finding the decadic logarithm of 3000 (type **log(3000)** and press the Enter key). There is obviously much more to TK!Solver than the Calculator mode. However, this mode comes in handy for assigning input values when their evaluation is required (for example, typing **34/8** instead of dividing manually and then assigning the resulting 4.25).

Now reset the sheets by typing /**RAY**. TK!Solver blanks all the sheets and returns the cursor to the first rule field in the Rule Sheet.

CREATING AND SOLVING A MODEL WITH ONE EQUATION

Consider two lots of land with areas a and b that are to be swapped for one rectangular lot of equal area with sides c and d. Using consistent units for length and area (say, miles and square miles), you can express the equality of the areas to be swapped by the equation

$$a + b = c * d$$

Suppose several different options are available, and you wish to examine them by solving the equation for different unknowns or for various combinations of the input and output variables given as follows:

Inputs	**Output**
a,b,c	d
a,b,d	c
a,c,d	b
b,c,d	a

You can create a single-equation model that can solve for any of these combinations without having to reformulate the equation.

Type the equation "as is" in the first Rule field of the Rule Sheet and press the Enter key. As TK!Solver checks the rule syntax, the variables encountered are displayed automatically in the Name field of the Variable Sheet. When the rule is parsed successfully, an asterisk appears in the corresponding Status field. You can examine the status of the equation by moving the cursor to the Status field (using the Left Arrow key). The message "Unsatisfied" appears in the Status line; this means that the equation has not been solved. The screen display will look like Figure 2-3.

Consider the following problem: what is the value of b when $a=3$, $c=4$, and $d=7$? Using the Switch command (;), move the cursor to the Input

```
(1s) Status: * Unsatisfied

==================== VARIABLE SHEET ===============...
St Input       Name     Output     Unit       Comment
-- -----       ----     ------     ----       -------

               a
               b
               c
               d


==================== RULE SHEET ===================...
S Rule
- ----
* a+b=c*d
```

Figure 2-3.
Variable and Rule Sheets after rule entry

field of variable a. Type its value, **3**, and press the Enter key. To move to the Input field of c, press the Down Arrow key twice. Type **4** and press the Down Arrow key. This assigns the value 4 to c and also moves the cursor to the Input field of d. Complete the problem definition by typing **7** and pressing the Enter key. The model is now ready to be solved; the Variable Sheet should look like Figure 2-4.

When you press the ! key (called the Action key), the message "Direct Solver" appears in the Prompt/Error line (indicating the solver being used) and disappears when b is evaluated and displayed in its Output field, as shown in Figure 2-5. Also note that there is no asterisk in the Status field of the rule; this indicates that the equation has been solved.

The same model can be used for working with any of the other input combinations as well. You can easily find out what the value of d should be when b=20 while a and c remain unchanged. With the cursor in the Input field of d, type /**B** and press the Enter key; the value is blanked out. Using

```
==================== VARIABLE SHEET ===============...
St Input       Name     Output     Unit       Comment
-- -----       ----     ------     ----       -------
   3           a
               b
   4           c
   7           d
```

Figure 2-4.
Variable Sheet with values assigned

```
==================== VARIABLE SHEET ===============...
St Input       Name     Output     Unit        Comment
-- -----       ----     ------     ----        -------
   3           a
               b        25
   4           c
   7           d


=================== RULE SHEET ==================...
S Rule
- ----
  a+b=c*d
```

Figure 2-5.
Variable and Rule Sheets after solution for unknown *b*

```
==================== VARIABLE SHEET ===============...
St Input       Name     Output     Unit        Comment
-- -----       ----     ------     ----        -------
   3           a
   20          b
   4           c
               d        5.75
```

Figure 2-6.
Variable Sheet after solution for unknown *d*

the Up Arrow key, move the cursor to the Input field of b. Assign the new value for b by typing **20** and pressing the Enter key. Press the Action key !, and d is evaluated as 5.75 (see Figure 2-6). Note that the cursor can be in any field in the Variable Sheet (or Rule Sheet) when you press the Action key to solve the problem.

CREATING AND SOLVING A MODEL WITH MORE THAN ONE EQUATION

The land-swapping problem in the previous section introduced the concept of a TK!Solver model and demonstrated its flexibility. The equation $a+b=c*d$ can be thought of as a common mathematical equation. Usually, however, mathematical models consist of more than one equation, rule, or constraint. Therefore, let us add one more equation,

$$sin(a-c) = e + f$$

to the model.

Move the cursor to the Rule Sheet with the Switch command ;. Next press the Down Arrow key to move the cursor to the second Rule field. Then type the new equation and press the Enter key. You will see the new variables e and f added to the Variable Sheet as the rule is being parsed. Figure 2-7 shows the Variable and Rule Sheets. Solve this model with input variables $a=0.1$, $d=4$, $e=0.2$, and $f=-0.5$.

Use the Switch command ; again to move the cursor to the Variable Sheet. Blank out all the variable values at once by typing /**RVY**. Using the Enter or Down Arrow keys, assign the values of the input variables.

Press the Action key !. The model is solved and the results are displayed in the Output field as shown in Figure 2-8. An examination of the known variable values and the rules makes it clear that TK!Solver evaluated the value of c from the second rule and used this value to calculate b from the first rule, thereby resolving the entire model.

```
==================== VARIABLE SHEET ===============...
St Input      Name    Output    Unit      Comment
-- -----      ----    ------    ----      -------
   3          a
   20         b
   4          c
              d       5.75
              e
              f

=================== RULE SHEET ===================...
S Rule
- ----
* a+b=c*d
* sin(a-c)=e+f
```

Figure 2-7.
Variable and Rule Sheets after entry of second rule

```
==================== VARIABLE SHEET ===============...
St Input      Name    Output      Unit      Comment
-- -----      ----    ------      ----      -------
   .1         a
              b       1.5187706
              c       .40469265
   4          d
   .2         e
   -.5        f
```

Figure 2-8.
Variable Sheet with input values and b,c evaluated

TK!Solver has the intelligence to select the solution path depending on the problem formulation. You tell it what you know, and it figures out the way to calculate the rest. TK!Solver evaluates as much as it can with the given information and stops when it cannot go any farther. If there are any rules that remain unresolved, asterisks will appear next to them in their Status fields.

Consider this modification of the problem. What is the value of *a* if the values of *d*, *e*, and *f* remain as they are and $b=1.2$? First you must blank out the input value of *a* and then assign 1.2 to *b*. Press the Action key !. The "Direct Solver" message comes on and disappears after a few seconds. But the asterisks remaining in the Status fields of the rules indicate that none of the equations has been solved. The reason is that the Direct Solver couldn't solve either equation for any single unknown. Don't despair, however. TK!Solver is equipped with the Iterative Solver which comes to the rescue.

A GLIMPSE AT THE ITERATIVE SOLVER

Iteration involves repeating a process and changing the parameters of that process along the way until some predefined conditions are satisfied. This technique can be used for solving the previous deadlocked problem: if you declare the variables *a* and *c* as free parameters, TK!Solver will iterate (that is, refine the guessed values of *a* and *c*) and resolve the model repeatedly until the equations are satisfied within a certain error limit. In this way, the original problem will be solved.

In fact, you only need to set up one parameter, either *a* or *c*. In this case, declare *a* as the parameter by typing **G** (for Guess) in *a*'s Status field. Then type **1** in *a*'s Input field (1 will be the initial guess value starting the iteration). The Variable Sheet will look as shown in Figure 2-9.

To solve the model, press the Action key. TK!Solver displays the message "Iterative Solver: 1 out of 10" in the Prompt/Error line. The value of *a* changes as the iteration proceeds, and after five iterations, the "G" disappears from the Status field and the calculated value of *a* appears in the Output field. TK!Solver also evaluates *c*, so the asterisks disappear entirely from the status field of Rule Sheet, indicating that the evaluated values of *a* and *c* along with the input values satisfy the equations. The Variable Sheet looks as shown in Figure 2-10.

```
==================== VARIABLE SHEET ===============...
St Input        Name     Output       Unit        Comment
-- -----        ----     ------       ----        -------
 G 1            a
   1.2          b
                c
   4            d
   .2           e
   -.5          f
```

Figure 2-9.
Variable Sheet with guess value for *a*

```
==================== VARIABLE SHEET ===============...
St Input        Name     Output       Unit        Comment
-- -----        ----     ------       ----        -------
                a        -.0062569
   1.2          b
                c        .29843578
   4            d
   .2           e
   -.5          f
```

Figure 2-10.
Variable Sheet after iterative solution

In the previous example, the Iterative Solver was used to solve a set of simultaneous equations. Now let's see it work in a real-life application. You may save the current model before resetting the sheets. Type /**SS** and TK!Solver responds with the prompt "Save: Filename:". Type **SIMULT** and press the Enter key; the model is saved under the name SIMULT. Now reset the sheets by typing /**RAY**.

THE ITERATIVE SOLVER AND INTEREST RATE ON A LOAN

Hardly any mathematical formula is used, abused, and misused as often as the formula for loan repayment. The formula is

$$R = \frac{(i/100) * P/N}{1-(i/(100*N) + 1)\hat{}-(N*Y)}$$

where

R — regular payment ($)
i — annual interest rate (%)

P — loan amount ($)
N — number of payments per year
Y — number of years over which the loan is repaid.

Let's say a sum of $6000 is borrowed from a bank at 16% interest to be repaid in monthly installments over a period of 5 years. What is the amount of each installment? In this case, $i=16$, $P=6000$, $N=12$, $Y=5$, and $R=?$. For now enter the formula as is in the Rule Sheet. Soon you will learn to use the unit conversion feature and will not have to divide *i* by 100 (for converting percent into the decimal form) when entering the formula in the Rule Sheet. Figure 2-11 shows the Rule Sheet with the formula. Move the cursor to the Variable Sheet and enter the known values of the input variables. To solve, press the Action key. The regular payment *R* is evaluated as $145.91.

Suppose, however, that the borrower wants to repay the loan at $140 per month instead of $145.91 over the same period. Obviously the interest rate has to be lower than 16%. To find the new interest rate, blank out the input value for *i*, assign 140 to *R*, and press the Action key. The equation remains unsolved and *i* is not evaluated. The reason is that the variable being solved for, *i*, occurs twice in the equation, and its value cannot be extracted from that equation by the Direct Solver. (This is discussed in detail in Chapter 8.)

So you must help TK!Solver by assigning a guess value for an unknown variable, in this case the interest, *i*. Let your guess be 15%. Enter **15** in the Input field of *i*, move the cursor to its Status field, and type **G**. Figure 2-12 shows the Variable Sheet after these operations.

When you press the Action key you invoke the Iterative Solver. The value of *i* converges to 14.13% in four iteration steps and moves into the Output field. You may save this model with the solution under the name LOAN.

Until now you have used the Direct and Iterative Solvers, the two main instruments that make TK!Solver a powerful and flexible problem-solving tool. We will now present some other features of TK!Solver.

```
=================== RULE SHEET ===========...
S Rule
- ----
* R=(i/100)*P/N/(1-(i/(100*N)+1)^-(N*Y))
```

Figure 2-11.
Rule Sheet with loan formula

```
==================== VARIABLE SHEET ===============...
St Input       Name    Output    Unit       Comment
-- -----       ----    ------    ----       -------
   140         R
 G 15          i
   6000        P
   12          N
   5           Y
```

Figure 2-12.
Variable Sheet with guess value for *i*

UNIT CONVERSION

Information about measurable quantities is meaningful only when both the numerical value and the unit of measurement are specified. Thus, to say "it weighs 5 pounds" is meaningful. To say "it weighs 5" is not. The Unit field in the Variable Sheet is used for associating units with variable values. The Unit Conversion feature in TK!Solver simplifies the conversions between the different units of measurement. To illustrate this feature, let's look at an example dealing with the concepts of electric current, power, and energy. The basic relationships are as follows:

Ohm's Law: $I = V/R$

Electric Power: $power = V * I$

Electrical Energy: $energy = power * time$

where

I — current in amperes (amp)
V — voltage in volts (volt)
R — resistance in ohms (ohm)
power — power in watts (W)
energy — energy in joules (J)
time — time in seconds (sec)

Reset the sheets by typing /**RAY** and enter the three relationships in the Rule Sheet.

You can add comments on the Variable Sheet to make your model self-explanatory and easier to use. In this instance, move the cursor to the Comment field of I in the Variable Sheet, type **current**, and press the Enter key. In the same way add appropriate comments to the other variables. A set of such comments is shown in Figure 2-13.

```
==================== VARIABLE SHEET =============================...
St Input      Name       Output      Unit       Comment
-- -----      ----       ------      ----       -------
              I                      amp        current
              V                      volt       voltage
              R                      ohm        resistance
              power                  W          power delivered
              energy                 J          energy supplied
              time                   sec        time period

=================== RULE SHEET =================================...
S Rule
- ----
* I=V/R                                       "  Ohm's Law
* power=V*I                                   "  Electric Power
* energy=power*time                           "  Electrical Energy
```

Figure 2-13.
Variable and Rule Sheets with units and comments

There is no Comment field in the Rule Sheet, so rule comments have to be appended to the rules if there is space. To do so, move the cursor to the first rule field in the Rule Sheet and invoke the Editor by typing /**E**. The Prompt/Error line reads "(Edit)" and a cue appears in the first character position of the rule.

Using the Right Arrow key, move the cue to the end of the rule and enter a few spaces with the space bar. Then type ", which signifies that anything following is a comment. Type **Ohm's Law** and press the Enter key. The field now displays the equation and also the comment in it. Similarly, add **Electric Power** to the second rule and **Electrical Energy** to the third rule. The Rule Sheet should look like Figure 2-13.

Now enter the appropriate unit names for each variable in the Unit field on the Variable Sheet. For example, with the cursor in the Unit field of *I* type **amp** and press the Enter key. Similarly, enter the units for the remaining variables. The Variable Sheet with the unit names appears as shown in Figure 2-13.

Some basics about specifying units for variables are worth noting here. Associated with each variable are two units called the Calculation Unit and Display Unit. By filling the Unit field of a variable for the first time in a model you establish the so-called Calculation Unit. As the name suggests, calculations will be performed with the value of the variable in this unit. The way in which the variable appears in the rules should be consistent with the chosen Calculation Unit.

The unit name displayed in the Unit field is the Display Unit. Whenever the Calculation and Display Units for a variable are different, the conversion of values is performed according to the unit conversion defined in the Unit Sheet. For example, the Calculation Unit for *time* in our model is sec. However, you would want to have 4500 sec displayed as 75 minutes, or 1.25 hour. This means the Display Unit for *time* should be either minute or hour, and the conversions between these two units and sec have to be defined in the Unit Sheet. Table 2-1 shows the list of appropriate units and conversion factors for the present model.

Display the Unit Sheet by typing **=U**. Move the cursor to the appropriate fields and key in the unit conversions given in Table 2-1. Notice that the first two definitions on the sheet have scrolled out of view. To see the entire sheet, type **/W1** so there is only one window on the screen. Now move the cursor to the first conversion definition. The Unit Sheet display is shown in Figure 2-14.

Once such a model (including unit conversions) has been built, it can be used to solve problems typically found in a physics textbook. For example,

Table 2-1.
Unit Conversions

From	To	Multiply By
hour	min	60
min	sec	60
m	cm	100
in	cm	2.54
m^2	cm^2	10000
W	cal/sec	0.239
hp	W	746
J	cal	0.239
kW	W	1000
kWh	J	3600000

```
==================== UNIT SHEET ===============...
From      To         Multiply By  Add Offset
----      --         -----------  ----------
hour      min        60
min       sec        60
m         cm         100
in        cm         2.54
m^2       cm^2       10000
J         cal        .239
W         cal/sec    .239
hp        W          746
kW        W          1000
kWh       J          3600000
```

Figure 2-14.
Unit Conversion table entered in the Unit Sheet

an electric motor takes 4.5 amp from a 110-volt line; determine the power input and energy, in W and kWh respectively, supplied to the motor in two hours.

Display the Variable Sheet by typing **=V** to assign the given input values. The Calculation Unit and also the Display Unit for *time* is sec. Since it is given in hours, the Display Unit for *time* should be changed to hours. Move the cursor to the Unit field of *time* and type **hour**. Enter **2**, the given value, in its Input field. Likewise, assign the values for *I* and *V*. The model is ready to be resolved.

When you press the Action key !, you invoke the Direct Solver, and both *power* and *energy* are evaluated with their values displayed in their respective Output fields. Since you want *energy* displayed in kWh, move the cursor to its Unit field, type **kWh**, and press the Enter key. The value in the Output field immediately changes to .99. The Variable Sheet appears as shown in Figure 2-15.

Save the model under the name ELECMOD. It can be used to solve other kinds of problems. As an example, you could find out how much current is drawn by a 100-watt bulb when it is connected to a 120-volt supply. Before solving this problem, blank out the variable values from the previous problem by typing **/RVY**. Assign **120** to *V* and **100** to *power;* then press the Action key.

USER FUNCTIONS

We now show you how to employ the User Function feature to expand the ELECMOD model. (Actually, since the user defines these functions, let's refer to them as "user-defined functions" rather than just "user functions" as in the TK!Solver documentation.) This feature is used to define

```
==================== VARIABLE SHEET =======================...
St Input      Name     Output     Unit       Comment
-- -----      ----     ------     ----       -------
   4.5        I                   amp        current
   110        V                   volt       voltage
              R        24.444444  ohm        resistance
              power    495        W          power delivered
              energy   .99        kWh        energy supplied
   2          time                hour       time period
```

Figure 2-15.
Variable Sheet with input values and *R*, *power*, and *energy* evaluated

functional relationships between variables. For example, the tax rate depends on income; that is, the tax rate is a function of income. Similarly, the gas mileage (miles per gallon) that you get from your car is a function of the make of the car.

We know from physics that the resistance R of a conductor depends on its length L, cross-sectional area A, and resistivity *rho*. This relationship is given by the following formula:

$$R = rho \frac{L}{A}$$

The units for R, *rho*, L, and A are ohm, ohmmeter (ohm-m), meter (m), and square meter (m ^ 2) respectively. The cross-sectional area for a circular conductor is given by the formula

$$A = \pi/4 * d\hat{\ }2$$

where d is the diameter of the conductor in meters. Resistivity is a characteristic of the material, as shown in Table 2-2.

This relationship between material and resistivity can be expressed by means of a user-defined function. Since there is a discrete relationship between the two variables, the so-called Table Lookup Mapping should be chosen for the function. Display the User Function Sheet by typing **=F**. Let *property* be the Name of the function, and let the Domain and Range of this function be populated, respectively, by the values of *material* and *resistivity*.

Enter the function name **property** in the Name field. The appearance of the word "Table" in the Mapping field denotes that the relationship is a Table Lookup. (This is discussed in more detail in Chapters 3 and 6.) Enter **material** in the Domain field and **resistivity** in the Range field. In

Table 2-2.
Resistivity of Materials

Material	Resistivity (ohm-m)
Aluminum	2.63E−8
Copper	1.62E−8
Gold	2.22E−8
Iron	1.1E−7
Platinum	1.11E−7
Silver	1.6E−8

the Comment field enter **Electrical Properties**. The User Function Sheet looks as shown in Figure 2-16.

To enter the values given in Table 2-2, dive into the User Function Subsheet using the Dive command >. The cursor moves to the Domain field of the User Function Subsheet. Since entries in the Domain field are names of materials, that is, symbolic values, they have to be prefixed with single quotes ('). To enter the first material, type **'aluminum** and press the Right Arrow key. The cursor moves to the corresponding Range field; now type either **2.63e−8** or **0.0000000263** and press the Enter key. In a similar manner, enter the rest of the table on the succeeding rows in the appropriate fields. Figure 2-17 shows the filled-out User Function Subsheet.

Change the display back to the User Function Sheet using the Return command <. Then display the Variable Sheet by typing **=V**. TK!Solver allows the entry of function names in the rules only after they have been defined in the User Function Sheet, so now you are able to enter the equation expressing the relationship between *resistivity* and *material* using the function *property*. Move the cursor to the first empty row on the Rule Sheet. Type **rho = property(material)** and press the Enter key. Then

```
(1r) Range: resistivity

==================== USER FUNCTION SHEET =====================..
Name        Domain      Mapping Range     Comment
----        ------      ------- -----     -------
property    material    Table   resistivi Electrical Properties
```

Figure 2-16.
User Function Sheet with function definition

```
==================== USER FUNCTION: property =======...
Comment:                         Electrical Properties
Domain List:                     material
Mapping:                         Table
Range List:                      resistivity
Element Domain          Range
------- ------          -----
1        'aluminum      .0000000263
2        'copper        .0000000162
3        'gold          .0000000222
4        'iron          .00000011
5        'platinum      .000000111
6        'silver        .000000016
```

Figure 2-17.
User Function Subsheet with Domain and Range values

enter the other two formulas given earlier for *R* and *A* to complete the model definition. The Rule Sheet including the comments for the new rules looks like Figure 2-18.

Now move the cursor back to the Variable Sheet and create a single window by typing **/W1**. Enter the units of the newly added variables in the Unit field: **ohm-m** for *rho*, **m** for *L*, **m^2** for *A*, and **m** for *d*. You may also fill the Comment fields of these new variables. Then blank out the old variable values by typing **/RVY**.

Consider the following problem: a copper coil develops 800 cal/sec (variable *power* in the model) when 20 V is applied across its ends. What is the resistance? If the wire has a diameter of 0.1 cm, what length is needed?

Since power is given in cal/sec, change the Display Unit of *power* to **cal/sec**. Similarly, change the Display Unit of *d* to **cm**. In the Input field of *material* type **'copper**. Assign the remaining known variable values, and press the Action key. The variables *rho*, *A*, and *R* are evaluated as shown in Figure 2-19. So the answer is 5.79 m of copper wire. Since the

```
==================== RULE SHEET ======================================...
S Rule
- ----
  I=V/R                                    "   Ohm's Law
  power=V*I                                "   Electric Power
  energy=power*time                        "   Electrical Energy
* rho=property(material)                   "   Functional Relationship
* R/rho=L/A                                "   Resistance
* A=pi()*d^2/4                             "   Cross-sectional area
```

Figure 2-18.
Rule Sheet with user-defined function

```
==================== VARIABLE SHEET ============================...
St Input     Name     Output      Unit       Comment
-- -----     ----     ------      ----       -------
             I        167.36402   amp        current
   20        V                    volt       voltage
             R        .1195       ohm        resistance
   800       power                cal/sec    power delivered
             energy               kWh        energy supplied
             time                 hour       time period
             rho      1.62E-8     ohm-m      electrical resistivity
   'copper   materia                         material of conductor
             L        5.7935235   m          length of conductor
             A        7.8540E-7   m^2        cross-sectional area
   .1        d                    cm         diameter of conductor
```

Figure 2-19.
Variable Sheet with input values and *R*, *rho*, *L*, and *A* evaluated

cross-sectional area A looks very small in m ^ 2, you may want to see it in cm ^ 2. Move the cursor to its Unit field and change m ^ 2 to **cm ^ 2**; the value changes to 0.007854 immediately.

This example illustrates how a user-defined function can be used to define and solve problems involving functional relationships between variables. There are two other kinds of Mappings, Linear Interpolation and Step Mapping, which are discussed in Chapters 3 and 6. You have also seen how TK!Solver can handle non-numerical values while solving a problem.

If you prefer to keep this more general model instead of the previous one, save it under the same name. Type **/SS** and, in response to the filename prompt, type **ELECMOD** and press the Enter key. The disk drive turns and the message "Overwrite filename: ELECMOD.TK: Y N" is displayed in the Prompt/Error line. Since you will lose the old model by saving the new one under the same filename, TK!Solver seeks confirmation prior to overwriting. Respond with **Y** and the new model is saved under the same name, ELECMOD.

LIST SOLVING

A commonly encountered task in science, engineering, and business is cause-effect or trend analysis—the examination of the effect of one or more variables on others in the system being modeled. These variables could be temperature and pressure in a manufacturing process or interest rate and money supply in a financial analysis. In the physics model developed earlier an example would be the dependence of the resistance of a conductor on the temperature.

One way to observe these cause-effect relationships is to solve the model over and over with different values of the input variables and note down the resulting values. However, this could get tedious if the model is fairly large with many relationships involving large numbers of independent and dependent variables.

The List Solving feature in TK!Solver greatly simplifies this task by processing lists of data without your intervention. Input data is drawn from the lists, and the calculated values of output variables are sent to lists during the instance-by-instance evaluation. You can use the Table feature to display lists of data in table form and the Plot feature to plot the data.

To illustrate, consider the following equation:

$$y = \frac{b}{b-a} \; (e^{-ax} - e^{-bx})$$

For fixed values of a and b, you can use the List Solver to examine the influence of x on y. An additional equation

$$t = log(x+1)$$

can be used to generate x values as t goes from 0 to 1 in steps of 0.05. This yields a higher density of x values in the region where the y values change more rapidly.

Reset TK!Solver by typing **/RAY** and enter the first equation in the Rule Sheet using TK!Solver's notation *exp* for exponentiation. Type

y = 1/(1−a/b) * (exp(−a*x)−exp(−b*x))

and press the Enter key. Enter the second equation as is. Declare t, x, and y as lists by typing **L** in their Status fields in the Variable Sheet. Now you must define the list of values for t in its List Subsheet. With the cursor in any field of t, access the List Subsheet using the Dive command twice. The Variable Sheet display is replaced by the List Subsheet, and the cursor is in the first Value field.

Enter the first value, t=**0**. The number 1 in the Element field indicates that it is the first element in the list. Assuming that you need 20 points between 0 and 1 in increments of 0.05, you could go to each Value field and enter 0.05, 0.1, 0.15, 0.2, 0.25, and so on, with 1 in the 21st position.

Fortunately, since you know the first and last values and the number of values needed, the Fill List feature will do the work for you. Invoke the Goto command by typing :. A prompt "Goto: Destination or Search:" appears in the Prompt/Error line. Type **21** and press the Enter key. The cursor jumps to the 21st position. Type **1** and press the Enter key. Then press the Action key ! to fill the intermediate values. The prompt "Fill List Y:N" will appear. Since you want the list filled, type **Y**. The gap between the first and last values is filled by 19 equally spaced intermediate values. To see all the values in the list, create a single window by typing **/W1**. A part of the list of values for t is shown in Figure 2-20.

Note that the Action key has a different role here from the one it has on the Variable and Rule Sheets. As we proceed, you will see that the Action key will perform different actions depending on the sheet from which it is invoked.

Return to the Variable Sheet by invoking the Return command < twice. Make t the input list by typing **I** in its Status field (*I* does not appear on the screen, and the default value 0 comes up in the Input field). Assign a=**0.5** and b=**0.9**. The Variable Sheet should look like Figure 2-21.

To solve, type /**L!**. The message "List Solver 1, Direct Solver" appearing in the Prompt/Error line indicates that the Direct Solver is being

```
==================== LIST: t ===...
Comment:
Display Unit:
Storage Unit:
Element Value
------- -----
1       0
2       .05
3       .1
4       .15
5       .2
6       .25
7       .3
8       .35
9       .4
10      .45
11      .5
12      .55
13      .6
14      .65
15      .7
16      .75
```

Figure 2-20.
List Subsheet with values of t

```
==================== VARIABLE SHEET ==============...
St Input      Name    Output    Unit      Comment
-- -----      ----    ------    ----      -------
L             y
   .5         a
   .9         b
L             x
L  0          t
```

Figure 2-21.
Variable Sheet with t, x, and y declared as lists

used. As each instance is processed, the values of x and y are displayed in their Output fields; the instance number also changes in the message and finally the message disappears when all the 21 instances have been processed. To see the calculated values of y in its List Subsheet, invoke the Dive command twice with the cursor in any field of y. A part of these values is shown in Figure 2-22. Similarly, you can see the values of x by diving into its List Subsheet.

The List Sheet contains the details of the lists defined in the model. Display the List Sheet by typing **=L**. As seen in Figure 2-23, the Name field contains the names of the three lists in the model. The number of elements in each list (21 in this case) is displayed in the Element field. Using the Dive command from either of the rows, you can access the corresponding List Subsheet.

```
==================== LIST: y ===...
Comment:
Display Unit:
Storage Unit:
Element Value
------- -----
1        0
2        .1008362707
3        .1944895901
4        .2784740135
5        .3503466633
6        .4078764726
7        .4492399465
8        .4732284061
9        .4794429551
10       .4684462593
11       .4418366029
12       .4022123628
13       .3530063792
14       .2981903641
15       .2418771827
16       .1878776043
```

Figure 2-22.
List Subsheet with calculated values of *y*

```
==================== LIST SHEET ========...
Name        Elements  Unit      Comment
----        --------  ----      -------
y           21
x           21
t           21
```

Figure 2-23.
List Sheet with listnames and number of elements

TABLE FEATURE

In order to examine how the values of *x* and *y* change (as *t* changes), you can use TK!Solver's table-generating feature to display the values in the form of a table. First, you must enter the necessary information in the Table Sheet. Display the Table Sheet by typing **=T**.

Enter **t**, the name of the first list, in the List field. The default value of 10 that appears in the Width field denotes the display width for the values in the list. Move the cursor to this field and enter **7** so that the column of *t* values in the display will be seven characters wide. The number in the First field, 1, indicates that the list will be displayed from the first value in the series. In the Header field, enter **t**, the heading for the column of *t* values. For the *x* list enter **x** in the List field, change the Width field setting to **13**, and leave the Header field blank. For the *y* list, enter **y** in the List field and **y=f(x)** in the Header field in the third row. Then enter the title **Table of t, x and y values** in the Title field. The Table Sheet looks as shown in Figure 2-24.

Press the Action key. The *t*, *x*, and *y* values appear in tabular form, as shown in Figure 2-25. Note the heading for the list of *x* values. When you leave the Header field blank, the list name is used for the heading. To change the display back to the Table Sheet, press any key.

TK!Solver also lets you print the table of values on the printer. To select this option, type **P** in the Screen or Printer field in the Table Sheet. Then press the Action key and the values are printed on the printer and also displayed on the screen. The printer parameters such as form length and left margin are set on the Global Sheet.

```
==================== TABLE SHEET ========================...
Screen or Printer:                 Screen
Title:                             Table of t, x and y values
Vertical or Horizontal:            Vertical
List       Width First Header
----       ----- ----- ------
t          7     1     t
x          13    1
y          10    1     y=f(x)
```

Figure 2-24.
Table Sheet with list information for generating table in Figure 2-25

Table of t, x and y values

t	x	y=f(x)
0	0	0
.05	.1220184543	.100836271
.1	.2589254118	.194489590
.15	.4125375446	.278474014
.2	.5848931925	.350346663
.25	.77827941	.407876473
.3	.995262315	.449239947
.35	1.238721139	.473228406
.4	1.511886432	.479442955
.45	1.818382931	.468446259
.5	2.16227766	.441836603
.55	2.548133892	.402212363
.6	2.981071706	.353006379
.65	3.466835922	.298190364
.7	4.011872336	.241877183
.75	4.623413252	.187877604
.8	5.309573445	.139288966
.85	6.079457844	.098196725
.9	6.943282347	.065550442

Figure 2-25.
Table generated from Table Sheet in Figure 2-24

PLOT FEATURE

The Plot feature in TK!Solver is used for graphic representations of data. First you must enter the necessary information for generating a plot on the Plot Sheet. To plot the x and y values obtained earlier, display the Plot Sheet by typing **=P**. Let the list of x values be the x coordinates. Therefore, in the X-Axis field, type **x** and press the Down Arrow key. The cursor is moved into the Y-Axis field. Type **y** and press the Enter key. You will see the default plotting character * displayed in the Character field. The data will be plotted using this character. You can change the plot character by typing the desired character in this field. This feature comes in handy when you plot several lists at the same time, and you want to use different characters for the different curves. The completed Plot Sheet should look like Figure 2-26.

Now press the Action key. The Plot Sheet disappears and the plot appears on the screen. This is shown in Figure 2-27. Pressing any key brings back the Plot Sheet.

It is possible to enter more than one list name in the Y-Axis field. Doing so results in multiple plots that allow you to observe the effect of one independent variable on several dependent variables at the same time. The title for the plot can be optionally entered in the Title field. Also the scale display can be turned off by setting the Display Scale On field to NO. The Screen or Printer field is used for printing the graph on a printer.

SUMMARY

Starting with a simple equation, we have taken you through a tour of the different features of TK!Solver. You have built several models and have also seen how textbook problems can be solved using TK!Solver.

```
==================== PLOT SHEET =====...
Screen or Printer:            Screen
Title:
Display Scale ON:             Yes
X-Axis:                       x
Y-Axis     Character
------     ---------
y          *
```

Figure 2-26.
Plot Sheet set up for plotting

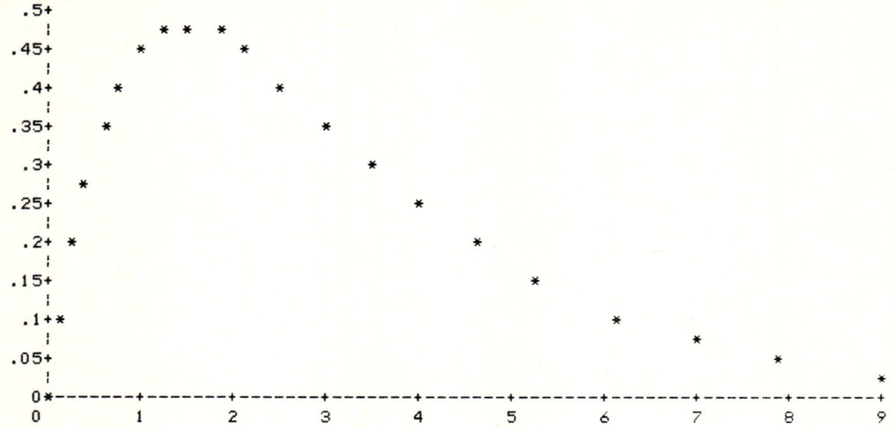

Figure 2-27.
Plot of x versus y

The following chapters explain in greater depth the details of the structure and usage of TK!Solver sheets and commands, the design of TK!Solver models, the working of Direct and Iterative Solvers, and additional TK!Solver features like list solving, tables, plots, and interfacing with other programs. All these functions and features are illustrated by numerous examples which may be seen as a continuation of our guided tour. Finally in Chapter 13 we take off for a few serious expeditions to solve real-life problems.

3

Sheet and Subsheet Composition

Compared with the previous chapter, which instructed the reader to go through the exercises with us, this chapter gives a descriptive account of the sheet and subsheet composition. Nevertheless, it is advisable to try the described features and operations on the computer.

Interaction with TK!Solver is carried out on eight sheets and three subsheets. These sheets and subsheets (called Information Sheets) each contain information about different aspects of a model. The sheet and subsheet names indicate the kind of information they contain. For example, the Rule Sheet contains the actual rules in the model while the Unit Sheet contains the unit conversions. This chapter discusses the composition of the different sheets and subsheets in TK!Solver and their interrelationships. The TK!Solver poster that comes with the program is an excellent guide for moving around the system of sheets and subsheets.

SCREEN COMPOSITION

TK!Solver's screen display is conceptually divided into two major areas: the Message Area at the top of the screen and the Information Area below (see Figure 3-1).

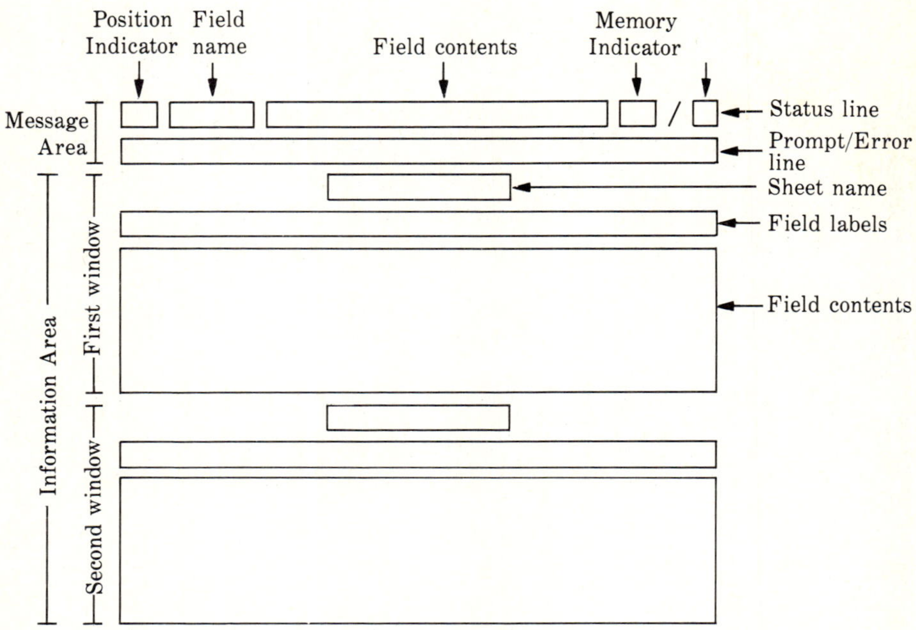

Figure 3-1.
The screen display

Message Area

The two lines at the top of the screen constitute the Message Area. The first line, the Status line, displays the current status of TK!Solver and provides such information as the amount of memory left, the current address of the cursor, and the state of the model (solved or awaiting solution). The second line, the Prompt/Error line, displays error messages and prompts and indicates which solver is being used.

The Position Indicator at the far left on the Status line displays the address of the field in which the cursor is currently positioned. In general, the field address consists of the row number followed by the field label. The field label is a character denoting the field name. For example, the Rule field is denoted by *r* and the Input field by *i*. The contents of the field containing the cursor are displayed next to the field name.

At the other end of the Status line are the Memory and Solution Indicators. The Memory Indicator shows the amount of memory available in kilobytes. When there is less than 1K of memory left, the indicator displays "LOW" and only a few actions are possible. When there is no memory left, the Memory Indicator displays "OUT" and almost all actions except saving the model fail until something is deleted. The Solution Indicator, "!", appears when the displayed values of variables do not reflect a valid solution of the model. This indicator also appears when a rule is added or edited, the status of the variables is changed, or an error is encountered during the solution process. It disappears when any equation is solved or no error is encountered.

Information Area

The various sheets are viewed through windows in the Information Area. The screen may consist of just one window displaying a single Information Sheet or two windows simultaneously displaying two different Information Sheets or different parts of the same Information Sheet. Table 3-1 lists the eight TK!Solver sheets along with their sheet labels and available subsheets. These labels are used to identify sheets in TK!Solver commands.

SHEETS AND SUBSHEETS—AN OVERVIEW

Figure 3-2 provides an overview of the sheets and subsheets and their interrelationships. You can access each of the eight major sheets from any other sheet or subsheet with the Select command by typing = followed by the sheet label.

Table 3-1.
Sheets, Sheet Labels, and Available Subsheets

Sheet	Sheet label	Subsheets
Variable Sheet	V	✓
Rule Sheet	R	
Unit Sheet	U	
Global Sheet	G	
List Sheet	L	✓
(User) Function Sheet	F	✓
Plot Sheet	P	
Table Sheet	T	

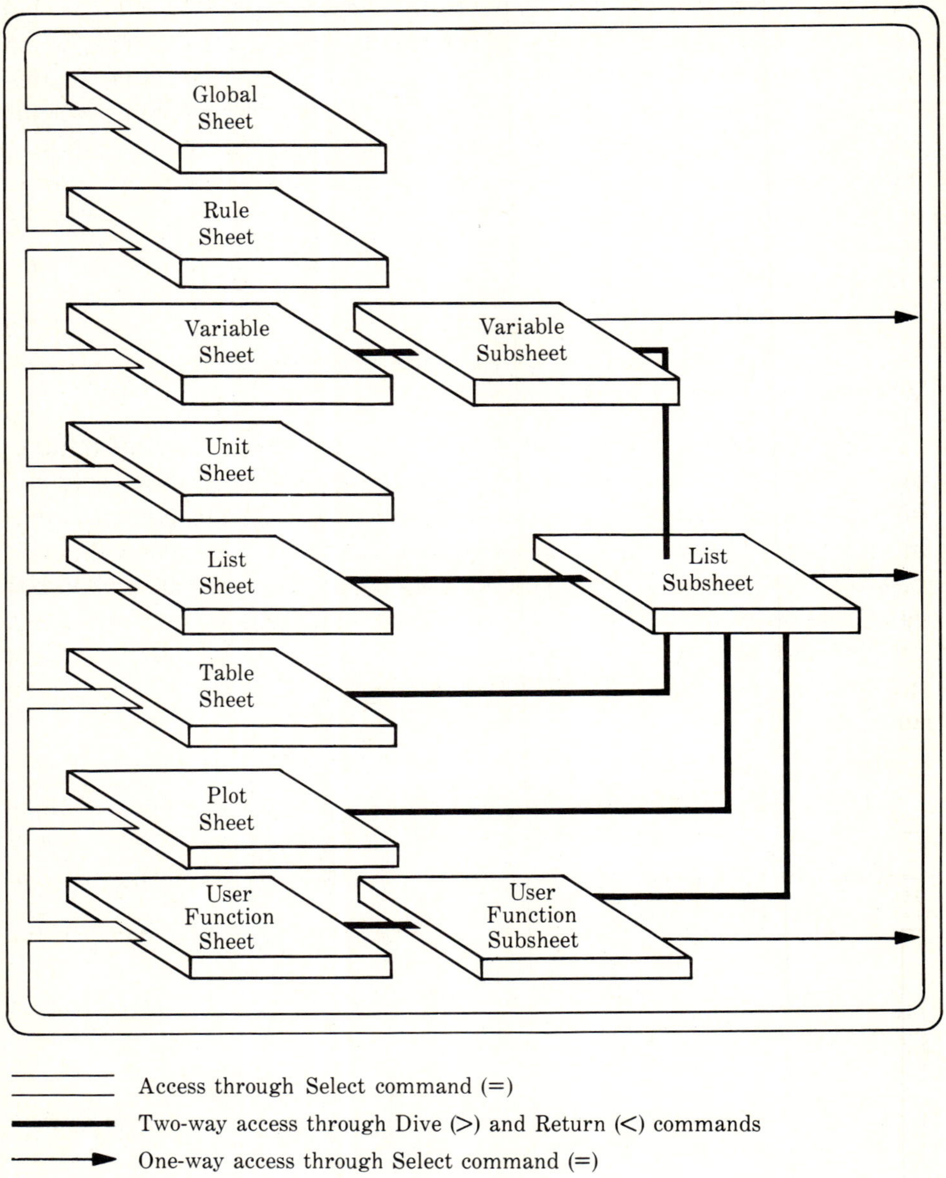

Figure 3-2.
Sheets and subsheets—an overview

To access the three subsheets—Variable, List, and User Function—from their respective sheets invoke the Dive command by typing >. The

Return command, <, returns you to the original sheet or subsheet from which you dived. For example, if the Return command is invoked from the Variable Subsheet, the Variable Sheet is displayed. The List Subsheet is not only accessible from the List Sheet, but, with the Dive command, from any of the following sheets or subsheets: Plot Sheet, Table Sheet, Variable Subsheet, and User Function Subsheet. With this overview in mind, let's discuss the different sheets and subsheets.

VARIABLE SHEET

When TK!Solver is first loaded, the Variable Sheet is displayed in the top window. You can also access it from any sheet or subsheet by typing =V. Each row of the Variable Sheet has different fields containing information associated with a single variable, as shown in Figure 3-3. The display width of these fields is fixed, and information longer than this width cannot be seen in full. The additional information may be seen in the Status line in the Message Area when the cursor is in that field. To view information longer than the Status line width, you must enter the Editor and scroll through it.

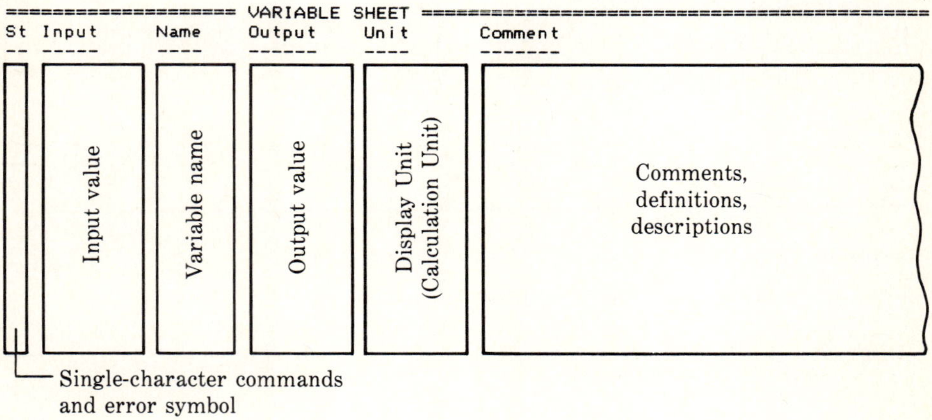

Figure 3-3.
The fields in the Variable Sheet

Name, Input, and Output Fields

The Name field contains the variable name used in the rules. The Input field is used for assigning input values to the variable; these values can be either numeric or symbolic. You may also assign input values using the Calculator mode by typing in expressions that evaluate to numeric or symbolic values. Invalid entries place you in the Edit mode with an appropriate message in the Prompt/Error line.

The evaluated results are displayed in the Output field. If any character is typed in this field, the message "Output Field Only" is displayed in the Prompt/Error line with a beep.

To see the different features, enter the rule

$$p * q = r$$

in the Rule Sheet. Then move the cursor to the Variable Sheet and do the following:

Action: Enter **3+5/8** in the Input field of *p*.
Result: The arithmetic expression is evaluated and displayed as 3.625.

Action: Enter **q+.87** in the Input field of *r*.
Result: TK!Solver beeps; the Prompt/Error line reads "(Edit) Unevaluated expression" and you are left in the Edit mode because *q* has no value (see Figure 3-4).

Action: Change *q* to ***p*** and press the Enter key.
Result: The arithmetic expression is evaluated and displayed as 4.495.

Action: Press the Action key.
Result: The equation is solved and the value of q=1.24 is displayed in the Output field.

```
(3i) Input:                                                       196/!
(Edit) Unevaluated expression
=================== VARIABLE SHEET ==...
St Input      Name    Output    Unit
-- -----      ----    ------    ----
   3.625      p
              q
   _q+.87     r
```

Figure 3-4.
Error message in the Prompt/Error line and user placed in Edit mode

Status Field and Single-Character Commands

When you examine different alternatives during problem-solving, you may not only change the variable values, but also their status. An input variable in one alternative may be an output variable in another. So you will need commands that can quickly alter the status of the variables. TK!Solver provides five single-character commands that can be typed in the Status field to change the variable status. These are shown in Figure 3-5. Three of these characters—B, I, and O—do not appear on the screen when they are typed.

Typing **B** (for Blank) clears the value displayed from either of the fields—Input or Output. Figure 3-6 shows the result of typing **B** in the Status fields of p and q.

Typing **I** (for Input) in the Status field of a variable makes it an input variable, and any value in its Output field is brought to the Input field. If a value has been blanked out, it is retrieved. In the Variable Sheet shown in Figure 3-6, typing **I** in the Status field of q brings back the value that was blanked earlier. If no value has previously been associated with a variable, a zero appears by default in that variable's Input field.

If an **O** is typed in a variable's Status field, the value from the Input field is moved to the Output field. In the present example, typing **O** in the

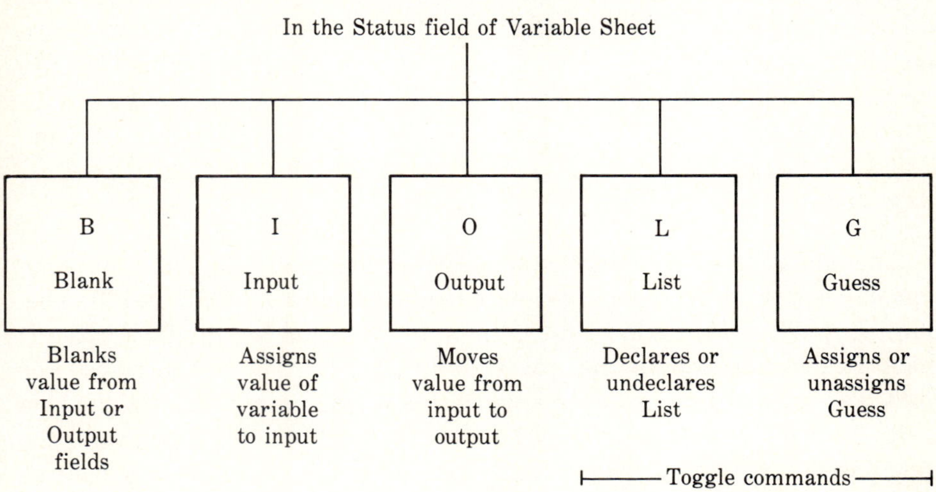

Figure 3-5.
Single-character commands in the Status field

```
(2s) Status:

==================== VARIABLE SHEET ==...
St Input      Name    Output     Unit
-- -----      ----    ------     ----
              p
              q
   4.495      r
```

Figure 3-6.
Typing **B** in Status fields of *p* and *q* blanks out their values

Status field of *r* moves the input value to its Output field. If no value has previously been associated with a variable, a zero appears by default in that variable's Output field.

Typing **L** in a variable's Status field declares it to be a list variable. Typing **G** in the Status field makes the variable a guess variable for the Iterative Solver. **L** and **G** are toggles. Typing **L** in the Status field of a variable already containing an "L" disassociates the list from the variable, and the "L" disappears from the Status field. (However, the list itself is not deleted and the name remains in the List Sheet.) Typing **L** again restores the association.

Similarly, typing **G** in the Status field of a variable already containing a "G" makes the variable an input variable and the guess status is lost. The "G" disappears and the value in the Input field is treated as the input value. Typing **I** in the field containing a "G" causes the "G" to disappear, and the variable becomes an input variable. The old guess value becomes the input value of the variable.

Unit Field

The unit of a variable may be specified in the Unit field. Actually, each variable has two units associated with it: the Calculation Unit and the Display Unit. The Calculation Unit is the unit specified for the first time. It must be consistent with the way the variable is used in the rules. For instance, by entering **margin=profit/sales**, you imply the Calculation Unit of *margin* to be the decimal fraction or "part of one." If you want the Calculation Unit to be percent (%), you have to formulate the rule as **margin=100*profit/sales.**

The second unit, called the Display Unit, is the unit seen in the Unit field and is the unit in which the value of the variable is displayed. The

Calculation Unit and Display Unit may be different; if this is the case, conversion of values is performed according to the unit conversion defined in the Unit Sheet. When you enter a unit for which no conversion from the Calculation Unit is defined on the Unit Sheet, a "?" appears in front of the value.

Occasionally you may define a conversion using a particular unit abbreviation and later on (inadvertently, of course) use a different one, only to be confronted by "?". Common examples are *sec* or *s* for second, *mt* or *min* for minute, *gm*, *g*, or *gram* for gram, and *mi/hr*, *mi/hour*, or *mph* for miles per hour. Typing errors can also cause problems. So if you encounter the "?", check the Unit Sheet first for a conversion and should there be one, check the abbreviations for spelling and consistency.

Comment Field

The Comment field may be used to describe variables or to enter any other message that makes the model readily understandable and easier to use.

RULE SHEET

The Rule Sheet is displayed in the bottom window when TK!Solver is first loaded. You can also access this sheet by typing **=R** from any sheet or subsheet. There are two fields on each row: the Rule field where the rules are entered and the Status field, which displays the status of the rule. Chapter 5 discusses rule composition and syntax.

The primary advantage of TK!Solver is that the formulas and rules can be typed in as we know them. We can have expressions on both sides of the equal sign. This represents a significant departure from conventional programming languages such as BASIC and FORTRAN, where the equal sign is used as an assignment operator with a variable name on the left side and the expression to be evaluated on the right. A TK!Solver rule can be as many as 200 characters long and must contain an equal sign.

An asterisk in the Status field of a rule indicates that it is syntactically valid and that it has not yet been solved by TK!Solver. When the cursor is moved to the Status field, the message on the Status line reads "Unsatisfied". When the rule is solved, the asterisk disappears and the message reads "Satisfied", indicating that the equality condition has been met.

Anything typed after a quotation mark (") in the Rule field is treated as a comment. In Chapter 2 you saw how to use this feature for explanatory remarks. Placing a quotation mark in front of a rule is equivalent to putting the rule out of operation, and removing the quotation mark brings the rule back into operation. This trick is frequently used during model development instead of alternately deleting and retyping the same rule.

The Status field of a row containing only a comment displays the message "Comment" in the Status line, and no asterisk appears in this field. For viewing rules that are longer than the display width, you have to enter the Editor and move the cue across the rule. (The cue is a tiny blinking marker that indicates the position where the next typed-in character appears.) There is no provision for continuing a rule longer than 200 characters on a different line. To overcome this limitation, you can use auxiliary variables in the rule and split long rules into several short ones.

ERROR SYMBOLS > IN STATUS FIELDS

When TK!Solver encounters an error during model resolution, an error symbol ">" is displayed in the Status field of the offending rule. Depending on the type of error, either one or all of the variables that appear in that rule are marked with the ">" in their Status fields in the Variable Sheet. This is illustrated on the rule $p*q=r$ used in the earlier discussion of the Variable Sheet.

When the equation is solved with $p=4$ and $q=3$, r is evaluated as 12. Now without changing the values of p and q, r is assigned 10 and the model is solved again. The resulting Variable and Rule Sheets are shown in Figure 3-7.

```
(1s) Status: > Inconsistent

==================== VARIABLE SHEET ==...
St Input        Name    Output    Unit
-- -----        ----    ------    ----
 > 4            p
 > 3            q
 > 10           r


=================== RULE SHEET ==...
S Rule
- ----
> p*q=r
```

Figure 3-7.
Variable and rules marked with error symbols; Status line displays the error message

The mathematical inconsistency

$$3 * 4 \neq 10$$

in the problem formulation has been detected, and the rule and the variables are marked. Moving the cursor to the Status field of the rule displays the message "Inconsistent" in the Status line. The message "Overdefined" is displayed in the Status line when the cursor is in the Status field of any of the variables p, q, or r. Likewise, other messages will point out other error conditions such as division by zero and invalid arguments for trigonometric functions. For a complete list of error messages refer to the *TK!Solver Reference Manual.*

ACTION KEY !

When the cursor is either in the Variable Sheet or the Rule Sheet and the Action key (!) is pressed, model resolution is initiated. This is different from other sheets where the Action key does not by itself initiate model resolution, but rather performs the action appropriate for that sheet or subsheet. For example, when the Action key is pressed with the cursor in the List Subsheet, intermediate values in the list are filled.

UNIT SHEET

The Unit Sheet is used for defining conversions between different units of measurement. This allows the use of two or more different Display Units with one variable. You can also access the Unit Sheet by typing =U from any sheet or subsheet. Each row containing the definition of a unit conversion may be "read" as follows:

> "To convert FROM <unit name> TO <unit name> MULTIPLY BY <number> and ADD OFFSET <number>".

For example, the *ft* to *in* conversion shown in the first row of the Unit Sheet in Figure 3-8 can be read as follows:

> "To convert FROM ***ft*** TO ***in*** MULTIPLY BY ***12*** and ADD OFFSET ***0***".

The Add Offset field is used to adjust the zeros of scales. The value in this field is added after the multiplication is done. If the field is left blank, the value is assumed to be zero. The Centigrade to Fahrenheit temperature

```
==================== UNIT SHEET ============...
From       To         Multiply By  Add Offset
----       --         -----------  ----------
ft         in         12
oC         oF         1.8          32
in         cm         2.54
m          cm         100
```

Figure 3-8.
Unit Sheet with defined unit conversions

conversion shown in Figure 3-8 illustrates the use of this field. The Multiply By and Add Offset fields accept values in the Calculator mode. For example, if, while defining a mile to kilometer conversion, we know that 5 miles is approximately equal to 8 kilometers, we can enter **8/5** in the Multiply By field. Recall the different conversions defined in Chapter 2.

TK!Solver can also perform conversion between two units defined in terms of a common unit. As seen in Figure 3-8, the units *ft* and *cm* have been defined in terms of the common unit *in*, so the conversion between all three units *ft*, *in*, and *cm* may be performed. In Figure 3-9*a*, the Calculation Unit and also the Display Unit for *dist* is *ft*. When the Display Unit is changed to *in*, the input value of 2 changes to 24 according to the conversion in the Unit Sheet in Figure 3-8. When the unit is changed to *cm*, the value changes to 60.96 since a conversion betwen *ft* and *cm* exists through *in*. However, when the Display Unit is changed to *m*, no conversion is performed and a "?" appears in the Input field, as shown in Figure 3-9*b*. Note also that the original value of *dist*, 2, reappears in the field.

```
==================== VARIABLE SHEET ==...
St Input      Name     Output    Unit
-- -----      ----     ------    ----
   2          dist               ft
```

a. Calculation and Display Units same for *dist*

```
==================== VARIABLE SHEET ==...
St Input      Name     Output    Unit
-- -----      ----     ------    ----
   ?2         dist               m
```

b. No conversion defined between Calculation Unit and Display Unit of *dist*

Figure 3-9.
Variable Sheets

The reason that no conversion takes place can be seen in Figure 3-8. No conversion is defined between *ft* and *m* either directly or through one common conversion unit. The conversion between *ft* and *cm* through *in* and also between *cm* and *m* in Figure 3-8 doesn't help to convert from *ft* to *m*. In other words, if there is no direct conversion between two units or if the conversion is spread over more than two rows in the Unit Sheet, TK!Solver doesn't perform the conversion and displays a "?" in front of the original value. In order to convert between all four units *ft*, *in*, *m*, and *cm* (or more), you have to make one of them common, *cm* in this example, and define the rest of them in terms of the common one.

The Action key has no role on the Unit Sheet. Pressing it produces the message "No Action for this Sheet" in the Prompt/Error line.

GLOBAL SHEET

The Global Sheet contains definitions that affect the behavior of TK!Solver on a global scale. For example, on the Global Sheet you can select the degree of accuracy you require in the solution of a particular problem and also define the printer settings. You can access this sheet by typing =G from any sheet or subsheet. The Global Sheet contents are divided into three groups separated by blank rows, as shown in Figure 3-10.

```
(v) Variable Insert ON: Yes

=================== GLOBAL SHEET ==...
Variable Insert ON:           Yes

Intermediate Redisplay ON:    Yes
Automatic Iteration ON:       Yes
Comparison Tolerance:         .000001
Typical Value:                1
Maximum Iteration Count:      10

Page Breaks ON:               Yes
Page Numbers ON:              Yes
Form Length:                  66
Printed Page Length:          60
Printed Page Width:           80
Left Margin:                  0
Printer Device or Filename:   PRN
Printer Setup String:
Line End (CR/LF or CR):       CR/LF
```

Figure 3-10.
Global Sheet

When the Variable Insert On field has the default setting of YES, newly encountered variables are automatically inserted in the Name field on the Variable Sheet when rules are being parsed. If the Variable Insert On field is set to NO, these variables are not added to the Variable Sheet by TK!Solver; if needed, they have to be entered manually.

When the Iterative Solver is used, the values of the guess variables (and other dependent variables) change as iteration proceeds. If you are not interested in these intermediate values, you may suppress their display by setting the Intermediate Redisplay On field to NO. Similarly, during List Solving, a YES setting will allow values to be displayed as each instance is processed, while a NO suppresses the display. The NO setting speeds up iteration and List Solving.

The Automatic Iteration On field controls the invocation of the Iterative Solver when the Direct Solver fails to find a solution. This feature is discussed in Chapter 9.

The Comparison Tolerance and Typical Value, discussed in Chapter 8, give you control over the allowed differences between left-hand side and right-hand side expressions in a rule. The default values are 0.000001 and 1 respectively.

The Maximum Iteration Count defines the number of iterations the Iterative Solver will try before it stops without finding a solution. The default value, 10, can be changed to any number between 1 and 10,000.

The next set of five fields sets the printer parameters. They are discussed in detail in the *TK!Solver Reference Manual.* The Printer Device or Filename field in this group is used for generating print files that can be incorporated in reports generated using word processing programs (see the section on "Interfacing With Word Processing" in Chapter 12).

LIST SHEET

The List Sheet contains a table of all the lists defined in a model. You access it by typing =L from any sheet or subsheet. The different fields in the List Sheet are shown in Figure 3-11. The Name field is used for entering the names of the lists. However, when a list is defined in any of the following places—Variable Sheet, Variable Subsheet, User Function Sheet, Plot Sheet, or Table Sheet—the listname is automatically recorded in the Name field. TK!Solver keeps track of the number of elements in the list and displays the number in the Elements field.

Two units are associated with the Unit field: the Storage Unit and the

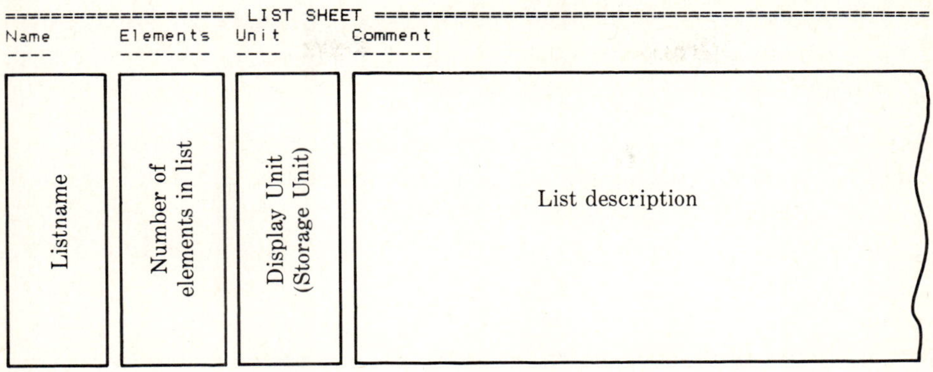

Figure 3-11.
Fields in the List Sheet

Display Unit; these are similar to the Calculation Unit and Display Unit on the Variable Sheet. The Storage Unit is the unit in which list values are stored in other programs and formats such as DIF, the Data Interchange Format. The first unit defined in the List Sheet is treated as the Storage Unit. The unit seen in the Unit field is the Display Unit, and the values are displayed in this unit. If the Storage and Display units are different, conversions between the two units have to be defined in the Unit Sheet.

Note the following important points concerning units on the List Sheet:

1. When you declare a variable as a list variable by typing **L** in its Status field on the Variable Sheet, the Calculation and Display Units of the variable become the Storage and Display Units, respectively, for the list. However, if you declare a variable to be a list variable and then assign units to it on the Variable Sheet, the units are not inherited by the list.

2. If a list with Storage and Display Units is associated with a variable (you do this by entering the listname in the Associated List field on the Variable Subsheet), a conversion between the Calculation Unit of the variable and the Storage Unit of the list must be defined on the Unit Sheet. Otherwise the calculated values will be incorrect.

3. If a list with defined units is used in a user-defined function as a Domain or Range list, the Display Unit of the list must be the same as the Calculation Unit of the variable. Otherwise, the results will be incorrect again.

4. When you save a list using the /**SS** command, both the Storage and Display Units are retained and the values are stored in the Display Unit. When the list is reloaded, the values are displayed in the Display Unit.

5. When you save a list in a DIF file using the /**S#S** command, the values are stored in the Storage Unit. When the DIF file is loaded, the values are displayed in the Display Unit of the list provided a conversion has been defined between the two units on the Unit Sheet.

USER FUNCTION SHEET

User-defined functions, as distinguished from built-in functions such as *sin, cos, min,* and *int,* are used for expressing the functional relationship between the Domain and Range lists. A function has to be defined in the User Function Sheet before it can be used in a rule. You can access the User Function Sheet by typing **=F** from any other sheet or subsheet.

The different fields in the User Function Sheet are shown in Figure 3-12. The name of the function being defined is entered in the Name field. The Range field is used for entering the name of the list containing the function values, the Range list. The listname containing the arguments of

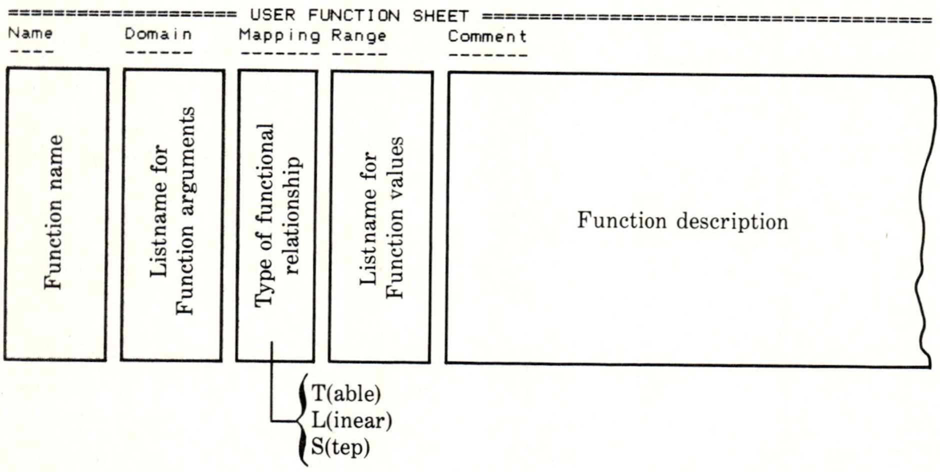

Figure 3-12.
Fields in the User Function Sheet

the function, the Domain list, is entered in the Domain field. (Names entered in the Range and Domain fields are automatically recorded in the List Sheet if they are not there already.) The actual values for the two lists may be assigned on the User Function Subsheet. This subsheet can be accessed through the Dive command. From the User Function Subsheet it is possible to dive into the List Subsheets for the Domain and Range lists. If you invoke the Dive command while the cursor is in the Range field of the User Function Subsheet, the List Subsheet for the Range list is displayed. (Note the connection between the User Function Subsheet and the List Subsheet in Figure 3-2.)

The type of functional relationship between the Range and Domain lists is defined in the Mapping field. TK!Solver provides the three types of Mappings which are discussed in brief in the following sections. A detailed discussion of the user-defined functions is found in Chapter 6.

Table Lookup

Table Lookup is the default option that comes up whenever a function name is entered in the Name field. You can also select Table Lookup by typing **T** in the Mapping field. This defines a discrete relationship between the corresponding elements of the Domain and Range lists.

Linear Interpolation

You may select the Linear Interpolation option by typing **L** in the Mapping field. This option approximates the relationship within each pair of consecutive points in the Domain and Range lists by a straight line. TK!Solver finds the interval within which the specified argument (or function value) lies and interpolates the corresponding function value (or argument).

Step Mapping

You may select Step Mapping by typing **S** in the Mapping field. For a given argument, TK!Solver finds the interval within which the argument lies. Step Mapping returns the value from the Range list corresponding to the starting point of the selected interval. Step Mapping, unlike Table and Linear Mappings, is non-invertible; in other words, given a value from the Range list, it is not possible to calculate the corresponding Domain value.

TABLE SHEET

The Table Sheet is used to enter information necessary for displaying lists in a tabular form. You can access this sheet from any other sheet or subsheet by typing =T. The different fields in the Table Sheet are shown in Figure 3-13.

The List field is used for entering the names of the lists that need to be displayed. The number in the Width field specifies the column width for that list in the table. A default value of 10 is automatically assigned when a listname is entered; the value can range from 3 to the width of the printed page as set on the Global Sheet. The number in the First field denotes the starting instance for that list in the table display. For example, entering 5 in this field results in the fifth element to the last element in the list being displayed in the table. The default value is 1, the first element.

The Header field is used to enter the caption for each individual list. If nothing is entered, the list name is used as the caption for that list. The Horizontal/Vertical field allows you to change the orientation of the table display. The table-of-values title can be entered in the Title field. The Screen or Printer field lets you indicate whether you want values displayed on the screen or printed on the printer (printing is governed by the settings on the Global Sheet). To initiate the table display you must press the Action key. If no values have been entered in the list, the message "No values to print" appears with a beep.

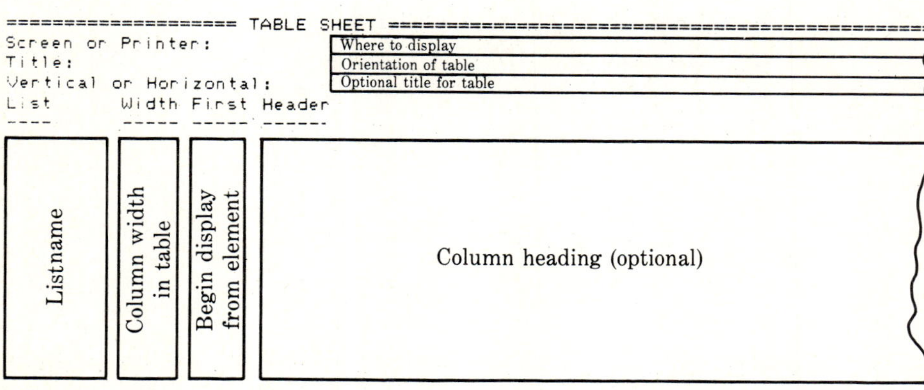

Figure 3-13.
Fields in the Table Sheet

```
=================== TABLE SHEET ===================...
Screen or Printer:              Screen
Title:                          Trigonometric Functions
Vertical or Horizontal:         Vertical
List        Width First Header
----        ----- ----- ------
x           7     1     x
sinx        15    1     sin(x)
cosx        15    1     cos(x)
tanx        15    1     tan(x)
```

Figure 3-14.
Table Sheet with information for generating table

Figure 3-14 shows the Table Sheet containing information about the four lists to be displayed. The values in the lists *sinx*, *cosx*, and *tanx* are the sine, cosine, and tangent, respectively, of *x* and were generated by List Solving with the *x* values as input. Figure 3-15 shows the table display. Pressing any key brings back the Table Sheet.

The Horizontal option is used to produce the table shown in Figure 3-16. (You select this option by typing **H** in the Horizontal/Vertical field.) The setting in the Width field is reduced to 8 for this purpose. Values have been rounded up for the display.

PLOT SHEET

The plotting feature in TK!Solver provides a valuable way of representing results. The information necessary to generate plots is entered in the Plot Sheet. You can access this sheet by typing **=P** from any sheet or sub-

```
                         Trigonometric Functions

x        sin(x)           cos(x)           tan(x)

0        0                1                0
15       .2588190451      .9659258263      .2679491924
30       .5               .8660254038      .5773502692
45       .7071067812      .7071067812      1
60       .8660254038      .5               1.732050808
75       .9659258263      .2588190451      3.732050808
90       1                1.947787445E-10  5134030422
```

Note: The value of 90 for *x* is actually 89.99999999. TK!Solver returns −212206590800 for *tan*(90). By changing it slightly, we obtain the value shown in the table.

Figure 3-15.
Table of *x*, *sinx*, *cosx*, and *tanx* values with the V option

Trigonometric Functions

x	0	15	30	45	60	75	90
sin(x)	0	.2588190	.5	.7071068	.8660254	.9659258	1
cos(x)	1	.9659258	.8660254	.7071068	.5	.2588190	1.95E-10
tan(x)	0	.2679492	.5773503	1	1.732051	3.732051	5.1340E9

Note: We input the last value of x as 89.99999999 degrees in order to obtain positive values of $tan(x)$. If x is assigned exactly 90 degrees, TK!Solver returns $tan(x) = -212206590800$.

Figure 3-16.
Table of x, $sinx$, $cosx$, and $tanx$ values with the H option

sheet. It is possible to plot several lists of values against a single list and examine the influence of one independent variable on several dependent variables simultaneously.

The different fields in the Plot Sheet are shown in Figure 3-17. The X-Axis field is used for entering the name of the list with the values of x or abscissa coordinates. More than one list of ordinates, or y values in the x,y plot, may be entered in the Y-Axis field. When a name is entered in the Y-Axis field, the default character "*" appears in the Character field and the values will be plotted using this character. Any other character can be entered in this field and used for plotting (with the exception of the command characters / ? = : ; < >, which have to be "edited in").

Plotting is done either on the Screen (the default) or on the Printer. You can make the selection by typing either **S** (for Screen) or **P** (for Printer) in

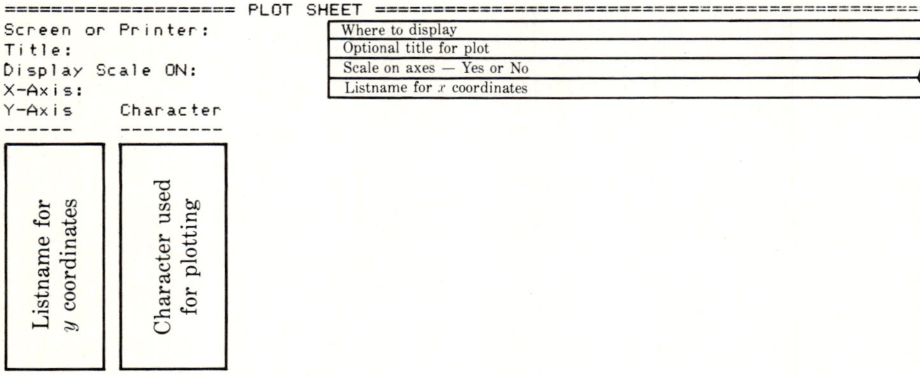

Figure 3-17.
Fields in the Plot Sheet

the Screen or Printer field. The Printer settings on the Global Sheet govern the plotting when the printer option is chosen. You initiate plotting by pressing the Action key. When the Display Scale On field is set to YES (the default), the scale is displayed on the axes. Typing **N** in the field suppresses the scale display. When a title for the plot is entered in the Title field, the title is displayed at the bottom of the plot. Pressing any key will return the display to the Plot Sheet.

The scales for the horizontal and vertical axes are automatically determined by the interval between the smallest and the largest values to be accommodated in the plot.

Figure 3-18 shows the Plot Sheet containing information for plotting the lists *x*, *sinx*, *cosx*, and *tanx*. The number of values in the list *x* is increased to 13 (compared to 7 in Figure 3-16) and the List Solver is used again to generate the values for the other three lists. If you keep all the lists as they are, the vertical scale will be chosen according to the interval of *tanx* (over 5E9), and the *sinx* and *cosx* points will lie flat on the x-axis. In order to generate good plots, you must remove the last nine values from the list *tanx* leaving the maximum value of 1.

Pressing the Action key produces the plots shown in Figure 3-19. Note that a few *s* dots are missing from the plot. The *sinx* and *cosx* values are equal at 45 degrees, and a few values of *sinx* are too close to *tanx*. One *c* and a few *t*'s overlay the *s*'s since on the Plot Sheet in Figure 3-18, *sinx* goes first, followed by *cosx* and *tanx*.

Suppose you want to reduce the width/height bias of the plot. You might add to the *x* and *sinx* lists additional "ghost values," say, 110 and 1 respectively. The result is shown in Figure 3-20.

Attempting a plot when the lists are empty, that is, they contain no values, produces the message "No points to plot" and a beep.

```
==================== PLOT SHEET =====================...
Screen or Printer:            Screen
Title:                        Trigonometric Functions
Display Scale ON:             Yes
X-Axis:                       x
Y-Axis    Character
------    ---------
sinx      s
cosx      c
tanx      t
```

Figure 3-18.
Plot Sheet set up for plotting

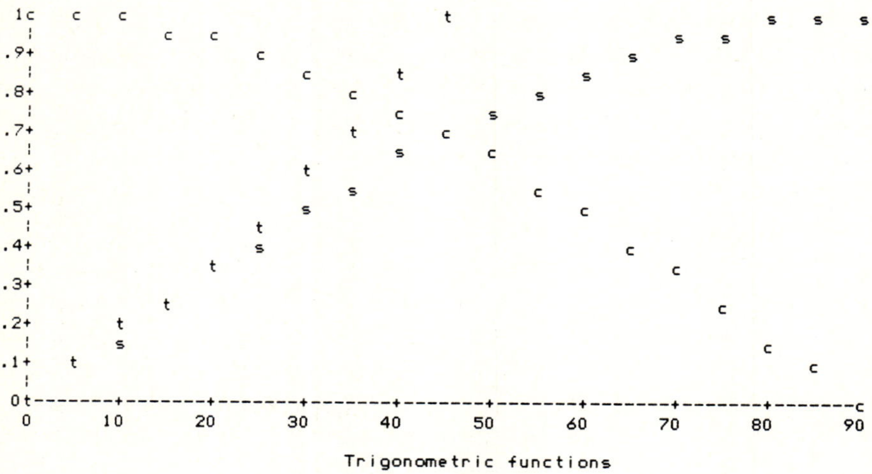

Figure 3-19.
Plots of *sinx*, *cosx*, and *tanx* vs. *x*

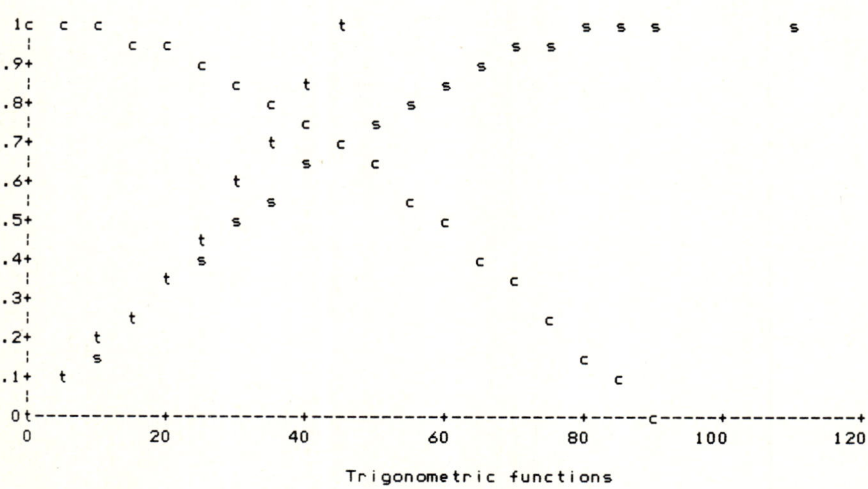

Figure 3-20.
Plot with reduced width/height bias

VARIABLE SUBSHEET

The Variable Subsheet contains detailed information about a particular variable. This subsheet is accessed from the Variable Sheet using the Dive command. Figure 3-21 shows the Variable Subsheet for the variable x. The variable name is displayed on top in the title line. The Input, Output, Status, and Comment fields are similar to those on the Variable Sheet. On the Variable Sheet only the Display Unit is seen, but here both the Calculation Unit and Display Unit are displayed.

The First Guess field is used for entering the initial guess value for Automatic Iteration (see Chapter 9). When you declare a variable as a list by typing **L** in the Status field (either here or on the Variable Sheet), the variable name becomes (by default) the Associated List name. On the other hand, if a listname is entered in the Associated List field, an "L" is automatically displayed in the Status field.

LIST SUBSHEET

The List Subsheet contains the values for a list defined in the List Sheet or in any of the following sheets or subsheets: Variable Sheet, Variable Subsheet, User Function Sheet, User Function Subsheet, Plot, or Table Sheets. The List Subsheet can be accessed from any of the previously mentioned sheets or subsheets with the Dive command. Figure 3-22 shows the List Subsheet with the name of the list, x, in the title line.

Only the Display Unit is seen on the List Sheet, but both the Storage Unit and Display Unit appear on the List Subsheet. The values for the list are entered in the Value field, and this field accepts entries in the Calculator mode as well. The Element field displays the position of the value in

```
==================== VARIABLE: x ==...
Status:                          L
First Guess:
Associated List:                 x
Input Value:                     0
Output Value:
Display Unit:                    deg
Calculation Unit:                rad
Comment:                         argument
```

Figure 3-21.
Variable Subsheet for x

```
=================== LIST: x ================...
Comment:                    list of x values
Display Unit:               deg
Storage Unit:               rad
Element Value
------- -----
1       0
2       7.5
3       15
4       22.5
5       30
6       37.5
7       45
8       52.5
9       60
10      67.5
11      75
12      82.5
13      90
```

Figure 3-22.
List Subsheet for *x*

the list. Thus 30, the fifth value in Figure 3-22, shows a "5" in the Element field. This feature is useful when you want to specify values from the list using the options in the List command.

Fill List Feature

The Fill List feature is very useful for creating a list of evenly spaced numbers. Given the number of values and the first and last values in the list, the Fill List feature interpolates the intermediate values and displays them in the Value field. This feature was used to fill in the intermediate values in the List Subsheet in Figure 3-22.

The first value, **0**, is entered in the first Value field in the List Subsheet of *x*. The cursor is moved to the 13th position with the Goto command (since 13 points are required) and the last value **90** is entered. Then the Action key is pressed to fill in the intermediate values. A message "Fill List: Y N" appears in the Prompt/Error line as shown in Figure 3-23. Typing **Y** results in the intermediate values being calculated and displayed; the resulting List Subsheet is shown in Figure 3-22.

USER FUNCTION SUBSHEET

The User Function Subsheet is accessible from the User Function Sheet through the Dive command. Figure 3-24 shows the User Function

```
(13v) Value: 90                                                    193/!
Fill List: Y N
===================== LIST: x =================...
Comment:                            list of x values
Display Unit:                       deg
Storage Unit:                       rad
Element Value
------- -----
1       0




13       90
```

Figure 3-23.
List Subsheet with Fill List prompt

Subsheet for the function *fun*; the function name is displayed in the title line. The Domain, Range, Mapping, and Comment fields contain the information entered in the User Function Sheet. The values for the two lists that make up the Domain and Range of the function are entered in their respective Value fields. These Value fields accept entries in the Calculator mode also.

The Element field associated with each Value field is similar to the Element field on the List Subsheet. The Fill List feature works on individual lists only; if the cursor is in any of the Value fields of the Domain

```
===================== USER FUNCTION: fun ==========================...
Comment:                            Atomic masses of elements (Periodic table)
Domain List:                        element
Mapping:                            Table
Range List:                         atomic_mass
Element Domain        Range
------- ------        -----
1       'hydrogen     1.008
2       'helium       4.003
3       'lithium      6.939
4       'beryllium    9.012
5       'boron        10.81
6       'carbon       12.011
7       'nitrogen     14.007
8       'oxygen       16
9       'fluorine     19
10      'neon         20.183
```

Figure 3-24.
User Function Subsheet for function *fun*

list and the Fill list feature is invoked, only the Domain values are affected. Similarly, if the cursor is in the Value field of the Range list, only the Range values are affected. You can dive directly into the individual List Subsheets from the User Function Subsheet.

4

Command Structure

The command structure of TK!Solver strikes a fine balance between simplicity and sophistication. It gives the user a broad range of options to suit individual needs. Even with the knowledge of a small fraction of the commands, you can use TK!Solver to set up a wide variety of models and to solve fairly complicated problems. The better you know the entire command structure, the more efficiently you can use TK!Solver, and the more complex the problems you can successfully attack. As with other aspects of TK!Solver, the best way to learn and get used to the command structure is to try the various commands and to observe their consequences. For those who have used VisiCalc, the command structure will look familiar. Despite the large number of commands and options, the logic of their structure makes them easy to master and use efficiently. When learning about the command structure, you will again find the TK!Solver poster to be an invaluable aid.

OVERVIEW

The commands in TK!Solver can be classified into the following six major groups:

1. Cursor Movement commands: Arrow keys, Switch, and Goto.
2. Slash commands: / followed by one or more characters.

3. Sheet Access commands: = followed by the Sheet letter, Dive >, or Return <.
4. Single-character commands: I, O, B, L, and G.
5. Action command: !.
6. Help command: ?.

When you are not sure of the command to use or how it works, type ? to invoke the Help facility, which will show and explain the options. If you attempt an invalid action (such as typing a non-existing option or interrupting a command), TK!Solver issues an error signal, a beep.

INTERACTION MODES

The interaction between the user and TK!Solver will always be in one of the following modes: Top Level, Command, Insert, Edit, or Help. This classification should help you understand the workings of the different commands.

Top Level

The Top Level represents the state in which TK!Solver is ready to accept commands—that is, after TK!Solver has been loaded, after a model has been loaded, after the solution of a problem, and, generally, after any command has been carried out and TK!Solver is waiting for the next one.

Command Mode

In the Command mode the different commands are typed in and executed. You may enter Command mode from the Top Level by typing any of the command characters.

Insert Mode

The Insert mode is the mode in which information is entered in a field. You may initiate this mode by typing the first character of your entry in the desired field. Pressing the Enter key terminates the Insert mode and also makes TK!Solver accept the entry. If the entered information is not valid for a particular field, an error message is displayed, and you remain in the Edit mode. Alternatively, any of the Arrow keys can be used instead of the Enter key. When an Arrow key is used to terminate the Insert mode, the entry, if valid, is accepted and the cursor is moved in the direction of the arrow. You may switch to the Edit mode from the Insert mode at any time by pressing **Control-E**, the Edit key.

Edit Mode

The Edit mode is the mode in which the contents of a field are edited. You may enter this mode either by using the /**E** command or by pressing **Control-E**. When the editor is in use, the message "(Edit)" is displayed in the Prompt/Error line. To leave the Edit mode and have the edited entry accepted, you must use the Enter key since the Arrow keys have a different function in this mode (see the section "Cursor Movement Commands").

Interrupting and Exiting the Modes

The Break key is used to interrupt or cancel any action. It leaves everything as it was before the action was initiated. For example, pressing the Break key while you are entering a value in the Input field terminates the Insert mode, restores the original contents, if any, and puts you back at the Top Level. Pressing the Break key in the Command mode terminates the Command mode and the command prompt disappears. The Break key can also be used to interrupt other actions like editing, printing, saving, loading, and solving.

Backspace Key

The Backspace key is used to delete the character to the left of the cue. The Backspace key can be used in Edit, Insert, and Help modes and also while you are responding to TK!Solver's prompt for filenames when the Storage command is invoked. If it is used any other place, it produces a beep.

Edit Key (Control-E)

The Edit key, **Control-E**, can be used instead of /**E** to enter the Edit mode. This alternative is especially useful when you are in the Insert mode and want to enter the Edit mode directly (/E would be treated as an entry rather than as a command). Also when responding to TK!Solver's prompts (to specify a filename for example), you can use the Edit key to correct the entry before pressing the Enter key.

CURSOR MOVEMENT COMMANDS

The different Cursor Movement commands can be classified as shown in Table 4-1. These commands are discussed in the following sections.

Arrow Keys

At the Top Level, the Arrow keys move the cursor in the designated direction. For example, pressing the Left Arrow key moves the cursor to the field on the left. However, the cursor can only be moved to the boundaries of the sheet. Attempting to move it beyond these boundaries results in a beep.

In the Insert mode, pressing an Arrow key causes any typed information to be entered if it is valid for that field and moves the cursor in the direction shown on the Arrow key. For example, when a number is typed in the Input field on the Variable Sheet and the Down Arrow key is pressed, the cursor moves to the Input field in the next row.

In the Edit mode, the Left and Right Arrow keys move the cue one character to the left and right respectively. The Up Arrow key moves the cue to the beginning of the item being edited. The Down Arrow key moves the cue to the end of the item.

Table 4-1.
Cursor Movement Commands

Command	Action
Arrow Keys (↑,↓,→,←)	Move from field to field; Move from row to row; Move within a field;
Switch (;)	Move from one window to another;
Goto (:)	Move to a specific address; search for a specific string and move to the field where string is found.

Switch Command (;)

When two windows are displayed on the screen, the Switch command is used to move the cursor from one window to the other. Pressing the ; key invokes this command, and the cursor moves to the most recent position in the other window. If the Switch command is invoked when only one window is displayed, TK!Solver beeps. The Switch command, one of the most frequently invoked commands, is also used with the Blank, Copy, Delete, Move, Print, and DIF Save commands for moving the cursor toward the destination.

Goto Command (:)

The Goto command provides a simple and fast way of moving the cursor directly to a field on the same sheet. Typing : initiates this command, and the prompt "Goto: Destination or search:" appears in the Prompt/Error line. Essentially there are two ways of specifying the final cursor position. In the first, the destination option, you must specify the address of the destination field and press the Enter key. In the second, the search option, you must specify the character string that needs to be searched and press the Enter key.

The Goto command is also used with the Blank, Copy, Delete, Move, Print, and DIF Save commands for pointing at the destination row or field.

Goto a Destination (:<address>)

The complete address of a field is made up of a row number and a field label letter. When specifying the address for the Goto command, you can use a partial address. The destination can be specified by

- The row number
- The * option
- The extended * option
- The row number and field label letter
- The field label letter

The row number option is used when the cursor is to be moved from a field on one row to the same field on a different row. For example, when moving from the first row to the sixth row on the Variable Sheet, you specify the address by typing **6** in response to the Goto command prompt.

Figure 4-1*a* and *b* shows the Variable Sheet before and after the execution of the command with the row number option. This is by far the most frequently used option.

You invoke the * option by typing an * and pressing the Enter key in response to the Goto command prompt. This action moves the cursor to the last non-empty row on a sheet. When experimenting with a model, you may frequently need to add a new rule or access the variables at the end of the sheet. In such cases, the * option provides a fast and convenient means of moving the cursor to the same field in the last non-empty row on the sheet. The Arrow key can then be used to move to the first empty row, if necessary.

Figure 4-2*a* shows a part of the List Subsheet as seen on the screen during an interaction. In order to move the cursor to the last value in the list, you would use the * option of the Goto command. Typing : invokes this

```
(1i) Input: 100000
Goto: Destination or search: 6_
==================== VARIABLE SHEET ==============================...
St Input      Name     Output      Unit        Comment
-- -----      ----     ------      ----        -------
   100000     H                    $           House price
              d        20000       $           Down payment
   20         dp                   %           Down payment percentage
              p        80000       $           Mortgage
   25         n                    yr          Term
   13.5       i                    %           Interest rate
              A        932.51591   $           Monthly payment
              T        279754.77   $           Total of payments
              Tip      199754.77   $           Total interest payments
```

a. Destination specified by row number

```
(6i) Input: 13.5

==================== VARIABLE SHEET ==============================...
St Input      Name     Output      Unit        Comment
-- -----      ----     ------      ----        -------
   100000     H                    $           House price
              d        20000       $           Down payment
   20         dp                   %           Down payment percentage
              p        80000       $           Mortgage
   25         n                    yr          Term
   13.5       i                    %           Interest rate
              A        932.51591   $           Monthly payment
              T        279754.77   $           Total of payments
              Tip      199754.77   $           Total interest payments
```

b. Cursor in destination field

Figure 4-1.
Variable Sheet with Goto command invoked

command. Then in response to the prompt you would type *. When the Enter key is pressed, the cursor moves to the last row on the List Subsheet, as shown in Figure 4-2*b*.

You specify the extended * option by using a field label letter along with the * in response to the Goto command prompt. This letter moves the

```
(5v) Value: 12                                                        192/
Goto: Destination or search: *_
==================== LIST: i ======= ...
Element Value
------- -----
5       12
6       12.5
7       13
8       13.5
9       14
10      14.5
11      15
12      15.5
13      16
14      16.5
15      17
16      17.5
17      18
18      18.5
19      19
20      19.5
21      20
```

a. Destination specified by *

```
(21v) Value: 20                                                       192/

==================== LIST: i ======= ...
Element Value
------- -----
5       12
6       12.5
7       13
8       13.5
9       14
10      14.5
11      15
12      15.5
13      16
14      16.5
15      17
16      17.5
17      18
18      18.5
19      19
20      19.5
21      20
```

b. Cursor moved to last row

Figure 4-2.
List Subsheet with Goto command invoked

cursor to the field specified in the last non-empty row of the sheet. Figure 4-3*a* shows the Variable Sheet with the cursor in the Input field of the first row. The destination is specified as ***o**. When the Enter key is pressed, the cursor moves to the Output field on the last row, as shown in Figure 4-3*b*.

When you specify both a row number and a field label letter, the cursor moves from one field on a given row to another field on a different row. For example, after building a model and entering comments, you will need to move the cursor from the Comment field on the last row to the Input field, say on the first row, for assigning input values.

Figure 4-4*a* shows the Goto command invoked when the cursor is in the Comment field on the last row of the Variable Sheet. The destination field, the Input field on the first row, has been specified as **1i** in response to the prompt. When the Enter key is pressed, the cursor moves to the specified destination, as shown in Figure 4-4*b*.

```
(1i) Input: 100000
Goto: Destination or search: *o_
==================== VARIABLE SHEET ================================...
St Input       Name     Output       Unit          Comment
-- -----       ----     ------       ----          -------
   100000      H                     $             House price
               d        20000        $             Down payment
   20          dp                    %             Down payment percentage
               p        80000        $             Mortgage
   25          n                     yr            Term
   13.5        i                     %             Interest rate
               A        932.51591    $             Monthly payment
               T        279754.77    $             Total of payments
               Tip      199754.77    $             Total interest payments
```

a. Destination specified by ∗ and field label letter

```
(9o) Output: 199754.771848

==================== VARIABLE SHEET ================================...
St Input       Name     Output       Unit          Comment
-- -----       ----     ------       ----          -------
   100000      H                     $             House price
               d        20000        $             Down payment
   20          dp                    %             Down payment percentage
               p        80000        $             Mortgage
   25          n                     yr            Term
   13.5        i                     %             Interest rate
               A        932.51591    $             Monthly payment
               T        279754.77    $             Total of payments
               Tip      199754.77    $             Total interest payments
```

b. Cursor in destination field

Figure 4-3.
Variable Sheet with Goto command invoked

When you specify only the field label letter, the cursor will move from one field to another on the same row. However, it is easier to use the Arrow keys than to remember the field labels.

Goto With Search (:"<string>)

You select the Search option by typing " in response to the Goto command prompt. The character string to be searched must then be typed in and the Enter key pressed to execute the command. The specified search string should be an exact match of what is displayed on the screen. When the command is invoked, the cursor should be in the column of fields in which the string being searched occurs. When an exact match is found, the cursor moves to that position. TK!Solver searches as follows: it looks for a match below the current cursor position; if it cannot find one, it scans

```
(9c) Comment: Total interest payments
Goto: Destination or search: 1i_
==================== VARIABLE SHEET ================================...
St Input      Name    Output    Unit       Comment
-- -----      ----    ------    ----       -------
              H                 $          House price
              d                 $          Down payment
              dp                %          Down payment percentage
              p                 $          Mortgage
              n                 yr         Term
              i                 %          Interest rate
              A                 $          Monthly payment
              T                 $          Total of payments
              Tip               $          Total interest payments
```

a. Destination specified by row number and field label letter

```
(1i) Input:

==================== VARIABLE SHEET ================================...
St Input      Name    Output    Unit       Comment
-- -----      ----    ------    ----       -------
              H                 $          House price
              d                 $          Down payment
              dp                %          Down payment percentage
              p                 $          Mortgage
              n                 yr         Term
              i                 %          Interest rate
              A                 $          Monthly payment
              T                 $          Total of payments
              Tip               $          Total interest payments
```

b. Cursor in destination field

Figure 4-4.
Variable Sheet with Goto command invoked

from the top of the column to the initial cursor position. A failure results in a beep. This command is especially useful when there are a large number of variables. However, for illustration, let's look at a simple example.

In the Variable Sheet shown in Figure 4-5*a*, the variable name *dpayment* is displayed as *dpaymen* in the Name field. So when searching for this variable name, you would enter the search string **dpaymen** and not the full name *dpayment*. In addition, the cursor should be in the Name field in any of the rows. Let's assume the cursor is initially in the Name field on the ninth row. To look for *dpayment* using the Search option, you would invoke the Goto command by typing :. In response to the prompt, you would type " followed by **dpaymen** and then press the Enter key. The cursor moves to the field containing the specified string. Note the full variable name in the Status line in Figure 4-5*b*.

```
(9n) Name: Tip
Goto: Destination or search: "dpaymen_
==================== VARIABLE SHEET ===============================...
St Input      Name     Output     Unit        Comment
-- -----      ----     ------     ----        -------
   90000      H                   $           House price
              dpaymen  18000      $           Down payment
   20         dp                  %           Down payment percentage
              p        72000      $           Mortgage
   25         n                   yr          Term
   14         i                   %           Interest rate
              A        866.70795  $           Monthly payment
              T        260012.39  $           Total of payments
              Tip      188012.39  $           Total interest payments
```

a. Search string specified

```
(2n) Name: dpayment

==================== VARIABLE SHEET ===============================...
St Input      Name     Output     Unit        Comment
-- -----      ----     ------     ----        -------
   90000      H                   $           House price
              dpaymen  18000      $           Down payment
   20         dp                  %           Down payment percentage
              p        72000      $           Mortgage
   25         n                   yr          Term
   14         i                   %           Interest rate
              A        866.70795  $           Monthly payment
              T        260012.39  $           Total of payments
              Tip      188012.39  $           Total interest payments
```

b. Cursor highlighting string

Figure 4-5.
Variable Sheet with Goto command invoked

SLASH COMMANDS

The commands that you initiate by typing a / are called Slash commands. They are shown in Table 4-2. When a / is typed, the characters corresponding to the different commands appear in the Prompt/Error line. The characters indicate the command—B stands for Blank, C for Copy, and so on. You choose the required command by typing the appropriate character. Some of these commands, like the Blank command, require additional information while others, like the Insert command, do not.

Blank Command (/B)

The Blank command is used to blank or clear a single entry or a range of entries on a sheet. You invoke this command by typing **/B**. The prompt "Blank: Point to last field <Pointer Indicator>" appears in the Prompt/

Table 4-2.
Slash Commands

Category	Command	Action
Field	/B	Blank fields
	/C	Copy field
	/E	Edit field
Row	/D	Delete rows
	/I	Insert row
	/M	Move row
Input/Output	/P	Print: sheet or file
	/S	Save or Load models or sheets
	/W	Display one or two windows
Action	/!	Solve model
	/L	List or Block solve; Put or Get instance
	/R	Reset Variables or Sheet or All
	/Q	Quit.

Error line. The current cursor location is shown by the Pointer Indicator. You are prompted to "point" to the last field to specify the final cursor position. Entries from the initial to the final cursor position (given by the Position Indicator and Pointer Indicator respectively) can be blanked out in this manner.

Pointing to the last field is done with any of the Cursor Movement commands or their combinations (discussed later). When the cursor is in the final position, the Enter key is pressed. The message "Blanking fields" is displayed and the fields are blanked out. The cursor returns to the initial position from which the command was invoked.

The blanked-out values in the Input and Output fields on the Variable Sheet can be retrieved by typing **I**, **G**, or **O** in the Status field of the variable. However, the contents of other blanked-out fields cannot be retrieved. For example, a blanked-out rule cannot be retrieved.

The Blank command works only in one dimension. Rectangular blanking, that is, blanking out both a column of fields and a row of fields at one time, is not possible. For example, blanking from the Input field on the second row through the Comment field on the fifth row of a Variable Sheet cannot be done simultaneously. Even if the cursor is moved to a different field in the destination row, blanking occurs only in the column in which the cursor was initially positioned.

Unblankable Fields

Some fields such as the Output field cannot be blanked out. Attempting to blank such fields produces the message "Unblankable field in block". If any unblankable fields appear in the range of fields specified for blanking, the same message is displayed and only the blankable fields in the range are blanked out.

Blanking a Single-Field Entry

Figure 4-6*a* shows a Variable Sheet on which the Blank command has been invoked. The prompt is displayed as well as the Position and the Pointer Indicators (in this case, both are 2i). Let's say that 30, the value in the current field, the Input field of *alpha*, is to be blanked out. This means that the destination is the same as the initial cursor position. So the Enter key is pressed and the value is blanked out, as shown in Figure 4-6*b*. (Generally, for blanking a single Input field in the Variable Sheet, you would type **B** in the Status field of the variable to save keystrokes.)

```
(2i) Input: 30
Blank: Point to last field (2i)
==================== VARIABLE SHEET ========================...
St Input        Name     Output      Unit       Comment
-- -----        ----     ------      ----       -------
   320          V0                   ft/sec     initial velocity
   30           alpha                deg        angle of departure
                time     10          sec        time taken
                maxht    121.92      m          maximum height
                range    844.68654   m          distance traveled
```

a. Cursor in Input field on second row

```
(2i) Input:

==================== VARIABLE SHEET ========================...
St Input        Name     Output      Unit       Comment
-- -----        ----     ------      ----       -------
   320          V0                   ft/sec     initial velocity
                alpha                deg        angle of departure
                time     10          sec        time taken
                maxht    121.92      m          maximum height
                range    844.68654   m          distance traveled
```

b. Value blanked out by pressing Enter key

Figure 4-6.
Variable Sheet with Blank command invoked

Blanking a Range of Entries

In order to blank out a range of entries, you must specify the destination using one of the Cursor Movement commands: the Arrow keys, or Goto, or their combinations.

Pointing Using Arrow Keys

The Arrow keys can be used to point to the destination. Figure 4-7*a* shows the Variable Sheet with the Blank command invoked. Assume that you would like to blank the values from the current cursor position in the Input field on the third row through the Input field on the first row. Using the Up Arrow key, you move the cursor to the destination field. Note the Pointer Indicator in Figure 4-7*b;* the cursor is in the destination field. When the Enter key is pressed, the input values in the third and first rows are blanked out. This is a very simple example, used here only for illustration purposes.

```
(3i) Input: 15
Blank: Point to last field (3i)
=================== VARIABLE SHEET ========================...
St Input       Name    Output       Unit       Comment
-- -----       ----    ------       ----       -------
   320         V0                   ft/sec     initial velocity
               alpha   48.590378    deg        angle of departure.
   15          time                 sec        time taken
               maxht   274.32       m          maximum height
               range   967.71000    m          distance traveled
```

a. Cursor in Input field on third row

```
(3i) Input: 15
Blank: Point to last field (1i)
=================== VARIABLE SHEET ========================...
St Input       Name    Output       Unit       Comment
-- -----       ----    ------       ----       -------
   320         V0                   ft/sec     initial velocity
               alpha   48.590378    deg        angle of departure
   15          time                 sec        time taken
               maxht   274.32       m          maximum height
               range   967.71000    m          distance traveled
```

b. Destination specified using Up Arrow key (note the Pointer Indicator (1i))

Figure 4-7.
Variable Sheet with Blank command invoked

Pointing Using Goto

When a long list of field entries must be blanked out, using the Arrow keys to point to the destination field can become tedious and time-consuming. In such cases, the Goto command comes in handy. The Blank command is invoked to blank out the first seven values in the List Subsheet shown in Figure 4-8*a*. In response to the prompt, you would invoke the Goto command by typing :. The Goto command prompt appears as shown in the figure. The destination is specified as 7, and the Enter key is pressed. The cursor moves to the destination field; the Blank command prompt reappears and the Pointer Indicator reads "7v" as shown in Figure 4-8*b*. Now when the Enter key is pressed, the specified values are blanked out.

Switch With Goto

When blanking out a long range of entries on a sheet, you will find it convenient to display different parts of the same sheet in the two windows. You invoke the Blank command in one window and, using the Switch command and the Goto command, you must specify the destination in the other window. Entries between the initial and final cursor positions (spanning over the two windows) are blanked out.

Arrow Keys With Others

The Arrow keys can be used in combination with the other Cursor Movement commands in order to point to the destination. In fact, this is more often the case when a combination of commands is used.

```
(1v) Value: 10
Goto: Destination or search: 7_
==================== LIST: alpha ==...
Comment:
Display Unit:                 deg
Storage Unit:                 rad
Element Value
------- -----
1         10
2         15
3         20
4         25
5         30
6         35
7         40
8         45
9         50
10        55
11        60
```

a. Destination specified using Goto command

```
(1v) Value: 10
Blank: Point to last field (7v)
==================== LIST: alpha ==...
Comment:
Display Unit:                 deg
Storage Unit:                 rad
Element Value
------- -----
1         10
2         15
3         20
4         25
5         30
6         35
7         40
8         45
9         50
10        55
11        60
```

b. Cursor in destination field
(note the Pointer Indicator (7v))

Figure 4-8.
List Subsheet with Blank command invoked

Copy Command (/C)

The Copy command is used to copy the contents of a field to a specified destination. With the cursor in the field to be copied, typing /C initiates copying. The prompt "Copy: Point to destination <Pointer Indicator>" is displayed in the Prompt/Error line. The destination field is pointed to with any of the Cursor Movement commands or their combinations discussed in connection with the Blank command (Arrow keys, Goto, Switch with Goto, and Arrow keys with others). With the cursor in the destination field, the Enter key is pressed. The contents are copied, and the cursor stays in the destination field.

The entry being copied should be a valid item for the destination field. For instance, it is not possible to copy a numerical value into the Name field on the Variable Sheet. Additionally, certain fields such as the Output and Status fields do not accept any entries. The Copy command is normally used for copying values, unit names, and also comments and rules that can be modified easily to suit the destination field (so you don't have to type them all over again).

If the rules in a model are only slightly different from each other, only one rule needs to be typed. Using the Copy command, you can copy this rule into the other rows, which can then be edited to make up the remaining rules.

Consider the set of rules in a model:

$$a11 * x1 + a12 * x2 + a13 * x3 = b1$$
$$a21 * x1 + a22 * x2 + a23 * x3 = b2$$
$$a31 * x1 + a32 * x2 + a33 * x3 = b3$$

Since the rules are almost identical, only the first one needs to be entered in the Rule Sheet. Figure 4-9*a* shows the Rule Sheet on which the Copy command has been initiated. The destination is specified with the Down Arrow key. When the Enter key is pressed, the rule is copied as shown in Figure 4-9*b*. This rule can be edited to form the second rule. The other rule can also be added with the same procedure.

An item from one sheet can be copied into a different sheet with the Copy command. In that case, the source sheet and the destination sheet must be displayed simultaneously in two windows, and the Switch command must be used to move from one sheet to the other.

```
(1r) Rule: a11*x1 + a12*x2 + a13*x3 = b1
Copy: Point to destination (1r)
==================== RULE SHEET ==========...
S Rule
- ----
* a11*x1 + a12*x2 + a13*x3 = b1
```

a. Cursor in field to be copied

```
(2r) Rule: a11*x1 + a12*x2 + a13*x3 = b1

==================== RULE SHEET ==========...
S Rule
- ----
* a11*x1 + a12*x2 + a13*x3 = b1
* a11*x1 + a12*x2 + a13*x3 = b1
```

b. Rule copied into destination field

Figure 4-9.
Rule Sheet with Copy command invoked

Delete Command (/D)

The Delete command is used to delete a row or a block of rows beginning with the current row. You initiate this command by typing **/D** with the cursor in the row to be deleted; the prompt "Delete: Point to destination <Pointer Indicator>" appears in the Prompt/Error line. You can specify the destination using the Cursor Movement commands and their combinations discussed in connection with the Blank command (Arrow keys, Goto, Switch with Goto, and Arrow keys with others). With the cursor in the destination field, the Enter key is pressed; the specified row or block of rows is deleted, and the contents of all the fields in the row are irretrievably lost. The non-empty rows move up to take the place of the deleted row or rows, and the remaining rows are renumbered. If rows in a List or User Function Subsheet are deleted, the elements are also renumbered, if necessary.

The variable names that occurred in a deleted rule remain on the Variable Sheet. Certain rows, such as those in the Global Sheet, cannot be deleted. In such cases, TK!Solver beeps when you type **/D**.

Deleting a Single Row

Figure 4-10*a* shows the Rule Sheet on which the Delete command has been invoked. To delete only the current row, you must press the Enter key in response to the displayed prompt. The Rule Sheet after the deletion is shown in Figure 4-10*b*. The next row has moved up to take the place of the deleted row.

Deleting a Block of Rows

The Delete command is invoked on the List Subsheet shown in Figure 4-11*a*. To delete the current row through the eighth row, you would use the Goto command to point to the destination. The Goto command prompt and the response are also shown. When the cursor is at the destination, the Enter key is pressed. The specified block of rows is deleted and the elements are renumbered as shown in Figure 4-11*b*.

Edit Command (/E)

The Edit command provides a convenient means of changing a field entry without retyping the complete entry. Placing the cursor in the field to be edited and typing **/E** invokes this command. The prompt then reads "(Edit)" and the edit cue appears at the beginning of the field entry. The

```
(2r) Rule: range = V0^2 * sin(2*alpha)/32
Delete: Point to last row (2r)
==================== RULE SHEET ===========...
S Rule
- ----
* maxht = V0^2 * sin(alpha)^2 / 64
* range = V0^2 * sin(2*alpha)/32
* time = .5 * sqrt(maxht)
* (range/time)^2 = V0^2 - maxht*64
```

a. Cursor in second row

```
(2r) Rule: time = .5 * sqrt(maxht)

==================== RULE SHEET ===========...
S Rule
- ----
* maxht = V0^2 * sin(alpha)^2 / 64
* time = .5 * sqrt(maxht)
* (range/time)^2 = V0^2 - maxht*64
```

b. After deletion, next row (rule) moves up

Figure 4-10.
Rule Sheet with Delete command invoked

```
(2v) Value: .5
Goto: Destination or search: 8_
==================== LIST: time ========...
Comment:                             time taken
Display Unit:                        sec
Storage Unit:                        sec
Element Value
------- -----
1       0
2       .5
3       1
4       1.5
5       2
6       2.5
7       3
8       3.5
9       4
10      4.5
11      5
12      5.5
13      6
```

a. Destination specified using Goto

```
(2v) Value: 4

==================== LIST: time ========...
Comment:                             time taken
Display Unit:                        sec
Storage Unit:                        sec
Element Value
------- -----
1       0
2       4
3       4.5
4       5
5       5.5
6       6
```

b. After deletion, elements are renumbered

Figure 4-11.
List Subsheet with Delete command invoked

Left Arrow and Right Arrow keys move the cue to the left and right. The Up Arrow key moves the cue to the beginning of the item being edited, and the Down Arrow key moves the cue to the end of the item. Characters can be typed as in the Insert mode. To exit the Edit mode, you must use the Enter key. Some fields like the Output and Status fields cannot be edited. Note that the Edit key, Control-E, can also be used to enter the Editor. The following examples illustrate the use of the Edit command.

Example 1:

The rule $p+q * r = t/s$ is to be changed to

$$(p + q) * r = t\ /cos(theta)$$

With the cursor highlighting the rule, you type **/E** to invoke the Edit command. The edit cue appears at the beginning of the rule, as shown in Figure 4-12*a*. Then you type **(** and using the Right Arrow key, move the cue beyond *q*. Now you type **)** and the rule looks as shown in Figure 4-12*b*. Then using the Down Arrow key, you move the cue to the end of the rule. The *s* is erased with the Backspace key. You type **cos(theta)** and the modified rule looks as shown in Figure 4-12*c*.

When the Enter key is pressed, the rule is parsed, and the new variable, *theta*, is inserted in the Name field on the Variable Sheet. An asterisk appears in the Status field of the rule indicating that the rule is to be solved. The variable *s* still remains on the Variable Sheet though it no longer appears in the rule.

Example 2:

Consider the Variable Sheet shown in Figure 4-13*a*. Suppose the Input value for *q* has to be changed from 9000 to 9100. With the cursor in this

```
(1r) Rule: p + q * r = t / s
(Edit)
==================== RULE SHEET ==...
S Rule
- ----
  _p + q * r = t / s
```

a. Cue in the first position

```
(1r) Rule: p + q * r = t / s
(Edit)
==================== RULE SHEET ==...
S Rule
- ----
  (p + q)_ * r = t / s
```

b. Rule after partial editing

```
(1r) Rule: p + q * r = t / s
(Edit)
==================== RULE SHEET ==...
S Rule
- ----
  (p + q) * r = t / cos(theta)_
```

c. Rule after complete editing and before the Enter key is pressed

Figure 4-12.
Rule Sheet with Edit command invoked

field, you type /**E** to enter the Edit mode. Using the Right Arrow key, you move the cue past the first 0. Then you erase it using the Backspace key. Now you type **1**, and the Variable Sheet looks as shown in Figure 4-13*b*. If the Enter key is pressed, 9100 will be entered in the field. But if you press the Break key instead, TK!Solver beeps, the Edit mode is canceled, and the original value, 9000, is left in the field.

Insert Command (/I)

The Insert command is used to insert a blank row in the sheet. You initiate this command by typing /**I**. Unlike the other commands, no prompt appears (and no response is required), and a new row is inserted above the current row. The other rows are renumbered accordingly. If a new row is inserted on a List Subsheet or a User Function Subsheet, the elements are renumbered, if necessary. It is not possible to insert several rows simultaneously using the Insert command.

Figure 4-14*a* shows the List Subsheet with the cursor in the fourth row. In order to add a new row above this row, you type /**I**. The List Subsheet with the blank row is shown in Figure 4-14*b*. Note that the elements have been renumbered—the old fourth element is presently the fifth one.

```
(1i) Input: 9000
(Edit)
==================== VARIABLE SHEET ==...
St Input      Name    Output     Unit
-- -----      ----    ------     ----
   _9000      q
```

a. Cue in the initial position

```
(1i) Input: 9000
(Edit)
==================== VARIABLE SHEET ==...
St Input      Name    Output     Unit
-- -----      ----    ------     ----
   91_00      q
```

b. Second digit changed to 1

Figure 4-13.
Variable Sheet with Edit command invoked

```
(4v) Value: 15

==================== LIST: x =========...
Comment:                     distance
Display Unit:                m
Storage Unit:                ft
Element Value
------- -----
1       0
2       5
3       10
4       15
5       20
6       25
```

a. Cursor is in the fourth row when command is invoked

```
(4v) Value:

==================== LIST: x =========...
Comment:                     distance
Display Unit:                m
Storage Unit:                ft
Element Value
------- -----
1       0
2       5
3       10

5       15
6       20
7       25
```

b. After insertion, elements are renumbered

Figure 4-14.
List Subsheet with Insert command invoked

List Command (/L)

The List command is used to solve the model for a list of values or to store or retrieve list values. Table 4-3 shows the different options. Typing /L initiates this command, and the prompt "! B P G" displays the different options. (These options are discussed in the following sections.)

Solver Option (/L!)

The Solver option of the List command is used for List Solving (solving the model repeatedly using lists of input values and generating lists of output values). Typing ! in response to the List command prompt initiates this option. Depending on the problem formulation, either the Direct Solver or the Iterative Solver is brought in to solve the model. The mes-

Table 4-3.
List Command

Command	Action
/L!	Solve all instances
/LB	Solve a block of instances
/LP	Put or Store an instance
/LG	Get a specific instance

sage in the Prompt/Error line indicates the solver being used. It reads either

"List Solver <element #>, Direct Solver"

or

"List Solver <element #>, Iterative Solver: m out of n"

where the <element #> indicates the element number being currently processed by the List Solver. The List Solver stops when the shortest input list is exhausted. If the Intermediate Display On field in the Global Sheet is set to YES (the default), the values of each instance are displayed as they are being processed. Make sure to designate at least one list of values as the input list; otherwise, the message "No input values for List Solver" appears and the solution process terminates. Chapter 10 contains a detailed discussion of List Solving.

Block Option (/LB)

Often after List Solving with the Solver option, you might want to change just a few of the values in the lists and solve again. However, if the Solver option is used now, all the elements, including the unchanged ones, will be processed. To avoid this unnecessary processing you may use the Block option of the List command. When Block Solving, the model is solved only for the specified block of elements.

You choose the Block option by typing **B** in response to the List command prompt. A new prompt "Block: first element:" appears, and you are asked for the first element number in the block of values to be processed. Typing the element number and pressing the Enter key produces the prompt for the last element in the block, "Block: last element:". When you respond to this, TK!Solver calls the Direct or the Iterative Solver, depending on the problem formulation, and the specified range of instances is processed. All other values outside this block remain unaffected. The use of the Block Solver is discussed further in Chapter 10.

Put Option (/LP)

The Put option of the List command is used to store (put) the instance displayed on the Variable Sheet (in either the Input field or the Output field) into a specified position in the lists. You choose this option by typing **P** in response to the List command prompt. The prompt for the position (the element number) in which the value has to be stored, "Put to element", appears. Typing the element number and pressing the Enter key executes the command. The values of all list variables, either in the Input field or in the Output field, are stored in the specified positions in the respective lists.

If the Display Units for a variable are different on the Variable Sheet and the List Subsheet, unit conversion is performed according to the conversions defined in the Unit Sheet.

Get Option (/LG)

The Get option of the List command is the opposite of the Put option; it is used to retrieve a specific instance from the lists and display it on the Variable Sheet. If the variable is an input variable, the value is displayed in the Input field; otherwise it is displayed in the Output field. You choose the Get option by typing **G** in response to the List command prompt. The prompt for the element number "Get from element" appears. Typing the element number and pressing the Enter key retrieves the specified element for all the list variables from the respective lists and displays it in the appropriate field in the Variable Sheet.

If the Display Units for a variable are different on the Variable Sheet and on the List Subsheet, unit conversion is performed according to the conversions defined in the Unit Sheet.

Move Command (/M)

The Move command is used to move a row to another location on the sheet. The contents of all the fields on the row are moved to the destination. You initiate this command by typing **/M**. The prompt "Move: Point to destination <Pointer Indicator>" appears in the Prompt/Error line. To point to the destination, you may use any of the Cursor Movement commands or their combinations discussed in connection with the Blank command (Arrow keys, Goto, Switch with Goto, and Arrow keys with others). Pressing the Enter key when the cursor is in the destination field moves the specified row to the destination, and the cursor remains at this destination. The other rows are moved up or down to eliminate the vacated row, and the remaining rows are renumbered. Moving a row in the List Subsheet or User Function Subsheet causes the elements to be renumbered. The Move command is commonly used for rearranging the display of the variables on the Variable Sheet to produce a more meaningful grouping. It is not possible to move several rows simultaneously using this command.

Figure 4-15*a* shows the User Function Subsheet on which the Move

```
(6d) Domain: 'sixth
Move: Point to destination (6d)
===================== USER FUNCTION: ==================...
Comment:                         Example of Move command
Domain List:                     words
Mapping:                         Table
Range List:                      numbers
Element Domain         Range
------- ------         -----
1        'first        1
2        'second       2
3        'third        3
4        'fourth       4
5        'fifth        5
6        'sixth        6
7        'seventh      7
8        'eighth       8
```

a. Cursor in sixth row of Domain values

```
(2d) Domain: 'sixth

===================== USER FUNCTION: ==================...
Comment:                         Example of Move command
Domain List:                     words
Mapping:                         Table
Range List:                      numbers
Element Domain         Range
------- ------         -----
1        'first        1
2        'sixth        6
3        'second       2
4        'third        3
5        'fourth       4
6        'fifth        5
7        'seventh      7
8        'eighth       8
```

b. After moving, elements are renumbered

Figure 4-15.
User Function Subsheet with Move command invoked

command has been initiated. The destination (in this case the second row) has been specified using the Goto command. When the cursor is in the destination row, the Enter key is pressed. The specified row is moved up and the elements renumbered, as shown in Figure 4-15*b*.

Print Command (/P)

The Print command is used to print all or part of a sheet or to write a file to a diskette. You initiate this command by typing **/P**. The prompt for the last line in the block of lines to be printed, "Print: Point to last line <Pointer Indicator>", appears in the Prompt/Error line. The last line can be specified using any of the Cursor Movement commands or their combinations discussed in connection with the Blank command (Arrow keys, Goto, Switch with Goto, and Arrow keys with others). Then the Enter key is pressed to carry out the command. The specified lines are printed along with the appropriate field labels, and these lines are also simultaneously echoed on the screen. The specific field in which the cursor is initially positioned in the row doesn't affect the printing. The Printer Device or Filename field on the Global Sheet can be set either to print the lines on a printer or to write them to a file.

Printing a Sheet

Figure 4-16*a* shows the Variable Sheet on which the Print command has been invoked. Say you want to print the complete sheet. You use the Goto command (with the * option) to move the cursor to the last row. Then the Enter key is pressed to print the sheet shown in Figure 4-16*b*.

The contents of the screen can be "dumped" to a printer using the IBM Personal Computer's Print Screen facility (hold down the Shift key and simultaneously press the PrtSc key).

Generating a Print File

The Print command can also be used to generate the so-called print files that can be saved on diskette. These files can be used in word processing programs for generating reports. (See the section on "Interfacing With Word Processing" in Chapter 12.) The authors made extensive use of this facility while writing this book.

The name of the print file under which the specified lines are to be stored on the diskette must be entered in the Printer Device or Filename field before the Print command is invoked on the Global Sheet. Executing

```
(1i) Input: 320
Print: Point to last line (1i)
=================== VARIABLE SHEET =========================...
St Input      Name    Output      Unit       Comment
-- -----      ----    ------      ----       -------
   320        V0                  ft/sec     initial velocity
   30         alpha               deg        angle of departure
              time    10          sec        time taken
              maxht   121.92      m          maximum height
              range   844.68654   m          distance traveled
```

a. Cursor in first row; destination specified using Goto command with * option

```
St Input      Name    Output      Unit       Comment
-- -----      ----    ------      ----       -------
   320        V0                  ft/sec     initial velocity
   30         alpha               deg        angle of departure
              time    10          sec        time taken
              maxht   121.92      m          maximum height
              range   844.68654   m          distance traveled
```

b. Printed Variable Sheet

Figure 4-16.
Variable Sheet with Print command invoked

the command writes the specified lines to the file. TK!Solver appends an extension to the specified filename. This extension is computer-specific and is given in the TK!Solver documentation. For the IBM Personal Computer, the extension is .PRF.

Quit Command (/Q)

The Quit command is used to exit TK!Solver and return to the DOS level. You initiate this command by typing /**Q**. The prompt "Quit: Y N" seeks confirmation to avoid unintentional quitting. Typing **Y** exits TK!Solver, while **N** cancels the command. Typing any other key evokes a protest beep and the prompt stays.

Reset Command (/R)

The Reset command is used to reset TK!Solver either partially or completely. The different reset options are shown in Table 4-4. You initiate this command by typing /**R**. The prompt "Reset: V S A" displays the options:

Table 4-4.
Reset Command

Command	Action
/RV	Blank variable values; reset their status
/RS	Reset entire sheet
/RA	Reset all sheets

Variable Values, current Sheet, or All Sheets. When you make a choice by pressing the appropriate key, TK!Solver seeks confirmation prior to executing the command.

Reset Variable Values Option (/RVY)

The Variable Values option of the Reset command is used for clearing or blanking the values and resetting the status of all the variables on the Variable Sheet. You select this option by typing **V** in response to the main prompt of the Reset command. A new prompt "Reset variable values: Y N" appears, seeking confirmation of the action. Responding with a **Y** displays the message "Resetting variable values"; the values are blanked out and the Status fields cleared. Typing **N** cancels the command with a beep, while any other key is ignored with a beep. The cursor can be in any sheet when you use this command.

Reset Sheet Option (/RSY)

The Sheet option of the Reset command is used to reset the entire contents of a sheet. The cursor must be on the sheet to be reset. You select this option by typing **S** in response to the main prompt of the Reset command, and TK!Solver displays a confirmation-seeking prompt "Reset current sheet: Y N". Typing **Y** displays the message "Resetting current sheet" and the contents are cleared. Typing **N** cancels the command while any other key is ignored with a beep and the prompt stays.

Reset All Sheets Option (/RAY)

The All Sheets option of the Reset command is used to reset all the sheets and is equivalent to loading TK!Solver again. You select this option by typing **A** in response to the main prompt of the Reset command. The prompt "Reset all: Y N" appears, seeking a confirmation. Typing **Y** produces the message "Resetting everything" and all the sheets are reset. Typing **N** cancels the command; any other key is ignored with a beep and the prompt stays. The cursor can be in any sheet when the All Sheets option is chosen. Recall that this option was used very often in Chapter 2 when different models were built in succession.

Storage Command (/S)

The Storage command is used to save, load, or delete files containing models or parts of models. You initiate this command by typing /**S**, and the prompt "Storage: L S V U F # D" displays the different options. These options are listed in Table 4-5.

A salient feature of the Storage command is that, apart from complete models, certain sheets in a model can be saved and loaded individually. For example, you can define a complete set of unit conversions that you would normally need and then save the Unit Sheet alone. Then any time you load a model, the Unit Sheet can be loaded separately and used. An example of this is the file TUNITS on the TK!Solver disk, which is used for the Travel model in the *TK!Solver Instruction Manual.*

The Storage command can also be used to merge models. It is possible to load a model into a model already on the sheets. All the rules from the new model are loaded, but common variable names are not duplicated.

The values in one or more List Subsheets can be saved using the DIF option, so that the values can be used by other application programs like VisiCalc, VisiPlot, and sequential programs written in BASIC.

Table 4-5.
Storage Command

Command	Action
/SL	Load model or sheet
/SS	Save model
/SV	Save Variable Sheet and Subsheets
/SU	Save Unit Sheet
/SF	Save User Function Sheet
/S#	DIF: Save or Load
/SD	Delete file

Filenames

Filenames must be unique, begin with a letter, and be no more than eight characters long. TK!Solver will append the extension .TK to a filename if no other extension is specified. However, when the DIF option is used for saving lists, TK!Solver appends .DIF. It is not necessary to specify the extension when you load a model or sheet that has either a .TK or a .DIF extension. After the filename is given, TK!Solver searches for the file in the directory and loads it if the filename is unique. Otherwise the name is displayed and confirmation is sought prior to loading.

When prompted by TK!Solver to specify a filename with "Load filename:", you can respond in one of two ways: (1) type the filename and press the Enter key; (2) invoke the Directory Scrolling feature by pressing the Right Arrow key. This causes TK!Solver to scroll through the diskette directory and display the first filename compatible with the TK!Solver format. While the Right Arrow key is kept down, the directory is scrolled and the filenames displayed one by one. When the desired filename appears, pressing the Enter key will load the file. It is possible to edit the filename displayed in the Prompt/Error line using the Edit key (Control-E). However, if the end of the directory is reached and no file has been selected, further scrolling results in exiting the command. The Directory Scrolling feature saves you the trouble of having to remember filenames.

Note: If the disk drive to be accessed is not the default drive (the drive from which TK!Solver was initially loaded), the drive specified must precede the filename. When using Directory Scrolling, you must specify the drive name (if it is not the default) before pressing the Right Arrow key.

Load Option (/SL)

The Load option of the Storage command is used to load a model or a sheet that has previously been saved. You select this option by typing **L** in response to the Storage command prompt. The prompt for the filename "Load: filename:" appears in the Prompt/Error line. When the filename is typed (prefixed by the drive name, if necessary) and the Enter key pressed, TK!Solver searches the diskette directory for the file. If the file is found, the message "Loading from <specified filename>" is displayed and the file is loaded. Otherwise, an error message "File does not exist" appears with a beep, and the command is exited. An alternative is to use the Directory Scrolling feature for loading a file.

Depending on the contents of the file, the appropriate sheets are loaded. For example, if the file contains the unit conversions saved with the Unit Save option (/SU), they are loaded into the Unit Sheet. Existing contents of the sheets are not lost.

Save Model Option (/SS)

The Save Model option of the Storage command is used for saving the entire model. You select this option by typing **S** in response to the Storage command prompt. After you give the filename and press the Enter key, the model is saved under the specified filename. A status message "Saving to <specified filename.TK>" is displayed as the file is being saved. If a file under the given name already exists on the diskette, TK!Solver seeks confirmation before overwriting, and the prompt "Save: Overwrite filename: <filename>: Y N" appears in the Prompt/Error line. Typing **Y** overwrites the file, while typing **N** cancels the Storage command with a beep. Directory Scrolling can also be used to specify a filename, though it is not something that you would normally use.

Save Variables Option (/SV)

The Variable Save option of the Storage command is used to save the contents of the Variable Sheet and Variable Subsheets. You select this option by typing **V** in response to the Storage command prompt. Specifying and confirming filenames are similar to the Save Model option previously described.

Save Unit Option (/SU)

Probably the most frequently invoked option after the Save Model option is the Unit Save option, which saves the contents of the Unit Sheet. You select this option by typing **U** in response to the Storage command prompt. Specifying and confirming filenames are similar to the Save Model option.

Save User-Defined Function Option (/SF)

When the same user-defined function can be used in different models, employing the User Function Save option can save time and effort. A function can be defined once, saved with this option, and loaded whenever required. For example, the element names and their atomic masses from the Periodic Table can be expressed as a function and saved with this option to be loaded and used in other models. You select this option by typing **F** in response to the Storage command prompt. Specifying and confirming filenames are similar to the Save Model option.

DIF Options (/S#)

DIF is a Data Interchange Format created by Software Arts that enables data to be exchanged between programs. TK!Solver lists can be saved in this format so that they can be used by other programs for further data analysis and presentation graphics. In order to Save or Load a file in DIF, you must position the cursor in the List Sheet. Then select this option by typing # in response to the Storage command prompt. A new prompt "DIF Storage: S L" asks whether the file is to be saved or loaded.

You select the DIF Load option by typing **L** in response to the DIF Storage prompt. If you specify the extension .DIF when responding to the prompt for filename, the file will be loaded. If the extension is not specified, TK!Solver searches the directory and, if it finds a file with the .DIF extension, it displays the name and seeks confirmation before loading. The file contents are loaded into the List Sheet and List Subsheets. Directory Scrolling can also be used to specify the filename.

You select the DIF Save option by typing **S** in response to the DIF Storage prompt. A prompt for the last list (in the block of lists) to be saved, "DIF Save: Point to last line <Pointer Indicator>", appears. After you point to the last line and press the Enter key, the prompt for the filename "DIF Save: Filename" appears. You can either type the filename directly or use Directory Scrolling. As the lists are being saved, the message "Saving to <specified filename.DIF>" is displayed. As mentioned earlier, TK!Solver appends the extension .DIF to files saved using this option.

Delete Option (/SD)

The Delete option of the Storage command is used for deleting files from the diskette. You select this option by typing **D** in response to the Storage command prompt. When the filename is specified with the extension, TK!Solver seeks confirmation before deleting the file. If the extension is not specified, TK!Solver searches the directory and then displays the filename with the .TK extension. When the Enter key is now pressed, a prompt appears seeking confirmation before the file is deleted. This command should be used with care.

Window Command (/W)

The Window command is used to display either a single window or two windows on the screen. Table 4-6 shows the different options.

You initiate this command by typing /**W**. The prompt "Window: 1 V R

Table 4-6.
Window Command

Command	Display
/W1	Single window
/WV	Variable Sheet
/WR	Rule Sheet
/WU	Unit Sheet
/WG	Global Sheet
/WF	User Function Sheet
/WL	List Sheet
/WP	Plot Sheet
/WT	Table Sheet

U G L F P T" appears in the Prompt/Error line. Then you select the desired option by typing the appropriate character. Thus, from a two-window display, typing **1** in response to the prompt displays a single window containing the sheet in which the cursor is positioned. The other options can be chosen only when there is one window on the screen. Otherwise TK!Solver protests with a beep. For example, when the Variable Sheet is displayed in the top window and the Rule Sheet in the bottom, typing **/WU** to display the Unit Sheet evokes a protest. When there is a two-window display, the Select command should be used to display the desired sheet. (See the section "Sheet Access Commands".)

The Switch command is used to move from one window to the other. Normally you would work with a two-window display. However, when working with large models containing many variables and rules, you will find it necessary to display just one sheet on the screen. In such cases, you can invoke the single window option by typing **/W1**.

The two windows scroll independently. If the same sheet is displayed in both the windows, changes made in any window affect the entire sheet.

Solve Command (/!)

The Solve Command is used from any sheet or subsheet to initiate model resolution. You initiate this command by typing /!. Depending upon the problem formulation, either the Direct Solver or the Iterative Solver is called. Since the Action key initiates model resolution only from the Variable and Rule Sheets, the Solve command is used when you are displaying any of the other sheets while playing with a model.

SHEET ACCESS COMMANDS

There are three different Sheet Accessing commands: the Select, Dive, and Return commands (see Table 4-7).

Select Command (=)

The Select command is used to display a specified sheet in a window. The different options are shown in Table 4-8. You initiate this command by typing = and the different options "Sheet: V R U G L F P T" appear in the Prompt/Error line.

You display the desired sheet by typing the appropriate character. To display the Unit Sheet, you would type **U** in response to the prompt. The Unit Sheet will replace the sheet currently displayed in the window. When there is a two-window display, you must use the Select command to change the displayed sheet, since the Window command /W doesn't work in such cases. The Select command can be used from any sheet or subsheet.

Table 4-7.
Sheet Access Commands

Command	Action
=	Display selected sheet
>	Dive into subsheet
<	Return from subsheet

Table 4-8.
Select Command

Command	Select
=V	Variable Sheet
=R	Rule Sheet
=U	Unit Sheet
=G	Global Sheet
=L	List Sheet
=F	User Function Sheet
=P	Plot Sheet
=T	Table Sheet

Dive Command (>)

The Dive command is used to access a subordinate subsheet from a higher level sheet or subsheet; for instance, to access the Variable Subsheet from the Variable Sheet. You execute this command by typing > (holding down the Shift key and pressing the > key simultaneously). If no dependent subsheet exists, TK!Solver beeps and the display does not change.

Return Command (<)

The Return command is the opposite of the Dive command. It is used to return to the sheet or subsheet from which the Dive command was executed. You execute this command by typing <. However, if this command is initiated at the Top Level, TK!Solver beeps.

ACTION COMMAND (!)

The Action command performs a variety of actions depending on the sheet from which it is invoked (see Table 4-9). For example, pressing the Action key ! on the Variable or Rule Sheets initiates model resolution. Depending on the problem formulation, either the Direct Solver or the Iterative Solver is called. Pressing the Action key on a Plot Sheet containing information for generating a plot displays the plot.

HELP COMMAND (?)

The Help command can be used from any sheet or subsheet to get information on available commands, actions, and options. It is especially useful when you have forgotten how a particular command works. Typing ? initiates this command and displays the Help prompt "Help: ? or topic:". There are two responses to this prompt. The first response is to type a ? to see instructions on using the Help facility. The second response is to specify a topic and press the Enter key. The requested information is then displayed. If necessary, the information will be displayed one page after another with the prompt "Help: Next Page: Y N" appearing at the end of

Table 4-9.
Action Command

Sheet/Subsheet	Action
Variable Sheet	Solve model
Rule Sheet	Solve model
Plot Sheet	Display plot
Table Sheet	Display table
List Subsheet	Fill list
User Function Subsheet	Fill list
All others	No action

each page. Responding with a **Y** displays the next page. An **N** terminates the information display and the Help prompt reappears.

If there is no help text available for a topic, the message "No topic <specified topic name>; More help: Y N" is displayed. Responding with a **Y** brings further help. Pressing the Enter key in response to the Help prompt exits the Help facility. The Break key may also be used to exit the Help command.

5

Rule Syntax and Semantics

Most of the power and originality of TK!Solver comes from the fact that the user communicates with the computer in terms of equations (or rules as they are called in TK!Solver) instead of programs made up of sequences of instructions. The TK!Solver user builds models consisting of sets of equations that express the mathematical relationships between the variables. Once a model has been set up, it can be used to solve any conceivable problem within the model's domain without the user having to reformulate the equations depending on the nature of the particular problem.

It is important that the user and the computer understand each other well when the user builds models, formulates the problems, and views the results, and when the computer interprets the models and generates the solutions to the problems. The user and the computer communicate through a simple "rule language." Like any other language, human or computer, this language has its syntax (which defines the various language elements and the way they may be combined) and its semantics (which defines the meaning of the various constructs).

The purpose of this chapter is to summarize the syntax and semantics of this rule language. We will show the syntax in terms of the so-called BNF notation which we will first describe. The compensation for learning BNF notation will be a precise and concise picture of the TK!Solver rule syntax—superior to a clumsy and wordy description in plain English. The following material may seem too technical for a TK!Solver or computer novice. It will do no harm to skip the formal BNF definitions and only browse through the text or to go on to the other chapters and then return to this one.

SYNTAX NOTATION

The BNF notational scheme (or Backus Naur Form) is named after John Backus and Peter Naur, who were the first to use it with computer languages. According to this scheme, an element of a language is defined as follows:

(element to be defined) : := (some combination of defined elements)

> **Note:** The symbol : := stands for "is defined as." The defined elements can be either previously or subsequently defined.

A definition may have two or more lines starting with : :=. In this case each line represents an alternative definition for a given element. In our modification of the BNF notation, we will use the following symbols for identifying, separating, and combining the syntactic elements:

- <> enclose and separate syntactic elements.
- | separates alternative elements.
- [ ] enclose optional elements.
- { } enclose repeatable elements that must occur at least once.

Note that we do not type in these symbols when entering a rule. Their only purpose is to facilitate the syntax description.

Now let's see how this system works using a familiar example—a house (the presentation loosely follows the introduction to BNF notation given in the Apple III *Business BASIC Reference Manual, Volume 2*).

<house> : := roof{door}{window}[fireplace][all-electric kitchen]

A house has a roof, one or more doors, and one or more windows, and may also have a fireplace and an all-electric kitchen.

<home> : := house | cottage | mansion

A home can be a house, a cottage, or a mansion.

<suburban neighborhood> : := house{ house}

Suburban neighborhoods have space between houses.

<urban neighborhood> : : = house{house}

Urban neighborhoods have no space between houses.

MODEL DEFINITION AND RULE SYNTAX

Now let's take a quick look "from the top" beginning with the definition of a TK!Solver model:

<model> : : = <rule>[{{newline}<rule>}]

This means that a model consists of at least one rule; each rule must start on a new line, and there may be any number of lines between the rules.

<rule> : : = <expression>=<expression>[<comment>]

This means that a rule is represented by two expressions linked by an equal sign and followed, optionally, by a comment. The length of a rule including blanks and comments must not exceed 200 characters. For easy viewing, it is preferable to accommodate a single rule within the visible part of the rule field (76 characters).

<comment> : : = "<character string>

This means that a rule comment consists of a quotation mark (") followed by a string of characters.

Now let's start from the other end by defining the basic elements and the way they are put together to form expressions.

Basic Elements

<letter> : : = A | B | C | D | E | F | G | H | I | J | K | L | M | N | O | P | Q | R | S | T | U | V | W | X | Y | Z | a | b | c | d | e | f | g | h | i | j | k | l | m | n | o | p | q | r | s | t | u | v | w | x | y | z

<digit> : : = 0 | 1 | 2 | 3 | 4 | 5 | 6 | 7 | 8 | 9

<special character> : : = @ | # | $ | % | _

<other character> : : = + | − | * | / | ^ | = | . | , | : | ; | ! | ? | & | ' | " | ~ | | | \ | (|) | [|] | { | } | < | >

<leading character> : : = <letter>|<special character>

<name character> : : = <leading character>|<digit>

<name> : : = <leading character>[{<name character>|<digit>}]

Note: The length of a name is limited only by the length of a rule, which must not exceed 200 characters.

<character> : : = <name character>|<other character>

<character string> : : = {<character>}

Operands

<variable name> : : = <name>

<whole number> : : = {<digit>}

<integer> : : = [+|−]<whole number>

<decimal fraction> : : = .<whole number>

<number in standard notation> : : = <integer>[.]
: : = <integer><decimal fraction>
: : = [+|−]<decimal fraction>

Note: The length of a number in standard notation is limited by the length of the rule, which must not exceed 200 characters.

<exponent symbol> : : = e | E

<number in scientific notation> : : = <number in standard notation>
<exponent symbol >[<integer>]

<numeric value> : : = <number in standard notation>|
<number in scientific notation>

<symbolic value> : : = '<name>

Operators and Functions

<unary operator> : : = +|−

<binary operator> : : = +|− | * | / | ^

<built-in function> : : = <function name>([<argument>
[{,<argument>}]])

<argument> : : = <expression>|<symbolic value>

Note: The syntax and semantics of built-in functions including the type of arguments will be summarized in the last section of this chapter.

<user-defined function> : : = <name>(<argument>)

<function> : : = <built-in function>|
<user-defined function>

Expressions

<arithmetic expression> : : = <unary operator><expression>|
<expression><binary operator>
<expression>

<expression> : : = <numeric value>|<variable name>|
<function>|<arithmetic expression>|
(<expression>)

Note: The variable name and function must evaluate into a numeric value.

<symbolic expression> : : = <symbolic value>|<expression>

Note: Expression must evaluate into symbolic value.

Numeric and Symbolic Values

As mentioned earlier, TK!Solver recognizes both numeric and symbolic values. However, unlike many common computer languages, TK!Solver variables are "type-less": a variable, for example *abc*, may be assigned either 1984 or 'dog as the input value during model resolution. (Note the single quote preceding *dog* indicating a symbolic value.) The same freedom applies to user-defined functions where both function and argument values may be numeric or symbolic.

However, when evaluating expressions, TK!Solver checks value types and rejects incompatibilities (TK!Solver cannot multiply 2.54 by *'blue*).

Blanks

Blanks may not appear within names, numeric values, or symbolic values as previously defined. However, any number of blanks (within the limits of the length of the rule) may appear around operands, operators, and expressions. If you wish to have a variable name consisting of two or more separate words, for instance *old value,* join them by using the underscore, that is, *old_value.*

SYNTAX CHECK (EXAMPLE)

The following example illustrates these concepts with an example of a syntactically correct rule:

$$(ABC\,\hat{}\,n-68.3*sin(th2))*(x+y)=1.67\mathrm{e}-4*(24*b+c)+exp(-x*y)$$

Here we can recognize the following syntactic elements:

Names:	*ABC n sin th2 x y a b c exp*
Variables:	*ABC n th2 x y a b c*
Built-in functions:	*sin exp*
Numbers in standard notation:	68.3 1.67 −4 24
Numeric values:	68.3 1.67e−4 24

and arithmetic expressions:

Left-hand Expression	Operator	Right-hand Expression	Resulting Expression
ABC	^	*n*	*ABC*^*n*
68.3	*	*sin*(*th2*)	68.3***sin*(*th2*)
ABC^*n*	−	68.3***sin*(*th2*)	*ABC*^*n*−68.3***sin*(*th2*)
x	+	*y*	*x*+*y*
(*ABC*^*n*−68.3***sin*(*th2*))	*	(*x*+*y*)	(*ABC*^*n*−68.3***sin*(*th2*))*(*x*+*y*)

and so on.

This summary of rule syntax is not meant to discourage the TK!Solver novice with no experience in computer programming from setting up the models. The syntax is easy to learn from examples and experience, whereas the BNF notation is good for settling arguments with the computer, computing friends, and software developers.

The TK!Solver parser (the part of the program interpreting the model prior to its resolution) will not accept any syntactic "spelling mistakes." It insists on correct syntax in rules and expressions and helps us achieve it by locating the mistakes and suggesting what might be wrong.

Assume our mind and fingers wander and we try to enter the previous

```
(1r) Rule:
(Edit) Missing operand
==================== VARIABLE SHEET =========================...
St Input      Name     Output     Unit       Comment
-- -----      ----     ------     ----       -------
              ABC


==================== RULE SHEET =============================...
S Rule
- ----
  (ABC*_*n-68..3*sin(th 2))*(x+y+1.67e^4*(24b+c)+exp(-x*y))
```

Figure 5-1.
First attempt to enter "misspelled" rule; parser rejects **

rule in a badly misspelled form:

(ABCn−68..3*sin(th 2))*(x+y+1.67e^4*(24b+c)+exp(−x*y))**

TK!Solver meticulously points to one mistake after another, keeping us in Edit mode until everything is fixed. The first response (see Figure 5-1) protests the illegal FORTRAN-like exponentiation operator. The parser interprets a double asterisk as two separate multiplication operators, leaves the cue between them, and asks for the "Missing operand". Note that *ABC* was recognized as a legal variable name and displayed in the Name field on the Variable Sheet.

Replacing ** with ^ and pressing the Enter key again brings the cue to a point where *n* is accepted as a variable name but **68..3** is rejected as a single operand (see Figure 5-2). The error message shows again that the

```
(1r) Rule:
(Edit) Invalid operator
==================== VARIABLE SHEET =========================...
St Input      Name     Output     Unit       Comment
-- -----      ----     ------     ----       -------
              ABC
              n


==================== RULE SHEET =============================...
S Rule
- ----
  (ABC^n-68._.3*sin(th 2))*(x+y+1.67e^4*(24b+c)+exp(-x*y))
```

Figure 5-2.
Parser's way of rejecting 68..3

```
(1r) Rule:
(Edit) Invalid operator
==================== VARIABLE SHEET ========================...
St Input      Name     Output     Unit       Comment
-- -----      ----     ------     ----       -------
              ABC
              n
              th

==================== RULE SHEET ============================...
S Rule
- ----
  (ABC^n-68.3*sin(th 2_))*(x+y+1.67e^4*(24b+c)+exp(-x*y))
```

Figure 5-3.
Parser dislikes blank space in *th2*

parser tries to guess (but cannot guarantee) the correct interpretation of our intention and may be slightly off in pointing to the location and the cause of the trouble.

The same applies to the next error (see Figure 5-3). The parser interprets an illegal blank in the middle of the variable name as an "Invalid operator". If we need a space within the variable name we can simulate it by using the special character _. Note that *th* has been treated as a variable name and will have to be removed from the Variable Sheet.

We fix *th2* but run into another "Invalid operator". This time the parser expects a regular operator after **24** rather than the letter *b* (see Figure 5-4).

After we insert an * between **24** and ***b***, the parser goes through to the

```
(1r) Rule:
(Edit) Invalid operator
==================== VARIABLE SHEET ========================...
St Input      Name     Output     Unit       Comment
-- -----      ----     ------     ----       -------
              ABC
              n
              th
              th2
              x
              y

==================== RULE SHEET ============================...
S Rule
- ----
  (ABC^n-68.3*sin(th2))*(x+y+1.67e^4*(24b_+c)+exp(-x*y))
```

Figure 5-4.
Parser does not recognize operand consisting of digits followed by a letter

```
(1r) Rule:
(Edit) Missing equal sign
==================== VARIABLE SHEET ========================...
St Input      Name     Output     Unit       Comment
-- -----      ----     ------     ----       -------
              ABC
              n
              th
              th2
              x
              y
              b
              c
==================== RULE SHEET ============================...
S Rule
- ----
  (ABC^n-68.3*sin(th2))*(x+y+1.67e^4*(24*b+c)+exp(-x*y))_
```

Figure 5-5.
Parser does not accept a rule without an equal sign

end of the rule and then it realizes that there isn't any equal sign (see Figure 5-5).

In Figure 5-6 the parser protests the "Equal sign within parentheses" (enclosing the whole rule within a pair of parentheses is not allowed).

We balance the parentheses in the left-hand expression by adding a parenthesis where it belongs (just before the equal sign), but now the parser detects "Unmatched right parenthesis" (see Figure 5-7). We must remove one of the two right parentheses at the right end of the rule.

After we fix that and press the Enter key, the rule is finally accepted. This is indicated by the absence of an error message and, more importantly, by the asterisk in the rule's Status field. The Memory Indicator

```
(1r) Rule:
(Edit) Equal sign within parentheses
==================== VARIABLE SHEET ========================...
St Input      Name     Output     Unit       Comment
-- -----      ----     ------     ----       -------
              ABC
              n
              th
              th2
              x
              y
              b
              c
==================== RULE SHEET ============================...
S Rule
- ----
  (ABC^n-68.3*sin(th2))*(x+y=_1.67e^4*(24*b+c)+exp(-x*y))
```

Figure 5-6.
The rule as a whole is not supposed to be embraced by parentheses

```
(1r) Rule:
(Edit) Unmatched right parenthesis
==================== VARIABLE SHEET ========================...
St Input      Name     Output     Unit       Comment
-- -----      ----     ------     ----       -------
              ABC
              n
              th
              th2
              x
              y
              b
              c
==================== RULE SHEET ============================...
S Rule
- ----
  (ABC^n-68.3*sin(th2))*(x+y)=1.67e^4*(24*b+c)+exp(-x*y)) _
```

Figure 5-7.
Excess of right parentheses in right-hand expression

drops by 1 and the Solution Indicator "!" appears in the Status line showing that the model (or a part of it) is in, but has not yet been solved. Figure 5-8 shows the situation after we move the cursor to the second line in the Rule Sheet by pressing the Down Arrow key (as if we were about to type in the second rule).

A close comparison with the correct equation given at the beginning of this section reveals that the numeric value 1.67e−4 was typed in incorrectly. Why wasn't this inconsistency spotted by the parser and rejected? The reason is that 1.67e^4 is syntactically correct. According to the definition of a number in scientific notation, 1.67e is interpreted as a legal

```
(2r) Rule:                                                        195/!

==================== VARIABLE SHEET ======================================
St Input      Name     Output     Unit       Comment
-- -----      ----     ------     ----       -------
              ABC
              n
              th
              th2
              x
              y
              b
              c
==================== RULE SHEET ==========================================
S Rule
- ----
* (ABC^n-68.3*sin(th2))*(x+y)=1.67e^4*(24*b+c)+exp(-x*y)
```

Figure 5-8.
Rule accepted, albeit with a semantic error, 1.67^4=7.77796321, instead of intended 1.67e−4=0.000167

operand meaning 1.67e^4=1.67^4=7.77796321, rather than 1.67e−4= 0.000167 as was intended. This, of course, is a semantic error, which the parser cannot detect.

A full list of error messages and remedial actions is found in the *TK!Solver Reference Manual* Appendix.

RULE SEMANTICS

In the previous section we saw how rules can be made syntactically correct so that TK!Solver will accept them. Having syntactically correct rules is the first and most basic condition for getting anything accomplished. The second condition is that rules be formulated so that TK!Solver will interpret them according to our intentions (it does not help if we wanted to say 0.000167, but this number became 7.77796321 in TK!Solver's interpretation, as shown in the previous section). The third condition is that in addition to TK!Solver accepting the syntax and interpreting our intention correctly, the intention must make sense to start with.

This scheme represents three aspects of computer-assisted problem solving:

Syntactic	Our entries have to make sense to the computer.
Semantic	Our entries have to make the same sense to the computer as they do to us; that is, the computer has to interpret them the way they are intended.
Pragmatic	The entries and consequent computer responses have to make sense when measured by our human values and goals.

Much of the time people spend with and around computers is devoted to reconciliations at these three levels—moving in what sometimes seems to be an endless (or worse, vicious) circle. TK!Solver does not automate this reconciliation process or eliminate any of its ingredients. It does, however, compact this process in space by bringing all the essential information on the screen and in time by providing an immediate response to our trials and thus speeding up the elimination of our errors.

Professionals using TK!Solver should be able to take care of the pragmatic aspects. There is not much left to do on the semantic level either: TK!Solver simplifies semantic considerations by letting the user rely more on his or her language of mathematical models and relationships.

Some of TK!Solver semantics is explained in the last section of this chapter, which deals with built-in functions. More information is given in the chapters dealing with special functions, model design, and solution process. The rest of this section examines three specific semantic considerations: the precedence of operations in the evaluation of expressions, number representation, and the issue of indeterminacy.

Precedence of Operations

In sequential programming, the precise order of computation is predetermined by the program. In TK!Solver, however, the solution of the model propagates whenever the opportunity arises. In other words, rules are scanned and operations performed whenever operand values are available. The order of operations coming up to execution depends on the formulation of the problem, that is, on the set of input variables.

What really matters is not the order in which the operations are performed, but the order in which they are recognized during scanning and parsing of the expressions. At that time TK!Solver has to decide unambiguously whether the expression *r*s+t* should be interpreted as *r* multiplied by the sum of *s* and *t* (the APL language interpreter would do that) or as the sum of *t* and the product of *r* and *s* (as in BASIC or FORTRAN).

Similar to the way of parsing in BASIC or FORTRAN, the TK!Solver parser looks for the subexpressions inside the innermost pairs of parentheses first. Having isolated a group of operands and operators, the parser interprets them in the following order of precedence:

+ −	unary plus and minus
^	exponentiation
* /	division and multiplication
+ −	addition and subtraction.

Once we know how TK!Solver interprets the expressions, we can formulate them so that they will be interpreted precisely the way we want by interspersing them with parentheses wherever necessary. For example, if we want to multiply the sum of *s* and *t* by *r*, we type **r*(s+t)**. If we want to use the Calculator mode to assign the negative value of 4^1.8, we type **−(4^1.8)**; if we leave out the parentheses, the unary minus takes precedence over ^ and TK!Solver refuses to raise −4 to power 1.8.

The arithmetic operations of equal level of precedence (* and / or + and −) are interpreted from left to right, and again the parentheses may affect the order of parsing and the results of computation. To illustrate, let's look at two sets of examples, each with four different setups of operators and parentheses and two different results:

$$18-4-6 = 18-(4+6) = 8 \quad \textit{versus} \quad 18-4+6 = 18-(4-6) = 20$$
$$84/6/7 = 84/(6*7) = 2 \quad \textit{versus} \quad 84/6*7 = 84/(6/7) = 98$$

Needless to say, if all the operators after 18 in the first set were pluses, the inclusion of parentheses would still affect the parsing, but it would not change the results of computation. The same could be said if the division operators after 84 in the second set were replaced by multiplication operators.

Representation of Numbers

Most of the communication between the user and TK!Solver and most of the problem-solving itself deals with numbers. The TK!Solver user has to know a few things about how the numerical entries should be formatted, how they may or may not be interpreted by TK!Solver, and how to interpret the numerical results that TK!Solver displays. At the source of these considerations are the physical limitations of computer memory and memory organization—all of which are present in all computing systems. The designers of TK!Solver shield users from many of the common worries and considerations concerning number representation, but not from all.

First, there is only one type of numerical constant and one internal format for storing numerical values in TK!Solver (unlike many programming languages that accept integer or floating point or single- or double-precision formats). As was shown in the rule syntax overview, numbers in standard or decimal form as well as in scientific notation* are accepted as numerical constants in TK!Solver rules. The same syntax applies to the numerical values entered in other TK!Solver sheets. Both "E" and "e" are equally good exponent prefixes in scientific notation. The plus sign doesn't

* In scientific notation a number is written in two parts separated by "E" or "e." The first part, called the mantissa, may contain a decimal point. The second part, called the exponent, must be an integer. The value is a product of the mantissa and 10 raised to the power of the exponent, for example,

```
   4.782E4  =  4.782 * 10^4   =   47820
 24.567e-5  =  24.567 * 10^-5 =   0.00024567
    -325e6  =  -325 * 10^6    =   -325000000
```

and so on. When TK!Solver displays a number in scientific notation, it uses "E" and makes the absolute value of the mantissa a number between 1 and 10 (the second and third numbers in this example would be displayed as 2.4567E−4 and −3.25E8 respectively).

need to precede an exponent. There is no need for (and no objection to) a period after an integer number or trailing zeros in the decimal part of the number.

We may type in a numerical constant or entry of any length up to 200 digits, but there is a limitation on the number of significant digits that TK!Solver accepts either in the standard format or in the mantissa of the scientific format. The trailing zeros (as in 16830000 or 2.56000) do not count as significant digits. Other than that, the limit on the number of significant digits is 11 or 12, depending on the distribution of the digits around the decimal point.

TK!Solver groups the digits by pairs on the left- and right-hand sides of the decimal point. It accepts the first six of them counting from left to right. In standard notation the excess digits are cut off. The pairs cut off from the left of the decimal point are replaced by zeros. Here are some examples:

Typed in	**Accepted by TK!Solver**	**Number of Significant Digits**
1234.1234	1234.1234	8
1234567890100	1234567890100	11
.0000123456123456	.0000123456123456	12
.00000123456123456	.0000012345612345	11
12345671234567	12345671234500	12
1234567.12345	1234567.1234	11
99999999999999	99999999999900	12

When the number are input in scientific notation much the same happens except TK!Solver rounds the numbers off instead of truncating them:

99999999999999e1	100000000000000	11
123456.123456e15	1.23456123456E20	11
123456.123456e16	1.23456123456E21	12

The numbers with the smallest absolute values different from zero that can be accepted or generated by TK!Solver are 1E−120 and −1E−120. An attempt to type in or generate any number with an absolute value smaller than 1e−120 results in an assignment of zero (this is unlike some other systems which indicate a so-called "underflow" in similar situations).

The numbers with the largest acceptable and representable absolute value are

.999999999999e120 and −.999999999999e120

that is, from just below 1e120 to just above −1e120. Attempts to enter or generate numbers with larger absolute values produce the error messages "Unevaluated expression" or "Exponent overflow".

The limits on the number of significant digits and on the magnitude of numerical values are generous enough to make TK!Solver understand and interpret correctly the user's numerical entries in the widest variety of applications.

The communication of numerical results from TK!Solver to the user, however, is a different matter. The fact that TK!Solver is limited to 11 or 12 significant digits may be responsible for a loss of accuracy throughout the computation process. For example, in TK!Solver the product of the two numbers 12345.6789 and 98765.4321 is 1219326311.13 (which is as much as can be expressed in 12 significant digits). The last six digits of the exact product

$$12345.6789 * 98765.4321 = 1219226311.12535269$$

are lost. The difference between the exact and approximate product is 0.00464731. This error by itself is very small relative to the numbers involved. However, as the solution to a problem propagates through the TK!Solver model, so does the error. An unlucky combination of subtractions, multiplications, and evaluations of mathematical functions may amplify the errors and, in extreme cases, produce untrustworthy results.

As an example of such an extreme let's consider the following expression:

$$\frac{1 - cos(x)}{x\ sin(x)}$$

This expression should evaluate very close to 1/2 for small values of x. The equivalent TK!Solver expression $(1-cos(x))/(x*sin(x))$ turns into zero when x is equal to or smaller than 0.00001. (It does not evaluate at all when x is smaller than 1e−60 because, in that case, both the numerator and denominator are approximated by 0, and TK!Solver ignores the 0/0 operation as indeterminate.)

In the next four chapters we will see how to take care of most of these precision and accuracy problems at the model design and problem-solving stage. Difficulties with error propagation and limited precision are common to all digital computers and to all programs dealing with numerical calculations. Actually, detection and prevention of these difficulties in TK!Solver is made easier thanks to the flexibility with which the most peculiar problems may be formulated and the models modified.

Indeterminacy

The semantic significance of a rule unfolds as the indicated operations are carried out during the problem-solving process. As we will see in Chapter 8, the solution propagates through the rules with TK!Solver performing one elementary operation (simple arithmetic operation or function evaluation) after another as the ingredients (operands or arguments) become available.

Let's assume an operation $a=b*c$ (or its equivalents $b=a/c$ or $c=a/b$) where a, b, and c stand for expressions as defined earlier in the chapter. TK!Solver will try to evaluate each one of them provided the values of the other two are available. The following three outcomes are possible:

1. The operation is performed, the unknown element is evaluated, and the solution process continues.
2. The operands or the implied results of the operation are outside the definition domain, the solution process terminates, and the appropriate error message is displayed.
3. The operands are satisfactory, but the information they carry is insufficient to determine the result. The operation is ignored and the solution continues.

The second outcome would occur if you attempted to divide a non-zero operand by zero with an implied result of infinity, which exceeds TK!Solver's limit of 1e120. The third outcome would occur if $a=b=0$ in this operation. Any value of c would satisfy the equation 0=0*c, and so no particular value could be determined and assigned to c. Consequently there is nothing that could be gained from the whole rule within which the 0/0 is spotted. At the same time there is no reason why the solution should not be allowed to propagate through the rest of the model. This situation is called "0/0 bypass" and we will take advantage of it when we design conditional rules (see Chapter 11).

In addition to the division of zero by zero, there are four other indeterminate situations related to the power operation

1 = 1^x   1 = x^0   0 = 0^x   x = 0^0

that also lead to a rule bypass. Last in this indeterminate category is the function *atan2(y,x)* which, as we will see later, serves for evaluation of the arctangent of y/x. Nothing is (and nothing can be) evaluated when $x=y=0$.

SYNTAX AND SEMANTICS OF BUILT-IN FUNCTIONS

TK!Solver offers the model designer a few dozen built-in functions to work with. Some of these are standard mathematical functions that bestow mathematical modeling powers on TK!Solver. Many of these functions may be found in common programming languages; others are unique to TK!Solver. These unique functions amplify the powers of TK!Solver by making it easier to design models, to formulate problems, and to reach desired solutions.

The built-in functions in TK!Solver may be subdivided into several categories. We will examine each category from the viewpoint of its formal setup (syntax) and its interpretation in problem-solving situations (semantics).

Built-in functions are not "case-sensitive": *sin*(x) or *SIN*(x) or *Sin*(x) all return the sine of x. This freedom does not apply to variable names: *ab*, *Ab*, *aB*, and *AB* would be interpreted as different variables.

Unlike most programming languages, there are no "reserved names" in TK!Solver. For instance, we can use *sin* as a variable name although that may be confusing and, therefore, not advisable. (TK!Solver would not have problems with *sin*(*sin*), but the user might.)

Mathematical Constants

The approximations of two widely used mathematical constants are available in TK!Solver as functions with no arguments. These are the transcendental numbers π (the ratio of the circumference to the diameter of a circle) and e (the base of natural logarithms). These are treated in TK!Solver as follows:

Mathematical notation	π	e
TK!Solver syntax	pi( )	*e*( )
Rounded-off display in Input or Output fields	3.1415927	2.7182818
Full internal representation displayed in Status field	3.1415926536	2.7182818285

Invertible Mathematical Functions

The following standard invertible mathematical functions are available in TK!Solver:

- Root function (square root)
- Exponential function
- Natural and decadic logarithms
- Trigonometric functions (sine, cosine, and tangent)
- Circular or inverse trigonometric functions (arcsine, arccosine, and arctangent)
- Hyperbolic functions (hyperbolic sine, cosine, and tangent)
- Inverse hyperbolic functions (arc hyperbolic sine, arc hyperbolic cosine, and arc hyperbolic tangent)

Table 5-1 summarizes the standard invertible mathematical functions including their TK!Solver syntax and definition intervals.

There are many other invertible mathematical functions we can use with TK!Solver that are not included in this table. Some of these may be expressed in terms of functions in the table (for instance, secant=1/cosine). Others (gamma function, integral logarithm) may be built by the model designer using the user-defined function feature.

Invertibility plays a crucial role in TK!Solver and needs to be discussed. If we have a rule *g*=*h*^2 with an assigned input value of *h* as 2.4 and we solve for *g*, TK!Solver responds with an output value for *g* equal to 5.76. Sometimes the same function value is associated with different values of an argument. For example, both *h*=2.4 and *h*=−2.4 as input values will yield *g*=5.76. Likewise, any of the equations *x*=−1.25**pi*( ), *x*=0.25**pi*( ), *x*=2.25**pi*( ), and so on will yield *sin*(*x*)=0.7071067812.

Should the inverse function (the square root of 5.76 in the first case) be 2.4 or −2.4? Should the arcsine of 0.7071067812 in the second example be −1.25**pi*( )=−3.926991 or 0.25**pi*( )=0.78539816 or 2.25**pi*( )=7.0685835? TK!Solver chooses a positive value in the case of the root function (2.4 in our example) and the so-called principal value in the case of inverse trigonometric functions (0.78539816 in our example). The non-uniqueness of some of the inverse built-in functions has to be taken into account when we design and use models with these functions.

Another potential source of problems is the limited precision of numerical approximation of function values. The TK!Solver documentation states that the functions in this category are typically evaluated to an

Table 5-1.
Built-in Invertible Mathematical Functions

Function	Syntax	Domain of Function Definition	Range of Function Values	Inverse Function
Square Root	*sqrt(x)*	$0 \le x <$ 1e120	$0 \le F <$ 1e60	$x = F$^2
Exponential Function	*exp(x)*	$-292.4283 < x <$ 276.3102	$0 < F <$ 1e120	$x =$ *ln(F)*
Natural Logarithm	*ln(x)*	$0 < x <$ 1e120	$-276.3102 < F <$ 276.3102	$x =$ *exp(F)*
Decadic Logarithm	*log(x)*	$0 < x <$ 1e120	$-120 < F <$ 120	$x =$ *exp(F)*/.43429448
Sine	*sin(x)*	$-$1e12 $< x <$ 1e12	$-1 \le F \le 1$	$x =$ *asin(F)*
Cosine	*cos(x)*	$-$1e12 $< x <$ 1e12	$-1 \le F \le 1$	$x =$ *acos(F)*
Tangent	*tan(x)*	$-$1e12 $< x <$ 1e12	$-$1e10 $< F <$ 1e10	$x =$ *atan(F)*
Arcsine	*asin(x)*	$-1 \le x \le 1$	$-$pi()/2 $\le F \le$ pi()/2	$x =$ *sin(F)*
Arccosine	*acos(x)*	$-1 \le x \le 1$	$0 \le F \le$ pi()	$x =$ *cos(F)*
Arctangent of x	*atan(x)*	$-$1e120 $< x <$ 1e120	$-$pi()/2 $\le F \le$ pi()/2	$x =$ *tan(F)*
Arctangent of y/x	*atan2(y,x)*	$-$1e120 $< y <$ 1e120	$0 \le F <$ 2*pi()	$y = x$**tan(F)*
		$-$1e120 $< x <$ 1e120		$x = y$/*tan(F)*
Hyperbolic Sine	*sinh(x)*	$-276.3102 < x <$ 276.31021	$-$5e119 $< F <$ 5e119	$x =$ *asinh(F)*
Hyperbolic Cosine	*cosh(x)*	$-276.3102 < x <$ 276.31021	$1 < F <$ 5e119	$x =$ *acosh(F)*
Hyperbolic Tangent	*tanh(x)*	$-276.3102 < x <$ 276.3102	$-1 < F < 1$	$x =$ *atanh(F)*
Arc Hyperbolic Sine	*asinh(x)*	$-$1e60 $< x <$ 1e60	$-138.8482 < F <$ 138.84824	$x =$ *sinh(F)*
Arc Hyperbolic Cosine	*acosh(x)*	$1 < x <$ 1e60	$0 < F <$ 138.84824	$x =$ *cosh(F)*
Arc Hyperbolic Tangent	*atanh(x)*	$-1 < x < 1$	$-11.85950 < F <$ 11.859499	$x =$ *tanh(F)*

Notes: 1. Definition limits are shown as would be seen in Input or Output fields of Variable Sheet (excess digits ignored).

2. The accuracy of function evaluation deteriorates when close to the definition limits (particularly the trigonometric functions should not be used for arguments far from the principal value region).

3. An attempt to evaluate a built-in function or its inverse outside the definition intervals results in termination of the solution with an appropriate error message.

accuracy of 10 significant digits. This is exactly what happened in the example with $sin(x)$. The exact value of $sin(-5\pi/4)=sin(\pi/4)=sin\ (9\pi/4)= sqrt(1/2)$ with 12-digit precision equals 0.707106781186. However, the *sin* evaluator in TK!Solver returns

$$sin(-1.25*pi()) = 0.707106781195$$
$$sin(.25*pi()) = 0.707106781195$$
$$sin(2.25*pi()) = 0.707106781201$$

All these numbers and also $sqrt(1/2)$ rounded off to 10 digits are indeed the same, 0.7071067812.

In the case of a function with extreme arguments, the accuracy of the evaluations may be even worse than that. TK!Solver, however, makes it easy to examine the situation using the Calculator mode and modified rules in order to remedy or circumvent this kind of problem.

Non-invertible Mathematical Functions Of One or Two Arguments

The non-invertibility of certain mathematical functions clashes with the TK!Solver spirit: if these functions are present in a rule, none of their unknown arguments can be evaluated even if the values of the rest of the variables are known. The reason is that the inverses may be ambiguous (absolute values, for example) or non-existent (as is the case when the *int* function is not equal to an integer value). We must take the consequences of non-invertibility into consideration when designing, analyzing, or using TK!Solver models. Table 5-2 summarizes the syntax and semantics of non-

Table 5-2.
Built-in Non-invertible Mathematical Functions

Function	Syntax	Returns
Absolute value	$abs(x)$	x if $x \geq 0$ $-x$ if $x < 0$
Signum	$sgn(x)$	1 if $x > 0$ 0 if $x = 0$ -1 if $x < 0$
Integer part	$int(x)$	Integer part of x
Remainder	$mod(x1,x2)$	Remainder of division of $x1$ by $x2$, $mod(x1,x2)=x1-x2*int(x1/x2)$
Step function	$step(x1,x2)$	1 if $x1 \geq x2$ 0 if $x1 < x2$

invertible mathematical functions of one or two arguments.

Non-invertible Mathematical Functions Of Multiple Arguments

The syntax of this class of functions is as follows:

<function of multiple argument> : : = <function name> (multiple argument)

<multiple argument> : : = <expression list>|<list name>

<expression list> : : = <expression>{,<expression>}

An expression list consists of two or more expressions (as defined in the section "Model Definition and Rule Syntax") separated by commas.

<list name> : : = <symbolic value>|<expression>

> **Note:** The list name is either a symbolic value or an expression that evaluates into a symbolic value; the symbolic value must represent a list and the name must appear in the List Sheet.

Naturally, a function can be evaluated only after all the ingredients are available. When a multiple argument is in the form of an expression list, all the constituent expressions must be evaluated from the input variables and rule information. When a multiple argument is in the form of a list name, the appearance of this name in the List Sheet and its definition in the List Subsheet are sufficient for function evaluation. Table 5-3 gives a summary of the functions of multiple arguments available in TK!Solver.

Special TK!Solver Functions

There are three functions—element, selection, and status—which do not fit any of these categories. These functions enhance the problem-solving powers of TK!Solver in specific ways.

Element Function

The element function is defined as follows:

(element function) : : = *element*([<list name>, <expression>[,<expression>]])

Table 5-3.
Functions of Multiple Arguments

Function	Syntax	Returns
Maximum value	*max(m)*	Maximum value of the multiple arguments
Minimum value	*min(m)*	Minimum value of the multiple arguments
Polynomial	*poly(x,m)*	Sum of the polynomial: $\sum_{i=1}^{n} m_i x^{(n-i)}$ where n is number of arguments in *m*
Net present value	*npv(x,m)*	Net present value of a cash flow series: $\sum_{i=1}^{n} m_i \left(\frac{1}{1+x}\right)^{(i-1)}$ where n is number of arguments in *m*
Element count	*count(m)*	Number of elements in a list or 0 if there are no defined elements for the specified list
Sum of series	*sum(m)*	Sum of values represented by the argument: $m_1 + m_2 + m_3 + ...$
Dot product	*dot(m1,m2)*	Sum of products of element pairs of *m1* and *m2*: $m1_1.m2_1 + m1_2.m2_2 + m1_3.m2_3 + ...$ where *m1* must be a list name and *m2* is a list name or expression list

Note: *m, m1,* and *m2* are multiple arguments as defined above; *x* represents expressions as defined in "Model Definition and Rule Syntax."

This function may be used in three different forms:

a. *element*( ), with no argument, returns the number of the instance currently being processed during List Solving or returns 0 if List Solving is not invoked.

b. *element(m,x)* returns the value of the *x*th element in the list *m*.

c. *element(m,x1,x2)* returns the value of the *x1*st element in the list *m*; if this element does not exist, the value of expression *x2* is returned.

The *element* function is non-invertible: none of its unknown arguments or argument components can be evaluated from a known function value.

Selection Function

The selection function is defined as follows:

(selection function) : : = *apply*(<symbolic expression>, <expression>)

The first argument must evaluate into a symbolic value representing a name that must appear on the User Function Sheet. The second argument, an expression, must evaluate into a value within the domain of the user-defined function specified by the first argument.

The selection function is used to select or invoke a particular user-defined function (for example, miles per gallon versus speed curve) depending on the circumstances of the problem (for instance the make and type of a car). Saying *apply('fun,x)* is equivalent to saying *fun(x)*, and we naturally prefer the latter form if we are happy with a fixed function name. The selection function *apply(car,x)* enables us to find the gas mileage for a given speed or vice versa depending on the assigned value of *car* (*'Horizon*, *'Datsun210*, *'Chevette*, and so on).

The invertibility of the selection function with respect to the second argument depends on the invertibility of the invoked user-defined function: the functions with Table or Linear Mapping are invertible, the functions with Step Mapping are not (see Chapter 6). The selection function is not invertible with respect to the first argument: we cannot expect the make of the car in return for given speed and gas mileage.

Status Function

The status function is defined as follows:

(status function) : : = *given*({<symbolic expression>,} <expression>,<expression>)

This function sorts the symbolic expression arguments into two groups:

a. Those that represent names of input variables

b. Those that represent names of variables with no assigned input values.

If all the symbolic expression arguments fall into group (a), the status function is evaluated from the first of the last two expressions. If any of the symbolic expression arguments fall into group (b), the status function is evaluated from the second (or last) expression.

The status function represents a valuable source of information about the status of the variables for use during model resolution. It is the only function that can be evaluated when the values of some of the arguments are unknown and consequently out of reach of any other function or operation. Without the status function, we would be unable to access and check an unknown variable and assign it, for instance, a default value.

Only the expression that is applicable according to the status of the symbolic expression arguments needs to be known for the evaluation of the status function. The status function is not invertible: none of the expression arguments or their components can be evaluated from a known function value.

6

Special Functions

The syntax and semantics of the built-in and user-defined functions were discussed in Chapter 5. Tables 5-1 and 5-2 summarized the built-in functions. This chapter discusses and illustrates the use of TK!Solver's special built-in functions. It also includes an in-depth discussion of user-defined functions—the different types, their features, how they should be defined, and facts to keep in mind when using them.

LIST FUNCTIONS

Functions such as *count, sum, max,* and several others operate on lists of values and are known as List functions. They can have one or more arguments, which can be specified in either of the following ways:

1. As a listname, that is, the name of a list containing the different values. Alternately, an expression that evaluates to a symbolic value representing a listname can be used.
2. As the values themselves separated by commas. Expressions that evaluate to numeric values can also be used.

The listnames need not appear in the Variable Sheet; they must, of course, be present in the List Sheet. The use of lists as arguments in List functions does not require List Solving. List functions and List Solving are two different features that may or may not be used together. This chapter focuses exclusively on List functions leaving the List Solving feature and the combination of the two for Chapter 10.

In the List function examples, the "experimental" list of values will be enclosed in square brackets; for example, *sample*[5,30,23] means a list named *sample* with three elements 5, 30, and 23.

Symbolic and Numeric Arguments

In the following examples, the *count*, *max*, *min*, and *sum* functions are discussed. In each example, the list *income*[20000,35000,24000,46000] is used.

Expression: *count('income)*
Result: 4

Expression: *count('income,*10,30000)
Result: 3
Reason: We might expect the result to be 6 since *income* is a list with four elements and there are two other values in the argument. However, TK!Solver ignores the fact that *income* is a list and treats it as a symbolic value, returning 3.

Expression: *max('income)*
Result: 46000

Expression: *max('income,*55000,23000)
Result: Returns the error message "Max: Argument error".
Reason: We might expect a result of 55000 since this is the largest value among all the values in the list *income* and the two other arguments specified along with it. However, TK!Solver treats *income* as a symbolic value, ignoring the fact that it is a list. When trying to compare symbolic and numeric values to find the maximum, TK!Solver obviously fails.

Expression: *min('income)*
Result: 20000

Expression: *min('income,*500,1000)
Result: Returns the error message "Min: Argument error".
Reason: The same as for the *max* function.

Expression: *sum('income)*
Result: 125000

Expression: *sum('income,*2000,3000)
Result: Returns the error message "Sum: Argument error".
Reason: We might expect to get 130000 (125000 from the list plus the other two values). However, TK!Solver treats *income* as a symbolic value, ignoring the fact that it is a list. So when TK!Solver tries to add the symbolic value *income* to the numbers, it obviously fails.

Partial and Empty Lists as Arguments

A basic principle behind TK!Solver is that if there is an unknown variable in a rule, the program will attempt to evaluate it from known information. If this attempt fails, the equation is left unsolved. However, this principle is not rigidly enforced when TK!Solver deals with List functions as explained in the following sections.

Partially Filled List

Figure 6-1 shows the List Subsheet for *info*. There is no second element in the list. When the rule *x=count('info)* is entered in the Rule Sheet and the model is solved, *x* is evaluated as 3. The answer is correct since there are three elements in the list in Figure 6-1. The purist might argue that since one element in the list is unknown, the equation should be left unsolved. On the other hand, returning 3 is only practical since there are three elements in the list, and this is what TK!Solver does. It ignores the blank element. TK!Solver does not treat missing elements as zeros; if it did, *x* would be equal to 4.

When the rule *y=sum('info)* is added to the model and solved, *y* is evaluated as 24. The blank element is not taken into account when TK!Solver evaluates the sum of the elements in the list.

```
=================== LIST: info ===...
Comment:
Display Unit:
Storage Unit:
Element Value
------- -----
1       3

3       9
4       12
```

Figure 6-1.
List Subsheet for *info* with blank element

Similarly, *max, min, npv,* and *poly* ignore blank elements in the lists. However, the *dot* function treats the blank element as a zero.

Empty List

Let's assume that all three elements in the list *info* are blanked out using the Blank command (/B) and the model *x=count('info), y=sum('info)* is solved again. In this case, x is evaluated as zero since there are no elements in the list. What might be a surprise is that y is also zero. This means that TK!Solver is assuming that when there are no elements in the list, the sum is zero.

If the rule

$$a + sum('b) = c * d$$

is solved with $a=4$, $c=8$, and b an empty list, then d is evaluated as 0.5. This happens because the sum of the empty list b is returned as zero. Since the rule will be marked "Satisfied", we might assume that everything is fine. In fact, however, the list b could have inadvertently been left empty. So you must take care to prevent empty lists from going undetected and corrupting the results. The interaction of this behavior of empty and partially filled lists with List Solving is discussed in Chapter 10.

When an empty list is used as an argument, the following functions also return zero: *dot, npv,* and *poly.* The functions *max* and *min* return argument error messages.

Dot Function

The *dot* function *dot(arg1,arg2)* returns the dot product of the two arguments *arg1* and *arg2*. Suppose *quant*[1,3,4] is a list with quantities of three different products and *price*[4,8,3] is a list with the unit prices of the three products. Then *dot('quant,'price)* returns 40. This is how it works:

quant:	1	3	4
price:	4	8	3

dot('quant,'price) = 1*4 + 3*8 + 4*3 = 40

The first argument for the *dot* function must be a listname and the second name may be a listname (as in the present example), or it may be expressions separated by commas. This function is especially useful in statistical analysis models (see the Linear Regression Analysis model in Chapter 10).

NPV Function

The *npv* function *npv(rate,listname)* returns the Net Present Value of a series of cash flow values, given in the list *listname*, at the discount rate specified in the first argument. The Calculation Unit for the first argument is assumed to be a decimal fraction rather than a percent. The *npv* function is used in financial analysis for capital investment decisions and budgeting.

Let's consider an investment proposal. An initial investment of $10,000 is expected to yield the following cash flows at the end of each succeeding year: $2000, $4000, $4000, $3000, and $2000. If the discount rate is 15%, what is the net present value of the investment?

First we enter these cash flows in the list *money*, as shown in Figure 6-2. Since the initial investment is a cash outflow, the first element of the list is entered as a negative value.

Then we enter the rule *value=npv(disct,'money)* in the Rule Sheet. Only the variables *value* and *disct* are recorded by TK!Solver in the Name field on the Variable Sheet. The listname *money* is treated as a symbolic value and is not recorded. Since the *npv* function assumes that the Calculation Unit for *disct* is a decimal fraction, we have to define a conversion between the decimal fraction and the percent on the Unit Sheet so that the value for *disct* can be entered as a percent. We assign 15% to *disct*, solve, and find *value* to be equal to 103.38324, as shown in Figure 6-3.

This is how the function works (see also the formula in Table 5-3):

```
value = -10000*(1/1.15)^0 + 2000*(1/1.15)^1 +
         4000*(1/1.15)^2 + 4000*(1/1.15)^3 +
         3000*(1/1.15)^4 + 2000*(1/1.15)^5
```

which yields 103.38324, as mentioned earlier.

```
=================== LIST: money =====================...
Comment:                     list of cash flow values
Display Unit:                $
Storage Unit:                $
Element Value
------- -----
1       -10000
2       2000
3       4000
4       4000
5       3000
6       2000
```

Figure 6-2.
List Subsheet with cash flow values; note that the investment is entered as a negative value

```
==================== VARIABLE SHEET ========================...
St Input      Name      Output      Unit      Comment
-- -----      ----      ------      ----      -------
              value     103.38324   $         net present value
   15         disct                 %         discount rate


==================== RULE SHEET ============================...
S Rule
- ----
  value = npv(disct,'money)
```

Figure 6-3.
Variable and Rule Sheets with Net Present Value evaluated; note the absence of the list-name *money* in the Variable Sheet

The use of the *npv* function is further discussed in Chapter 15 in conjunction with capital investment problems. With this function it is possible, for instance, to find the internal rate of return (IRR) using the Iterative Solver.

Poly Function

The *poly* function *poly*(x,*coeff*) returns the sum of the polynomial in x with the coefficients *coeff*. Let's assume *coeff* is a list with three elements [6,−3,4] and $x=2$; then *poly*(x,*'coeff*) returns 22. This function works as follows:

$$6 * 2\wedge(3-1) + (-3) * 2\wedge(3-2) + 4 * 2\wedge(3-3) = 22$$

The general formula is given in Table 5-3.

TK-SPECIFIC FUNCTIONS

The three functions *element*, *given*, and *apply* are unique to TK!Solver and greatly enhance its problem-solving capabilities. This section discusses each of the functions in detail and provides suitable examples.

Element Function

The *element* function can essentially be used in three different ways: with no arguments, with two arguments, and with three arguments.

```
==================== VARIABLE SHEET ==...
St Input      Name     Output     Unit
-- -----      ----     ------     ----
L             index
L  0          p
L             q
L  0          r


==================== RULE SHEET ======...
S Rule
- ----
  index = element()
  p * q = r
```

Figure 6-4.
Variable and Rule Sheets of the model using the *element* function with no argument

Element Function With No Argument: *element*( )

This form returns the number of the instance being currently processed during List Solving. It can play a role similar to that of the loop index in FOR/NEXT loops in BASIC.

Let's consider, for example, the Variable and Rule Sheets in Figure 6-4. Here, *p*[5,10,15,20,25] and *r*[10,20,30,40,50] are declared as input lists. In addition, *q* and *index* are also declared as lists. Typing /L! initiates List Solving. As each instance is processed, the instance number is displayed in the Output field of *index*. Figure 6-5 shows the values obtained after List Solving displayed using the table feature.

We can use this changing value of *index* as the second argument in the two-argument format of the *element* function to access a particular element in a list during List Solving.

Element Function With Two Arguments: *element*(*listname*,*x*)

This form returns the value of the *x*th element in the list whose name is specified in the first argument. The variable *x* can be an expression that

p	r	q	index
5	10	2	1
10	20	2	2
15	30	2	3
20	40	2	4
25	50	2	5

Figure 6-5.
Table of values after List Solving of model in Figure 6-4

evaluates to a numeric value, and *listname* can also be an expression that evaluates to the name of a list.

If p=[5,10,15,20,25] and n=3, then *element('p,n)* returns the value 15, since 15 is the third element in the list p.

If n=6, *element('p,n)* returns an error message: "Element: Argument error". This error occurs because of the attempt to access the non-existent sixth element (list p contains only five elements). In such cases the *element* function with three arguments comes in handy.

Element Function With Three Arguments: *element(listname,x,y)*

This form returns the value of the xth element in the specified list; if this element does not exist, it returns the value of the third argument y. Variable y can be an expression that evaluates to a numeric or symbolic value.

If p=[5,10,15,20,25], m=6, and r=50, then *element('p,m,r)* returns 50. Since there are only five elements in list p and m=6, the value of r (the default value) is returned. Thus with this third format, it is possible to avoid generating error messages when non-existent elements are accessed and instead return default values or model-specific messages. This process is similar to array-bounds checking in conventional programming.

The *element* function is not invertible. It cannot be used for "feeding" (assigning values to) a list. Consider the following rule:

$$f = element('exam,num)$$

where *exam*[30,40,50,60], f=70, and *num*=5.

When this rule is solved, TK!Solver returns an "Element: Argument error" message because there is no value corresponding to *num*=5 in the list *exam*. We might say that since f=70, TK!Solver should assign this value to the fifth position in the list *exam*; but it doesn't. TK!Solver can assign values to list elements only during List Solving as discussed in Chapter 10.

Generating Fibonacci Numbers

The *element* function with three arguments can be used for finding the famous Fibonacci sequence of numbers. The story goes as follows:

> A certain man put a pair of rabbits in a place surrounded by a wall. How many pairs of rabbits can be produced from that pair in a year, if every month each pair begets a new pair that is productive from the second month on?

The numbers of pairs of rabbits form the Fibonacci sequence which is given by the general formula

$$F(n) = F(n-1) + F(n-2)$$

where F(n) is the nth number (or rabbits in nth month), and F(1)=1.

This formula produces the following results:

$$\begin{aligned} n = 2&: F(2) = F(2-1) + F(2-2) = F(1) = 1 \\ n = 3&: F(3) = F(3-1) + F(3-2) = F(2) + F(1) = 1+1 = 2 \\ n = 4&: F(4) = F(4-1) + F(4-2) = F(3) + F(2) = 2+1 = 3 \end{aligned}$$

The first twelve Fibonacci numbers derived in this manner are 1, 1, 2, 3, 5, 8, 13, 21, 34, 55, 89, and 144. What transpires is that the values computed in the previous two steps have to be used in the present step to get the number, and the value calculated in this step has to be used in the next two steps, and so on. This sequence suggests that the *element* function can do the job.

Since we need an index like n, we use the *element* with no argument. This leads to the first rule *num=element*() in the Rule Sheet shown in Figure 6-6. Suppose we use the list *fibnum* to store the generated numbers. In the ith step we should access the ($i-2$)th element and also the ($i-1$)th element, and we should add them up to get the ith element and store it back in *fibnum*. This suggests the following rule:

fibnum = *element('fibnum,num−2)* + *element('fibnum,num−1)*

Let's assume that the list *fibnum* initially contains 1 in the first position. When List Solving is initiated, the first instance sets *num* to 1 from the first rule. When *num*=1, the second rule becomes

fibnum = *element('fibnum,*1−2) + *element('fibnum,*1−1)

This rule will generate an error because the second arguments in the two element functions are −1 and 0 respectively. To prevent this "out of bounds" error, we use a third argument for the element function. We use 0 and 1 as the default values, as shown in Figure 6-6.

Since we have just one element in the list *fibnum*, if we type /**L**! to initiate List Solving, only one instance will be processed and the solution process will terminate. Instead, we use the Block Solving option and specify how many numbers we want to generate. We initiate Block Solving by typing /**LB**. In response to the "Block: First element:" prompt, we enter **2**, and for the last element prompt, we enter **12**. The specified number of Fibonacci numbers is generated (see the List Subsheet in Figure 6-7).

```
==================== VARIABLE SHEET ========================...
St Input      Name    Output    Unit      Comment
-- -----      ----    ------    ----      -------
              n       12                  index
L             fibnum                      fibonacci numbers


==================== RULE SHEET ============================...
S Rule
- ----
  n = element()
  fibnum = element('fibnum,n-2,0) + element('fibnum,n-1,1)
```

Figure 6-6.
Variable and Rule Sheets for generating Fibonacci numbers

Given Function

The Status function *given('v1,'v2,'v3,...,'vn,x,y)* returns the value of x if all the variables *v1, v2, v3,..., vn* have input values; if any one of them has not been assigned an input value, the value of y is returned. Note that the variable names have to be expressed as symbolic values; thus the variable *v1* is expressed as *'v1*. The arguments x and y can be expressions that evaluate to either numeric or symbolic values. This function should have a

```
==================== LIST: fibnum ===...
Comment:
Display Unit:
Storage Unit:
Element Value
------- -----
1       1
2       1
3       2
4       3
5       5
6       8
7       13
8       21
9       34
10      55
11      89
12      144
```

Figure 6-7.
List Subsheet with Fibonacci numbers

minimum of three arguments, and TK!Solver treats the last two arguments as the values to be returned.

In TK!Solver, all other functions or operations are ignored unless the values of all arguments are known (either input or evaluated). The *given* function plays a special role in TK!Solver in that it works regardless of whether or not the values of the arguments *V1, V2, V3, ..., Vn* are known. The information about a variable's status may be used to control the model resolution process or to assign a default value. Before looking at specific examples, let's see how the function works.

Consider the Variable and Rule Sheets shown in Figure 6-8. Since the variable *p* has an input value, the first rule sets *w* to 5, the value of *A*. Note how the variable name *p* is expressed as a symbolic value by prefixing it with a quote (') in the Rule Sheet.

In the second rule, *x* is set to 10, the value of *B*, since the variable *q* does not have an input value. Out of the four variables whose status is being checked in the third rule, *q* does not have an input value. So *y* is set to 10, the value of *B*. Even if a variable does not appear on the variable sheet, it still is considered to have an input value. Since *ne* does not appear on the Variable sheet, *z* is set to the value of *A* in the last rule.

Of the two last arguments, only the argument that is used for the function evaluation needs to be known. Thus, even if *A* has no value (and there is no additional rule for it), *given('p,'q,A,B)* returns 10 (the value of *B* since *q* has no input value).

```
==================== VARIABLE SHEET ==...
St Input      Name     Output    Unit
-- -----      ----     ------    ----
   3          p
              q
   4          r
   23         s
   5          A
   10         B
              w          5
              x         10
              y         10
              z          5

==================== RULE SHEET ======...
S Rule
- ----
  w = given('p,A,B)
  x = given('q,A,B)
  y = given('p,'q,'r,'s,A,B)
  z = given('p,'ne,A,B)
```

Figure 6-8.
Variable and Rule Sheets with *given* function example

The *given* function is non-invertible. In Figure 6-9, since r has an input value, and Z is known, we might expect TK!Solver to assign 16, the value of Z, to X. It doesn't and the rule remains unresolved.

How the Given Function Works

During problem solving, there are three typical situations in which the *given* function comes in handy. First, the *given* function can be used when we need to assign default values to variables that have input value. For example, in a model involving g, the acceleration due to gravity, a default value can be assigned to the value of g using the *given* function in a rule, instead of entering it every time on the Variable Sheet. Further, if a value is assigned as input on the Variable Sheet it is used instead of the default value set in the rule. Second, the *given* function can be used to round off values of variables to make them more meaningful. While the *int* function can be used for this purpose, it is noninvertible and so TK! Solver will not be able to solve for its argument. Using the *given* function avoids this loss of back solvability. Finally, the *given* function can be used to select only those equations in the model that are applicable under the particular conditions. The solution strategy can thus be controlled with the help of the *given* function. We will now look at the examples of these three situations.

Using Given to Assign a Default Value

The *given* function may be used to assign a default value to a variable. Let's assume that the inflation rate, *infl*, in a model has to be assigned a default of 5%. This can be expressed as follows:

$$infl = given('infl, infl, 5)$$

If *infl* is assigned an input value, this equation becomes *infl*=*infl*; otherwise it is *infl*=5.

```
==================== VARIABLE SHEET ==...
St Input       Name     Output     Unit
-- -----       ----     ------     ----
   4           r
               x
   2           y
   16          z

==================== RULE SHEET ======...
S Rule
- ----
* z = given('r,x,y)
```

Figure 6-9.
Variable and Rule Sheets illustrating the non-invertibility of the *given* function

Note, however, that if *infl* is evaluated from any other rule and is not equal to 5, TK!Solver will detect a contradiction. One of the two rules will be marked with the error symbol ">" and the solution process will terminate. (You will find an additional example of using *given* for returning default values in Chapter 12.)

Using Given With Int to Return Integer Values

Integer-valued solutions are sometimes required because it is not possible to buy 495.3 items of something or employ 5.7 persons. Generally, calculations are performed with the actual numbers and only the final displayed results are rounded off. Numbers can be rounded up or down depending on the circumstances.

Assume that the variable *Qcal* is calculated from the rule

$$Qcal = sqrt(2*ad*oc/hc)$$

and needs to be rounded up to the nearest integer and displayed as *Qorder*. This suggests the following rule:

$$Qorder = int(Qcal+.5)$$

But there is a problem with using this rule. What happens if *Qorder* is given and *ad* is to be calculated? Since *int* is a non-invertible function (see Table 5-2), *Qcal* cannot be evaluated from the second rule and so *ad* remains unevaluated.

So we need a rule that will check if *Qorder* is given, and if so, set *Qcal* equal to *Qorder*. This leads to the rule

$$Qcal = given('Qorder, Qorder, Qcal)$$

Figure 6-10*a-c* shows the Variable and Rule Sheets with illustrative examples.

Using Given to Control Solution Strategy

Let's examine a model dealing with the analysis of chemical compounds for this explanation. The gram molecular mass *gmm* of a chemical compound consisting of three elements is given by the equation

$$gmm = am1*n1 + am2*n2 + am3*n3$$

where *am1*, *am2*, and *am3* are the atomic masses of the three elements and *n1*, *n2*, and *n3* are the numbers of each of the elements in the compound. A user-defined function relating the element names and their

```
==================== VARIABLE SHEET ============================...
St Input        Name      Output      Unit        Comment
-- -----        ----      ------      ----        -------
   1000         ad                                annual demand
   5            oc                    $           ordering cost
   1.25         hc                    $           holding cost
                Qorder    89                      ordering quantity
                Qcal      89.442719               calculated quantity
```

a. Variable Sheet with *Qorder* evaluated and displayed as an integer

```
==================== VARIABLE SHEET ============================...
St Input        Name      Output      Unit        Comment
-- -----        ----      ------      ----        -------
                ad        1250                    annual demand
   5            oc                    $           ordering cost
   1.25         hc                    $           holding cost
   100          Qorder                            ordering quantity
                Qcal      100                     calculated quantity
```

b. Variable Sheet with *Qorder* given and *ad* evaluated

```
==================== RULE SHEET ================================================
S Rule
- ----
  Qcal = sqrt(2*ad*oc/hc)                   "  original equation
  Qorder = int(Qcal+.5)                     "  round up Qcal to Qorder
  Qcal = given('Qorder,Qorder,Qcal)         "  if Qorder is given, Qcal=Qorder
```

c. Rule Sheet with the rules in the model

Figure 6-10.
Using the *given* function to display an integer solution

atomic masses can be used to return the atomic masses when the elements are specified. Figure 6-11 shows the User Function Subsheet for the function *fun*.

Rules of the form

$$am1 = fun(e1)$$

can be used to do the Table Lookup when the element *e1* is specified. When there are two more similar rules for the other two elements, everything will work fine, provided the model is used for compounds with three elements.

When there are only two elements, however, *e3* will not have any input value and so the rule *am3=fun(e3)* will not be solved. Consequently, the rule for evaluating *gmm* will remain unresolved and the model becomes useless for two-element compounds. However, the *given* function can be used in the rule for *am3* so that the Table Lookup is performed when *e3* is specified; if *e3* is not specified, *a3* is assigned zero. The modified rule will be

$$am3 = given('e3,fun(e3),0)$$

```
==================== USER FUNCTION: fun ========================================
Comment:                    atomic masses of elements from the periodic table
Domain List:                element
Mapping:                    Table
Range List:                 atomic_mass
Element Domain      Range
------- ------      -----
1       'hydrogen   1.008
2       'helium     4.003
3       'lithium    6.939
4       'beryllium  9.012
5       'boron      10.81
6       'carbon     12.011
7       'nitrogen   14.007
8       'oxygen     16
9       'fluorine   19
10      'neon       20.183
11      'sodium     22.9898
12      'magnesium  24.312
```

Figure 6-11.
User Function Subsheet for function *fun*

Since *n3* is also involved in the *gmm* rule, the *given* function can be used to set *n3* to zero if *e3* is not given, as follows:

$$n3 = given('e3,n3,0)$$

With these two rules, *gmm* can be evaluated even when there are only two elements in the compound. Figure 6-12 shows the Rule Sheet with all the

```
==================== RULE SHEET ================================================
S Rule
- ----
  "            * * * * *     Chemical Compound Analysis     * * * * *"

* gmm = am1*n1 + am2*n2 + am3*n3            "  molecular mass

* p1 = am1*n1/gmm                           "  proportion of e1
* p2 = am2*n2/gmm                           "  proportion of e2
* p3 = am3*n3/gmm                           "  proportion of e3

* tw = w1+w2+w3                             "  total amount
* w1 = p1*tw                                "  amount of e1
* w2 = p2*tw                                "  amount of e2
* w3 = p3*tw                                "  amount of e3

* am1 = fun(e1)                             "  atomic mass of e1
* am2 = fun(e2)                             "  atomic mass of e2
* am3 = given('e3,fun(e3),0)        "  if e3 is given do table lookup, else am3=0

* w3 = given('e3,w3,0)              "  if e3 is not given, set w3=0
* n3 = given('e3,n3,0)              "  if e3 is not given, set n3=0
```

Figure 6-12.
Rule Sheet with rules for chemical compound analysis; note the use of the *given* function

rules in the model. The Variable Sheets with the analysis of compounds with two and three elements are shown in Figures 6-13*a* and 6-13*b* respectively.

```
=================== VARIABLE SHEET ==================================
St Input       Name    Output      Unit        Comment
-- -----       ----    ------      ----        -------
   'hydrogen   e1                              first element
   'oxygen     e2                              second element
               e3                              third element

   2           n1                              # of atoms of first element
   1           n2                              # of atoms of second element
               n3      0                       # of atoms of third element

               gmm     18.016      amu         molecular mass of compound
               tw      28.15       g           total amount of compound

               w1      3.15        g           amount of first element
   25          w2                  g           amount of second element
               w3      0           g           amount of third element

               p1      11.190053 %             proportion of first element
               p2      88.809947 %             proportion of second element
               p3      0         %             proportion of third element

               am1     1.008       amu         atomic mass of first element
               am2     16          amu         atomic mass of second element
               am3     0           amu         atomic mass of third element
```

a. Two-element compound

```
=================== VARIABLE SHEET ====================================
St Input       Name    Output      Unit        Comment
-- -----       ----    ------      ----        -------
   'calcium    e1                              first element
   'carbon     e2                              second element
   'oxygen     e3                              third element

   1           n1                              # of atoms of first element
   1           n2                              # of atoms of second element
   3           n3                              # of atoms of third element

               gmm     100.091     amu         molecular mass of compound
               tw      208.33195 g             total amount of compound

               w1      83.423528 g             amount of first element
   25          w2                g             amount of second element
               w3      99.908417 g             amount of third element

               p1      40.043560 %             proportion of first element
               p2      12.000080 %             proportion of second element
               p3      47.956360 %             proportion of third element

               am1     40.08       amu         atomic mass of first element
               am2     12.011      amu         atomic mass of second element
               am3     16          amu         atomic mass of third element
```

b. Three-element compound

Figure 6-13.
Variable Sheets with analysis of compounds

Apply Function

The selection function *apply(symbolic_arg,arg)* returns the range value corresponding to the Domain value specified in the second argument *arg* for the user-defined function specified in the first argument *symbolic _arg*. We may use the *apply* function to select a particular user-defined function under certain conditions. For example, different cars have different speed versus gas mileage performances. If the speed versus gas mileage relationships are expressed as user-defined functions, then, depending on the type of the car, TK!Solver can select the appropriate function and for a given speed can determine the gas mileage. If the gas mileage is known, TK!Solver can find the speed. Another example is that different materials have different load-deformation characteristics; depending on the particular material, the appropriate set of values can be selected.

Using the Apply Function

Figure 6-14 shows the User Function Subsheet for the function *econ* relating the speed *spd* and gas mileage *emlg* of economy cars. All performance figures used in this chapter that relate to particular car models are fictitious and are for purposes of illustration only. The Mapping is Linear.

Figure 6-15 shows the Variable and Rule Sheets with the solution to the problem: what is the gas mileage of an economy car traveling at 30 mph? Note that *ecomlg* and *mileage* are the same. This is obvious because when *type* was assigned *'econ*, the *apply* function returned the value corresponding to *speed*=30 from the function *econ*. Thus, saying *apply('fun_name,*

```
=================== USER FUNCTION: econ ====================...
Comment:                          mileage vs. speed, economy cars
Domain List:                      spd
Mapping:                          Linear
Range List:                       emlg
Element Domain          Range
------- ------          -----
1       20              38
2       30              43
3       40              42
4       50              37
5       60              32
```

Figure 6-14.
User Function Subsheet for *econ* relating the speed and mileage of economy cars

```
==================== VARIABLE SHEET ============================================
St Input      Name     Output    Unit       Comment
-- -----      ----     ------    ----       -------
   'econ      type                          class of car
   30         speed              mi/hr      speed
              mileage  43        mi/gal     mileage using apply
              ecomlg   43        mi/gal     mileage from econ function

==================== RULE SHEET ================================================
S Rule
- ----
  mileage = apply(type,speed)           "  calculate mileage using apply
  ecomlg = econ(speed)                  "  mileage from user-def function
```

Figure 6-15.
Variable and Rule Sheets with solution showing that *apply* (*fun_name, arg*) is equivalent to *fun_name*(*arg*)

arg) is equivalent to saying *fun_name*(*arg*). Then what is the use of the *apply* function?

Suppose the function *mid* for midsized cars shown in Figure 6-16*a* is added to the model. If the *apply* function were not available, we would have to add the rule *midmlg=mid*(*midspd*) to calculate the gas mileage. If we wanted to use this calculated gas mileage in a different rule, for example, *amount=distance/mileage*, then, depending on whether the function *econ* or *mid* was used, this rule would have to be modified. The *apply* function comes in handy here because different functions are to be used depending on the circumstances.

To find the *mileage* of a midsized car at 40 mph, we assign *type* as *'mid* and *speed* as 40 and solve the model. The solution is 24 miles per gallon.

The speed/mileage relationship for big cars is given by the function *big* shown in Figure 6-16*b*. With these three functions and the *apply* function, the gas mileage for a specific speed (within the function limits) for any of the three types of cars can be found.

Figure 6-16*c* shows the User Function Subsheet with names of cars and their classification into one of the three categories. In Figure 6-17 a new rule has been added to the Rule Sheet relating the *type* of car and its *make*. This figure also shows the Variable Sheet with the evaluated gas mileage for a Malibu traveling at 55 mph.

Invertibility

The invertibility of the *apply* function with respect to the second argument depends on the invertibility of the invoked user-defined function. In this example, all three functions *econ*, *mid*, and *big* have Linear

```
==================== USER FUNCTION: mid ==========================...
Comment:                        speed vs. mileage for mid-sized cars
Domain List:                    spd
Mapping:                        Linear
Range List:                     mmlg
Element Domain      Range
------- ------      -----
1       20          15
2       30          22
3       40          24
4       50          23
5       60          19
```

a. Function *mid* relating the speed and mileage of midsized cars

```
==================== USER FUNCTION: big ==========================...
Comment:                        speed vs. mileage for big cars
Domain List:                    spd
Mapping:                        Linear
Range List:                     smlg
Element Domain      Range
------- ------      -----
1       20          13
2       30          15
3       40          16
4       50          15
5       60          13
```

b. Function *big* relating the speed and mileage of big cars

```
==================== USER FUNCTION: class ========================...
Comment:                        make and type of car
Domain List:                    name
Mapping:                        Table
Range List:                     category
Element Domain      Range
------- ------      -----
1       'Rabbit     'econ
2       'Datsun_210 'econ
3       'Horizon    'econ
4       'Duster     'mid
5       'Malibu     'mid
6       'Cadillac   'big
7       'LeBaron    'big
```

c. Function *class* relating the make and type of cars

Figure 6-16.
User Function Subsheets

Mapping which is invertible. Given a particular *mileage*, you can compute the *speed* for a given *make* of car using the *apply* function. If the user-defined function had Step Mapping, it would be non-invertible.

The *apply* function is not invertible with respect to the first argument. This means that even if both *mileage* and *speed* are known, it is not possible to find *type* (and also *make*).

```
=================== VARIABLE SHEET ======================================...
St Input      Name     Output     Unit        Comment
-- -----      ----     ------     ----        -------
              type     'mid                   class of car
   55         speed               mi/hr       speed
              mileage  21         mi/gal      mileage using apply
   'Malibu    make

=================== RULE SHEET ==========================================...
S Rule
- ----
  mileage = apply(type,speed)                 "  calculate mileage using apply
  type = class(make)                          "  determine type from make
```

Figure 6-17.
Variable and Rule Sheets with gas mileage evaluated for Malibu traveling at 55 mph

Using Apply for Two-Dimensional Table Lookup

Table 6-1 shows the distances between each of five different cities. To find the distance from Albany to each of the cities, we define a function named *Albany* using the values in the first column of the table. The User Function Subsheet is shown in Figure 6-18.

Similarly, we can define funcitons for the other four places using the appropriate data in Table 6-1. Since the names of the places are the same in each function, the same Domain list can be used for the other functions as was used for Albany. The User Function Sheet with the names of the functions and the Domain and Range lists is shown in Figure 6-19.

To find the distance between two cities, we must first select the function corresponding to the first of the two cities. Then the distance to the other city can be found out using the function. The question is how to select the proper function when the city name is given. Figure 6-20 shows the Rule and Variable Sheets with the rule and the distance from *'New_York* to *'Providence.*

Table 6-1.
Distances Between Different Cities

Place	Albany	Boston	Hartford	New York	Providence
Albany	0	176	107	152	174
Boston	176	0	102	215	45
Hartford	107	102	0	113	74
New York	152	215	113	0	183
Providence	174	45	183	183	0

Since *place_A* is assigned *'New_York*, the *apply* function uses *New_York* as the function name and finds the distance corresponding to *Providence*, which is the value of *place_B*, the second argument.

```
==================== USER FUNCTION: Albany ====================...
Comment:                               dist from Albany to other places
Domain List:                           place
Mapping:                               Table
Range List:                            dist1
Element Domain       Range
------- ------       -----
1       'Albany      0
2       'Boston      176
3       'Hartford    107
4       'New_York    152
5       'Providence  174
```

Figure 6-18.
User Function Subsheet for *Albany;* the Range values correspond to the distances in the first column in Table 6-1

```
==================== USER FUNCTION SHEET ==============================...
Name       Domain    Mapping Range    Comment
----       ------    ------- -----    -------
Albany     place     Table   dist1    dist Albany to other places
Boston     place     Table   dist2    dist Boston to other places
Hartford   place     Table   dist3    dist Hartford to other places
New_York   place     Table   dist4    dist New_York to other places
Providenc  place     Table   dist5    dist Providence to other places
```

Figure 6-19.
User Function Sheet with the five functions

```
==================== VARIABLE SHEET ===============...
St Input      Name     Output     Unit       Comment
-- -----      ----     ------     ----       -------
              distanc  183        mi
   'New_York  place_A
   'Providen  place_B


=================== RULE SHEET ===================...
S Rule
- ----
  distance = apply(place_A,place_B)
```

Figure 6-20.
Variable and Rule Sheets with rule and distance between New York and Providence evaluated

USER-DEFINED FUNCTIONS

Sometimes the relationship between variables cannot be expressed in terms of analytical functions or mathematical formulas. Three such examples are

1. Gas mileage versus make of the car.
2. Experimentally observed load-deformation characteristics of plastic materials.
3. Tax table.

All three relationships can be expressed in TK!Solver with the help of the user-defined function feature. Three different types of functional relationships are involved in these three examples:

1. A discrete relationship exists between the gas mileage and the make of the car. Table Lookup Mapping in TK!Solver can be used to express this relationship.
2. The intervals within successive experimental points on the load-deformation curve can be approximated by straight lines using the Linear Interpolation Mapping.
3. The amount of tax paid depends on the tax bracket within which the income lies. The tax brackets progress in steps and this stepwise relationship can be expressed using Step Mapping in TK!Solver.

Defining a Function

The User Function Sheet is used to define a function. The function name is entered in the Name field. The name of the list containing the arguments is entered in the Domain field, and the name of the list with function values is entered in the Range field. The type of relationship is expressed in the Mapping field. A user-defined function needs to be supported by the lists of related function values (Range) and argument values (Domain). One way of defining these lists is to dive into the User Function Subsheet and enter the values. Alternately, the corresponding List Subsheets can be accessed independently from the List Sheet or Variable Subsheet and the values entered. The user-defined function can be saved using the Function Save option of the Storage command (/SF) discussed in Chapter 4.

The name of a function can be entered in the Rule Sheet only after it has been defined on the User Function Sheet. The variable names for the argument and function values in the rules can be different from the Domain and Range list names. In the example of countries and capital names in the Table Lookup example discussed later, the Domain and Range listnames are *couname* and *capname* respectively (Figure 6-21), while *country* and *capital* are used in the Variable Sheet for the argument and function value (Figure 6-22).

TK!Solver's built-in function names cannot be used for user-defined functions. If you try, you will get the message "Built-in function already exists" and a beep. Using the function name for its argument or value in the rule should also be avoided. Although TK!Solver will accept *value= indic(indic)* and give correct results, this form is likely to cause confusion, especially when others use the model.

Using Table Lookup

Table 6-2 gives the names of some countries and their capitals. If we wanted to know what the capital of France was, we could find France in the table and then "look up" the corresponding entry in the capital column. Similarly, to find the country of which Tokyo is the capital, we would again do a "lookup," but this time in the country column. Table Lookup Mapping in TK!Solver works the same way. On the other hand, if we look in the table for the capital of Italy, we won't find it; in such cases TK!Solver returns the message "User Function: Argument error".

Figure 6-21 shows the User Function Subsheet with the definition of the function *capfun*. The rule containing the function and the illustrative examples are shown in Figure 6-22*a-d*.

Values should be unique: Figure 6-23 shows the User Function Subsheet with the function *type* relating the species of timber *species* and the modulus of elasticity *elasmod*.

Table 6-2.
Countries and Capitals

Country	Capital
England	London
France	Paris
Japan	Tokyo
USA	Washington, D.C.
USSR	Moscow

```
=================== USER FUNCTION: capfun ==========...
Comment:                     Countries and Capitals
Domain List:                 couname
Mapping:                     Table
Range List:                  capname
Element Domain       Range
------- ------       -----
1       'England     'London
2       'France      'Paris
3       'Japan       'Tokyo
4       'USA         'Washington
5       'USSR        'Moscow
```

Figure 6-21.
User Function Subsheet for function *capfun*

```
=================== RULE SHEET ======...
S Rule
- ----
  capital = capfun(country)
```

a. Rule Sheet

```
=================== VARIABLE SHEET ==...
St Input      Name    Output     Unit
-- -----      ----    ------     ----
              capital 'Paris
   'France    country
```

b. Variable Sheet with *capital* evaluated

```
=================== VARIABLE SHEET ==...
St Input      Name    Output     Unit
-- -----      ----    ------     ----
   'Tokyo     capital
              country 'Japan
```

c. Variable Sheet with *country* evaluated

```
(1r) Rule: User Function: Argument error

=================== VARIABLE SHEET ==...
St Input      Name    Output     Unit
-- -----      ----    ------     ----
>             capital
   'Italy     country
```

d. Variable Sheet with error message since Italy is not defined in the function in Figure 6-21

Figure 6-22.
Table Lookup

The rule *modulus=type(timber)* is entered in the Rule Sheet. When *timber* is assigned *'spruce* and the model is solved, *modulus* is evaluated as 1.2E6. When *modulus* is assigned 1.2E6 and the model is solved, *timber* is evaluated as *'redwood*. You can see from Figure 6-23 that the result is correct. However, it is not possible to get *'spruce*, despite the fact that

```
==================== USER FUNCTION: type ====================...
Comment:                         Modulus of Elasticity of Timber
Domain List:                     species
Mapping:                         Table
Range List:                      elasmod
Element Domain        Range
------- ------        -----
1         'white_oak  1700000
2         'redwood    1200000
3         'tamarack   1300000
4         'spruce     1200000
5         'soft_pine  1000000
```

Figure 6-23.
User Function Subsheet for *type* relating the timber species and modulus of elasticity; note the two identical values in the Range

'spruce also has the same value (1.2E6). The reason is that when you specify an argument (or function value), TK!Solver scans the Domain (or Range) list from the top, and when it finds a match, it returns the corresponding value from the Range (or Domain) list.

Linear Interpolation

Linear Interpolation works as follows: the relationship within each pair of consecutive points in the Domain and Range lists is approximated by a straight line. TK!Solver finds the interval within which the specified argument (or function value) lies and interpolates the corresponding function value (or argument).

Consider the points $(x1,y1)$ and $(x2,y2)$ shown in Figure 6-24. The point (x',y') is interpolated according to the following formula:

$$\frac{y2 - y1}{x2 - x1} = \frac{y' - y1}{x' - x1}$$

If x' is given, TK!Solver looks for the values of $x1$ and $x2$ in the list of x values within which x' lies. Then using the formula and the corresponding values in the y list, TK!Solver computes y'. Conversely, if y' is given, x' is evaluated in a similar manner.

A function named *relate* is defined in the User Function Sheet with x and y as the Domain and Range lists respectively. Typing **L** in the Mapping field selects Linear Mapping. Figure 6-25 shows the User Function Subsheet with the function definition.

The rule $y=relate(x)$ is entered in the Rule Sheet. When x is assigned 4 and the model is solved, y is evaluated as 35. Likewise the value of x corresponding to $y=50$ can also be found. Attempts to interpolate outside the

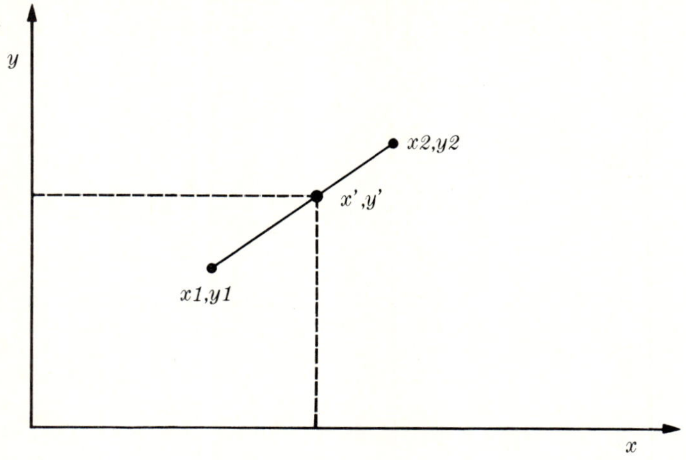

Figure 6-24.
Graphical representation of Linear Interpolation

defined limits of the function result in error messages. For example, when the equation is solved with y=70, an error occurs, the message "User Function: Argument error" is displayed, and the solution process is terminated.

Consider the function *sinfun* shown in the User Function Subsheet in Figure 6-26. The values in the Range list are the sine of the values in the Domain list. (These Range list values were generated by List Solving with the rule *ysin*=*sin*(*xsin*).) Using this function, let's interpolate the values for arguments between 0 and 60 degrees in steps of 3 and compare the results with the values returned by the *sin* function for the same arguments.

```
==================== USER FUNCTION: relate ================...
Comment:                    Linear Interpolation example
Domain List:                x
Mapping:                    Linear
Range List:                 y
Element Domain      Range
------- ------      -----
1       1           10
2       3           25
3       5           45
4       8           60
```

Figure 6-25.
User Function Subsheet for function *relate*

```
==================== USER FUNCTION: sinfun =================...
Comment:                          xsin values from sin function
Domain List:                      xsin
Mapping:                          Linear
Range List:                       ysin
Element Domain        Range
------- ------        -----
1       0             0
2       45            .7071067812
3       15            .2588190451
4       30            .5
5       60            .8660254038
```

Figure 6-26.
User Function Subsheet for *sinfun;* the *ysin* values are the sine of *xsin*

Figure 6-27 shows the Variable and Rule Sheets used in the model. Here x is declared as the Input list containing the arguments mentioned. The Table feature is used to display the values obtained from List Solving (see Figure 6-28). The plot of the error *yerr* against x is shown in Figure 6-29.

We can see that the error *yerr* is zero for the points that have been defined in the Domain list of the function. At the interpolated points, however, there is an error, and it increases as x increases. This trend is due to the nature of the Sine function.

In general, the interpolation error can be reduced if the function is defined by a greater number of points. For example, if the points in the function *sinfun* are defined in intervals of 5 degrees (instead of the 15 degrees shown), then the interpolated values will be much closer to the actual ones.

```
==================== VARIABLE SHEET =============================================
St Input      Name     Output     Unit       Comment
-- -----      ----     ------     ----       -------
L  30         x                   deg        function argument
L             y        .5                    value from sin function
L             yfun     .5                    value from Linear Interpolation
L             yerr     .0                    error due to interpolation

==================== RULE SHEET =================================================
S Rule
- ----
  y = sin(x)                          " actual y
  yfun = sinfun(x)                    " interpolated y
  yerr = y - yfun                     " interpolation error
```

Figure 6-27.
Variable and Rule Sheets in the model; the Calculation Unit for x is radians

x	sin(x)	yinterp	yerror
0	0	0	0
.052360	.05233595624	.05176380902	.000572147222
.104720	.1045284633	.103527618	.001000845227
.157080	.156434465	.1552914271	.001143037979
.209440	.2079116908	.2070552361	.000856454736
.261799	.2588190451	.2588190451	0
.314159	.3090169944	.3070552361	.001961758293
.366519	.3583679495	.3552914271	.003076522483
.418879	.4067366431	.403527618	.003209025035
.471239	.4539904997	.451763809	.002226690719
.523599	.5	.5	0
.575959	.544639035	.5414213562	.003217678778
.628319	.5877852523	.5828427125	.004942539818
.680678	.6293203911	.6242640687	.005056322338
.733038	.6691306064	.665685425	.00344518141
.785398	.7071067812	.7071067812	0
.837758	.7431448255	.7388905057	.004254319771
.890118	.7771459615	.7706742302	.006471731232
.942478	.8090169944	.8024579547	.00655903963
.994838	.8386705679	.8342416793	.004428888681
1.04720	.8660254038	.8660254038	0

Figure 6-28.
Table of values after List Solving; note the increase in *yerr* at higher values of x

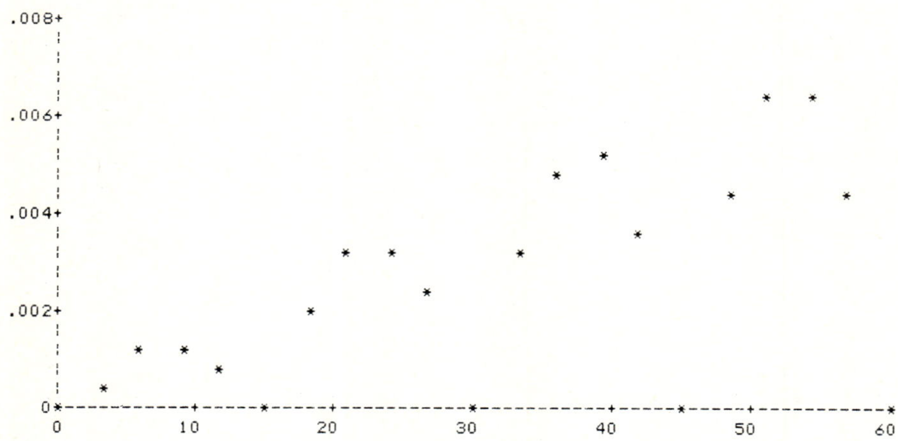

Figure 6-29.
Plot of error *yerr* as a function of x

When non-monotonous functions (functions with same Range value corresponding to two or more Domain values) are interpolated for a given Range value, the interval first encountered in the Domain list is chosen for estimating the corresponding Domain value.

Step Mapping

Step Mapping is chosen when the function must return a constant value over a certain interval of values. When an argument is specified, TK!Solver scans the Domain list from the top and finds the interval within which it lies. Then TK!Solver returns from the Range list the value corresponding to the beginning of the Domain interval (the value encountered first while scanning the Domain list). A graphical representation of Step Mapping is shown in Figure 6-30.

Consider the tax table example given earlier. Here we have a stepwise relationship, meaning that there are several income brackets and people in the same income bracket pay taxes at the same rate. A hypothetical tax structure is given in Table 6-3. The User Function Subsheet with the function *amount* is shown in Figure 6-31. Typing **S** in the Mapping field selects Step Mapping.

The rule *rate=amount(income)* is entered in the Rule Sheet.

Now let's calculate the tax rate if a person earns $18,000 annually. In this case, *income* is assigned **18000** and the model is solved; *rate* is found to be 15%. We can see from the User Function Subsheet that 18000 falls between 15000 and 20000 and so TK!Solver returns the value corresponding to 15000 from the Range list.

Now what is the tax rate for an income of $19,500? When the model is solved with this new value of *income*, the tax rate remains the same, 15%.

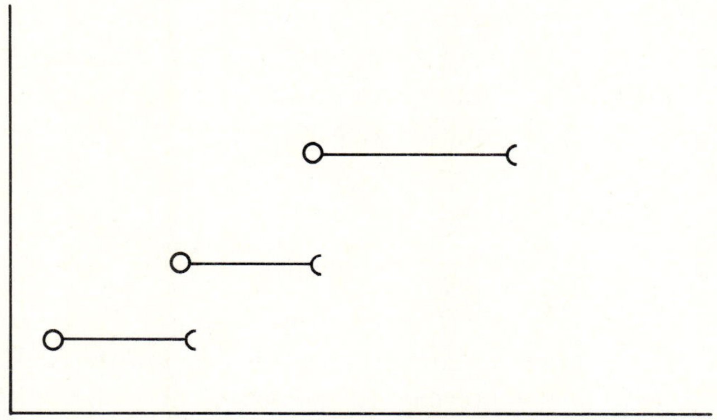

Note: (indicates open interval (<)
0 indicates closed interval (≥)

Figure 6-30.
Graphical representation of Step Mapping

Table 6-3.
A Hypothetical Tax Structure

Income ($)		Tax Rate (%)
At least	Not over	
0	5,000	0
5,000	10,000	5
10,000	15,000	10
15,000	20,000	15

```
=================== USER FUNCTION: amount ===================...
Comment:                      Income vs. Tax Rate relationship
Domain List:                  income
Mapping:                      Step
Range List:                   tax_rate
Element Domain       Range
------- ------       -----
1       0            0
2       5000         5
3       10000        10
4       15000        15
5       20000        15
```

Figure 6-31.
User Function Subsheet for *amount* relating income and rate

The reason is that this income also falls in the same income bracket, 15000 to 20000.

Step Mapping, unlike Table and Linear Mapping, is non-invertible; in other words, given a value from the Range list, it is not possible to calculate the corresponding value from the Domain list. As we saw in the preceding example, the income corresponding to a tax rate of 15% can be either 18000 or 19500; in fact, it can be 15000 or anything from 15000 to 20000. Rather than returning a value that may be incorrect, TK!Solver does not return any.

Problems With Interpolation

Since all interpolation is done on an interval-by-interval basis, the list values should be in either increasing or decreasing order. TK!Solver does not attempt to order the values in the lists prior to evaluating the function, so the results may not be what we "expect." This applies to both Linear Interpolation and Step Mapping.

For example, in Figure 6-26, if the fourth row corresponding to $xsin=45$ is moved to become the second row (using the Move command /M), and the model is solved with $x=30$ degrees, it yields $y=0.5$, $yfun=0.47140452$, and $yerr=0.02859548$. The reason is that when the list of *xsin* values is scanned (top down), TK!Solver finds that the argument 30 degrees lies between 0 and 45, the first two values in the list, and chooses the corresponding (first two) values from the *ysin* list to arrive at the value of $yfun=0.47140452$.

Units

As mentioned in the "List Sheet" section of Chapter 3, when a list with defined units is used in a user-defined function, the Display Unit of the list must be the same as the Calculation Unit of the variable. In Figure 6-26 the values of *xsin* are displayed in degrees for purposes of explanation. When the model was solved, the Display Unit for the list *xsin* was changed to radians to correspond to the Calculation Unit of x in Figure 6-27. (Note that x is used as the argument of the function *sinfun* instead of the Domain listname *xsin*.) If the Display Unit of *xsin* were not changed to radians, TK!Solver would give incorrect results.

For example, when $x=30$ degrees and the Display Unit of *xsin* is degrees, TK!Solver returns $y=.5$, $yfun=.517638092$, and $yerr=-.0176380902$. Compare these with the values in Figure 6-27. When $x=30$ degrees, y=.5, $yfun=.5$, and $yerr=0$. Therefore, care should be taken when using lists with associated units in user-defined functions.

7

Model Design

TK!Solver shortcuts the distance between the mathematical description of a problem and its numerical solution. It obviates programming of an explicit sequence of instructions that the computer must follow when solving a problem. In other words, the TK!Solver program takes care of the operation-sequencing role of conventional programs.

TK!Solver models, consisting of a number of rules (and optionally, additional information), represent the subject-matter component of the knowledge involved in the problem-solving process. Therefore, model design is a crucial step in the use of TK!Solver. Based on the discussion in Chapters 5 and 6 on the syntax and semantics of model components and subcomponents, this chapter explores the pragmatic aspects of building models.

GENERAL CONSIDERATIONS

A TK!Solver model is, in essence, a mathematical description of the relationships between variables representing various objects in the real world. This mathematical description is based on the concept of equality of expressions; each such equality is called a rule in TK!Solver. The rule's building blocks are not limited to algebraic operations and analytical functions; they may be supplemented by empiric data and relationships.

Every TK!Solver model that has been designed with a purpose reflects a segment of knowledge represented as relationships. Embedded in the TK!Solver framework, the model is not just an abstract and passive description. It opens up a concrete multidimensional space full of situations that can be actively explored and analyzed. In this process, we take advantage of the solvers, Editor, standard sheet formats, and other TK!Solver tools, features, and capabilities.

At present TK!Solver's mathematical power covers only a tiny fraction of the apparatus of applied mathematics. Not available or unattended to are such topics as complex variables, vectors, matrices, differential equations, and mathematical optimization. However, those features and capabilities that are available in TK!Solver cover an overwhelming majority of the total usage of mathematical techniques.

In many situations when TK!Solver cannot handle the general mathematical, analytical part of the problem-solving process, we can still use it for practical problem-solving employing analytically derived formulas. Let's consider as an example the problem of a curve formed by a perfectly flexible cable that is suspended from its ends. This situation may be described by the following ordinary differential equation:

$$\frac{d^2y}{dx^2} = k\sqrt{1 + (dy/dx)^2}$$

Each of the first two pairs of rules in the Rule Sheet shown in Figure 7-1 represents the analytical solution of this equation. The model may be used for investigating the shape of suspended cables under any particular conditions. Figure 7-2 shows the shape of a cable 5m long with the horizontal and vertical distance of suspension points 4m and 1m respectively.

Model Generalization

When we use a pocket calculator (including a programmable one), we usually enter the numerical data of a particular problem to get the numerical results in the quickest way. We can do the same in TK!Solver, but the quickest way is not always the most efficient. Because of the knowledge-representation nature of TK!Solver models, you should usually try to make and keep the models as general and comprehensive as possible.

Suppose we want to find the roots of the following cubic equation:

$$5x^3 + 8x^2 - 12x + 23 = 0$$

It is preferable to generalize the problems of cubic equation by expressing

```
==================== VARIABLE SHEET ==========================...
St Input      Name     Output      Unit       Comment
-- -----      ----     ------      ----       -------
                                              Point of symmetry:
              x0       1.6396240                 x-coordinate
              y0       1.1886618                 y-coordinate
                                              Left branch:
   0          x1                                 x-coordinate
   2          y1                                 y-coordinate
              s1       1.8822137                 length
                                              Right branch:
   4          x2                                 x-coordinate
   3          y2                                 y-coordinate
              s2       3.1177863                 length

              k        .56255839              Constant
   5          S                               Total length

==================== RULE SHEET ==============================...
S Rule
- ----
  " " "     C A B L E   C U R V E  " " "

  y1 = y0 + 1/k*(cosh(k*(x1-x0)) - 1)       "  left branch
  s1 = 1/k*sinh(k*(x0-x1))

  y2 = y0 + 1/k*(cosh(k*(x2-x0)) - 1)       "  right branch
  s2 = 1/k*sinh(k*(x2-x0))

  S = s1 + s2
```

Figure 7-1.
Cable curve model: Variable and Rule Sheet with a solution obtained using guesses $k=1$ and $x0=1$.

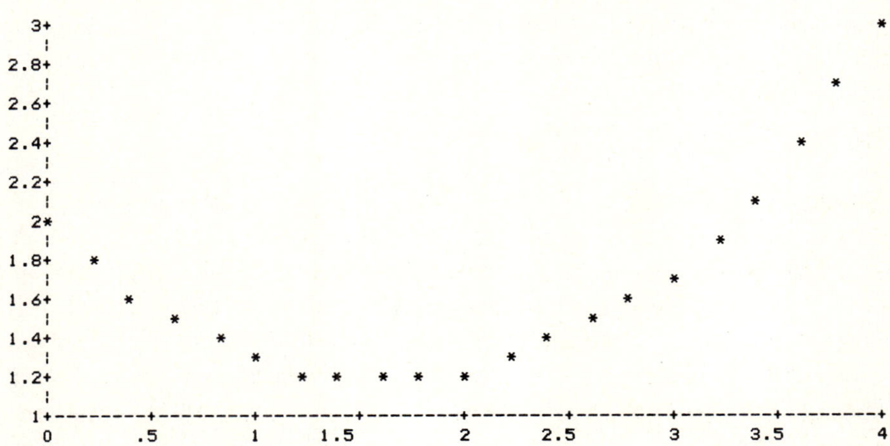

Figure 7-2.
Cable curve (shape of flexible cable suspended at two points)

the coefficients as generally applicable variables rather than as particular numerical constants, that is

$$a*x\hat{}3 + b*x\hat{}2 + c*x + d = 0$$

or, even better, using the TK!Solver function *poly:*

$$poly(x,a,b,c,d) = 0$$

This way we can clearly see that the equation defines the relationship between a, b, c, d, and x. When written in one of these general forms, the equation may be used to evaluate any of the five variables when the rest of them are known. This is the strongest point of TK!Solver. Even if the roots of the equation (the values of x) are the only object of our interest in a particular application, it is still better to have the equation in a general form with the coefficients a,b,c,d in the Variable Sheet. The reason is that we can easily assign and reassign the variable values without editing the rule. Or we can make them into lists in order to get multiple solutions, tables, graphs, or, in other words, to take full advantage of TK!Solver's flexibility and exploratory powers.

Balance of Variables and Rules

Another of TK!Solver's strong points is the ease with which the model can be built piecemeal with rules added, removed, modified, and tested as we gain a better appreciation for the subject matter and for the peculiarities of the problem-formulation and problem-solving processes. However, we must be clear about one thing: the model (or any part of it) may be solved for only as many unknown variables as the number of independent equations available.

Assume we have two rules:

$$(a + x) * (b - x) = (a + y) * (b + y) \quad (7\text{-}1)$$

$$b * (x - y) - a * (x + y) = x\hat{}2 + y\hat{}2 \quad (7\text{-}2)$$

A simple algebraic manipulation reveals that one follows from the other. They are not independent, and consequently, they have the worth of only one equation and can be used to evaluate only one variable. Should we keep both of them in the model? The answer, at least in this case, is that we shouldn't. There are situations when so-called "redundant equations" help (see Chapter 11); however in this case, one of the equations is useless and should be deleted from the model. In the next section, we will see why it is best to retain the second equation.

At some stage of the model design, we may check on the independence of the equations and make sure that the whole model can be resolved when

$$\text{NOV} = \text{TNV}-\text{NIV} = \text{NIE}$$

or

$$\begin{pmatrix}\text{Number of}\\ \text{Output}\\ \text{Variables}\end{pmatrix} = \begin{pmatrix}\text{Total}\\ \text{Number of}\\ \text{Variables}\end{pmatrix} - \begin{pmatrix}\text{Number of}\\ \text{Input}\\ \text{Variables}\end{pmatrix} = \begin{pmatrix}\text{Number of}\\ \text{Independent}\\ \text{Equations}\end{pmatrix}$$

Resolvability of Rules

The possibility of telling TK!Solver **a+b=c*d** and allowing TK!Solver's power to come up with a value for any one variable when the other three are known is undoubtedly the program's strongest syntactic and semantic feature. Of course, we only see the result, but internally TK!Solver must resort to the time-honored way of evaluating any of the following:

$$a = c*d-b$$
$$b = c*d-a$$
$$c = (a+b)/d$$
$$d = (a+b)/c$$

depending on which is the unknown. In order for TK!Solver to do this, the rule must be resolvable or backsolvable* with respect to each variable. Resolvability with respect to a particular variable means that there has to be a sequence of legal TK!Solver arithmetic and function operations that isolates the variable on one side of the equation. In other words, this sequence must lead to expressing that variable explicitly as a function of all the other variables. (Remember, the arithmetic and function operations are all TK!Solver can play with; it is incapable of performing algebraic manipulations and other mathematical tricks.)

---

* The terms "backsolving" and "backsolvable" come from TK!Solver folklore and literature. They aptly reflect the fact that if a rule is written in the form of an assignment statement, say

$$r = sqrt(x\verb|^|2 + y\verb|^|2)$$

then TK!Solver is said to "backsolve" it for unknown x or y working back past the equal sign. This is, however, only a part of the TK!Solver story. We can write this rule equally well as

$$x\verb|^|2 + y\verb|^|2 = r\verb|^|2$$

(actually, it looks better this way). In this case, the word "backsolving" does not do justice to the fact that the rule can be solved for either x, y, or r.

When you design a TK!Solver model, you should apply your mathematical skills and common sense to making the rules resolvable with respect to as many variables as possible. In the section "Balance of Variables and Rules," rule (7-1) cannot be solved for any of the variables. The equivalent rule (7-2) can be solved at least for a and b, and therefore, it is better to include this rule in the model.

If you have a choice, try to formulate the rules so that they will be resolvable with respect to those variables that you will be solving for most frequently. For instance, the equation

$$a * y + b * x = c * x * y$$

cannot be resolved directly for either x or y. If you expect to use this formula in the model quite frequently for evaluating y, you should formulate the rule as

$$y * (c * x - a) = b * x$$

which is resolvable for y, a, b, and c, but not for x. If x is usually the unknown, you would instead use

$$a * y = x * (c * y - b)$$

Now let's look at a small model that appeared in a review of TK!Solver in one of the popular computer magazines:

$$\begin{aligned} markup &= (sales - costs)/sales \\ margin &= (sales - costs)/costs \end{aligned}$$

The model in this formulation may be completely resolved for the following sets of unknowns:

markup and *margin*
markup and *costs*
margin and *sales*

However, it would have to be iterated on if the unknowns are

markup and *sales*
margin and *costs*
sales and *costs*

The obvious reason is that the first and second rules are not resolvable for *sales* and *costs* respectively. The first two of these unresolvable cases may be taken care of if the rules are formulated as follows:

$$margin = 1 - costs/sales \tag{7-3}$$
$$markup = sales/costs - 1 \tag{7-4}$$

This still would not solve the last problem with known *margin* and *markup* and unknown *sales* and *costs* (not a very likely situation). Nevertheless, by substituting for *sales/costs* into (7-4), we arrive at the final formulation, which is directly resolvable for any combination of knowns and unknowns:

$$markup = sales/costs - 1$$
$$(1 + markup) * (1 - margin) = 1$$

Model Size Limitations

The maximum possible physical size of the model in terms of the number of rules and variables depends primarily on the amount of available memory. Practically speaking, you will hardly ever reach these limits before one (or both) of the following two things happen:

- The time necessary for resolution of a huge model reaches the limit of your patience.
- The sight of the Rule Sheet and the Variable Sheet spanning over a large number of screenfuls will erode the beauty of "having the world within your eyesight and under your fingertips."

TK!Solver's sophisticated human-computer interface and extraordinary problem-solving power show up best in models with no more than three screenfuls of variables and no more than two screenfuls of rules. (However, you may wish to ignore this limitation if a large proportion of your model consists of rules that solve quickly by the Direct Solver and if a large proportion of the variables doesn't need to be observed and changed too often.)

Obviously, computer memory limitations do affect the maximum size of models or the efficiency of running the TK!Solver program. Usually it is the number and length of the lists that are responsible for "running out of memory" rather than the number of rules and variables alone.

BASICS OF MODEL DESIGN

The keystone of most programming languages is the so-called assignment statement. If the programmer writes

$$A = B - 2*A \tag{7-5}$$

the computer first evaluates the right-hand expression (that is, retrieves the values of variables A and B from the memory locations reserved for these variables and subtracts twice the value of A from the value of B). Then the value of the evaluated expression is sent back to the memory location reserved for A. The previous value of A is overwritten and lost.

In TK!Solver variable names also represent memory locations where the values of the variables are stored, but the similarity ends there. The values of individual variables cannot be overwritten during the course of model resolution by the Direct Solver.

Suppose the values of A and B are 2 and 3 respectively. When equation 7-5 is processed as an assignment statement in a conventional programming language, B remains the same and A becomes -1. In contrast, TK!Solver will, under similar circumstances, retrieve the values of A and B, check the consistency of the equation $2=3-2*2$, stop the evaluation, and issue an error message. If only A were known, B would be evaluated and assigned the value 6. If only B were known, nothing would happen.

Thus to write a rule in the form of an assignment statement as shown does not make much sense in TK!Solver. The rule would be interpreted as an equality, $3*A=B$. So why not write it this way in the first place? (Actually, we will see later that this is the *only* sensible way to write it.)

So the first important precept of TK!Solver model design is that rules or equations need not look like assignment statements. There may be a full-blown expression on the left-hand side, not just a single variable name. However, if the rule or equation represents a definition of one variable in terms of others (like the time it takes an object to fall, $t=sqrt(2*h/g)$), or if it is more pleasing mathematically or aesthetically, we should feel free to write

<variable name> = <expression>

We should keep in mind, however, that

<expression> = <variable name>

is also admissible, and

<one expression> = <another expression>

is very often preferable because it stresses the "relationship" nature of the rules and makes them more readable.

Ordering Rules in a Model

The concept of TK!Solver rule formation offers more freedom during the process of rule formulation than the computer programming concept of assignment statement. The same applies to the ordering of rules in a TK!Solver model versus the ordering of assignment and other statements in ordinary computer programs.

Suppose we need a program in BASIC for calculating the discriminant *D* and the roots *X1,X2* of a quadratic equation. Ignoring the input/output statements and checking the sign of the discriminant *D*, we can write

```
50 D  =  B^2 - 4*A*C
60 X1 =  (SQRT(D) - B)/(2*A)
70 X2 =  C/(A*X1)
```

When this program is run, the computer uses the BASIC interpreter to execute one statement after another. Any change in the order of these statements would destroy the function of the program.

TK!Solver operates differently: it scans through the rules and evaluates any single unknown variable from any particular rule it can. It stops only when there is nothing more that can be evaluated. Consequently, TK!Solver results do not depend on the order of the rules in the Rule Sheet. For instance, in the case of the quadratic equation mentioned earlier, the results will be the same if the model is entered as

```
    d  =  b^2 - 4*a*c
   x1  =  (sqrt(d) - b)/(2*a)
x1*x2  =  c/a
```

or

```
x1*x2  =  c/a
   x1  =  (sqrt(d) - b)/(2*a)
    d  =  b^2 - 4*a*c
```

or in any other order.

This flexibility should not encourage us to set up models in a haphazard manner. Generally, the order of the rules in the model should follow some logic dictated by the subject matter. The resulting model will be easier to read and use for reference purposes.

The same principle applies to the ordering of variable names on the Variable Sheet. (This may require inserting the variable names separately from the rules or reshuffling the lines in the Variable Sheet if the rules were inserted with the automatic Variable Insert option on.) If we first insert the rule defining the discriminant *d*, the automatically generated sequence of variables will be *d,b,a,c;* however, the manually ordered sequence *a,b,c,d* makes more sense.

When deciding on the order of the rules on the Rule Sheet, the second factor we must consider is the speed of the model resolution. If the model will usually be used with a particular set of input variables, we should insert the rules in the order of their use to avoid unnecessary scanning. In fact, we may even express the anticipated unknowns explicitly in terms of known or evaluated variables (as was done in the preceding BASIC program for evaluating *D*, *X1*, and *X2*). Practically, however, such measures don't make too much difference.

Selection of Variable Names

We are free to choose any variable names within the syntax limitations stipulated in Chapter 5. Generally, it is a good idea to use mnemonic abbreviations or even whole words (*time, load, price*) whenever possible and convenient. At the same time, if the rules are long and complicated, it is better to stick to short names for the sake of rule clarity. Remember too that the display in the Name field is restricted to seven characters. (Longer variable names can be seen in full on the Status line when the cursor is in the Name field.)

The longer the variable names, the longer the rules; excessive rule length is even worse than excessive length of variable names. Only 76 characters can be seen on the visible part of the rules in the Rule Sheet. To see the obscured part of the rule, we must enter the Editor and scroll the line to the left.

Selection of Operations

Different operations require different execution times. For instance, taking a square root usually takes longer than raising to the power of 2. However, it doesn't make any difference in TK!Solver if the rule about the relationship between the time to fall, height, and gravitational constant of a falling object is written as

$$t = sqrt(2*h/g)$$

or

$$t^{\wedge}2 = 2*h/g$$

The reason is that the choice of the operation during model resolution depends on the combination of input and unknown variables that determines the solution path, rather than on the type of operation (direct or inverse) written in the rule. If h and g are known, the square root always has to be taken in order to evaluate t. Conversely, if t is known and h or g is to be evaluated, t power 2 will be evaluated regardless of the rule formulation.

Reducing the Number of Operations

Complete resolution of a model implies execution of all operations that appear in the rules. The fewer operations there are, the faster is the resolution of the model. Consequently, we should formulate rules in the simplest possible way for the sake of efficiency, and we should replace operations over constants by the results instead of leaving them in the model to be repeated all over again during the model resolution.

For example, if the gravitational constant g in the free-fall formula is always equal to 9.8 m/s^2, there is no point in having a rule $t{=}sqrt(2*h/9.8)$ when we can write it more simply as $t{=}sqrt(h/4.9)$.

Another way to improve models is to reduce the number of repetitious subexpressions. It is possible, but rather inefficient, to formulate the quadratic equation model as follows:

$$\begin{aligned} x1 &= (-b + sqrt(b^{\wedge}2 - 4*a*c))/(2*a) \\ x2 &= (-b - sqrt(b^{\wedge}2 - 4*a*c))/(2*a) \end{aligned}$$

Replacing repetitious subexpressions by single variables reduces the number of operations. This process does have a cost, however. Additional rules are required to define the added variables. Thus the quadratic equation model might be written as

$$\begin{aligned} d &= b^{\wedge}2 - 4*a*c \\ x1 &= (-b + sqrt(d))/(2*a) \\ x2 &= (-b - sqrt(d))/(2*a) \end{aligned}$$

If we don't need to check the sign of the discriminant d, we can go even further. For example:

$$\begin{aligned} bah &= 0.5*b/a \\ srd &= sqrt(bah\hat{\ }2-c/a) \\ x1 &= -bah + srd \\ x2 &= -bah - srd \end{aligned}$$

This cuts the original number of operations to be performed by half.

Checking and Testing

Simplifications of formulas may be laborious and error-prone. As was mentioned earlier, TK!Solver does not have the intelligence to perform algebraic manipulations and simplifications on its own. However, the fact that rules can be edited, added, or removed with ease facilitates checking the correctness of simplifications and modifications during the model build-up.

For example, in order to test the correctness of the versions of a quadratic equation model, we would add the following rules:

$$\begin{aligned} a*x1\hat{\ }2 + b*x1 + c &= 0 \\ a*x2\hat{\ }2 + b*x2 + c &= 0 \end{aligned}$$

and run the model for a few sets of input values a, b, and c. If no contradictions are detected, the model is probably correct, and the added rules may be deleted.

A convenient way to delete a rule temporarily is to "comment it out," that is, to make a comment of the rule or part of it by inserting a quotation mark (") in front of the part to be ignored. Removing the quotation mark returns the rule to its original function.

The designed models should be thoroughly tested to check not only on subject matter and mathematical integrity, but also on potential accuracy and convergency problems (the latter applies to the use of the Iterative Solver). It is advisable to test-solve the model for various combinations of known and unknown variables, for very small values and very large values, and in sensitive areas anywhere within the application domain.

VEC MATRICES AND R-GRAPHS

Traditionally, computer problem-solving involves designing or choosing an algorithm (a precise description of how a computation is to proceed) and writing it in terms of programming language statements. Frequently the programmer uses a diagram called a "flowchart" to facilitate the design and understanding of the algorithm or the program structure. Flowcharts consist of boxes representing various operations and directed lines representing the flow of information and the time sequence of these processes.

There is not much use for a flowchart in the world of TK!Solver because the user and the computer interact at the level of mathematical models or relationships between variables and because the computer automatically takes care of sequencing the operations. However, you still may find a need for a diagrammatic or pictorial representation of the structure of the model during its design and use. In response to this need, let's look at the concepts of Variable-Equation Coincidence matrix (VEC matrix) and Relationship graph (R-graph). Examples of their use will be given in later sections and chapters.

Variable-Equation Coincidence Matrix

The Variable-Equation Coincidence or VEC matrix is an $m \times n$ array or matrix with m rows representing equations and n columns representing variables. The occurrence of the jth variable in the ith equation is indicated by a cross (x) in the cell which belongs to the ith row and the jth column.

The VEC matrix for the Travel model

$$cost = gas*price$$

$$mlg = dist/gas$$

$$speed = dist/time$$

is shown in Figure 7-3. For example, in row 1 representing the first equation, the crosses appear in cells belonging to the columns denoted *cost*, *gas*, and *price*.

Let's add to the model another equation defining the gas mileage as a function of speed:

$$mlg = a*speed\hat{\ }2 + b*speed + c$$

	cost	gas	price	mlg	dist	speed	time
1	x	x	x				
2		x		x	x		
3					x	x	x

Figure 7-3.
VEC matrix of the simple Travel model

	1	2	3	4
cost	x			
gas	x	x		
price	x			
mlg		x		x
speed			x	#
dist		x	x	
time			x	
a				x
b				x
c				x

Figure 7-4.
VEC matrix of the extended Travel model

The variables in this equation are *mlg* and *speed*, and the empiric coefficients *a*, *b*, and *c*. Note that the variable *speed* appears twice in this equation. This means that TK!Solver will be unable to solve the equation for *speed* when *mlg*, *a*, *b*, and *c* are known. As we will see later, the resolvability of an equation or rule for a particular unknown variable may determine whether a particular problem can be solved by the more efficient Direct Solver or the slower Iterative Solver. The VEC matrix will be more useful if it shows for which variables the equation is not directly resolvable. We indicate this situation by a double cross (#) as shown in Figure 7-4. According to this convention, all the variables that appear in the arguments of the non-invertible functions, such as *abs*, *int*, and *max* (see Tables 5-2 and 5-3), have to be marked # in the VEC matrix.

In Figure 7-4, the disposition of the variables and rules along the rows and columns is opposite to that in Figure 7-3. It really does not matter what goes where. The number of variables is almost always larger than the number of equations; so the arrangement in Figure 7-4 fits better the standard bias of sheets of paper.

Relationship Graphs

In an R-graph each rule or equation is represented by a polygon with nodes for each of the variables (see Figure 7-5*a-c*). For better clarity the polygons may be shaded. If there are only two variables in the rule, the rule is represented by a line connecting the two nodes.

A complete or partial model may be represented by an R-graph composed of polygons representing constituent rules (see Figure 7-6). The nonresolvability of a particular equation for a particular variable is denoted by a mark around the node as is shown around the node for *speed* in Figure 7-6.

OTHER MODEL COMPONENTS

The concept of a TK!Solver model covers more than the rules and the variables. Some of the contents of the other sheets (Unit, List, Global, and Function) are the subject of concern in the course of model design; they

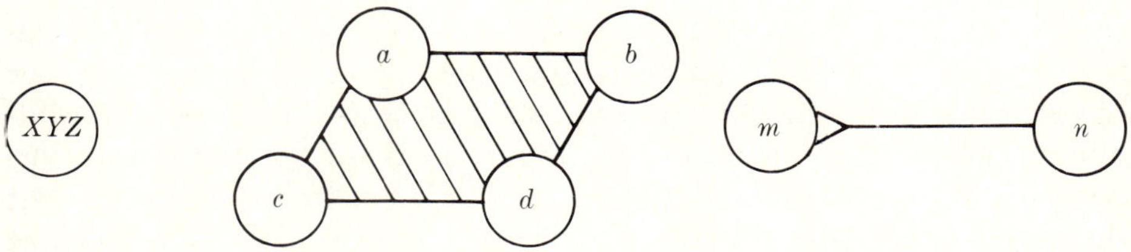

a. Node representing variable *XYZ*

b. Polygon representing the rule $a+b=c*d$

c. Line representing the rule $3*n=\text{int}(m)$ (not resolvable with respect to m)

Figure 7-5.
Building blocks for R-graphs

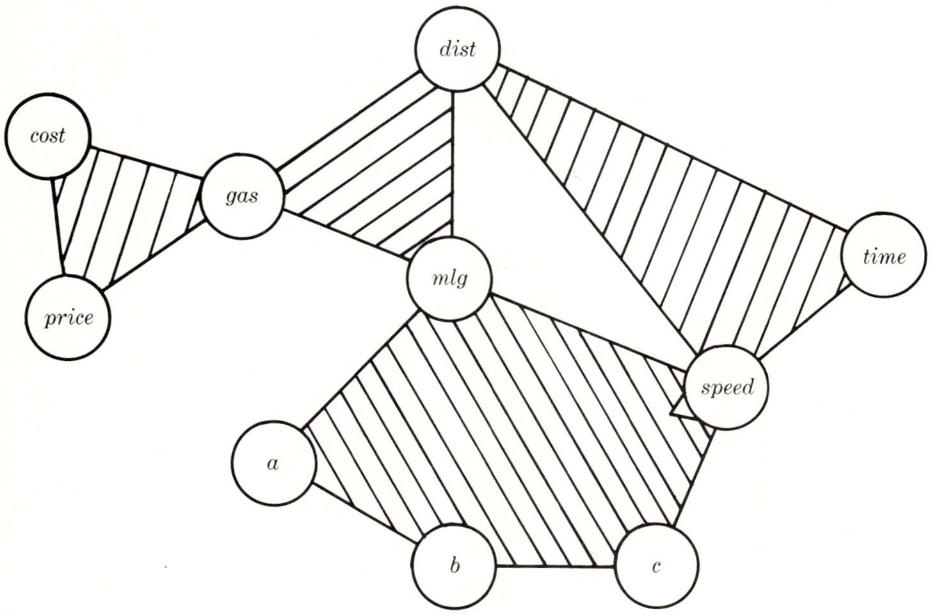

Figure 7-6.
R-graph for extended Travel mode.

represent valuable information and should be considered a part of the model. Also, you should take advantage of the fact that the Variable Sheet, Unit Sheet, User Function Sheet, and List Sheet can be saved and loaded separately.

Units

Generally, when you build a model, you should associate units with the appropriate variables wherever applicable. The unit associated with the variable for the first time becomes the Calculation Unit. It must be consistent with the appearance of the variable in the rule. Also, the Calculation Units of the variables in each rule must be compatible with one another.

Sometimes the equations used for building a model may imply different units for the same variable. Since there can be only one Calculation Unit associated with a particular variable in the model, you must make the conversion factor a part of one of the rules so that the rule's dimensional integrity is maintained.

As an example, let's look at the following situation. The perimeter of a rectangle equals twice the sum of the sides, and its area equals the product of the sides. For reasons of compatibility with other parts of the model, we may want to have the Calculation Unit for *area* be acres and for *perimeter* feet. If we choose feet to be the Calculation Units for the sides as well, we may say

$$perimeter = 2 * (a + b)$$

but we cannot say $area = a*b$, which would imply that the Calculation Unit for *area* is square feet. In order to have acres as the Calculation Unit for area and to preserve the integrity of this rule, we have to build the conversion in the rule and enter it as

area = a * b / 43560

Formulas in engineering and science drawn from different sources may use different systems of units. You should take advantage of TK!Solver's Unit Conversion feature so that the model can handle a variety of commonly used units. The conversion between the Calculation Unit and the Display Unit (the unit in which the values are entered and displayed) should be defined on the Unit Sheet. If you omit declaring the correct Calculation Unit and later on assign the desired Display Unit that is different from what is implied by the usage of the variable in the rules, you will be in trouble. The values of a variable look "funny" after a solution, although the equation is known to be correct. In this case, the first thing to do is to check the units of the variable and make sure that Calculation and Display Units are correctly defined and converted.

Lists

When you want to solve a model repeatedly for different values of one or more variables, you should take advantage of the provision for associating a set of values with a variable. Lists and List Solving simplify and speed up cause-effect analysis commonly used in problem-solving. You may find it helpful to set up the lists in advance during the model design phase so that they can be associated with variables when needed.

TK!Solver's built-in List functions open up the field of statistical analysis and other important applications. Here again, the lists have to be an integral part of a model from its inception.

Unit compatibility is very important when associating lists with variables. If the Storage Unit on the List Subsheet and the Calculation Unit of the variable are different, you should define a conversion on the Unit Sheet. Otherwise, you will not obtain the correct results.

The lists of values generated by List Solving can be saved in DIF files for use with other application programs. Similarly, lists of values from other programs can also be brought into TK!Solver with the DIF feature. If you plan to use the designed model routinely with other programs, interfacing through DIF should be a part of the model design process.

User-Defined Functions

The user-defined function feature is employed when the relationship between the variables cannot be expressed by any of the available arithmetic operators or built-in functions or their combinations. This applies specifically to empiric relationships relating experimental data. Depending on the type of relationship, one of three types of Mapping—Table Look-up, Linear Interpolation, or Step Mapping—can be chosen.

If you intend to use the user-defined functions, you must plan ahead. In fact, the rule parser will not accept a rule referring to a function name that has not been declared in advance in the User Function Sheet. This could be quite irritating if you typed a complicated rule with an undeclared function name *fun* in it. (Rather than lose your line, change *fun* for, say, *sin* when still in Edit mode, have your rule accepted, declare *fun* in the User Function Sheet, and then edit the rule replacing *sin* with *fun*. Alternately, you can make a comment out of the rule by typing a " at the beginning of the rule. After declaring the function, you can edit out ".)

Setting up all the lists with argument and function values for the user-defined function is an integral part of model design. When lists have units associated with them, you should ensure that the Display Unit on the List Subsheet is the same as the Calculation Unit of the variable. Otherwise, your results will be incorrect.

The naming of a function, the list of argument values (Domain) and list of function values (Range), and referencing these in the rules are other potential sources of confusion. The function name (let's assume it is *fun* again) will obviously appear in both the User Function Sheet and the Rule Sheet. The Domain and Range lists on one hand and the variables representing argument and function values in the rules on the other hand are different entities, and it is preferable to name them differently. For instance, in the Rule Sheet you may refer to your function several times in several ways, for example:

$$
\begin{aligned}
a + b &= fun(k) \\
n &= fun(m) \\
t &= fun(u*v)
\end{aligned}
$$

In the User Function Sheet and Subsheet, the function may be defined as $y=fun(x)$; that is, the Domain and Range values may be defined in lists x and y without either of these two variable names ever appearing in the Variable or Rule Sheets.

Global Sheet Settings

Global Sheet settings govern the behavior of a model as a whole. Obviously, the desired behavior will differ depending on the nature and purpose of the model. Therefore the Global Sheet settings should be a part of the model design. The Comparison Tolerance and Typical Value settings affect the guaranteed accuracy with which the problems are solved (Chapter 8 discusses this in detail). You can speed up Iterative and List Solving by setting the Intermediate Redisplay ON field to NO. The Automatic Iteration On field can be set to invoke the Iterative Solver when the Direct Solver fails. Automatic iteration is activated only when there are guess values set in the First Guess field in the Variable Subsheets. Again it is a model design decision whether or not to use this feature and what the standard guess values should be.

MODEL DOCUMENTATION

A certain amount of information about the contents and the purpose of the model follows directly from the rules themselves. Generally they are much easier to read and understand than computer programs written in BASIC, Pascal, or other computer languages. Yet additional information about the contents and use of a model is always useful and often necessary, especially when we consider the role of TK!Solver models as depositories of knowledge, elementary expert systems, and problem-solving tools.

This section does not discuss specific hard copy documentation related to the design and usage of particular models. Good examples of such documentation are found in the manuals accompanying the TK!SolverPacks. An even more detailed account of why and how the rules were set up in a particular way, what sources and assumptions they are based on, how the models should or should not be used, VEC matrices, R-graphs, and recommended values of initial guesses for iteration may be extremely useful to gather and maintain.

This section focuses on the provisions for the model documentation presented by the TK!Solver program itself. Two major areas for keeping additional information about models and their usage are the Comment fields in the Variable Sheet and the Rule fields in the Rule Sheet. Most of the comments in the Variable Sheet will relate to particular variables (giving their definitions and explaining their usage). The Comment field is not that useful for other purposes because of its limited field width and its need to compete for screen space with the variables and their comments.

The space in the Rule field is more readily available for comments (preceded by a quotation mark); the field is wider and the number of rules is usually smaller than the number of variables. Some other sheets (User Function, Table, and Plot) also have a little space available for comments. A convenient feature is that sheet comments automatically appear on the corresponding subsheets.

Typical problem formulations and solutions are important components of the computer-retrievable model documentation. You can store these as whole models (with rules, unit conversions, and functions), but in this form they take up a lot of diskette space. Alternatively, you can create files with variables and their values so that you can continue from where you left off. Another memory-efficient way to solve particular problem formulations and solutions is to use the /LP (list put) and /LG (list get) features.

8

Direct Solver

The Direct Solver is the heart and the workhorse of TK!Solver. It is extremely easy and almost effortless to use with other TK!Solver features for solving simple problems; it is not even essential that you master the concepts and theories presented here before touching the keyboard. Yet occasionally the Direct Solver fails to deliver because of its own limitations or the user's oversight. Difficulties are easy to untangle thanks to TK!Solver's transparency and flexibility. With accumulated experience and the information presented in this chapter, you should be able to extricate yourself from problem situations.

Three major components of the TK!Solver program contribute to the function of the Direct Solver: (a) a mechanism for performing the arithmetic operations and for function evaluations; (b) the means of controlling the propagation of the solution to the problem through the model; and (c) the tools for spotting errors in model design and problem-formulation as they surface during the problem-solving process. The capabilities of the first component were discussed in Chapter 5. This chapter concentrates on the latter two.

DIRECT SOLVER OVERVIEW

You activate the Direct Solver by pressing the Action key !. This clears the Output field on the Variable Sheet (if there was anything there) and displays the solution of a new problem (if input values had previously been assigned to some of the variables and rules had been entered in the Rule Sheet). At least this is what a casual onlooker may observe. The TK!Solver user needs to know some though not necessarily all of the inner workings of the Direct Solver in order to use it efficiently and to interpret its response correctly—especially if the response points to an error condition.

Rule Resolution

The elementary action performed by the Direct Solver is to resolve a particular rule with respect to a particular variable. This amounts to solving an equation, represented by a rule, for an unknown variable, provided the values of all the other variables in that equation are known.

Suppose we have the rule

$$a+b = c*d$$

which the Direct Solver "hits" at a point when it is already known that $a=5$, $b=6.7$, and $d=3$. TK!Solver then evaluates

$$c = (a+b)/d = (5 + 6.7)/3 = 3.9$$

For another example, consider that one of the formulas of "Projectile Motion" states

$$sin(2*angle)/g = range/velocity\hat{\ }2$$

The values of *range* and *velocity* of a projectile and the gravitational constant g are known. The Direct Solver evaluates the *angle* of departure as

$$angle = asin((range/velocity\hat{\ }2)*g)/2$$

As was mentioned in the previous chapter, the Direct Solver can resolve a rule for a particular variable only if it can find its way through by performing a sequence of TK!Solver-supported arithmetic operations and built-in or user-defined function evaluations. This would not be possible if, in the first example, the rule had been written as

$$(c-d)/(a+b) = 1/d-1/c$$

Although this is mathematically equivalent to the original equation, $\boldsymbol{a+b=c*d}$, there is nothing the Direct Solver can do to extract from it the value of the variable c.

Similarly, in the second example the Direct Solver would be unable to evaluate the variable *angle* if the equivalent rule

$$2*sin(angle)*cos(angle)/g = range/velocity \wedge 2$$

had been used.

In addition, the Direct Solver cannot resolve a rule with respect to an unknown variable that appears in the argument of a non-invertible function. This situation is like being on a dead-end one-way street. Suppose we have \$4.50 and want to buy three cups of coffee for $c=40$ cents each and the maximum possible number of doughnuts for $d=30$ cents each and an equal number N of doughnut holes for $h=6$ cents each. The Direct Solver can find the number N from the rule

$$N = int((money-3*c)/(d+h))$$

which shows N to be 9.

The Integer truncation function *int* is non-invertible. If someone knew the value of N and the prices d, m, and c, it would be impossible for him or her to find out from this equation how much money we had to start with (it could be anything from \$4.44 to \$4.79).

The capabilities and the limitations of the Direct Solver have to be taken into account when building models and using TK!Solver for solving problems. This is the reason why we have been stressing the advantage of formulating the rules in the general form of

<expression1> = <expression2>

and why we have put so much emphasis on the issue of function invertibility and rule resolvability in Chapters 5, 6, and 7.

Consecutive Substitution Procedure

Resolving a rule with respect to a variable (with the restrictions just explained) is only one of the Direct Solver's two major functions. The other is scanning through the rules of the model and resolving them one after another until there is nothing left that can be evaluated. This process does automatically what we do when we manually solve one equation for one variable, then substitute the value for this variable into another equation and solve that for another variable, and so on. This process is called the consecutive substitution procedure.

We may follow the consecutive substitution procedure using the R-graph and analyze this procedure using the concept of VEC matrix introduced in the previous chapter. Let's take another look at the R-graph of the Travel model of Figure 7-6. Assume we know (or more precisely, TK!Solver is given input values of) *price* of gas per gallon, distance to travel *dist*, gas mileage *mlg*, and *speed*. You can mark the respective nodes with a "w." When the Action key ! is pressed, the Direct Solver comes up and "looks" at the first rule. There are two unknowns (*cost* of trip and amount of *gas*), so nothing can be evaluated. Then the Direct Solver moves to the second rule, finds that *mlg* and *dist* are known, and evaluates the sole unknown *gas* (mark the node with "v"; keep marking this way all variables that are evaluated). Now the Direct Solver moves to the third equation and evaluates *time* from *dist* and *speed*. Next it looks at the fourth rule, finds that it cannot do anything with the unknowns *a*, *b*, and *c*, and moves to the first rule again. This time there is only one unknown, *cost*. It is evaluated, all the rules are browsed through again, and once nothing else can be done, the Direct Solver stops.

In this case, TK!Solver is only able to solve the model partially. This situation is not unusual; TK!Solver is often used for solving problems when only part of the model and only some of the variables may be involved.

Following the Solution on the VEC Matrix

Suppose the situation changes so that we know all the *a*, *b*, and *c* coefficients, but we don't know the gas mileage. You may want to work out the Direct Solver's way through the R-graph (meaning through the model) yourself. Let's see how to interpret the solution of this problem using the VEC matrix concept and the VEC matrix for the Travel model shown in Figure 7-4. First we reduce the matrix by excluding all the rows related to the variables with input values. The reduced square 4×4 matrix is shown in Figure 8-1. The matrix size is determined by the number of unknown variables and the number of equations available for their solution.

When the Direct Solver "operates" on the model, it in fact performs implicitly the so-called triangularization of the reduced VEC matrix. A triangular matrix is a matrix with all the elements above or below a diagonal equal to zero (or empty cells in our representation). We may transform the reduced VEC matrix in Figure 8-1 into a diagonal matrix by reshuffling columns and rows, as shown in Figure 8-2. The diagonal of the transformed matrix clearly shows which unknown variables are evaluated from which equations and in what order. So *time* and *mlg* are evaluated first from the third and fourth rules respectively. The variable *gas*, taking advantage of the already evaluated *mlg*, is evaluated from the second rule.

	1	2	3	4
cost	x			
gas	x	x		
mlg		x		x
time			x	

Figure 8-1.
VEC matrix of the Travel model from Figure 7-4 reduced for a problem with unknowns *cost, gas, mlg,* and *time*

	3	4	2	1
time	x			
mlg		x	x	
gas			x	x
cost				x

Figure 8-2.
Reduced VEC matrix from Figure 8-1 after triangularization

Finally, *cost* is evaluated from the first rule using the already evaluated *gas*. Your exercise with the R-graph will confirm all this.

In essence, having all the cells either above or below the diagonal of a reduced and transformed VEC matrix free of the x's or #'s means that the Direct Solver, when scanning through the rules, always finds at least one rule with just one variable that it can evaluate. This also implies that no double crosses (#) should appear along the diagonal. Nor should there be any gaps or empty cells along the diagonal; their presence indicates problems with an infeasible set of input variables.

Note that there is one double cross on the diagonal in Figure 8-3. The figure shows a reduced transformed matrix for a problem similar to the previous one, except that *cost* has been assigned as an input value rather

	1	2	3	4
gas	x	x		
mlg		x	x	
speed			#	
time				x

Figure 8-3.
An attempt to triangularize VEC matrix for Travel model with unknown *gas, mlg, speed,* and *time;* the double cross in the diagonal means that the Direct Solver cannot solve the problem

than *speed*, and TK!Solver has been asked at what speed a person should drive to keep within the budget. The Direct Solver cannot find the solution, as we may see from the imperfect matrix diagonal in this figure or from the R-graph in Figure 7-6 (see the mark on the node *speed*) or from the fourth rule itself (it cannot be solved for the unknown *speed*).

Of course, all this does not imply that the model designers and users have to spend time and effort drawing R-graphs and filling VEC matrices. The Direct Solver follows the imaginary R-graphs and VEC matrices automatically. Nevertheless, these two concepts can help us understand how the Direct Solver works. Occasionally, analyzing an R-graph or VEC matrix of the whole model or part of it may help us figure out why the Direct Solver does not work and what we can do in order to make it work. This is analogous to computer programmers occasionally needing a flowchart in order to figure out what they or the computer is doing, right or wrong.

The complete VEC matrix as well as the R-graph offer a quick indication of whether and under what circumstances the reduced VEC matrix will not triangularize and the Direct Solver cannot solve a particular problem. The presence of a closed ring in the R-graph and an equivalent closed loop connecting a set of crosses in the VEC matrix indicates potential difficulties.

In Figure 8-4*a-c* the model and the corresponding VEC matrix and R-graph illustrate this point. There are five rules for ten variables in the model. When, for instance, *b, c, d, g,* and *u* are input variables, the entire model may be solved by the Direct Solver without a hitch. If, however,

```
=================== RULE SHEET ===...
S Rule
- ----
* 10*e = b*c*d                "  1
* f = b/a                     "  2
* a^2 = 4e-5/pi()*c*g         "  3
* d = u*v                     "  4
* w = u/v                     "  5
```

a. Rule Sheet

	1	2	3	4	5
a		x	x		
b	x	x			
c	x		x		
d	x			x	
e	x				
f		x			
g			x		
u				x	x
v				x	x
w					x

b. VEC matrix

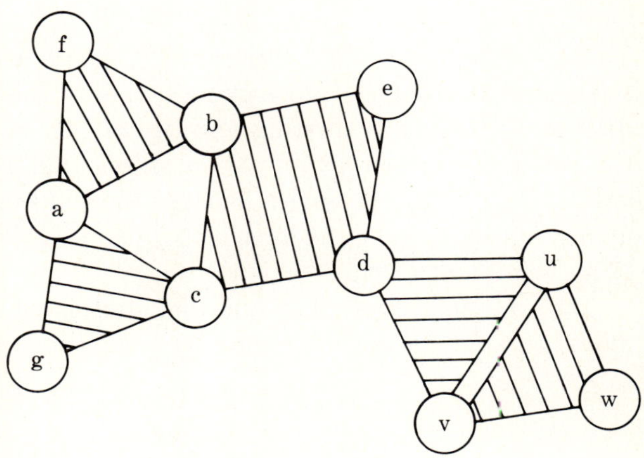

c. R-graph

Figure 8-4.
Potential problems for the Direct Solver

neither *a*, *b*, nor *c* is known, the Direct Solver gets stuck and cannot do anything with the first three rules even if the values of *d*, *e*, *f*, and *g* are available. The same is the case with rules 4 and 5 if only *d* and *w* are known. Both problems are reflected by closed loops in the VEC matrix in Figure 8-4*b* (the closed loops imply that it is impossible to triangularize a reduced matrix with the variables and rules in question). The closed rings on the R-graph in Figure 8-4*c* are just another reflection of this situation. In Chapter 11 we will see how this model can be resolved by the Direct Solver when we add the so-called redundant equations.

Solution Feasibility

There is no way the Direct Solver can solve the problem if the reduced matrix does not triangularize. The converse, unfortunately, is not true; the matrix may work out fine, but the Direct Solver may still be unable to solve the problem. The reason is that VEC matrices only show the distribution of variables over the rules and ignore possible mathematical fallacies. As a simple example, let's look at the following two rules with three unknowns:

$$x+3 = sin(z)$$
$$y = ln(x)$$

The corresponding VEC matrix and R-graph are trivial and, considering the distribution of variables over the rules, the Direct Solver should not have any problem evaluating any two of the variables given the value of the third. Yet closer examination shows that no solutions exist for any value of any of the variables because the solution process will always end up attempting to take the logarithm of a negative argument or the arcsine of an argument greater than 1.

Let's recall the issue of the distribution of variables and rules in a model and the condition of solution feasibility introduced in Chapter 7:

$$NOV = TNV - NIV = NIE$$

where

TNV = total number of variables
NIV = number of input variables
NOV = number of output variables
NIE = number of independent equations.

The Direct Solver can perform successfully only if this relationship holds for the whole model or for the particular part we may be solving.

Two types of troublesome situations may arise due to a violation of these relationships: (a) the problem is underdetermined and NOV fails to include the variable (or variables) for which we are trying to solve; (b) the problem is overdetermined and the solution is terminated because in one of the rules a discrepancy is discovered between the values of the left-hand and the right-hand expressions (they are supposed to be equal within the tolerance limit).

Sometimes a model may contain both problems with each occurring in different parts of the model; in this case the difficulty still shows up during the solution attempt as (b), as may be seen in Figure 8-5.

The model in Figure 8-5 consists of two parts: the first three rules with variables a, b, e, and f, and the last rule with the variables b, c, d, and f. The variables b and f link the two parts together. If e and f are input variables, the first part of the model is obviously overdetermined (there are three rules for four variables and consequently just one input variable would turn the first part into three equations for three unknowns). On the other hand, the second part (the last rule) is underdetermined: knowing the input variable f and the calculated value of b still leaves two unknowns, c and d, which cannot be evaluated from that rule. A closer look at the VEC matrix (built into the Rule Sheet as a comment) reveals the gap in the diagonal of the reduced matrix indicating this situation.

Reformulating the problem provides another twist to the story, as we can see in Figure 8-6. With the input variables b and c, the Direct Solver evaluated the variable f from the first rule belonging to the first part of the model. That made it possible to solve the second part ($b+c+$...) for the unknown d. The Direct Solver "got exhausted" at that point because the reduced matrix could not be fully triangularized. (The rules were reshuffled in the figure in order to show the reduced VEC matrix; the same result would be obtained if they were left in the original order.)

If we make a an additional input variable, the first part of the model

```
(5s) Status: > Inconsistent

==================== VARIABLE SHEET ===============...
St Input      Name      Output     Unit       Comment
-- -----      ----      ------     ----       -------
 >            a         .75
 >            b         16
              c
              d
 > 3          e
   4          f

=================== RULE SHEET ==================...
S Rule
- ----
  "             VEC matrix:  a  b  c  d  e  f
  "             ------------------------------
  a = e/f          "         x           x  x
  b = f^2          "            x           x
> a+b = e^3        "         x  x  ?     x
* b+c+d+f=1        "            x  x  x     x

  "        reduced matrix      gap        diagonal
```

Figure 8-5.
The gap in the diagonal of the reduced matrix reflects the blend of overdeterminacy and underdeterminacy (the VEC-matrix is built into the Rule Sheet as comments)

```
(4s) Status:   Satisfied

==================== VARIABLE SHEET ===============...
St Input       Name    Output     Unit       Comment
-- -----       ----    ------     ----       -------
               a
   16          b
   20          c
               d       -39
               e
               f       4

==================== RULE SHEET ===================...
S Rule
- ----
  "            VEC matrix:  f   d   a   e   b   c
  "           --------------------------------
  b = f^2             "         x               x
  b+c+d+f=1           "         x   x           x   x
* a = e/f             "         x       x   x
* a+b = e^3           "                 x   x   x

  "         reduced matrix                       diagonal
```

Figure 8-6.
The reduced VEC matrix failed to triangularize; the Direct Solver stopped halfway through the model

```
(6s) Status: > Inconsistent

==================== VARIABLE SHEET ===============...
St Input       Name    Output     Unit       Comment
-- -----       ----    ------     ----       -------
 > .75         a
 > 16          b
   20          c
               d       -39
 >             e       3
               f       4

==================== RULE SHEET ===================...
S Rule
- ----
  "            VEC matrix:  f   d   e   a   b   c
  "           --------------------------------
  b = f^2             "         x               x
  b+c+d+f=1           "         x   x           x   x
  a = e/f             "         x       x   x
> a+b = e^3           "                 x   x   x

  "         reduced matrix                       diagonal
```

Figure 8-7.
Example of overdeterminacy: the reduced VEC-matrix shows that f, d, and e can be evaluated from the first three equations and the fourth equation becomes inconsistent (in some versions of TK!Solver the solution terminates before evaluating d)

gets overconstrained again and the Direct Solver will "die" on the last equation (Figure 8-7). Note a perfect triangular matrix for the first three equations and all the unknowns *f*, *d*, and *e*; the fourth equation naturally becomes inconsistent.

To finish, let's look a chapter ahead, make *a* a guess, and use the Iterative Solver to complete the solution of the problem (Figure 8-8). Assigning *a* as a guess variable gives it a temporary input status and takes it out of the reduced VEC matrix. The generated error in the fourth equation comes in as an additional unknown. The reduced matrix is triangular and thus the Iterative Solver can do the job.

Checking for Model Inconsistency

Both the rules and the input variables (or more precisely, the number of independent equations *NIE* and the number of input variables *NIV*) are susceptible to the following errors:

1. *Errors of omission.* These occur when an essential rule is left out of the model or a crucial variable is not assigned an input value.
2. *Errors of commission.* These occur when an unwanted constraint is imposed on the model or the solution (either by including an unnecessary or incorrect rule or by assigning an excess input value).

```
==================== VARIABLE SHEET ===============...
St Input        Name    Output      Unit        Comment
-- -----        ----    ------      ----        -------
                a       .63822777
   16           b
   20           c
                d       -39
                e       2.5529111
                f       4

==================== RULE SHEET ==================...
S Rule
- ----
  "            VEC matrix:  f  d  e  *  a  b  c
  "            ---------------------------------
  b = f^2            "      x              x
  b+c+d+f=1          "      x  x           x  x
  a = e/f            "      x     x     x
  a+b = e^3          "            x  x  x  x

  "       reduced matrix                diagonal
```

Figure 8-8.
Solution obtained by the Iterative Solver

It should be noted that the *NIE* and *NIV* represent the numbers of *independent* equations and *independent* input variables*; any misconceptions in this respect may lead to infeasibility problems even if the feasibility equation seems to hold.

The variety of combinations of things that can go wrong is formidable. (Here we are talking about the balance of variables and equations; in addition, there may be mathematical or subject matter inconsistencies.) To make the Direct Solver work (if it can) may require some debugging effort on the user's part. Fortunately, thanks to the ease with which the rules may be switched on and off and the input values assigned, reassigned, and unassigned, and thanks to the dependability of the Direct Solver itself, debugging is not hard.

There are three points to keep in mind when we use the Direct Solver for solving problems:

1. We will not discover problems with model design or problem formulation until we actually use the Direct Solver. For instance, the TK!Solver parser happily accepts two rules, say, one stating $A=4$ and the next one $A=2$. It will not protest against this obvious nonsense until the Action key ! is pressed and the Direct Solver finds out that $TNV=1$, $NIV=1$, and $NIE=2$ do not fit the basic condition of the solution feasibility. (Here again the Direct Solver does not count and compare *TNV*, *NIV*, and *NIE;* it evaluates *A* from the first rule and finds the second rule to be in error.)

2. It is a good idea to pull larger models apart and to check or debug their components separately. (We can do this by selective assignment of input values without even splitting the large model into smaller separate ones.)

3. Quite frequently the failure of the Direct Solver to solve the model or to return the value of a particular variable tempts us to assign one more input variable (that is, to increase *NIV*) to see if that helps. More often than not, TK!Solver's response is to terminate the solution and indicate an overdeterminacy error. It may be that we trial-assigned a wrong variable and made one part of the model over-determined while keeping another part still underdetermined.

*How can we be sure that the input variables are independent? They are not, for instance, if all the variables marked "Overdefined" have input values assigned to them (see Figure 8-5); the message comes up in the Status line when the cursor covers any of the ">" marks on the Variable Sheet. How can we be sure that the equations in the model are independent? They are not, if for some particular set of input variables, there are more rules marked "Satisfied" (that is, the Status fields of the rules are blank) than output values, if at the same time all input variables are independent (see Figure 8-15).

However, quite frequently TK!Solver's response means that the reduced VEC matrix cannot be triangularized, the Direct Solver cannot help, and we have to resort to using the Iterative Solver (which will be discussed in Chapter 9). Let's assume, for example, that we try to overcome the impasse in solving the travel problem shown in Figure 8-3 by an additional assignment of, say, *time*. This will make $NIV=7$, while $TNV=10$, and $NIE=4$. The contradiction $10-7\neq 4$ will be detected in the fourth equation and the solution will be terminated.

Error Conditions

Two classes of error conditions cause the Direct Solver to terminate the solution. One consists of all the errors detected while TK!Solver performs particular operations or evaluates built-in or user-defined functions. In this group belong attempts to divide by zero, to take the arcsine or the arccosine of an argument with an absolute value larger than 1, to take a logarithm of a negative argument, and so forth. (For a listing and an explanation of these errors, see the Appendixes of the *TK!Solver Reference Manual.*)

In the second group are the so-called rule inconsistency errors caused by overdetermining the problem. As you saw previously, overdeterminacy is caused by an excessive number of input variables *NIV*.

Overdeterminacy leads to a situation in which the Direct Solver finds out, during its scanning tour through the rules, that the values of all variables in that rule are known although the rule itself has not been used for evaluating any of them. The Direct Solver "gets suspicious," evaluates the left-hand and right-hand expressions, and checks on their equality. If the rule passes the scrutiny, the Direct Solver ignores the overdeterminacy and moves on. If an intolerable discrepancy is found, the solution is terminated and the rule and all its variables are marked ">" in their respective Status fields. The error message "Inconsistent" is associated with the rule and "Overdefined" with the variables.

In other words, overdeterminacy itself does not represent an error condition per se and is not even indicated unless it causes a serious discrepancy in the rule. It is not the rigor of the problem formulation but the integrity of the rules that is held sacrosanct by TK!Solver.

This point is illustrated in Figure 8-9*a-c*: Figure 8-9*a* shows examples of a simple Direct Solver run, Figure 8-9*b* shows a Direct Solver run through an overdetermined problem with non-contradictory input values,

```
==================== VARIABLE SHEET ==...
St Input      Name    Output     Unit
-- -----      ----    ------     ----
   32         a
   8          b
              c       4
   10         d
              e       20
   4          f

==================== RULE SHEET ======...
S Rule
- ----
  a+b = c*d
  c^2 = e-f
```

a. Solving two equations for two unknowns

```
(2s) Status:   Satisfied

==================== VARIABLE SHEET ==...
St Input      Name    Output     Unit
-- -----      ----    ------     ----
   32         a
   8          b
              c       4
   10         d
   20         e
   4          f

==================== RULE SHEET ======...
S Rule
- ----
  a+b = c*d
  c^2 = e-f
```

b. Two equations and one unknown; problem overdetermined—no contradiction detected

```
(2s) Status: > Inconsistent

==================== VARIABLE SHEET ==...
St Input      Name    Output     Unit
-- -----      ----    ------     ----
   35         a
   8          b
 >            c       4.3
   10         d
 > 20         e
 > 4          f

==================== RULE SHEET ======...
S Rule
- ----
  a+b = c*d
> c^2 = e-f
```

c. Two equations and one unknown; problem overdetermined—model overconstrained

Figure 8-9.
Another look at overdeterminacy

and Figure 8-9*c* shows an overdetermined problem with contradictory input values.

PROPAGATION OF SOLUTION

The operation of the Direct Solver may be visualized in many ways: as a contagious disease spreading all over the R-graph from a few infection centers or nodes representing variables with input values; or as a chain reaction initiated at those nodes and proliferating through the links of the R-graphs; or as airborne commandos descending at selected points (using the input values for getting the footholds at these points) and gradually taking over the whole land (model) following the path of least resistance on the map represented by the R-graph. The attacking forces may not be strong enough (that is, there may be not enough input information) and the invasion may exhaust itself before the whole R-graph land is occupied. Or the attack may be overdone and brought to a halt when the attacking forces get involved in conflict with each other.

These and other allegories—more appropriate and less extreme—will reinforce appreciation for the principle of the Direct Solver, which, essentially, propagates the solution of a given problem through the rules of the model. There is one subtle difference between these analogies and the real world of TK!Solver: the propagation or proliferation of the solution does not happen haphazardly or simultaneously. There is the "big finger" of TK!Solver pointing to one rule after another and controlling the sequence of events.

Order of Rules

Here we have to qualify our previous assertions that the solution of the model does not depend on the order of the rules in the model. This statement is valid if everything goes smoothly and no error condition is detected that would cause the termination of the solution process.

Suppose we add a rule $c=5$ to the model in Figure 8-9*a* leaving the other rules and values of input variables intact to produce Figure 8-10*a*. We can see in the figure that the Direct Solver generated the same solution as before (that is, $c=4$ and $e=20$) except for finding an inconsistency when it came upon the additional rule and labeling variable c as "Overdefined." If, however, we move the additional rule from the last position to the first position in the Rule Sheet and solve again, *c* is evaluated from the current first rule as equal to 5, the contradiction is detected in the second rule, and the solution is terminated without moving to the third rule and evaluating *e* (see Figure 8-10*b*).

The next example (Figure 8-11*a*) shows two independent equations with four variables. The third rule was derived by manipulating algebraically the first two in order to eliminate variable *b* (it is a so-called redundant equation added in order to obviate the use of the Iterative Solver

```
(3s) Status: > Overdefined

==================== VARIABLE SHEET ==...
St Input      Name   Output    Unit
-- -----      ----   ------    ----
   32         a
   8          b
 >            c      4
   10         d
              e      20
   4          f

==================== RULE SHEET ======...
S Rule
- ----
  a+b = c*d
  c^2 = e-f
> c=5
```

a. Discrepancy detected in third rule

```
(2s) Status: > Inconsistent

==================== VARIABLE SHEET ==...
St Input      Name   Output    Unit
-- -----      ----   ------    ----
 > 32         a
 > 8          b
 >            c      5
 > 10         d
              e
   4          f

==================== RULE SHEET ======...
S Rule
- ----
  c=5
> a+b = c*d
* c^2 = e-f
```

b. Discrepancy detected in second rule

Figure 8-10.
Effect of the position of the mischievous rule $c=5$ (in some versions of TK!Solver the position of $c=5$ is irrelevant)

```
(3s) Status: Inconsistent

==================== VARIABLE SHEET ==...
St Input      Name    Output    Unit
-- -----      ----    ------    ----
 > 2          a
              b       -8
 >            u       6
 > 10         v

==================== RULE SHEET ======...
S Rule
- ----
  a - b = v
  (a+b)^2 = u^2
> 2*a = u + v
```

a. Positive u evaluated from second rule

```
(2s) Status:   Satisfied

==================== VARIABLE SHEET ==...
St Input      Name    Output    Unit
-- -----      ----    ------    ----
   2          a
              b       -8
              u       -6
   10         v

==================== RULE SHEET ======...
S Rule
- ----
  a - b = v
  2*a = u + v
  (a+b)^2 = u^2
```

b. Negative u evaluated from second rule

Figure 8-11.
The position of the redundant equation affects the Direct Solver's response (in some versions of TK!Solver $u=-6$ is evaluated in (a) and no error conditions occur)

when both a and b are unknown—more about this process in Chapter 11). With input variables $a=2$ and $v=10$, the Direct Solver yields $b=-8$, $u=6$, and an inconsistency message pointing to the third rule. The reason is that the third rule implies $u=-6$, which contradicts the positive u evaluated as the square root of (2−8)^2. Swapping the second and third rules makes the Direct Solver run through smoothly (see Figure 8-11*b*). However, this should not satisfy us. Now we must decide how to treat the ambiguity of the square root function (whether and how to choose positive or negative values of square roots) and how to amend the model as required.

Similar problems may occur in equations involving trigonometric functions. We must bear in mind that inverse trigonometric functions routinely return the principal values (see Table 5-1 and comments). If we regularly want the inverse from another interval, or if the choice of the interval depends on some other variables, the rule has to be formulated accordingly.

Finally, Figure 8-12*a* and *b* shows another problem with redundant equations—this time caused by a trig function evaluation error. TK!Solver may be used for proving theorems by allowing us to compare the evaluations of expressions that are supposed to be equal. The figure deals with the well-known relationship

$$sin(phi)\hat{}\,2 = (1-cos(2*phi))/2$$

```
(2s) Status: > Inconsistent

==================== VARIABLE SHEET ==...
St Input        Name      Output      Unit
-- -----        ----      ------      ----
 > .01          a                     deg
 >              b         .01999615   deg

==================== RULE SHEET ======...
S Rule
- ----
  sin(a)^2 = .5*(1-cos(b))
> b = 2*a
```

a. Error amplified beyond tolerance level

```
(1s) Status:   Satisfied

==================== VARIABLE SHEET ==...
St Input        Name      Output      Unit
-- -----        ----      ------      ----
   .01          a                     deg
                b         .02         deg

==================== RULE SHEET ======...
S Rule
- ----
  b = 2*a
  sin(a)^2 = .5*(1-cos(b))
```

b. Error within tolerance level

Figure 8-12.
The function evaluation error depending on the rule order (in some versions $b=2*a$ is evaluated in both cases and no error condition occurs)

The solution for *phi*=0.01 degrees in Figure 8-12*a* shows a contradiction in the second rule (this rule expresses the assumed ratio of the arguments of the sine and cosine). The culprit is the imprecise evaluation of *b*=0.01999615 from the first rule due to the sensitivity of the arccosine function to small arguments. With default values of the Comparison Tolerance and Typical Value (0.000001 and 1), the second rule implying 0.02=0.01999615 simply did not pass the test. If the first and second rules are swapped, as shown in Figure 8-12*b*, the precise value of *b* is evaluated from the first rule. The difference between the values of the left-hand side and right-hand side expressions in the second rule (*error*=1.174e−11) is small enough to be ignored.

Generally, we will still find that the correct solution of a particular problem does not depend on the order of rules in the model. However, the Direct Solver's response in a broad sense (that is, the solutions as well as detected error conditions) may be affected by rule reshuffling as was shown in the previous examples. In other words, the detected error conditions may differ depending on the rule order. It even is possible to have one rule sequence that results in an error condition and another that produces an error-free solution. You should be careful in this latter case and make sure that the solution is correct and that the error condition in the first version comes from benign causes. If you cannot get a valid solution when using the Direct Solver, it is naive to expect that changing the order of rules will produce one.

On the other hand, changing the rule order may occasionally help the Iterative Solver work better or work at all. When we use the Iterative Solver, we purposefully generate contradictions in one or more rules and then, during the iteration process, reduce the contradictions below a certain limit. The magnitude and slope of the generated error may differ from rule to rule. Changing the rule order may change the rule on which the Iterative Solver pivots. When the rule changes so do the convergency conditions (for better or worse) of the iteration process.

Solution Propagation Control

The Direct Solver controls the solution propagation and relieves the user from deciding which way to go. Excluding the special situations, the TK!Solver user really does not have and does not need to have too much control over the solution propagation process. Occasionally, however, the user may want to take over (especially during model design and debugging).

Swapping and reshuffling the rules in the model may not be the best way of gaining such control; the sequence of evaluating unknown variables, especially in larger models, is hard or impossible to predict. There are other methods available:

1. Commenting out some of the rules so that the remaining part of the model is smaller and its solution path is easier to analyze.
2. Blanking out some of the input variables so that the effect of the remaining ones on the proliferation of the solution is easier to follow.
3. Including "ballast" variables in the form of harmless multiplication by u/u or addition of $v-v$ to a particular rule so that we can control when that rule is brought into the game by the availability of the values of u or v. Needless to say, we must remove the "ballast" when we are through debugging.

PROPAGATION OF ERRORS

In TK!Solver, the solution propagates through a sequence of arithmetic operations and function evaluations. Because of the limited number of digits available for number representation (see Chapter 5), each of these operations is a potential source of rounding error. The errors propagate and accumulate in parallel with the propagation of the solution itself.

There are two kinds of problems to cope with:

1. Integrity and reliability of the solution: We don't want to generate unknowingly imprecise or wrong answers.
2. Error magnitude: We don't want to be falsely alarmed by solution termination and by error messages when, in fact, the generated results are sufficiently close to true values.

There is little we can do about the first problem except to estimate the maximum possible error and set up the rules in the models in a way that will reduce the magnitude of the error. Therefore, this discussion begins with the second kind of problem, which is more visible and causes more concern in day-to-day TK!Solver use.

Comparison Tolerance

Let's review the two causes of overdeterminacy: one occurs when we overdetermine the problem being solved by assigning input values to more variables than the truly independent ones; another occurs when we overdetermine the model by including in it rules that are not truly independent (we will see the purpose of these so-called redundant equations or rules in Chapter 11). In both cases, overdeterminacy may lead to the violation of one or more of the rules or, in other words, to the failure of one or more of the equations "to obtain."

The Direct Solver is equipped with a built-in "fuse" that either lets through only those discrepancies that are most likely caused by rounding errors or forces the termination of the solution with the display of an error message when the likely source of the discrepancy is a wrong rule or a contradictory input value. This fuse is set on the Global Sheet by two parameters called Comparison Tolerance (*CT*) and Typical Value (*TV*). Their default values are $CT=0.000001$ and $TV=1$.

Absolute and Relative Errors

There are two more concepts to introduce. The first is the difference between the values of the rule's left-hand side expression *LHE* and the right-hand side expression *RHE*:

$$\text{absolute error} = abs(LHE-RHE)$$

The second is the magnitude of error in relation to the magnitude of the values involved:

$$\text{relative error} = \frac{\text{absolute error}}{max(abs(LHE),abs(RHE))}$$

The difference between *LHE* and *RHE* is considered acceptable and the rule is considered satisfied if either of the following two conditions holds:

1. relative error $\leq CT$
2. $max(abs(LHE),abs(RHE)) \leq CT * TV$

The first condition reflects the fact that TK!Solver works with the same number of significant digits regardless of the magnitude of values (regardless of whether we deal with billions or tens or billionths). The rounding errors creep in from the right. The correctness of a limited number of the most significant or leftmost digits (out of TK!Solver's 11 or 12) is the best we can expect, and it also satisfies most of the numerical problem-solving needs.

The default value $CT=1e-6$ implies expected correctness of the six leftmost digits or about half of the digits representing a number in

TK!Solver. This is only the worst-case limit; in most of the practical situations we can count on about 9 or 10 digits being correct. We can reduce the CT value on the Global Sheet to, say, 1e−5 if we anticipate heavy error accumulation and don't want to be bothered by error messages. On the other hand, we can raise CT to 1e−7 or 1e−8 if we want to be told when the discrepancies reach the 7th or 8th digit.

The second condition comes up when the values of both LHE and RHE are very close to zero and when it is not possible to maintain a low relative error. As an example, let's consider the $a+b=c*d$ rule with the following values:

$$a = 0.000000014$$
$$b = 10$$
$$c = 2.500000018$$
$$d = 4$$

In this case

$$LHE = 10.000000014$$
$$RHE = 10.000000078$$
$$\textit{absolute error} = 0.000000058$$
$$\textit{relative error} = 0.58\text{e}{-8}$$

which means that the discrepancy easily passes the test against CT=1e−6. If, however, the rule is written as $a=c*d-b$, then for the same values of a, b, c, and d,

$$LHE = 0.000000014$$
$$RHE = 0.000000072$$
$$\text{absolute error} = 0.000000058$$
$$\text{relative error} = 0.8056$$

which is far from passing the first relative error test although the situation is basically the same as before. This is the reason for having the alternative condition. TK!Solver can pass the "error-loaded" rules regardless of the relative error, provided both the LHE and RHE are close enough to zero.

We can see from this example why a situation when the values of the left-hand side and right-hand side expressions are close to zero must be judged differently from a situation when they are not. It is also obvious that "proximity to zero" means different things depending on the values of the variables. If millions are involved, then 1 or less may be close enough.

On the other hand, if the values are typically in thousandths, then the value should drop at least to 1e−9 before qualifying for close-to-zero treatment. The Typical Value parameter (*TV*) serves the purpose of scaling up or down the criterion for passing a contradictory rule when the values of *LHE* and *RHE* are close to zero.

Example

To illustrate the effect of the *CT* and *TV* parameters, let's look at a simple example of an overconstrained rule, $p*q=r$. The testing ground was set up as shown in Figure 8-13. Assume we have declared all the variables as lists, created lists of values of p, q, and r, made these input variables, commented out the rule $p*q=r$, and list-solved. The results (that is, the values of absolute and relative errors for all 17 instances of given p, q, and r) are shown in Table 8-1. Then we reactivated the first rule and list-solved again with nine different combinations of *CT* and *TV*. The account of the Direct Solver's response is given in Table 8-2. It is interesting to see and analyze the distinction between the regions of inconsistency errors and regions where the test is passed thanks to the tolerable relative error, or the proximity of values to zero, or both.

```
(3i) Input: 2.6666666667

==================== VARIABLE SHEET ==...
St Input      Name     Output     Unit
-- -----      ----     ------     ----
L  1.3333333  p
L  2.6666667  q
L  3.5555556  r

L             abserr   1.E-10
L             relerr   2.813E-11

==================== RULE SHEET ======...
S Rule
- ----
  p*q = r

  abserr = abs(p*q-r)
  relerr = abserr/max(p*q,r)
```

Figure 8-13.
Model for exploring the concepts of absolute and relative error (the instance displayed shows the effect of rounding errors in $p*q=r$ for $p=4/3$, $q=8/3$, and $r=32/9$ assigned as input)

Table 8-1.
Absolute and Relative Errors for Overdefined Problem in Figure 8-13

n	p	q	r	abserr	relerr
1	3.	4.	12.0000001	1.E−7	8.3333333E−9
2	3.	4.	12.000001	1.E−6	8.3333326E−8
3	3.	4.	12.00001	1.E−5	8.3333264E−7
4	3.	4.	12.0001	1.E−4	8.3332639E−6
5	3.E−1	4.E−1	12.0001E−2	1.E−6	8.3332639E−6
6	3.E−2	4.E−2	12.0001E−4	1.E−8	8.3332639E−6
7	3.E−3	4.E−3	12.0001E−6	1.E−10	8.3332639E−6
8	3.E−3	4.E−4	12.0001E−7	1.E−11	8.3332639E−6
9	3.E−4	4.E−4	12.0001E−8	1.E−12	8.3332639E−6
10	3.E−4	4.E−4	12.001E−8	1.E−11	8.3326389E−5
11	3.E−4	4.E−4	12.01E−8	1.E−10	8.3263947E−4
12	3.E−4	4.E−4	12.1E−8	1.E−9	8.26446281E−3
13	3.E−4	4.E−4	13.0E−8	1.E−8	7.692307692E−2
14	3.E−4	4.E−4	22.0E−8	1.E−7	4.545454545E−1
15	3.E−4	4.E−4	11.2E−7	1.E−6	8.928571429E−1
16	3.E−4	4.E−4	10.12E−6	1.E−5	9.881422925E−1
17	3.E−4	4.E−4	10.012E−5	1.E−4	9.988014383E−1

Table 8-2.
Results of Passing Consistency Check in Table 8-1

CT:	1E−5	1E−5	1E−5	1E−6	1E−6	1E−6	1E−7	1E−7	1E−7
TV:	1E−1	1E0	1E2	1E−1	1E0	1E2	1E−1	1E0	1E2
1	1	1	1	1	1	1	1	1	1
2	1	1	1	1	1	1	1	1	1
3	1	1	1	1	1	1	err	err	err
4	1	1	1	err	err	err	err	err	err
5	1	1	1	err	err	err	err	err	err
6	1	1	1	err	err	err	err	err	err
7	1	1	1,2	err	err	err	err	err	err
8	1	1,2	1,2	err	err	2	err	err	err
9	1,2	1,2	1,2	err	2	2	err	err	2
10	1,2	1,2	1,2	err	2	2	err	err	2
11	2	2	2	err	2	2	err	err	2
12	2	2	2	err	2	2	err	err	2
13	2	2	2	err	2	2	err	err	2
14	2	2	2	err	2	2	err	err	2
15	err	2	2	err	err	2	err	err	err
16	err	err	2	err	err	err	err	err	err
17	err	err	err	err	err	err	err	err	err

Note: err = indicates inconsistency
1 = indicates passing relative error check
2 = indicates passing zero proximity check

There are two facts to bear in mind in order to avoid illusion and confusion when using the Direct Solver:

1. Setting the *CT* and *TV* values higher or lower does not affect the actual magnitude of errors; it only affects error monitoring and reporting.
2. If there are no redundant equations and no excess input values (that is, if all equations and all input variables are independent and the results are generated by a single pass of the Direct Solver), the set values of *CT* and *TV* do not affect anything.

This is not true with respect to the Iterative Solver. As we will see in the next chapter, assigning guess values to one or more variables is what invokes the Iterative Solver. This is equivalent to having too many input variables and overconstraining the rules. The artificially generated errors are then brought below the tolerance limit during the iteration process. Here the set values of *CT* and *TV* control the degree to which the contradictions that we created by assigning the guesses have to be reconciled, and consequently the precision and correctness of the overall solution of the problem.

Error Management

During ordinary use of TK!Solver it is unlikely that you will face serious error propagation problems that require rigorous error-analysis. Adhering to the following rules of thumb will help keep you out of trouble when designing and using models:

1. Be careful about combinations of summations and multiplications. Avoid subtracting close-to-equal numbers especially when the result is to be multiplied by large or divided by small numbers. Here are classical examples easy to play with using TK!Solver:

$$\frac{e^x - \mathbf{1}}{x} = 1 + \frac{x}{2} + \frac{x^2}{6} + \frac{x^3}{24} + \cdots$$

$$1 - cos(x) = \frac{x^2}{2} - \frac{x^4}{24} + \frac{x^6}{720} - \cdots$$

   The right-hand sides represent Taylor series approximations of the expressions on the left-hand sides. Yet for x near zero, the right-hand side approximations yield much more accurate values than the original left-hand side expressions.

2. The approximation of trigonometric and other continuous built-in functions introduces so-called truncation errors, which are usually larger than the rounding and propagation errors from basic arithmetic operations. These functions should therefore be used sparingly and in the simplest possible way. Naturally, it is better to use

   $$sin(2*phi)$$

   than

   $$2*sin(phi)*cos(phi)$$

   or (even worse)

   $$sqrt(1-cos(2*phi)\hat{}\,2)$$

   Likewise, it is better to use

   $$poly(x',a,b,c,d,e)$$

   than

   $$a + b*x + c*x\hat{}\,2 + d*x\hat{}\,3 + e*x\hat{}\,4$$

   The *poly* function seems to be using only additions and multiplications whereas the evaluation of higher powers of x goes through the error-prone evaluation of logarithms.

3. Scale the variables up or down so that most of the calculations will be performed with numbers between, say, hundredths and hundreds so that very small and very large numbers will not be mixed. It is more important to follow this advice when there are some summations in the model than when there are multiplications (and divisions) only.

4. Distribute the operations between the left-hand side and the right-hand side expressions in such a way that the relative error checking will most likely take place and not be skipped because both the *LHE* and *RHE* are close to zero.

5. Examine the accuracy and error conditions during model development. It is especially important to check the model's performance at extreme values (0, 1, very small values, very large values, and so on—depending on the structure of the model and on the anticipated solution domain).

Let's review the most efficient response to the messages "Inconsistent" and "Overdefined," which may indicate a problem with error propagation. The correct response is to add an error term to one of the sides of the culprit rule and solve again in order to find out how big the error is and what its source may be. This will also show how far the solution with the same input variables can go without the constraining rule (the error term relieves the constraint) and whether there is another rule or constraint causing trouble.

All error tests are performed on the values in Calculation Units. The unit conversion itself is a part of the solution propagation process and as such may contribute to the propagation of errors. Occasionally you may come across a dubious result like the one in Figure 8-14 where you would expect a plain 1 as the difference between 75.5 and 74.5. The trailing zeros in the Output field indicate that, in fact, they are not trailing. Positioning the cursor over the number reveals its true value in the Status field, 1.0000000046. The source of the error is the conversion from degrees (Display Unit) to radians (Calculation Unit) and back.

Generally, TK!Solver is "well-behaved" with respect to rounding and other errors. Even harmless situations like this one are not frequent: it took the authors a while to find this case and generate the example. The example in Figure 8-15*a* and *b* is more characteristic. Here we see a projectile model with six variables and three independent equations. The fourth rule is added as the so-called redundant equation in order to avoid the use of the Iterative Solver when both *angle* and *velocity* are unknown. For given *angle*, *range*, and *g*, the range is evaluated from the first equation and the redundant equation is just checked (and passed because the relative error is only 1.12e−10). Figure 8-15*b* shows the solution of the same problem with the first equation commented out so that the variable *range* is evaluated from the fourth equation. The difference between the two values of *range* is only 0.000000003 and appears in the last (the 12th) significant digit.

```
(2o) Output: 1.0000000046

==================== VARIABLE SHEET ==...
St Input       Name     Output      Unit
-- -----       ----     ------      ----
   74.5        a                    deg
               b        1.0000000   deg
   75.5        c                    deg


=================== RULE SHEET ======...
S Rule
- ----
* a+b=c
```

Figure 8-14.
Error due to unit conversion (Calculation Unit for *a*, *b*, and *c* is radians)

```
(3o) Output: 1400.71410366

==================== VARIABLE SHEET ==...
St Input      Name     Output     Unit
-- -----      ----     ------     ----
   15         angle               deg
   100000     range               m
              velocit  1400.7141  m/s
              height   6698.7298  m
              time     5462.7766  s
   9.81       g                   m/s^2

              relerr   1.120E-10
==================== RULE SHEET ======...
S Rule
- ----
  sin(2*angle)*velocity^2 = g*range
  (sin(angle)*velocity)^2 = 2*g*height
  g*time = 8*height
  tan(angle)*range = 4*height

  relerr = abs(tan(angle)*range-4*height)/(4*height)
```

a. Relative error in redundant equation

```
(3o) Output: 1400.71410369

==================== VARIABLE SHEET ==...
St Input      Name     Output     Unit
-- -----      ----     ------     ----
   15         angle               deg
   100000     range               m
              velocit  1400.7141  m/s
              height   6698.7298  m
              time     5462.7766  s
   9.81       g                   m/s^2

              relerr   1.120E-10
==================== RULE SHEET ======...
S Rule
- ----
  "sin(2*angle)*velocity^2 = g*range
  (sin(angle)*velocity)^2 = 2*g*height
  g*time = 8*height
  tan(angle)*range = 4*height

  relerr = abs(tan(angle)*range-4*height)/(4*height)
```

b. Negligible difference in the value of *velocity* due to different rule used for its evaluation

Figure 8-15.
Two solutions of the projectile model

9

Iterative Solver

In the introduction to Chapter 8, we called the Direct Solver the workhorse of TK!Solver. By the same token, we can introduce the Iterative Solver as the most powerful tool in the TK!Solver kit.

Chapter 7 and Chapter 11 discuss techniques that we can use at the model's design stage in order to avoid using the Iterative Solver. Why move in the heavy artillery if we can achieve the same objective with a shotgun? Yet there are millions of real-world situations described by sets of simultaneous and, more often than not, non-linear and transcendental equations that do not solve easily. Their solutions cannot be derived through algebraic manipulations or worked out by the Direct Solver. This is when the Iterative Solver is a blessing, even though it may require more involved problem formulation and a longer solution time.

ITERATION

"Iteration" implies a succession of computations that produce a sequence of intermediate results that converge (that is, come closer and closer) to a desired solution. Each successive $(i+1)$th solution may be found as some function of the previous ith one; in general terms this would be

$$x_{i+1} = F(x_i)$$

The concept of iteration may be illustrated by an example involving the search for a root of the cubic equation

$$x^3 - 9x + 4 = 0$$

which may be rewritten as

$$x = 4/(9 - x\,\hat{}\,2)$$

We may consider the right-hand side of this equation as an iteration function and evaluate a sequence of

$$x_{i+1} = \frac{4}{9 - x_i^{\,2}}$$

for $i = 1, 2, 3,$ and so on until a satisfactory solution is reached.

We can build an iterative procedure using the TK!Solver list feature and the *element* function. We enter the following two rules:

$$xi = element('x, element(\,) - 1)$$
$$x = 4/(9 - xi\,\hat{}\,2)$$

where xi and x stand for x_i and x_{i+1} respectively; they are declared as lists.

Next we assign a "seed" or initial guess value (for example, 1) to the first element of list x and initiate Block Solving by typing **/LB**; we specify the solution interval from 2 to 12.

In each solution step or instance, the first rule transfers the value of x from the previous instance to xi (initially it will be the guess value). The second rule will calculate the next approximation of x. Block Solving yields the following list of x values:

1
0.5
0.4571428571
0.4550097502
0.4549090651
0.4549043253
0.4549041022
0.4549040917
0.4549040912
0.4549040912
0.4549040912
0.4549040912

We would get the same result if we worked with just one rule, $x = 4/(9 - element('x, element(\,) - 1)\,\hat{}\,2)$. This form, however, obscures the iteration function.

The full precision value of the 10th and subsequent elements of the list x is 0.454904091223, which is indeed the solution of the original cubic equation. We can check it by typing in the rule

$$y = x\hat{}3 - 9*x + 4$$

and by assigning the final value of x to input and solving for y; the result is 0 as expected.

This example of the so-called "direct substitution" method illustrates the general concepts of the iteration process. Notice that although the process converged reasonably fast to a desired solution, the preparatory work and formulation of the model were rather involved. Fortunately, TK!Solver's Iterative Solver works differently, using the so-called Newton-Raphson procedure. Let's look into its principles before proceeding to explore its implementation in TK!Solver.

NEWTON-RAPHSON PROCEDURE

Looking for a root of a function means looking for a point x,0 at which the graph of the function $y=f(x)$ intersects the horizontal axis X. The Newton's method of finding a root may be explained in geometrical terms as follows:

1. We take a guessed or approximate value of x and find the corresponding point $x,f(x)$ on the function graph.
2. We draw a tangent to the function graph at the point $x,f(x)$; the x coordinate of the intersection of the tangent with the X axis is considered to be a new estimate of x. Then we go back to step 1 and repeat the process.

This cycle is repeated until the value of $f(x)$ is smaller than a chosen error limit.

According to Figure 9-1, we have the formula

$$\frac{f(x_i)}{x_i - x_{i+1}} = \text{ slope of tangent } = f'(x_i)$$

where $f'(x)=df(x)/dx$ is the derivative of the function $f(x)$ with respect to x. From here we can derive Newton's iteration formula:

$$x_{i+1} = x_i - f(x_i)/f'(x_i)$$

Let's try Newton's iteration method on the cubic equation introduced earlier. We substitute for the function $f(x)$ and its derivative $f'(x)$ in the

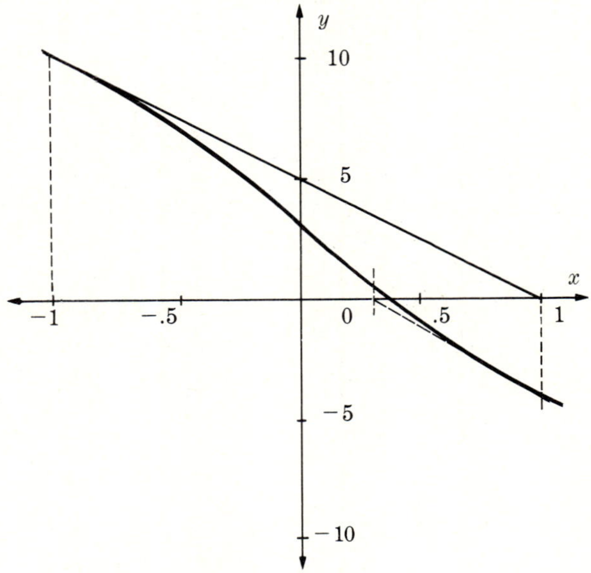

Figure 9-1.
Graphical representation of Newton's iteration method applied to a search for the middle root of $y=x^3-9*x+4=0$. (For illustration purposes an initial guess of $x=-1$ is used; the next approximation is $x=1$, and so on.)

iteration formula from

$$f(x) = x \hat{} 3 - 9*x + 4$$
$$f'(x) = 3*x \hat{} 2 - 9$$

and write TK!Solver rules for simulating the iteration process along the pattern introduced previously:

xi = element('x,element( )−1)
*x = xi − (xi^3−9*xi+4)/(3*xi^2−9)*

Block Solving (starting again from the second element) yields the following values of list x:

1
0.333333333
0.52991453
0.549034975
0.549040912
0.549040912
....

From the 5th element on, the values remain the same: 0.454904091221 in full precision. Although this result differs in the last digit from the result obtained previously, it also represents a correct solution of our cubic equation (in fact, any x equal to 0.454904091217 through 0.454904091227 turns the function $y=f(x)$ evaluated by TK!Solver into zero).

Advantages

Newton's iteration method converged significantly faster than the direct substitution method, requiring only four iteration steps instead of nine to find the root. Newton's iteration method is superior in other respects too.

First, the iteration function is more clearly defined; the slope of the tangent of the function graph may be approximated by numerical differentiation, that is,

$$\text{slope} = f'(x) = \frac{f(x+dx) - f(x)}{dx}$$

where dx is a small increment in the variable x. This makes it possible for us to simplify and automate the derivation of the iteration function and of the whole iteration process without engaging ourselves or TK!Solver in symbolic differentiation and algebraic manipulation. (We used a manually derived symbolic derivative in the example to illustrate Newton's method; the Iterative Solver uses a numerical differentiation scheme and does everything automatically.)

Second, Newton's iteration method gives us a chance to influence the convergence of the solution to a particular root (if there are more roots than one) by allowing us to select the guess value. Our cubic equation has three roots, as may be seen in Figure 9-2. If we choose a guess $x=-3$, 1, or 3, Newton's iteration converges to -3.201 or 0.455 or 2.747, respectively. The direct substitution method, on the contrary, inevitably converges to 0.455 regardless of the guess value.

Third, the Newton-Raphson method may be easily generalized for sets of equations with two or more unknowns. There is a geometric interpretation even in the case of two equations with two unknowns, for instance,

$$f1(x,y) = exp(x) + x*y - 1 = 0$$
$$f2(x,y) = sin(x*y) + x + y - 1 = 0$$

The functions $f1(x,y)$ and $f2(x,y)$ may be represented by two surfaces in three-dimensional space with two coordinate axes for x and y and a third

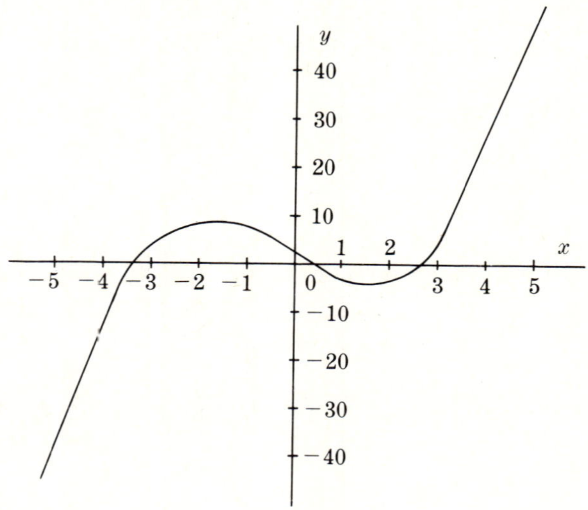

Figure 9-2.
Graph of the function $y=x\wedge 3-9*x+4$

for the values of the functions *f1* and *f2*. Both may be represented by surfaces relative to the plane *x,y*. We can imagine tangential planes to each of these surfaces at the point, with coordinates $x=x0$ and $y=y0$ representing the initial guesses. Those two tangential planes intersect with the *x,y* plane along straight lines, and these lines, in turn, intersect the plane *x,y* at one point; this point represents new estimated values of *x* and *y*.

Mathematical Interpretation

It is hard to use a geometrical interpretation to explain the iterative solution of problems with three and more unknowns. Our imagination does not work too well in four-dimensional space and beyond. Therefore we have to resort to more difficult (but also more powerful) mathematical interpretation.

Suppose we have *n* functions of *n* unknowns, that is,

$$f_1(x_1,x_2,\ldots,x_n)$$
$$f_2(x_1,x_2,\ldots,x_n)$$
$$\cdots\cdots\cdots$$
$$f_n(x_1,x_2,\ldots,x_n)$$

In the case of a single unknown, the iteration function in Newton's method makes use of the rate of change in $f(x)$ relative to a change in x—this is what the concept of the derivative or the slope of the tangent to the function graph is about. In a multi-function and multi-variable case, the role of a single derivative is played by the so-called Jacobian matrix or table of partial derivatives of each of the functions with respect to each of the variables:

$$\begin{matrix} \frac{\partial f_1}{\partial x_1} & \frac{\partial f_1}{\partial x_2} & \cdots & \frac{\partial f_1}{\partial x_n} \\ \frac{\partial f_2}{\partial x_1} & \frac{\partial f_2}{\partial x_2} & \cdots & \frac{\partial f_2}{\partial x_n} \\ \cdots & \cdots & \cdots & \cdots \\ \frac{\partial f_n}{\partial x_1} & \frac{\partial f_n}{\partial x_2} & \cdots & \frac{\partial f_n}{\partial x_n} \end{matrix}$$

As in the case of the single unknown, we would again use numerical differentiation to approximate the derivative of each ith function with respect to the jth variable:

$$\frac{\partial f_i}{\partial x_j} = \frac{f_i(x_1,x_2,...,x_j + \partial x_j,...,x_n) - f_i(x_1,x_2,...,x_j,...,x_n)}{\partial x_j}$$

In the case of a single variable, evaluating each new estimate of the unknown x may be interpreted as solving a single linear equation with the coefficient $\partial f(x)/\partial x$. Similarly, in a multi-variable, evaluating the new estimate of the unknowns $x_1,x_2,...,x_n$ is accomplished by solving a system of n linear equations

$$\begin{matrix} a_{11}\, x_1 & + & a_{12}\, x_2 & + & \cdots & + & a_{1n}\, x_n & = b_1 \\ a_{21}\, x_1 & + & a_{22}\, x_2 & + & \cdots & + & a_{2n}\, x_n & = b_2 \\ & & \cdots & \cdots & \cdots & \cdots & & \\ a_{n1}\, x_1 & + & a_{n2}\, x_2 & + & \cdots & + & a_{nn}\, x_n & = b_n \end{matrix}$$

with the Jacobian matrix playing the role of the system matrix (or, in other words, derivatives $\partial f_i/\partial x_i$ playing the role of a_{ij} coefficients).

We need to appreciate this much in order to understand the behavior of the Iterative Solver and to follow the explanations given in the following sections.

ITERATIVE SOLVER OVERVIEW

Knowing the principles of iteration in general and the Newton-Raphson iterative procedure in particular, we now look at some of the practicalities of using the Iterative Solver. The Iterative Solver is a powerful and convenient tool; however, solving problems with the Iterative Solver is less straightforward than with the Direct Solver in two respects:

- The solution depends on guessing one or more unknowns and the success is not guaranteed.
- Using the Iterative Solver increases the solution time because a repeated resolution of the model is involved.

When to Use the Iterative Solver

As we saw in earlier chapters, the Iterative Solver is to be used whenever the Direct Solver fails to yield the solution, or more precisely, whenever the Direct Solver stumbles over (1) the non-resolvability of a rule with respect to an unknown variable, (2) the simultaneity of equations, or (3) both these factors at the same time.

Examples of (1) are the cubic equation (discussed in the previous section) that cannot be resolved with respect to unknown x because x appears in the equation more than once, and also loan repayment models, which cannot be resolved with respect to an unknown interest rate for the same reason. An example of (2) is the model in Figure 8-6 in which the last two equations could not be resolved simultaneously with respect to the unknowns a and e.

How can we be sure that the Iterative Solver will do the job if the Direct Solver fails? The answer is that, generally, we cannot. The Direct Solver may fail for a number of reasons. Some may still present problems when we switch to the Iterative Solver (for example, problems caused by contradictory rules or domain errors).

There are two sorts of unmistakable symptoms that indicate the Iterative Solver has to be used to move the solution forward. The first kind is related to the concept of balance of variables and equations and the second is rooted in the concept of resolvability of equations.

1. The number of independent equations in the model (or in a part of it), *NIE*, is equal to the number of unknowns left after input values have been assigned to *NIV* independent variables; nevertheless, the Direct Solver returns less than the same number of output values. If

at this point we attempt to assign an input value to one of these unknown variables, the response "Inconsistent" and "Overdefined" follows.

2. Some of the unknown variables form a ring in the R-graph and a closed loop in the VEC matrix (see Figure 8-4 and consider the case with unknowns *a,b,c*). Some of these variables may be arguments of a non-invertible function or may appear more than once in rules they are supposed to be evaluated from. In other words, the reduced VEC matrix discussed in Chapter 8 does not triangularize. Obviously, we may not see that clearly when we look at the model. What we do see are peculiar-looking rules that often contain complicated nonlinear expressions and multiple appearances of the same groups of variables.

Before moving further, let's consider a complementary question: when *not* to use the Iterative Solver (even if the Direct Solver fails for the reasons discussed here). The answer is not to use the Iterative Solver whenever we can help the Direct Solver do its job. The ways of "helping" the Direct Solver—modifying the rules or adding one or more redundant equations to the model—are discussed in detail in Chapter 10. These situations are generally few and far apart, so it is highly advisable to master the use of the Iterative Solver.

How the Iterative Solver Works

The Iterative Solver is launched the same way as the Direct Solver—by pressing the Action key ! (or /! from other than the Variable or Rule Sheet, or /L! when List Solving). TK!Solver automatically invokes the Iterative Solver whenever there is at least one variable marked "G" in the Status field—indicating a guess variable with a guess value showing up in the Input field.

The Iterative Solver adopts the guess variables temporarily as input variables. This overconstrains some of the rules. Instead of interpreting the resulting discrepancies as inconsistency errors (as the Direct Solver would), the Iterative Solver treats these discrepancies as if they were values of regular variables called, say, *err1*, *err2*, ... (for "error terms") built in the rules. The Newton-Raphson algorithm takes over and, as described in the beginning of this chapter, manipulates the guess values to bring the error terms below the error limit. Reaching the error limit is equivalent to finding guess variable values, which, if assigned as input values, would make all the original rules (rules without added error terms) easily pass the comparison tolerance test described in Chapter 8.

To be on the safe side, the Iterative Solver does not stop when the error term is reduced below the Comparison Tolerance setting; it continues until

```
==================== VARIABLE SHEET ==...
St Input      Name     Output     Unit
-- -----      ----     ------     ----
   1          a
   0          b
   -9         c
   4          d
 G 1          x


==================== RULE SHEET ======...
S Rule
- ----
* a*x^3 + b*x^2 + c*x + d = 0
```

a. Variable and Rule Sheets with problem set up for iterative solving

```
(5o) Output: .454904091218

==================== VARIABLE SHEET ==...
St Input      Name     Output     Unit
-- -----      ----     ------     ----
   1          a
   0          b
   -9         c
   4          d
              x        .45490409
```

b. Variable Sheet and Status line after solution

```
(1s) Status:    Satisfied

==================== VARIABLE SHEET ==...
St Input      Name     Output     Unit
-- -----      ----     ------     ----
   1          a
   0          b
   -9         c
   4          d
   .45490409  x


==================== RULE SHEET ======...
S Rule
- ----
  a*x^3 + b*x^2 + c*x + d = 0
```

c. The root satisfying the equation

Figure 9-3.
Iterative solution of a cubic equation

the difference between successive guess values is below the Comparison Tolerance as well.

Let's see how the iteration process works on the cubic equation example introduced earlier. Figure 9-3*a* shows the cubic equation entered in the Rule Sheet in the general form, the coefficients, and the guess $x=1$ assigned in the Variable Sheet. Pressing the Action key ! initiates a fast sequence of changes of the guess value of x and the display in the Prompt/Error line and eventually moves the x value to the Output field and clears the Prompt/Error line (see Figure 9-3*b*). This indicates that the solution is successfully completed. The resulting value of x indeed represents the solution of the problem, as we may prove by moving it to the Input field and pressing the Action key again. (This time there is no "G" in the Status field, so the Direct Solver goes through the model and, not finding anything wrong, marks the rule "Satisfied", as shown in Figure 9-3*c*.)

What is all the information that flashes on the screen when the Iterative Solver is on? If we could observe faster, we would see what is compiled

```
(5i) Input: .33333
Iterative Solver: 2 out of 10
==================== VARIABLE SHEET ==...
St Input      Name     Output      Unit
-- -----      ----     ------      ----
   1          a
   0          b
   -9         c
   4          d
 G .33333     x
              err      1.0370659

==================== RULE SHEET ======...
S Rule
- ----
   a*x^3 + b*x^2 + c*x + d = 0
   a*x^3 + b*x^2 + c*x + d = err
```

a. Variable and Rule Sheets after step 2

	x	x (full prec.)	err	N1	N2
before step 1	1	1	-4	1	10
after step 1	.33333	.33333	1.0370659	2	10
after step 2	.45299145	.452991452988	.01603134	3	12
after step 3	.45490350	.454903502402	4.9339E-6	4	5
after step 4	.45490409	.45490409123	-1.E-10	5	5
after step 5	.45490409	.454904091218	0		

b. Contents of different fields

Figure 9-4.
Monitoring the iteration process

in tabular form in Figures 9-4*a* and *b*. (The authors added another rule to the model so that the changes in the error term *err* could be followed; they also moved the cursor over the guess value so that its full precision value was displayed in the Status line.) Figure 9-4*b* demonstrates how nicely the value of x converges to the correct solution and the value of *err* to zero.

This would be a good time to say a few words about the "N1 out of N2" message that appears on the Prompt/Error line. The first number N1 counts the iteration steps as they proceed. The second number N2 represents an estimate of the number of iteration steps needed to complete iteration. This estimate is based on the changes during the past several steps. Naturally, during the first two steps there is no such history available, and the Iterative Solver displays instead the maximum number of iteration steps set on the Global Sheet (the default value 10 is seen in Figure 9-4*a*). The progress of the iteration process depends on both the global and local characteristics of the error terms as functions of guesses. Consequently, the number of steps is very hard to predict and the prediction should not be taken too seriously. Generally, however, large numbers indicate ragged error functions and the danger that iteration will diverge and the solution will not be found (TK!Solver has mercy on our nerves and limits this

```
==================== VARIABLE SHEET ==...
St Input       Name      Output     Unit
-- -----       ----      ------     ----
 G 0           x
 G 0           y
   2           a
   3           b

=================== RULE SHEET ======...
S Rule
- ----
* exp(x) + x*y = a
* sin(x*y) + x + y = b
```

a. Variable and Rule Sheets with problem setup

```
==================== VARIABLE SHEET ==...
St Input       Name      Output     Unit
-- -----       ----      ------     ----
               x         .30625583
               y         2.0952099
   2           a
   3           b
```

b. Variable Sheet with solution

Figure 9-5.
Problem with two guess variables

number to 1000). On the other hand, numbers (N2) close to the current iteration count (N1) mean that the Iterative Solver is close to the solution.

Figures 9-5*a* and 9-5*b* show the formulation and solution of another problem introduced in the previous section, this time a set of two simultaneous equations for two unknowns. The trace of the iteration process with some dramatic ups and downs is shown in Figures 9-6*a* and 9-6*b*.

How to Select Guess Variables

In order to assign guess status to a variable, we have to move the cursor to the Status field and type **G**. There are four possibilities: a previously assigned input value becomes the guess value; a value in the Output field becomes the guess value; a "hidden" value, left from a previous assign-

```
Iterative Solver: 3 out of 149
==================== VARIABLE SHEET ==...
St Input       Name     Output     Unit
-- -----       ----     ------     ----
 G .73799177   x
 G .51791262   y
   2           a
   3           b
               err1     -.4739459
               err2     1.3711188

==================== RULE SHEET ======...
S Rule
- ----
   exp(x) + x*y = a
   sin(x*y) + x + y = b

   err1 + exp(x) + x*y = a
   err2 + sin(x*y) + x + y = b
```

a. Variable and Rule Sheets after step 2

	x	y	err1	err2	N1	N2
before step 1	0	0	1	3	1	10
after step 1	.99998000	2.00002	-2.718207	-.9093057	2	10
after step 2	.73799177	.51791262	-.4739459	1.3711188	3	149
after step 3	.19005179	1.8132944	.44606793	.65881495	4	23
after step 4	.32146162	2.0704292	-.0447056	-.0093933	5	26
after step 5	.30622069	2.0949077	2.1389E-4	4.7048E-4	6	8
after step 6	.30625583	2.0952099	-1.29E-8	-2.77E-10	7	7
after step 7	.30625583	2.0952099	-1.E-10	6.E-11		

b. Contents of different fields

Figure 9-6.
Monitoring the iteration process using a problem with two guesses

ment, is brought up in the Input field and becomes the guess value; no value was assigned, so a zero comes up in the Input field and becomes the guess value. The **G** is a toggle switch. When pressed repeatedly, it alternately assigns and deassigns guess status. If guess status is deassigned, the guess value stays and becomes the input value. The guess status may be assigned to a list variable and vice versa. The guess status and the list status are mutually independent.

An alternate way of assigning guess status to a variable is with the so-called Automatic Iteration option. This option is invoked if all the following conditions apply:

1. The First Guess field in the Variable Subsheet is filled with a value.
2. The Automatic Iteration switch on the Global Sheet is set to YES.
3. There is no variable with guess status.
4. The variable does not have an input value.
5. The variable was not evaluated by the Direct Solver.

After the Direct Solver finishes, the variable in question is automatically made a guess (with the value from the First Guess field) and the solution process is taken over by the Iterative Solver.

The question of what variable or variables should be selected as guesses is more important than these technicalities. As stated previously, the selection process starts when the Direct Solver fails to evaluate the desired unknown variable or the entire model—if that was the objective. Obvious candidates for guess status are the variables whose values we are looking for or any of the other unknown variables that the Direct Solver fails to evaluate. Often we will need more than one guess variable. It is possible to assign guess variables piecemeal and to try the Iterative Solver after each assignment. We don't need to have everything planned and decided beforehand; we can develop the formulation of the problem gradually as we go along. This is an important advantage especially with large and complicated models when it is hard to see the whole picture.

Using this gradual approach or doing a preliminary analysis of the model itself with R-graph and VEC matrices may help us to get away with the minimum number of guess variables. The solution time for each step is approximately proportional to the square of the number of guess variables. Sometimes the number of steps increases with an increasing number of guess variables. (This is partially because of increased uncertainty about what initial guess values to assign to all those guess variables.) We could have assigned all the unknown variables a,d,e,f in Figure

8-8's guess values and the model would be solved; however, why should we slow down the solution process if a single guess variable a is sufficient for triggering the solution of the whole model?

Here is a rule of thumb that will minimize the number of guess variables: we select the first one so that, when applied alone, it will produce the solution of the maximum number of unknown variables. If this selection is not sufficient, we select the second guess variable following the same principle, and so on.

How to Select Guess Values

The closer the initial guess is to the final solution, the higher the probability that the Iterative Solver will converge to it, and the fewer the iteration steps that will be required. This is another reason for using as guesses those variables that you are solving for, know something about, and can make intelligent guesses for—rather than some auxiliary or intermediate variables with obscure values.

The "more non-linear" the equations to be solved, the more important it is to start the iteration from a good guess. When the Iterative Solver is used for solving sets of simultaneous linear equations, the choice of guesses is almost immaterial. Everything is permissible (including zero) and the iteration converges very rapidly. Solving a single quadratic equation is usually straightforward too except for two details: a quadratic equation may have no real root at all, in which case the Iterative Solver oscillates in vain within a broad interval of values (try x^2+x+1=0 and see for yourself), or the equation may have two roots; that is, the graph of the function, which is a parabola, intersects the X-axis in two different points. In that case the Iterative Solver converges to the root belonging to the same branch of the parabola as the point chosen as a guess.

We will illustrate the issues of the "goodness" of guesses and the multitude of roots on two examples. The first is our experimental cubic equation x^3−9*x+4=0. As we know from earlier in this chapter, the equation has three real roots. If we did not know this, the best and quickest way to find out would be to use the List Solving and Plotting features for generating a graph of the function y=x^3−9*x+4 for a certain interval of x, for example, $-4 \le x \le 4$. Alternatively we may use the Table feature for tabulating the guess and error values.

Let's review the sequence of keystrokes required to use the List Solving, Plotting, and Table features for the example. The following routine is frequently used and is very important for efficient use of the Iterative Solver:

1. Declare the variables x and y as lists.
2. Make x an input.
3. Generate the list of x values by the following:
   a. Move the cursor to row x on the Variable Sheet.
   b. Dive to the List Subsheet by typing >>.
   c. Type the first list value, **−4**, and press the Enter key.
   d. Move to, say, the 33rd position by typing **:33** and press the Enter key.
   e. Type the last list value, **4**, and press the Enter key.
   f. Fill the list by typing **!Y** and return to the Variable Sheet by typing <<.
   g. List solve by typing **/L!**.
4. Plot the $y=f(x)$ graph by the following:
   a. Go to the Plot Sheet by typing **=P**.
   b. Press the Down Arrow key three times (skipping the options).
   c. Associate the variable x with the X-axis by typing **x**.
   d. Press the Down Arrow key once.
   e. Associate the variable y with the Y-axis by typing **y** and press the Enter key.
   f. Type ! to plot the graph.

Sometimes a table of the guess and error values is a good complement to the graph. There are even some advantages to using tables: we can tabulate the values of some other important variables more easily than by plotting them together with the error term (scaling problems). More important, if we see, for instance, the following in a part of the table:

x	Error
0.25	1.765625
0.5	−0.375

we can quickly interpolate in our minds with higher accuracy (say, $x=0.45$) than when we take the information from the graph (which yields no better than $x=0.5$). The correct root was found at $x=0.4549$.

The keystroke sequence for displaying a table (after we generate list x and List Solve for y) is as follows:

1. Go to the Table Sheet by typing **=T**.
2. Press the Down Arrow key three times to skip the options.
3. Type **x** and press the Down Arrow key.
4. Type **y** and press the Enter key.
5. Press ! to display the table.

The graph and table are shown in Figure 9-7*a* and *b*. If we did not see any or all roots, we would have to shift or widen our search. In our case we see clearly that the curve intersects the y=0 line at three points—the first in the neighborhood of −3, the second somewhere between $x=0$ and $x=1$ (let's say, x=0.5), and the third close to $x=3$. These three points make reasonable guesses and the Iterative Solver indeed converges to the following:

1st root $x=-3.201472$ from guess value −3 in 4 steps

2nd root $x=0.45490409$ from guess value .5 in 3 steps

3rd root $x=2.7465682$ from guess value 3 in 5 steps

What happens if we choose as a guess a certain point close to a peak of the graph? According to Newton's method (discussed in the beginning of the chapter), the intersection of the imaginary tangent to the curve at that point with the horizontal axis (or more precisely, with the line of zero error term) gives the next guess value. If the tangent is almost parallel to the axis, the point of intersection may be pretty far from the root we are iterating for, especially when we deal with a multi-root function. In such a case, the Iterative Solver may converge to a wrong root (for instance to a negative one even if only positive values of an unknown make sense), or it may not converge at all.

Let's take a simple equation $y=x*sin(1/x)$ to illustrate this point. The equation is not as innocent as it looks. As the value of x decreases from 1 to 0 there is a decrease in the amplitude and an accelerating increase in the frequency of the sine curve. Suppose we were aiming at the second largest root, which is actually $x=0.15915494$. If we have the foresight to make an initial guess between 0.135 and 0.195, the Iterative Solver converges. If

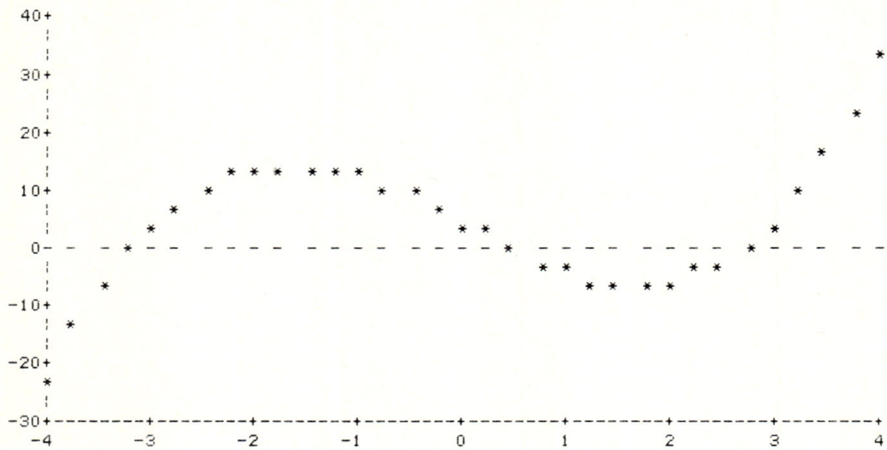

a. Graph

x	y
-4	-24
-3.75	-14.984375
-3.5	-7.375
-3.25	-1.078125
-3	4
-2.75	7.953125
-2.5	10.875
-2.25	12.859375
-2	14
-1.75	14.390625
-1.5	14.125
-1.25	13.296875
-1	12
-.75	10.328125
-.5	8.375
-.25	6.234375
0	4
1	-4
1.25	-5.296875
1.5	-6.125
1.75	-6.390625
2	-6
2.25	-4.859375
2.5	-2.875
2.75	.046875
3	4
3.25	9.078125
3.5	15.375
3.75	22.984375
4	32

b. Table

Figure 9-7.
TK!Solver solution for $y=x\hat{}3-9*x+4$. (The zero-axis is plotted as a $y=0$ function using "–" as the plotting character.)

our guess is slightly smaller or slightly larger, we get the following peculiar responses:

Guess	Converges to
0.127	0.01872411
0.128	−0.0636620
0.129	−0.3183099
0.130	−0.0397887
0.131	0.31830989
0.132	0.31830989
0.133	0.02893726
0.134	0.06366198
⋮	⋮
0.196	divergence
0.197	divergence
0.198	0.03183099

Here again investigative List Solving, tabulating the function values, and plotting the graph of the function can help to choose a good guess on the first try. Using these techniques will quickly show that the largest root is somewhere around $x=0.3$ and the second largest around 0.15. (Could you find out what the third, fourth, and fifth largest roots of this function are?)

A few words about divergence: if, in this example, we set the initial guess as $x=10$, iteration seems to go forever with the value of x creeping up and up. The graph of the function in Figure 9-8 (as well as a closer look at the equation itself) shows why. The function approaches 1 as the value of x increases. The changes of y with respect to changes of x become so small that the Iterative Solver gets lost in the abyss of numerical instabilities as it looks for a root which does not exist in the first place.

Looking for non-existing solutions or infinities (which cannot be expressed numerically in a computer with a finite amount of memory) may lead to all kinds of fallacies. For instance, if we have the same equation $y=x*sin(1/x)$ and assign $y=1$ and guess $x=10$, the Iterative Solver after some 20 steps returns a "solution" of $x=467.07243$ (although mathematically speaking $y=1$ only for an infinitely large x). Moving the resulting x to input and solving for y reveals $y=0.99999924$; that is, the result was right from the Iterative Solver's viewpoint (the error in the rule was reduced below the Comparison Tolerance, which in this case was equal to

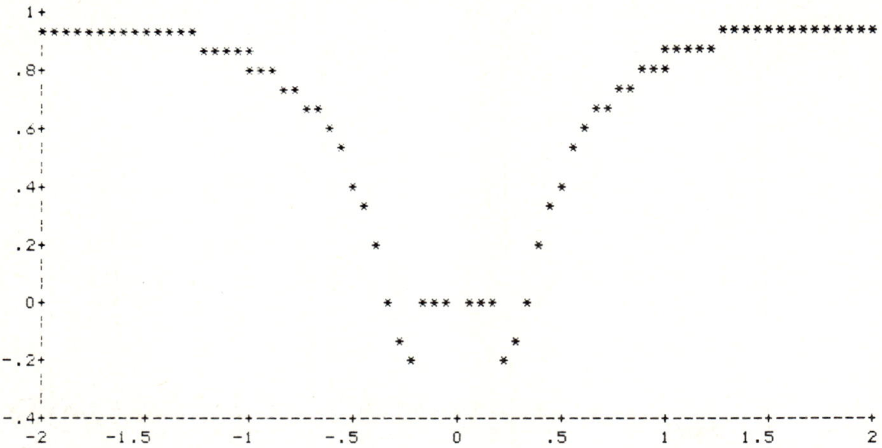

Figure 9-8.
Graph of the function $y=x*sin(1/x)$

the default 1e−6), but from a mathematical viewpoint the solution was incorrect.

Both our examples considered a single equation with one unknown. However, if we have a whole set of non-linear or linear simultaneous equations with many unknowns, quite often only one unknown has to be made a guess to trigger the complete solution. In that case, we have one guess variable and one error term, and consequently we use the techniques described above—List Solving, plotting, and tabulating—to search for a reasonable guess.

With two or more guess variables, the search for reasonable initial guess values becomes trickier. The subject matter, common sense, and past experience are the best guides. A good systematic approach is to relax the constraints by spelling out the error terms in the rules so that the whole model can be resolved with guesses assigned as regular input values. Then we vary these "input" values to get a feeling for their effect on the error terms. Next we fix the first error term by assigning an input value 0 to it, make one of the guess-turned-input variables a guess value again, and try to iterate. If it works, we do the same with another error-guess pair, and so on. At each step of this process, we can use List Solving, plotting, and tabulating for guidance.

Not only is finding good initial guesses more difficult with two or more guess variables, but it is also much harder to make sure that the Iterative

Solver is converging to a correct root and that there isn't a better one hiding around the corner or over the hill. The best way to find good initial guesses is to combine your mathematical grasp of the problem with the TK!Solver features that permit you to set up, run, and evaluate relevant experiments easily in the TK!Solver environment.

How to Control the Iterative Solver

If you sit in front of your computer and struggle with a nasty set of simultaneous, non-linear equations, you may have a feeling that the Iterative Solver is controlling you and not the other way around. If this is the case, you could be dealing with a situation which, without TK!Solver, would require a large computer, a large dedicated program, and formidable human effort to get under control.

Let's summarize all the strings available to you for controlling the performance of the Iterative Solver:

1. You have complete flexibility in selecting and reselecting guess variables (parameters are free to vary during the iteration process) and in assigning and reassigning initial values.

2. The solution is considered successful and the iteration is terminated when the rule discrepancies, caused by less than perfect guesses, are reduced to a level below the error limit. You can control this limit by the values of Comparison Tolerance and Typical Value, which you set on the Global Sheet. A smaller value of Comparison Tolerance implies a more precise solution and often also a larger number of iteration steps before the solution is reached. The Comparison Tolerance value has a subtle effect on the whole iteration process, not just on its outcome. Depending on the problem, it does not make sense to reduce the Comparison Tolerance below a certain limit. The default value of 0.000001 is usually the best bet. (Experiment with the effect of different Comparison Tolerances on the solution of the cubic equation and other models and you will see our point.)

3. Another "control point" is the Maximum Iteration Count, which is also set on the Global Sheet. The default value is 10. The iteration of well-behaved problems from reasonable guesses usually does not take more than 10 steps. Requiring more than 10 steps often implies that there is a divergency or oscillation problem and that the iteration could go on forever if there were no limit set. Generally, this is not important. If you see that the iteration goes nowhere even before

the limit is reached, you can always stop it by pressing the Break key. If, on the other hand, the Iterative Solver fails to reach the solution within the preset number of steps, the iteration stops, but the guess variables retain their status and the latest guess values. You only have to press the Action key again and the iteration continues automatically for another preset number of steps. The most frequent and helpful use of this feature is probably setting the Maximum Iteration Count to 1, which makes it possible to run the Iterative Solver step-by-step to investigate the iteration path and convergency patterns.

4. The Automatic Iteration feature is another control string that makes the Iterative Solver easy to use to solve routine problems. (Do not use this feature when you are still searching for a meaningful problem formulation and feasible guess values.) The default status of the Automatic Iteration switch on the Global Sheet is YES. Let us suppose that Automatic Iteration is ON and there are guess values assigned in the First Guess field of one or more Variable Subsheets. When the Direct Solver finishes solving the model and TK!Solver finds out that any of the variables with preassigned First Guess values remain unknown, it automatically assigns guess status to the variables and launches the Iterative Solver using the First Guesses as guess values. This feature is convenient to use for solving standard models when particular values of guesses are applicable to the whole range of problems, for example, solving loan repayment and similar models for an unknown interest rate. An assignment of 10% (or 0.1) on the First Guess line of the Variable Subsheet covers nearly all practical needs (see the section "Eight in One" in Chapter 12 for an illustration of Automatic Iteration). Specifying NO on the Global Sheet turns off this feature without losing the First Guess values on the Variable Subsheets.

5. You may speed up the iteration process somewhat by turning off the Intermediate Redisplay On switch on the Global Sheet. If you do so, you may gain a few seconds here and there, but you will deprive yourself of the pleasure of viewing how nicely the iteration process converges to the desired solution. Or more important, you will not see how the trouble develops and what to do about it.

6. You can easily experiment with the feedback information you receive. This is probably the most important aspect of the iteration

process control. When you get used to what TK!Solver and particularly the Iterative Solver do for you, you will naturally want more. You may want maps and three-dimensional images of surfaces representing the error terms as functions of two or more guess variables. You may want an iterative procedure that will shoot not just along the slopes of the hills, but over and around their tops if necessary. You will want a detailed trace of the iteration process, and so on. You will develop these and other ideas thanks to all the features already available. You can trace the iterative process by setting the Maximum Iteration Count to 1 and proceeding one step at a time. (On an IBM Personal Computer you can interrupt the iteration by printing the screen dump with all the information about guesses and error terms.) You can use List Solving in conjunction with the Table and Plot features for reconnaissance of the terrain before assigning guess values or after the first attempt has failed.

7. Expanding on the last point and reiterating on what has been said elsewhere, let us note that the way the rules are formulated and ordered in the model may determine (a) which rules become overconstrained and pivoted on by the Iterative Solver, (b) the character of the error function (steep or level, hilly or monotonous), and (c) the generation and propagation of rounding and other errors which may hamper the convergency. Consequently, rule modification and reshuffling represent another tool for controlling the Iterative Solver (the ease with which rules and models can be modified and the consequences of observing these modifications makes this tool very powerful indeed). As a rule of thumb, try to smooth the environment in which the Iterative Solver is to operate, avoid erratic behavior of the error terms as functions of guess variables, and make sure that if possible, the guess values and error terms are not too big, too small, or too different.

Error Conditions

In Chapter 8 we discussed two classes of error conditions that cause termination of the solution by the Direct Solver:

1. *Domain errors.* These errors occur when an attempt is made to contradict the definitions of arithmetic operations or built-in or user-defined functions, for example, dividing by zero, taking the square

root of a negative argument, or looking up the capital of a country unknown to the model.

2. *Consistency errors.* These errors occur when the problem is overdefined and the equal sign in one of the rules does not tolerate the difference between the values of the left-hand and right-hand side expressions that exceeds the error limit. When the Iterative Solver is invoked, TK!Solver reacts the same way in both these situations—by terminating the solution and displaying an error message.

The additional power of the Iterative Solver implies additional sources of problems. We already discussed the failure to converge to a solution indicating that the guesses were not good enough or that the solution does not exist at all. Before we explore other error conditions specific to the Iterative Solver, we will again look at the familiar domain errors as these may have a special flavor when they come up during iteration.

In contrast to direct solving, which reflects a particular state of the model, the iterative solving moves the solution all around the solution space. Consequently, everything may seem okay at the initial guess stage or during the first few steps, but we may suddenly be confronted with a domain error because the value of one of the variables moves out of the domain of a particular operation. This happens quite often with arguments of arcsine or arccosine functions becoming greater than 1, arguments of square roots or logarithms becoming negative, and so on.

Let's consider, as an example, the $y=x*sin(1/x)$ function mentioned before. Suppose we modify it slightly by adding the square root of x to the denominator of the sin argument so that we have

$$x*sin(1/(x+sqrt(x))) = 0$$

We try to iterate from the initial guess $x=0.3$ (before modification this was close enough to the root $x=0.31830989$). The Iterative Solver moves the guess value to $x=-0.14673196$, and the solution stops with the message "SQRT: Argument error".

The model may be valid only for certain intervals of the variables involved. It is possible that moving out of that interval during iteration may even cause inconsistency conditions. These "dynamic" (as we can call them) domain and inconsistency errors are caused by the Iterative Solver wandering in large circles. This may indicate either that the initial guesses were too far from the solution and we need a closer guess or that no solution exists.

The Direct Solver rejects outright any rule inconsistency that it finds. In contrast, the Iterative Solver cannot function and improve initial guesses without inconsistencies or discrepancies to hinge on. Most of the Iterative Solver-specific error conditions or irregular behavior is related to the imbalance or dissonance between the guesses and rule inconsistencies. Let's illustrate these irregularities on a sequence of simple examples.

Needless Guess I

Consider the model with the problem formulation shown in Figure 9-9*a*. When the Action key ! is pressed, TK!Solver finds out that x is a guess variable and activates the Iterative Solver. The latter "borrows" $x=1$ as input, runs through the model, and evaluates everything it can. It does not find any discrepancy, so it terminates the solution without iterating, as the Direct Solver would if x were a regular input. Because it was a guess, the value of x moves to the Output field (see Figure 9-9*b*). This really is not an error situation even though the solution with all the values in the Output field looks as if three unknowns were evaluated from two equations. The $x=1$ should have been made an input rather than a guess.

```
==================== VARIABLE SHEET ==...
St Input      Name     Output     Unit
-- -----      ----     ------     ----
 G 1          x
              y
              z

==================== RULE SHEET ======...
S Rule
- ----
* x + y = 7
* x * z = 12
```

a. Problem formulation

```
==================== VARIABLE SHEET ==...
St Input      Name     Output     Unit
-- -----      ----     ------     ----
              x        1
              y        6
              z        12
```

b. Solution

Figure 9-9.
No need to assign $x=1$ as a guess (input status is enough)

Needless Guess II

What happens if, in addition to keeping x as a guess variable, we assign an input value to, say, variable z (see Figure 9-10*a*)? In this case, the Iterative Solver takes the input value $z=4$, resolves the model completely finding that $x=3$, ignores the formerly assigned guess value, and displays the solution, as shown in Figure 9-10*b*. This time the displayed solution, showing one input value and two variables evaluated from two equations, makes sense. Having $z=4$ assigned as input would be sufficient for the Direct Solver to reach the same results.

Too Many Guesses

Suppose we have the same rule and make an even greater mistake by assigning two guesses, $x=1$ and $y=1$ (see Figure 9-11*a*). This time our mistake is fatal: the Iterative Solver evaluates z, finds only one discrepancy as opposed to two guesses, advises us about the excess guesses on the Status line by pointing to the last contradictory rule it looked at, and terminates the solution process. (In Figure 9-11*b*, note the little shift in the values of x, y, and z—a residue from the numerical differentiation.) The guess status of the variables x and y remains; this is always the case when the Iterative Solver cannot come up with a solution.

```
=================== VARIABLE SHEET ==...
St Input          Name     Output    Unit
-- -----          ----     ------    ----
 G 1              x
                  y
   4              z
```

a. Problem formulation

```
=================== VARIABLE SHEET ==...
St Input          Name     Output    Unit
-- -----          ----     ------    ----
                  x        3
                  y        4
   4              z
```

b. Solution

Figure 9-10.
No need to assign $x=1$ as a guess (input $z=4$ is enough)

```
==================== VARIABLE SHEET ==...
St Input       Name     Output     Unit
-- -----       ----     ------     ----
 G 1           x
 G 1           y
               z
```

a. Problem formulation

```
(1s) Status: > Iteration: Too many guesses

==================== VARIABLE SHEET ==...
St Input       Name     Output     Unit
-- -----       ----     ------     ----
 G 1.0001839   x
 G 1.0000566   y
               z        11.997794


==================== RULE SHEET ======...
S Rule
- ----
> x + y = 7
  x * z = 12
```

b. Response

Figure 9-11.
Too many guesses assigned

Entangled Inconsistency

Let's consider the same guess and input variables as in Figure 9-10*a* and the first rule from Figure 9-9*a*, but add two more rules constraining the values of $x*y$ and $x*z$, as shown in Figure 9-12. It is obvious that the problem in this figure is overdefined. The guess for x would be sufficient for evaluating y from the first rule, generating a discrepancy in the second and iterating on it until the final values of x and y are found, and, eventually, evaluating z from the third rule. The input variable z definitely overconstrains the model: you don't need an additional constraint when there are three equations for three unknowns.

Yet the placement of the error symbols in Figure 9-12 may seem strange. Here is the explanation: the Iterative Solver at first evaluates everything it can without the help of guess variables. So it evaluates $x=5$ from the third rule (the output is not displayed because x is also a guess variable), then $y=2$ (which is displayed) from the first rule, and—the Iterative Solver gets stuck on the second equation even before the guess value of x is brought up. This is why the solution is terminated and the

```
(2s) Status: > Inconsistent

==================== VARIABLE SHEET ==...
St Input      Name     Output     Unit
-- -----      ----     ------     ----
 G 1          x
>             y        2
   4          z


==================== RULE SHEET ======...
S Rule
- ----
  x + y = 7
> x * y = 12
  x * z = 20
```

Figure 9-12.
Inconsistency detected prior to bringing in the guess variable

inconsistency attributed to the second rule. Note that only y is marked as overdefined in the Variable Sheet; the error mark ">" does not overwrite "G."

Disparate Inconsistency

Inconsistency may be detected in a rule that is only indirectly connected with the rule and variables involved in the iteration process or that is not connected at all. The latter case is seen in Figure 9-13. The first two variables constrained by the first two rules would iterate happily with x as a guess; the input values for a and z clearly contradict the third rule.

```
(3s) Status: > Inconsistent

==================== VARIABLE SHEET ==...
St Input      Name     Output     Unit
-- -----      ----     ------     ----
 G 1          x
              y
 > 4          z
 > 6          a


==================== RULE SHEET ======...
S Rule
- ----
* x + y = 7
* x * y = 12
> a * z = 20
```

Figure 9-13.
Inconsistency separate from guess variable and iterated-on rule

```
==================== VARIABLE SHEET ==...
St Input      Name     Output     Unit
-- -----      ----     ------     ----
              x        4
              y        3
    4         z
              a        5
```

Figure 9-14.
Flawless solution of the model in Figure 9-13

Lucky Guess

If in the example shown in Figure 9-13 we blank the input value of a and solve again, the Iterative Solver comes up with the solution shown in Figure 9-14. What would happen if, by sheer luck or providence, we assign a guess $x=3$ to start with? After assuming x as input, the Iterative Solver will not detect any contradiction and, fully satisfied with the state of affairs, will display the same solution as in Figure 9-14. This iteration shortcut takes place only when all the guesses are correct; otherwise the iteration goes on as usual. You will find that it is easier to win a state lottery than to guess a correct answer for $x \neq 0$ in $x * cos(x) = sin(x)$.

Too Few Guesses

Let's consider Figure 9-15*a* and *b*. Figure 9-15*a* shows one guess entered for three unknowns, and the bottom of Figure 9-15*b* shows three equations in three unknowns x,y,z. We assign $x=1$ as a guess (as was sufficient in previous examples) and press the Action key !. Nothing happens except that the variable x loses its guess status and the value moves to the Output field. All the rules remain unresolved. The reason is clear: even with $x=1$ used as an input, the Iterative Solver could not evaluate any additional variable from any of the equations. Generally, such a meager output indicates a need for more input or guess variables. In our case, assigning an input value to y or z would overconstrain the model. An additional guess was the key to success as may be seen in Figure 9-16*a* and *b*. The "too few guesses" condition is not indicated by any specific message.

```
==================== VARIABLE SHEET ==...
St Input      Name     Output     Unit
-- -----      ----     ------     ----
 G 1          x
              y
              z
```

a. Problem formulation

```
(2s) Status:   Unsatisfied

==================== VARIABLE SHEET ==...
St Input      Name     Output     Unit
-- -----      ----     ------     ----
              x        1
              y
              z

==================== RULE SHEET ======...
S Rule
- ----
* x + y + z = 7
* x * y * z = 12
* x + y * z = 20
```

b. Variable Sheet with the response and Rule Sheet

Figure 9-15.
Under-guessed situation

```
==================== VARIABLE SHEET ==...
St Input      Name     Output     Unit
-- -----      ----     ------     ----
 G 1          x
 G 1          y
              z
```

a. Variable Sheet with problem formulation

```
==================== VARIABLE SHEET ==...
St Input      Name     Output     Unit
-- -----      ----     ------     ----
              x        19.380832
              y        -.0502139
              z        -12.33062
```

b. Variable Sheet with results

Figure 9-16.
Successful solution

Dependency Error

If the number of independent equations in the model doesn't match the number of unknowns, the guesses cannot help to solve the problem (unless they happen to be right answers). This situation is illustrated by yet another set of three equations in three unknowns in Figure 9-17*a* and *b*. These are linear equations; thus two guesses with zero values should suffice. The attempt to solve the problem failed because the Iterative Solver found out that only two of the three equations were independent (the third equation is a sum of the first two).

```
==================== VARIABLE SHEET ==...
St Input      Name    Output    Unit
-- -----      ----    ------    ----
 G 0          x
 G 0          y
              z


==================== RULE SHEET ======...
S Rule
- ----
* x    +    y +   z = 6
* 2*x  +    y +   z = 7
* 3*x  + 2*y  + 2*z = 13
```

a. Variable Sheet with problem formation and Rule Sheet

```
(2s) Status: > Iteration: Dependency error

==================== VARIABLE SHEET ==...
St Input      Name    Output    Unit
-- -----      ----    ------    ----
 G 0          x
 G 0          y
>             z


==================== RULE SHEET ======...
S Rule
- ----
  x    +    y +   z = 6
> 2*x  +    y +   z = 7
> 3*x  + 2*y  + 2*z = 13
```

b. Dependency error pointed out

Figure 9-17.
Problem underdefined (two independent equations with three unknowns)

FINE POINTS

Using the Direct Solver is like riding a bus. Your route is predetermined. Once you are on, short of mix-ups, unexpected delays, or accidents, you will get where you planned when you planned. Using the Iterative Solver is more like doing the driving yourself. A lot depends on you. And it makes a difference if you are on an expressway or negotiating a curving, unpaved mountain road. In the latter case success depends on your knowledge of the terrain, your skills, and your access to a good map. The next few stories were conceived as an advanced driving lesson.

Simultaneous Linear Equations

In linear equations all the unknown variables occur only to the first power. For instance, the equations

$$a*y + b*x\hat{\ }2 = exp(x*y)$$
$$a*(x+y) + b/y = sin(x-y)$$

are solved as linear ones if x and y are known. If, however, a and b are known and x and y are not, we have non-linear equations, which are much harder to deal with.

As with any other set of simultaneous equations, when we solve a set of linear equations we have to assign guesses and use the Iterative Solver. Although we are not taking a bus ride, we still have a pretty straightforward drive on an expressway. The reason is that the derivatives in the world of linear equations are constant; consequently, the Jacobian matrices of the Newton-Raphson procedure replicate the equations themselves and the solution for new guesses is equivalent to the solution for the unknowns. One or two iteration steps are sufficient for getting the solution, regardless of the values of the original guesses.

You can try solving linear equations yourself with the model LINEAR on the TK!Solver program diskette; LINEAR is a set of five linear equations for unknowns a,b,c,d,e with 100% dense coefficient matrix (or VEC matrix); every unknown appears in every equation. We have a choice of assigning only four guesses so that the fifth variable will be evaluated from the first equation and the contradictions in the next four equations will serve as pivots for the iteration. However, this will slightly distort the Jacobian matrices and the iteration will take longer. Generally, in the use of linear equations with dense VEC matrices, it is faster to make all the unknowns guesses (with, say, zeros as guess values) because then only one or two steps are required.

The Fewer the Guesses, The Better (With Exceptions)

Even with non-linear equations, there are situations in which the minimum number of guesses is not the best. It is possible to solve the equations in Figure 9-18 for unknown x and y with only one guess value, x. If we assign a positive value, for example, $x=0.5$, the Iterative Solver seems to oscillate forever. The graph of the error function in Figure 9-19 shows why the Newton-Raphson procedure cannot traverse the discontinuity at $x=0$.

Surprisingly, if we assign two guess variables, $x=y=0.5$, the solution in Figure 9-18 is reached within six steps. This is so because an additional guess variable y helps to bridge the discontinuity and to bring the guess x to the negative semiplane where the root lies.

Iteration and Discontinuities

Iteration is problem-prone when the environment contains discontinuities and sharp corners in error functions and their derivatives. A discontinuity in the error function (coming, for instance, from a *step*, *int*, or *abs* function or from a conditional rule) will cause a sudden change in the convergence pattern and possibly a convergence to an undesirable root, divergence, or oscillation.

```
==================== VARIABLE SHEET ==...
St Input      Name     Output       Unit
-- -----      ----     ------       ----
              x        -.3851379
              y        1.2472335
   .2         a
   .4         b


==================== RULE SHEET ======...
S Rule
- ----
  exp(x) + x*y = a
  sin(x*y) + x + y = b
```

Figure 9-18.
Set of non-linear equations with a solution

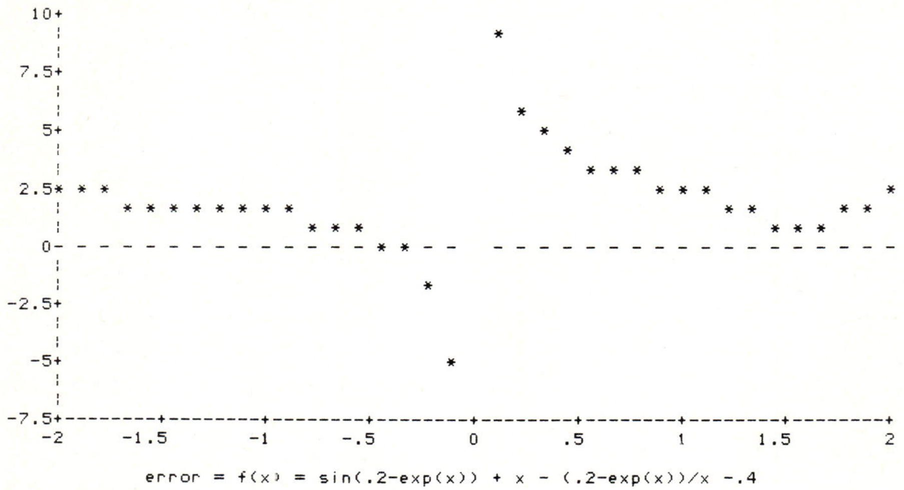

Figure 9-19.
Error function for the problem in Figure 9-18 (applies when solving with a single guess variable x)

As an example let's consider a simple loan repayment formula $R=(i/100)*P/N/(1-(i/(100*N)+1)\wedge-(N*Y))$ and modify it so that the monthly payment is returned in dollars and cents:

$$R = int(i*P/N/(1-(i/(100*N)+1)\wedge-(N*Y)) + 0.5)/100$$

Suppose we managed to borrow $P=8000$ dollars for $Y=5$ years at an annual interest $i=9.5\%$. TK!Solver returns a monthly ($N=12$) payment of \$168.01. If we want to know what the interest should be for a monthly payment of exactly \$168, we make $R=168$ an input, $i=9.5$ a guess, and iterate. A rule without the dollars and cents rounding would return an interest $i=9.496$. The rule as shown here returns nothing. The Iterative Solver goes around in circles because the *int* operation results in the error function being a non-differentiable step function of the guess variable i. (Chapter 11 shows you how to round off to dollars and cents and still be able to iterate when the interest is unknown.)

Hard Problems

The following two examples show how TK!Solver can shortcut the solution of hard and ill-defined problems. These examples are taken from

K. L. Hilbert's "The Evaluation of Mathematical Software That Solves Systems of Non-linear Equations," based on a study at Sandia National Laboratories and reported in *ACM Transaction on Mathematical Software,* Vol. 8, 1982, pp. 5-20. Both samples deal with solving chemical equilibrium problems.

The first is a set of four simultaneous linear and two non-linear equations shown in Figure 9-20. The best candidate for the guess variable is *x1* since it appears in four equations, which is more than any other variable. Attempting to solve (after assigning guess value $x1 = 1$) yields the values of three unknowns, *x2*, *x3*, and *x4*. The variables *x5* and *x6* remain unsolved and the second, third, and sixth rules are not used. A closer examination shows that the unknowns *x5* and *x6* appear in each of these equations. Consequently, we make $x5 = 1$ a guess and solve again. Now the Iterative Solver converges to a solution.

The resulting values range wildly from −1e-11 to 55, and we have to make sure that they don't suffer excessively from accumulated errors. We transfer all the evaluated values *x1* through *x6* to input, introduce error terms (one for each rule), and solve again. The error in the third rule is 1.11e−9, that is, of approximately the same order of magnitude as the values of *x1*, *x2*, and *x3* in this rule. A closer examination shows that if we subtract the second rule from the third two times, we get

$$x1 + x2 + x3 - x6 = 0.001$$

Using this as the third rule instead of the one in Figure 9-20 should not only make the relative error in this rule smaller, but should also eliminate *x5* from this rule, thus making it possible to have one guess variable only. Now the full precision results are as follows:

$x1 = -1.0000227714\text{e-}10$ $\quad$ $x4 = 0.00100000110003$

$x2 = -1.0000227714\text{e-}9$ $\quad$ $x5 = 55.0009999929$

$x3 = -1.0000252818\text{e-}11$ $\quad$ $x6 = -0.0009999929$

```
=================== RULE SHEET =======...
S Rule
- ----
* x1 + x2 + x4 = .001
* x5 + x6 = 55
* x1 + x2 + x3 + 2*x5 + x6 = 110.001
* x1 = .1*x2
* x1 = 10000*x3*x4
* x5 = 55e14*x3*x6
```

Figure 9-20.
Example of a poorly scaled problem

The new error terms $er1=-1.1e\text{-}17$, $er2=2.e\text{-}9$, $er3=1.597e\text{-}16$, and $er4=er5=er6=0$ don't seem to compromise the accuracy of the results.

The second example describes the combustion of propane in air; there are 11 equations for 11 unknown variables $x1$ through $x10$ and the sum of these is TOT:

$$x1 + x4 - 3 = 0$$
$$2*x1 + x2 + x4 + x7 + x8 + x9 + 2*x10 - R = 0$$
$$2*x2 + 2*x5 + x6 + x7 - 8 = 0$$
$$2*x3 + x5 - 4*R = 0$$
$$x1*x5 - 0.193*x2*x4 = 0$$
$$x6*sqrt(x2) - 0.002597*sqrt(x2*x4*TOT) = 0$$
$$x7*sqrt(x4) - 0.003448*sqrt(x1*x4*TOT) = 0$$
$$x8*x4 - 0.00001799*x2*TOT = 0$$
$$x9*x4 - 0.0002155*x1*sqrt(x3*TOT) = 0$$
$$x10*x4\hat{}2 - 0.00003846*x4\hat{}2*TOT = 0$$
$$x1 + x2 + x3 + x4 + x5 + x6 + x7 + x8 + x9 + x10 = TOT$$

The amount of air, R, present in the combustion is known. The article states that "This problem was very sensitive to the starting values used. Every compared code got into trouble by taking a step that caused some of the variables to become negative which, in turn, caused a negative argument for the square root function." As you will see, this seemingly hard problem posed little challenge to TK!Solver.

The VEC matrix of the model is not very dense. The reduced matrix (not counting R's) has 50 cells occupied out of 121, three with double crosses. This means that the Iterative Solver should manage with many fewer than 11 guesses, especially if the equation can be simplified further. Indeed, we can divide the sixth equation by $sqrt(x2)$, the seventh equation by $sqrt(x4)$, and the tenth equation by $x4\hat{}2$ (this simplification also reduces the danger of *sqrt* domain errors during iteration). We also modify the second equation by substituting into it from the eleventh so that

$$x1 - x3 - x5 - x6 + x10 + TOT = R$$

This reduces the number of the non-zero cells in the VEC matrix by 4.

The first choice of guesses is $TOT=10$ and $x1=1$ (as these variables participate in seven and six equations respectively). An attempt to solve falls short of evaluating $x2$, $x3$, $x5$, $x8$, and $x9$. A look at a partial VEC matrix for unsolved variables and unused equations (Figure 9-21) shows that the model can be resolved entirely if we add $x5$ as a guess, or, even

Unsolved variables

Unused equations	$x2$	$x3$	$x5$	$x8$	$x9$
2		x	x		
3	x		x		
4		x	x		
5	x		x		
8	x			x	
9		x			x
11	x	x	x	x	x

Figure 9-21.
A residual VEC matrix halfway through the solution of the second "hard problem"

better, if we can eliminate *x3* or *x5* from either the second or fourth equations (in that case the two guesses *TOT* and *x1* would suffice). We eliminate *x5* from the second equation by adding the fourth equation to it. The final version of the model and its solution is shown in Figure 9-22*a* and *b*. The solution was obtained in eight iteration steps from the previously mentioned initial guesses for *TOT* and *x1*. No problems with domain errors were encountered.

The article also mentioned that "If *R* is too small, the mass balance equations cannot be satisfied." Trial solution for decreasing *R* shows that *x1* is decreasing rapidly and is the first variable to give us *sqrt* errors in the seventh equation if its value becomes negative. Taking advantage of TK!Solver's flexibility, we make *x1*=0 an input and *R* a guess, iterate, and find that the critical (smallest allowable) value of *R* is 3.0008471.

Teaser

Let us consider a "proper rational function":

$$\frac{x^3 - 6x^2 + 11x - 6}{x^5 - 10x^4 + 39x^3 - 74x^2 + 68x - 24} = 10000$$

Could you find the roots with the help of TK!Solver? You should be able to, although the process may not be as simple as the solution of most of the

```
==================== RULE SHEET ======...
S Rule
- ----
* x1 + x4 = 3
* x1 + x3 - x6 + x10 + TOT = 5*R
* 2*x2 + 2*x5 + x6 + x7 = 8
* 2*x3 + x5 = 4*R
* x1*x5 = .193*x2*x4
* x6 = .002597*sqrt(x4*TOT)
* x7 = .003448*sqrt(x1*TOT)
* x8*x4 = .00001799*x2*TOT
* x9*x4 = .0002155*x1*sqrt(x3*TOT)
* x10 = .00003846*TOT

* TOT = x1+x2+x3+x4+x5+x6+x7+x8+x9+x10
```

a. Rule Sheet

```
==================== VARIABLE SHEET ==...
St Input        Name     Output      Unit
-- -----        ----     ------      ----
                x1       2.8801060
                x2       3.9506750
                x3       19.984130
                x4       .11989400
                x5       .03174078
                x6       .03468458
                x7       .03048398
                x8       .01608812
                x9       .12055940
                x10      .00104378
                TOT      27.139405
   10           R
```

b. Variable Sheet

Figure 9-22.
Final version of the model for the second "hard problem" with solution

other problems in this book. First, the form may not be the easiest to investigate. If, for instance, the polynomials in both the numerator and the denominator happen to be equal to zero at the values of x we are looking for, there is no way to get the solution because of the 0/0 bypass (see Chapter 5). So we should multiply both sides by the denominator. It also may be better to divide both sides by 100 in order to reduce the inaccuracies due to mixing small and large numbers. Finally, expressing the polynomials using the *poly* function is more precise. Thus the equivalent TK!Solver rule is as follows:

$$poly(x,1,-6,11,-6)/100 = poly(x,1,-10,39,-74,68,-24)*100$$

Another clue: there are a total of five real roots, which are not hard to find if you examine the error function graph and zoom down to the intervals of apparent interest.

If your friends, to whom you demonstrate the powers of TK!Solver, find out that they can solve the problem by factorizing the polynomials, that is, without TK!Solver, don't argue because it's true. Just change the left-hand side polynomial to

$$poly(x,1,-6,11,-(5+cos(2*pi()*x)))$$

This cannot be factorized, and there are still five roots to look for. There is one trick that may help the Iterative Solver to converge to another root and prevent slipping to the root that has already been found: divide both sides of the equation by the difference between the unknown x and the already known roots, for instance $x-2$. Happy hunting!

10

Lists and List Solving

During problem solving, we frequently want to know the effect of changing one or more variable values on the other variables. For example, we may want to know how mortgage payments change as the interest rate changes, how the resistance of a metal changes as the temperature changes, or how the radioactive decay of a substance progresses over time. We can examine all these cause-effect relationships quickly and easily using the List Solving feature in TK!Solver. In this chapter we see how this feature can be used and how the List functions interact with List Solving.

We will use the term *List Solving* rather than *List Solver* as is used in the TK!Solver documentation and in the program itself because we are not talking about a special solver like the Direct or Iterative Solver. All the so-called List Solver does when we type /L! is invoke the Direct or Iterative Solver repeatedly on lists of values.

LIST MANAGEMENT

A list is a set of values stored under a particular name. All lists in a model are recorded in the List Sheet by their names along with associated information.

Declaring Lists

In order to get the list recorded in the List Sheet, we have to declare it in one of the following ways:

1. Enter the listname in the Name field on the List Sheet.
2. Type an **L** in the Status field of a variable.
3. Enter the listname in the Domain or Range field of the User Function Sheet or Subsheet.
4. Enter the listname in the Associated List field of the Variable Subsheet.
5. Enter the listname in the List field of the Table Sheet.
6. Enter the listname in the X-axis or Y-axis fields of the Plot Sheet.

Generating Values in Lists

We may generate the list values by performing the following steps:

1. Entering the list values in the List Subsheet.
2. Entering the list values in the User Function Subsheet.
3. List Solving.
4. Using the Put option of the List command (/LP).
5. Reading via DIF format.

Associating Lists With Variables

There are two ways of associating lists with variables:

1. Typing **L** in the Status field of a variable to declare a list; a list of the same name as the variable is automatically associated with the variable.
2. Entering the name of the list in the Associated List field on the Variable Subsheet.

In addition, the listname can be an input value for a variable, as we will see in the Linear Regression model described later in this chapter.

Lists and Units

There are two units associated with a list: the Storage Unit and Display Unit (see Chapter 3). Let's review the important points about these units.

1. If the Calculation Unit of a variable is different from the Storage Unit of the associated list, a conversion must be defined on the Unit Sheet. Otherwise the results based on the list values will be incorrect.

2. If a list with defined units is used in a user-defined function, the Display Unit of the list must be the same as the Calculation Unit of the variable. Otherwise, once again the results based on the list values will be incorrect.

3. When we declare and associate a list by typing an **L** in the Status field of a variable and the variable has units associated with it, the Calculation Unit and Display Unit become, respectively, the Storage Unit and Display Unit of the list. However, if after association, units are assigned to the variable, they are not inherited by the list.

Accessing List Values

The Dive command can be used from any of the following sheets and subsheets to access the list values: List Sheet, Variable Sheet, User Function Sheet, Table Sheet, Plot Sheet, User Function Subsheet, and Variable Subsheet. See Figure 3-2 for an overview of the sheets and subsheets in TK!Solver.

Dissociating Lists From Variables

There are two ways of dissociating lists from variables:

1. Typing **L** in the Status field of a variable already containing an "L". The listname remains on the List Sheet and the values are not lost. We can restore the association by typing **L** again.

2. Blanking the listname from the Associated List field on the Variable Subsheet. The listname remains on the List Sheet and the values are not lost.

USING LISTS AND LIST SOLVING

Let's look at three examples of the use of lists and List Solving.

Interstellar Flights and List Solving

Einstein's famous twin paradox goes as follows: Imagine twins at age 21. One becomes an astronaut and volunteers for the first interstellar flight. He takes off and travels at a speed of 2.99×10^8 meters per second. The astronaut travels for what he measures to be a year, at which time he fires retro rockets and navigational engines and turns around and heads toward Earth. The journey naturally takes another year. He is now 23 years old; but when he steps from the ship, his twin is over 48 years old!

The subjective and real time for the twin on earth and for the other twin traveling near the speed of light is given by the equation

$$Ts = Te \sqrt{1 - v^2/c^2}$$

where

Ts = time passed on board ship
Te = time passed on earth
v = ship velocity relative to earth
c = speed of light (2.9979×10^8 m/s).

List Solving can be used to find out how the time passed on earth Te changes as the ship velocity v changes for a given time in space Ts. Let's consider the following example: how does Te change as v varies from 10% to 90% of the speed of light when Ts=10 years?

The equation is entered in the Rule Sheet as shown in Figure 10-1*a*. The Calculation Unit for c and v is the speed of light itself and is entered in the Unit Sheet as **sol** (see Figure 10-1*b*). The Display Unit **m/s** is entered in the Unit fields of v and c in the Variable Sheet (see Figure 10-1*c*). A conversion between sol and m/s is defined on the Unit Sheet. The velocity of light in *m/s* **2.9979*10^8** is assigned to c. Ts is assigned **10**.

The first step in List Solving is to identify the variables that will take on multiple values and assign the necessary variables as input. Here, of the two variables v and Te that will have multiple values, v is the input. So we type an **I** (for input) in its Status field and declare (and associate at the same time) v and Te as lists by typing **L** in their Status fields (The Variable Subsheet for v is shown in Figure 10-2. The Associated List field displays the name of the list associated with the variable, in this case v, the variable name.

```
==================== RULE SHEET ===============================...
S Rule
- ----
* Ts = Te * sqrt(1 - v^2/c^2)
```

a. Rule Sheet

```
==================== UNIT SHEET ===============================...
From        To          Multiply By   Add Offset
----        --          -----------   ----------
sol         m/s         299790000
```

b. Unit Sheet

```
==================== VARIABLE SHEET ==========================...
St Input       Name    Output     Unit       Comment
-- -----       ----    ------     ----       -------
L              Te                 yr         time on earth
   10          Ts                 yr         time in spaceship
L  0           v                  m/s        spaceship velocity
   299790000   c                  m/s        velocity of light
```

c. Variable Sheet (Calculation Unit for v and c is velc)

Figure 10-1.
Model for Einstein's Twin Paradox

```
==================== VARIABLE: v ================...
Status:                    L
First Guess:
Associated List:           v
Input Value:               0
Output Value:
Display Unit:              m/s
Calculation Unit:          sol
Comment:                   spaceship velocity
```

Figure 10-2.
Variable Subsheet for v (note the Associated List field)

For entering the values of v, we access the List Subsheet for v by diving. As seen from Figure 10-3*a*, the Calculation Unit and Display Unit of the variable have become the Storage Unit and Display Unit, respectively, of the list. Since the first value of v is 10% of c, we enter **10/100*c** in the first Value field and let TK!Solver evaluate it in the Calculator mode. It displays 0.1 as seen in the figure. The Display Unit of the list is m/s, the Display Unit of c is m/s, and the value of c in the Variable Sheet is

299790000. But the value in the List Subsheet is 0.1. The reason is that when we use a variable name (that has a value) in the Calculator mode, TK!Solver returns its value in the Calculation Unit. In this example, the Calculation Unit of *c* is sol, so its displayed value in m/s is converted to sol (which results in 1) and is substituted for *c* in the expression entered in the Value field; hence the 0.1. So we must be careful when using the values of variables with units in the Calculator mode.

To get the correct value, we enter **10/100*2.9979E8** in the first Value field. In the ninth field we enter **90/100*2.9979E8**, the last value. The intermediate values are filled using the Fill List feature (see Chapter 3). The List Subsheet with the values is shown in Figure 10-3*b*.

We change the display to the Variable Sheet using the Select command =. Before List Solving, solving the model with one set of input values helps check whether the problem is formulated correctly. We invoke the List command by typing /**L**. Then to select the Solve option we type ! in response to the "! B P G" prompt. The message "List Solver 1, Direct Solver" is displayed in the Prompt/Error line. The first value from the list

```
==================== LIST: v ====================...
Comment:                        spaceship velocity
Display Unit:                   m/s
Storage Unit:                   sol
Element Value
------- -----
1       .1
```

a. In the Calculator mode (*c* is returned in its Calculation Unit sol though the Display Unit is m/s)

```
==================== LIST: v ====================...
Comment:                        spaceship velocity
Display Unit:                   m/s
Storage Unit:                   sol
Element Value
------- -----
1       29979000
2       59958000
3       89937000
4       119916000
5       149895000
6       179874000
7       209853000
8       239832000
9       269811000
```

b. List Subsheet with the different speeds

Figure 10-3.
List Subsheets for *v*

of v is displayed in its Input field and Te is evaluated and displayed in its Output field. We say that an instance has been processed. Each instance corresponds to one set of values of all the variables. The instance is displayed as it is being processed since the Intermediate Redisplay On field on the Global Sheet is set to YES. We can suppress this display and reduce the solution time by setting the field to NO. After all the nine instances are processed, the message disappears and the Variable Sheet looks as it did before List Solving was initiated. We can see the values of Te by diving into its List Subsheet.

Generally, Table and Plot features are used together with List Solving. Figure 10-4 shows the values displayed with the table-generating feature. The Plot Sheet is used to produce the plot shown in Figure 10-5. We can see on the plot that as the ship speed increases, more time passes on earth for the same time in space.

Modifying the Problem

We would now like to find out how Te changes as Ts varies from 1 to 10 for each of the values of v. We declare Ts as a list by typing **L** in its Status field and then enter the values from 1 to 10 in its List Subsheet. Since there is a value of Ts in the Input field, we do not need to declare it again as an input by typing I (as was done earlier for v). After List Solving, the values are displayed in a table as shown in Figure 10-6.

There are only 9 values of Te instead of 10*9=90 (10 different times and 9 different speeds). The reason is that TK!Solver processes the values in the list serially. It takes the first value from all the input lists, processes it, and then moves on to the next one and so on. So it is not possible to do what we might call two-dimensional List Solving.

speed (m/s)	years on earth
29979000	10.05037815
59958000	10.20620726
89937000	10.48284837
119916000	10.91089451
149895000	11.54700538
179874000	12.5
209853000	14.00280084
239832000	16.66666667
269811000	22.94157339

Figure 10-4.
Time passed on earth during ten years in space at different speeds

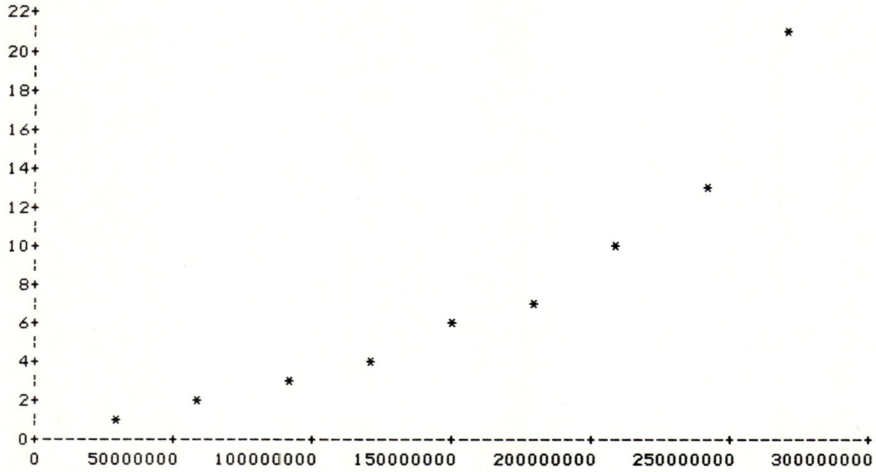

Figure 10-5.
Plot of speed vs. time on earth

Ts (yr)	speed (m/s)	Te (yr)
1	29979000	1.00503782
2	59958000	2.04124145
3	89937000	3.14485451
4	119916000	4.36435781
5	149895000	5.77350269
6	179874000	7.5
7	209853000	9.80196059
8	239832000	13.3333333
9	269811000	20.6474161
10		

Figure 10-6.
Time on earth for different periods in space at different speeds (note there are no values corresponding to *Ts*=10 under speed and *Te*)

Blank Elements Ignored

Another point to note in Figure 10-6 is that there are only 9 values of *Te*, though there are 10 values in *Ts*. Not only is List Solving serial in nature, but it also terminates when the shortest input list is exhausted. In this example, v had only 9 elements, so List Solving stopped after that. There is no value corresponding to the 10th position in *Te*. During List

Solving, blanks in lists are ignored and the corresponding positions are left blank in the output list.

If an empty list is used as an input, TK!Solver displays the message "List Solver: No input list values" and the solution is terminated with a beep. This is different from the way empty lists are treated by List functions (for example, the *sum* function returns a zero for an empty list).

Errors During List Solving

When TK!Solver encounters an error during List Solving, the solution of the particular instance is terminated with a beep, the error symbol ">" appears, and the solution proceeds to the next instance. The corresponding positions in the output lists are left blank.

Steps in List Solving

To summarize, the steps involved in List Solving are as follows:

1. Identify variables that will have multiple values and assign the necessary variables as input.
2. Declare and associate the lists with the appropriate variables.
3. Enter the values for the lists associated with input variables in their List Subsheets.
4. Check to see if the problem is well formulated by solving it once by pressing the Action key.
5. If desired, to save time change the setting in the Intermediate Redisplay On field in the Global Sheet to NO to suppress the display of the different instances.
6. Solve by typing /**L!**.

Generating Factorials

The Block Solving option of the List command processes a specified block of elements (see Chapter 4). This feature can be used to generate a table of factorials. The expression "n factorial" is defined as follows if n is an integer greater than zero:

$$n! = 1 \cdot 2 \cdot ... \cdot (n-1) \cdot n$$

This definition is not unlike the expression for Fibonacci numbers given in Chapter 6. Here we get the ith number by multiplying the $(i-1)$th number by *i*. This means that all the operations have to be performed on the same list, so the *element* function has to be used. This definition translates into the rule shown in Figure 10-7. The first *element* function retrieves the ($i-1$)th element in the list *factorial; element*() returns the instance number, and the product is stored in the *i*th position in *factorial*.

To declare the variable *factorial* as a list, we type **L** in its Status field. Then when we invoke List Solving by typing **/L!**, the message "List Solver: No input list values" is displayed and the solution is terminated with a beep. There is a funny situation here: *factorial* is both an input list and also the output list. If it is declared as an input list, TK!Solver can do nothing since no elements are defined. We cannot specify the elements in the list because that is what the model is supposed to find out. Here is where the Block Solving option comes in. Recall that we used this option for a similar purpose with the Fibonacci numbers in Chapter 6.

To invoke the Block Solving option, we type **/LB**. The prompt "List Block: First element:" is displayed, and we type **1** and press the Enter key. The prompt for the last element in the block "List Block: Last element:" is displayed. To generate the factorials for the first ten numbers, we type **10** and press the Enter key. The "List Solver 1, Direct Solver" message comes on and the factorials are generated as each instance is processed. The message disappears when the specified block is processed. The List Subsheet with the generated factorials is shown in Figure 10-8.

The Get option of the List command can be used to display the factorial of a desired number on the Variable Sheet. For example, to display "6 factorial", we invoke the List command by typing **/L** and select the Get option by typing **G** in response to the List command prompt. The prompt "Get from element:" is displayed. We type **6** and press the Enter key. The value of 6 factorial, 720, is displayed in the Output field of *factorial*.

```
(1n) Name: factorial
List Solver 1, Direct Solver
==================== VARIABLE SHEET ===========================...
St Input      Name     Output     Unit       Comment
-- -----      ----     ------     ----       -------
L             factori                        factorial

==================== RULE SHEET ===============================...
S Rule
- ----
* factorial = element('factorial,element()-1,1) * element()
```

Figure 10-7.
Variable and Rule Sheets for generating factorials (note message in the Prompt/Error line)

```
=================== LIST: factorial ====...
Comment:                     factorials
Display Unit:
Storage Unit:
Element Value
------- -----
1       1
2       2
3       6
4       24
5       120
6       720
7       5040
8       40320
9       362880
10      3628800
```

Figure 10-8.
List Subsheet with factorials

How Far Can We Go?

To determine the largest number whose factorial TK!Solver can generate, we use the Block Solving option and find that 80 factorial (7.157E118) is the maximum. The factorials of numbers greater than 80 are greater than 1E120 and thus exceed TK!Solver's limits. In such cases, TK!Solver beeps and displays the "Exponent Overflow" error message. In fact, values are actually accurate only up to 16 factorial (which has 14 digits with the last three being zero, giving 11 significant digits). Beyond this, the accuracy goes down and the errors start accumulating.

Number of Combinations

The factorial model can be expanded to generate the number of combinations of n things taken r at a time. This is given by the following formula:

$$C(n,r) = \frac{n!}{(n-r)!\, r!}$$

Since the formula requires the factorials of different numbers, the values generated earlier can be used as the Range list of a user-defined function that relates the number and its factorial through a Table Mapping.

Figure 10-9 shows the User Function Subsheet for the function *fact* with *factorial* as the Range list and *number* as the Domain list. By definition 0!=1, so 1 is added at the top of the *factorial* list. (The Insert command /I is used to insert the blank row.) A new rule based on the given formula

```
==================== USER FUNCTION: fact ===========...
Comment:                         factorials of numbers
Domain List:                     number
Mapping:                         Table
Range List:                      factorial
Element Domain        Range
------- ------        -----
1        0            1
2        1            1
3        2            2
4        3            6
5        4            24
6        5            120
7        6            720
8        7            5040
9        8            40320
10       9            362880
11       10           3628800
```

Figure 10-9.
User Function Subsheet for *fact* using the factorials generated in Figure 10-8 (note that 0!=1 has been added at the top of the list)

```
==================== VARIABLE SHEET ==============================...
St Input      Name    Output     Unit       Comment
-- -----      ----    ------     ----       -------
L             c                             number of combinations
   10         n                             number of things
L  0          r                             number taken at a time

==================== RULE SHEET ===================================...
S Rule
- ----
  "factorial = element('factorial,element()-1,1) * element()
  c = fact(n) / (fact(n-r) * fact(r))
```

Figure 10-10.
Variable and Rule Sheets for generating number of combinations; the factorial rule has been commented out and the variable is deleted from the Variable Sheet

is added to the Rule Sheet as shown in Figure 10-10. Since the factorial rule is not required, we comment it out by typing a " in front of the rule, as shown in the figure. The variable *factorial* is deleted from the Variable Sheet, but the list *factorial* remains.

Let's find out the number of combinations of 10 things (n=10), taken r (varying from 0 to 10) at a time. For this, r is declared as a list and the values from 0 to 10 are entered in its List Subsheet. Then n is assigned **10** in its Input field and we initiate List Solving by typing /**L**!. After the

```
==================== VARIABLE SHEET ==============================...
St Input      Name    Output    Unit        Comment
-- -----      ----    ------    ----        -------
L             c       252                   number of combinations
   10         n                             number of things
L  5          r                             number taken at a time
```

Figure 10-11.
Variable Sheet with the sixth instance displayed using the List Get option

r	0	1	2	3	4	5	6	7	8	9	10
c	1	10	45	120	210	252	210	120	45	10	1

Figure 10-12.
Table of combinations of ten things taken r at a time (table displayed using the Horizontal option on the Table Sheet)

solution, the Get option of the List command is used to display the sixth instance. Figure 10-11 shows the Variable Sheet. Note that the value of r is displayed in its Input field while that of c is displayed in its Output field.

All the values generated are displayed in a table as shown in Figure 10-12. It can be seen from the figure that the resulting values are binomial coefficients, and naturally $C(n,0)=C(n,n)$, $C(n,1)=C(n,n-1)$, and so on.

In Chapter 7 we saw that models should be developed in stages. Here the scope of a model has been widened by our adding a new rule and using the results generated from an earlier solution of the model.

Linear Regression Analysis

List Solving is not necessary when List functions are used as this Linear Regression Analysis model will show. The Linear Regression technique is used for fitting a straight line of the form $y=c+m\times x$ to a set of x and y data points that may have been obtained experimentally. The resulting equation can be used to make predictions of one value, let us say y, given a particular x value. We can also calculate the correlation coefficient using this model.

The Formulas

If x and y are two sets of n data points each, then for the straight line $y=c+m\times x$, the slope (m), intercept (c), and correlation coefficient (r) are defined as follows:

$$m = \frac{n\ \Sigma xy - \Sigma x\ \Sigma y}{n\ \Sigma x^2 - (\Sigma x)^2}$$

$$c = \frac{\Sigma y - m\ \Sigma x}{n}$$

$$r = \sqrt{\frac{m\left(\Sigma xy - \dfrac{\Sigma x \Sigma y}{n}\right)}{\Sigma y^2 - \dfrac{(\Sigma y)^2}{n}}}$$

Building the Model

In TK!Solver lists have to be used for entering the data points. When we look at the formulas, two functions come to mind immediately—*sum* for the sum of values and *dot* for the sum of the dot product of the two lists of values. In addition, the *count* function can be used to find out n, the number of values.

Sometimes it is a good idea to enter the variable names in the Variable Sheet in the desired order *before* entering the rules. This model is an excellent illustration of such a choice. Note also that the variable names are mnemonic and that the comments in the Variable Sheet in Figure 10-13 explain what each variable stands for. The Rule Sheet in the figure contains the rules in the model. We can see that the rules are structured very much like the formulas.

Using the Model

Table 10-1 shows the height and weight of 11 male college students. The problem is to fit a straight line to these points.

We display the List Sheet and declare two lists *height* and *weight* on it. We then enter the values from the table into the two List Subsheets. We

Table 10-1.
Height and weight of 11 male college students

Height	71	73	64	65	61	70	65	72	63	67	64
Weight	160	183	154	168	159	180	145	210	132	168	141

```
==================== VARIABLE SHEET ==========================================
St Input      Name     Output     Unit      Comment
-- -----      ----     ------     ----      -------
              x                             x values
              y                             y values
              n                             # of values
              sx                            sigma(x)
              sy                            sigma(y)
              sxy                           sigma(xy)
              sx2                           sigma(x^2)
              sy2                           sigma(y^2)
              sxsy                          sigma(x)*sigma(y)

              slope                         slope of straight line
              inter                         y intercept
              corr                          Pearson's correlation coefficient

==================== RULE SHEET ==============================================
S Rule
- ----
* n = count(x)
* sx = sum(x)
* sy = sum(y)
* sxy = dot(x,y)
* sx2 = dot(x,x)
* sy2 = dot(y,y)
* sxsy = sx * sy

* slope = (n*sxy - sxsy) / (n*sx2 - sx^2)
* inter = (sy - slope*sx) / n
* corr = sqrt(slope * (sxy - sxsy/n) / (sy2 - sy^2/n))
```

Figure 10-13.
Variable and Rule Sheets for Linear Regression Model; the Variable Sheet was generated first

enter the listname **'height** in the Input field of x on the Variable Sheet and the listname **'weight** in the Input field of y. We press the Action key to solve the model and the solution is shown in the Variable Sheet in Figure 10-14.

General Applicability

The *count* function in the first rule in the Rule Sheet (see Figure 10-13) has the argument x, which is not a symbolic value. We recall from Chapter 6 that List Functions should have symbolic values as their arguments. In the present example, x has been assigned a symbolic value, *'height*, which also is a listname. Likewise, y has been assigned the symbolic value *'weight*. We used x and y (and not the symbolic values *'height* and *'weight*) as the arguments for the List Functions in order to make the model more general.

If the model had been built with the listnames *height* and *weight* as the arguments for the List functions, then every time different lists were to be used, all the rules would have to be edited. In Chapter 7, we used the cubic equation model to emphasize the need to make the models more general when building them. Now we have another model to illustrate the same point. For example, to fit a straight line for the data given in Table 10-2, all we need to do is create two new lists *brother* and *sister*, assign them as input values to x and y, and press the Action key. Figure 10-15 shows the Variable Sheet with the solution. The Linear Regression model can be expanded for curvilinear regression.

```
==================== VARIABLE SHEET ============================================
St Input      Name    Output     Unit      Comment
-- -----      ----    ------     ----      -------
   'height    x                            x values
   'weight    y                            y values
              n       11                   # of values
              sx      735                  sigma(x)
              sy      1800                 sigma(y)
              sxy     120935               sigma(xy)
              sx2     49275                sigma(x^2)
              sy2     299364               sigma(y^2)
              sxsy    1323000              sigma(x)*sigma(y)

              slope   4.0472222            slope of straight line
              inter   -106.7917            y intercept
              corr    .74582851            Pearson's correlation coefficient
```

Figure 10-14.
Variable Sheet with sclution for data in Table 10-1 (note the listnames are specified as symbolic values in the Input fields of x and y)

```
==================== VARIABLE SHEET ============================================
St Input      Name    Output     Unit      Comment
-- -----      ----    ------     ----      -------
   'brother   x                            x values
   'sister    y                            y values
              n       11                   # of values
              sx      759                  sigma(x)
              sy      704                  sigma(y)
              sxy     48615                sigma(xy)
              sx2     52445                sigma(x^2)
              sy2     45122                sigma(y^2)
              sxsy    534336               sigma(x)*sigma(y)

              slope   .52702703            slope of straight line
              inte~   27.635135            y intercept
              corr    .55805471            Pearson's correlation coefficient
```

Figure 10-15.
Variable Sheet for data in Table 10-2

Table 10-2.
Heights of brothers and sisters

Brother	71	68	66	67	70	71	70	73	72	65	66
Sister	69	64	65	63	65	62	65	64	66	59	62

With TK!Solver, fitting a straight line is not the only objective of linear regression. The equation can also be used for playing around with the variables and for predicting and analyzing the trends. We enter the equation of the fitted straight line *yest=inter+slope*xest* in the Rule Sheet. For a given *xest* the corresponding *yest* can be found from the calculated values of *inter* and *slope*. Figure 10-16 shows the Variable Sheet with the weight estimated for a five-foot, eight-inch tall student. The variables *x* through *sxsy* are retained on the Variable Sheet but are scrolled out of view.

LIST SOLVING AND LIST FUNCTIONS

Let's use a model for DC circuit analysis to examine how List Solving interacts with List functions. In a circuit, the total resistance of resistors in series is given by the sum of their individual resistances. A list can be used to enter the individual resistance values, and the *sum* function is then used to evaluate the total resistance. This leads to the first rule shown in Figure 10-17.

The voltage drop across each resistor is the product of its resistance and the current through the circuit; this is shown by the second rule. The total drop in the circuit is the sum of the individual drops, and this leads to the third rule in the figure.

Let's consider the following problem: calculate the total resistance, the

```
=================== VARIABLE SHEET ==========================================
St Input       Name    Output     Unit       Comment
-- -----       ----    ------     ----       -------

   4.0472222   slope                         slope of straight line
   -106.7917   inter                         y intercept
               corr                          Pearson's correlation coefficient

   68          xest                          x estimate
               yest    168.41944             y estimate
```

Figure 10-16.
Variable Sheet with *yest* calculated for a given *xest* using the slope and intercept of the obtained straight line

```
=================== RULE SHEET ===========================...
S Rule
- ----
  serres = sum('res)        " total resistance in series
  vdrop = iser * res        " voltage drop across each res.
  vtot = sum('vdrop)        " total voltage drop in circuit
```

Figure 10-17.
Rule Sheet for DC series circuit analysis

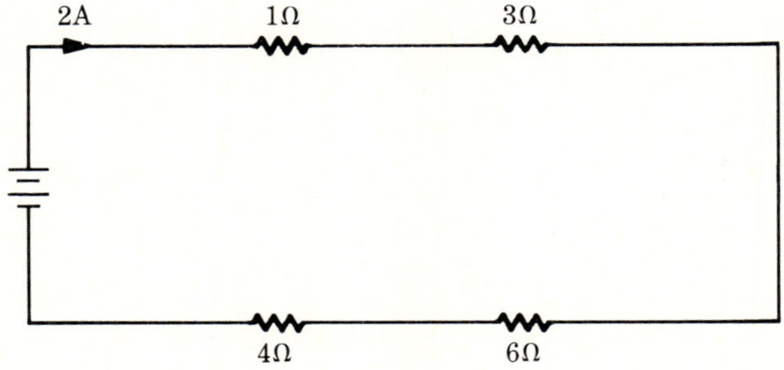

Figure 10-18.
The DC circuit to be analyzed

individual voltage drops, and the total voltage drop for the circuit shown in Figure 10-18.

Since the resistances are given, *res* is made as an input variable. We declare it as a list by typing **L** in its Status field. Then we also declare *vdrop* as a list since the individual voltage drops have to be stored and summed up to find the total voltage drop *vtot*. The resistance values **1**, **3**, **6**, **4** are entered in the List Subsheet for *res*. Then *iser* is assigned 2. We invoke List Solving by typing /L!. As seen in Figure 10-19, *vtot* is evaluated as 20.

Figure 10-20 shows the values of *res* and *vdrop* displayed in tabular form. We can see that the sum of *vdrop* is 2+6+12+8=28, whereas the Variable Sheet displays 20 for *vtot*.

The difference of 8 between the actual value and the value of *vtot* is the last value of *vdrop*. The *sum* function in the third rule does not take into account the last instance generated by List Solving and hence the difference.

When the Action key is now pressed, the correct value of 28 for *vtot* is displayed on the Variable Sheet. The reason is that now all four elements

```
==================== VARIABLE SHEET ====================================...
St Input      Name      Output    Unit       Comment
-- -----      ----      ------    ----       -------
L  0          res                 ohm        list of resistors
   2          iser                amp        current in circuit
              serres    14        ohm        total resistance in series
L             vdrop               volt       voltage drop across resistor
              vtot      20        volt       total voltage drop
```

Figure 10-19.
Variable Sheet after List Solving (note the value of *vtot* is 20)

```
resis (ohm)  1            3            6            4
vdrop (volt) 2            6            12           8
```

Figure 10-20.
Table of resistance and the voltage drop across each resistor (note that the sum of voltage drops is 28, whereas the *vtot* in Figure 10-19 displays 20)

are present in the list *vdrop*, so the *sum* function returns their sum correctly.

It is worth noting the following facts about the interaction between List Solving and List functions when they are used together:

1. The last instance evaluated by List Solving is not taken into account by the List function, so the Direct Solver should be invoked after List Solving to get the correct answer.
2. If the last element in an input list is changed, then after List Solving again, the Direct Solver has to be invoked.
3. Similarly if the last element is deleted, then after List Solving, the Direct Solver has to be invoked.
4. If a new element is added to the end of the list, the Direct Solver should be used after List Solving.
5. If any of the intermediate values are changed, there is no need to use the Direct Solver after List Solving.

ITERATIVE SOLVING WITH LISTS

In the models discussed until now, the Direct Solver was used on lists of values to solve the problem. However, the Iterative Solver can also be invoked on lists of values. The guesses for the variables have to be entered in the List Subsheet of the guess variable. As seen in the earlier chapters, we declare a variable as a guess variable by typing a **G** in its Status field. Then when we initiate List Solving by typing **/L!**, the Iterative Solver is called and the model solved repeatedly for the different values in the lists. A guess value has to be assigned for each instance. Each solution is stored in the corresponding position in the list.

However, if an instance does not converge in the specified number of steps, TK!Solver beeps and proceeds to the next instance. The initial guess value stays in the corresponding position. The fact that TK!Solver does not automatically record the value reached during the last iteration step is a disadvantage, especially when we want to continue the iteration after a convergency failure.

Vapor Pressure Model

The pressure and temperature of a material are related by the following equation:

$$ln(P) = a + b/T + c*ln(T)$$

where

P = the pressure in atmospheres
T = the temperature in Kelvin
a, b, c = constants for a particular material.

Given a=18.19, b=−23180, c=−0.8858 for lead, we are asked to find the temperatures as the pressure changes from 0.01 to 0.1 atmospheres in steps of 0.01 atm.

We can see from the equation that the Iterative Solver has to be used to evaluate T (since it appears twice in the equation). The equation is entered in the Rule Sheet. We make P an input variable and then make T the guess variable by typing **G** in its Status field.

We will use the second method for associating a list with a variable. The List Sheet is displayed and we enter the listname **pres** in the Name field. Then we enter the unit name **atm** in the Unit field. Using the Dive command, we access the List Subsheet for entering the different values of pressure. The first and last values 0.01 and 0.1 are entered in the first and tenth positions respectively. We then fill the intermediate values using the Fill List feature. The List Sheet and List Subsheet are shown in Figure 10-21.

The Variable Subsheet for *P* is displayed and we enter the name of the list **pres** in the Associated List field. The list *pres* is associated with *P* and an "L" appears in the Status field. It is possible to dive into the List Subsheet for *pres* from where we are. Figure 10-22 shows the Variable Subsheet for *P*.

The given values of *a*, *b*, and *c* are assigned on the Variable Sheet. *T* is assigned **oK** as the Calculation Unit and **oC** as its Display Unit. Then we declare *T* as a list by typing **L** in its Status field (see Figure 10-23*a* and 10-23*b*). The Unit Sheet with the conversion between oK and oC is shown in Figure 10-23*c*. The List Subsheet for *T* is accessed to enter the guess values for the Iterative Solver. Initial guesses from 600 to 1500 are assigned as shown in Figure 10-24.

```
==================== LIST SHEET ==========...
Name         Elements  Unit        Comment
----         --------  ----        -------
pres         10        atm         pressures


==================== LIST: pres ==========...
Comment:                        pressures
Display Unit:                   atm
Storage Unit:                   atm
Element Value
------- -----
1       .01
2       .02
3       .03
4       .04
5       .05
6       .06
7       .07
8       .08
9       .09
10      .1
```

Figure 10-21.
List Sheet and List Subsheet for *pres* with values

```
==================== VARIABLE: P ======...
Status:                         L
First Guess:
Associated List:                pres
Input Value:                    0
Output Value:
Display Unit:                   atm
Calculation Unit:               atm
Comment:                        pressure
```

Figure 10-22.
Variable Subsheet for *P* (note the listname *pres* in the Associated List field)

We initiate List Solving by typing /**L**!; the prompt "List Solver 1, Iterative Solver 1 out of 10" is displayed in the Prompt/Error line indicating that the Iterative Solver has been invoked. As each value of T converges, it

```
==================== RULE SHEET =============================...
S Rule
- ----
  ln(P) = a + b/T + c*ln(T)
```

a. Rule Sheet

```
==================== VARIABLE SHEET =========================...
St Input      Name      Output      Unit      Comment
-- -----      ----      ------      ----      -------
   18.19      a                               constant for lead
   -23180     b                               constant for lead
   -.8858     c                               constant for lead
LG 0          T                     oC        temperature
L  0          P                     atm       pressure
```

b. Variable Sheet (list *pres* is associated with P)

```
==================== UNIT SHEET =============================...
From      To      Multiply By    Add Offset
----      --      -----------    ----------
oC        oK      1              273
```

c. Unit Sheet

Figure 10-23.
The Vapor Pressure Model

```
==================== LIST: T =============...
Comment:                          temperature
Display Unit:                     oC
Storage Unit:                     oK
Element Value
------- -----
1       600
2       700
3       800
4       900
5       1000
6       1100
7       1200
8       1300
9       1400
10      1500
```

Figure 10-24.
List Subsheet with guess values of T

is stored in its List Subsheet and the next instance is processed. When all the instances are processed, we can see the values of T by diving into its List Subsheet. Figure 10-25 shows the values displayed with the table generating feature, while a plot of pressure vs. temperature is shown in Figure 10-26.

pres (atm)	temp (oC)
.01	1143.172772
.02	1209.639012
.03	1251.588281
.04	1282.868363
.05	1308.058684
.06	1329.274594
.07	1347.676716
.08	1363.974095
.09	1378.633234
.1	1391.97823

Figure 10-25.
Table of pressure and temperature values

```
1400+                                                                       *
    :                                                               *
1375+                                                       *
    :                                               *
1350+
    :                                       *
1325+                               *
    :
1300+
    :                       *
1275+
    :
1250+               *
    :
1225+
    :       *
1200+
    :
1175+
    :
1150+
    *
1125+-------+-------+-------+-------+-------+-------+-------+-------+-------+
   .01     .02     .03     .04     .05     .06     .07     .08     .09     .1
```

Figure 10-26.
Plot of pressure vs. temperature

11

Advanced Model Design

In this chapter we will first look at model-design techniques that can help circumvent the use of the Iterative Solver. Following this we will see how "conditional" rules can be implemented in TK!Solver. In the last section we will explore some more tricks that can be incorporated into models in order to make TK!Solver more friendly, powerful, and versatile.

CIRCUMVENTING THE ITERATIVE SOLVER

The flexibility with which we can set up different problems (that is, assign input values to different combinations of variables) is one of the key features of TK!Solver. Depending on the nature and design of the model, some of these combinations may be handled by the Direct Solver, and some may require the slower Iterative Solver. The model should be set up so that many practical or frequently encountered problems can be solved using the Direct Solver.

In this section we look at several model-design techniques serving this purpose (some of them were already touched on in Chapter 7, but they are mentioned again here for the sake of completeness). However, let's first look at the total number of ways in which problems may be formulated so that we may determine the resolvability of each of them by the Direct Solver.

Number of Input Combinations

We have already seen that if *NIE* is the number of independent equations in a model, *TNV* is the total number of variables, and *NIV* is the number of input variables, then

$$NIV = TNV - NIE$$

Input variables are required to use the *NIE* equations for evaluating the same number (*NIE*=*TNV*−*NIV*) of unknowns. The number of input combinations (*NIC*) is equal to the number of combinations of *NIV* variables out of *TNV*, that is,

$$NIC = \binom{TNV}{NIV} = \frac{TNV!}{NIV!\,(TNV-NIV)!}$$

Some of the combinations of input variables may not lead to a solution because they may overdetermine one part of the model, leaving the other parts underdetermined. This happens when a combination contains all the variables present in a particular equation, or, in other words, when some of the input variables are not independent because they are constrained by that equation. This situation reduces the true number of combinations.

Let's consider the following set of equations in a model:

$$\begin{aligned} p + q &= u + r*v \\ s &= r/q \\ t &= p \end{aligned}$$

Here *TNV*=7 and *NIE*=3, and so *NIV*=*TNV*−*NIE*=4. The number of combinations of input variables *NIC*=7!/(3!*4!)=35. However, there are 4 input combinations involving *q*,*r*,*s* and 9 with *p*,*q*, which make a total of 13, overdetermining one of the rules. So the number of valid combinations of input variables is 35−13=22.

Simplification

The expressions in a rule must be simplified to make every variable appear only once whenever possible. The equation

$$y/x = a*x$$

cannot be solved for x by the Direct Solver since x appears twice in the equation. It can be solved for x if it is written as

$$y = a*x^2$$

Factorization

The expressions must be factorized whenever possible so that every variable appears only once in the equation. The equation

$$y = x*y - a$$

cannot be solved for y by the Direct Solver, while it can be if it is factored and written as

$$a = y*(x-1)$$

Modifying the Rules—Reducing VEC Matrix Density

Using basic algebraic simplification techniques, we can modify the equations so that the Direct Solver can solve for a larger number of input combinations than would otherwise be possible. These modifications are equivalent to reducing the density of the VEC matrix; the sparser the matrix, the higher the likelihood that after reduction for any particular set of input variables, the matrix can be triangularized. In Chapter 7, we looked at the example of the Markup and Margin model. Now we will look at one more example to emphasize this point.

Let's consider the following equations:

$$x1 + x2 = y1 + y2 \tag{11-1}$$

$$cxy = (x1 - x2 + y1 - y2)/2 \tag{11-2}$$

The VEC matrix and R-graph for the set of equations are given in Figure 11-1*a*.

Since $NIE{=}2$ and $TNV{=}5$, given the values of three variables ($NIV{=}3$), it should be possible to solve for the other two variables. The number of input combinations NIC for which the model can be solved is 10. Let's assume we know the values of $x1$, $x2$, and $y2$. From the VEC matrix we can see that $y1$ can be evaluated from the first equation and cxy from the second. Thus the model can be completely resolved by the Direct Solver. However, for the input combination cxy, $x1$, $y2$, the set of equations remains unresolved. In fact, unless three of the four variables $x1$, $x2$, $y1$, and $y2$ are known, the Direct Solver cannot solve the set of equations.

The equations can be modified as follows so that the Direct Solver can resolve the model for a larger number of input combinations. Substituting for $x1$ from equation 11-1 into equation 11-2 we get

$$cxy = y1 - x2 \tag{11-3}$$

	1	2
$x1$	x	x
$x2$	x	x
$y1$	x	x
$y2$	x	x
cxy		x

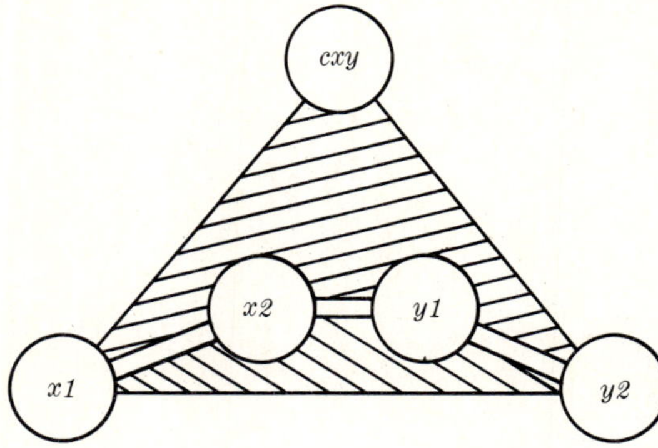

a. Before modification
$x1+x2=y1+y2$
$cxy=(x1-x2+y1-y2)/2$

	1	2
$x1$	x	
$x2$		x
$y1$		x
$y2$	x	
cxy	x	x

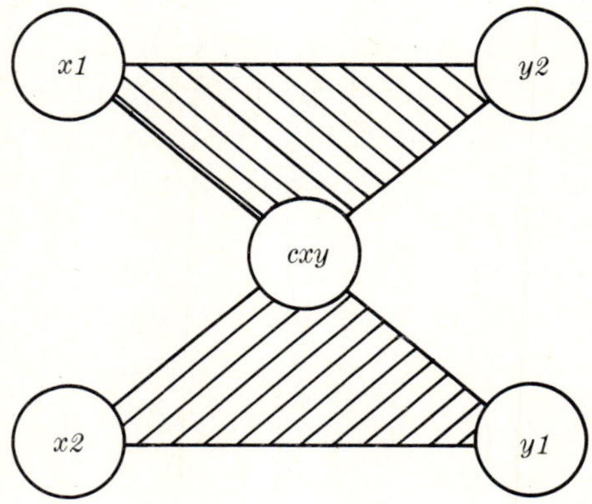

b. After modification
$cxy=y1-x2$
$cxy=x1-y2$

Figure 11-1.
VEC-matrix and R-graph for the set of equations

Since $x1-y2=y1-x2$ from equation 11-1, we have

$$cxy = x1 - y2 \tag{11-4}$$

Equations 11-1 and 11-2 have thus been reduced by simple algebraic manipulations to equations 11-3 and 11-4. The VEC matrix and R-graph for this set of equations are given in Figure 11-1*b*. We can see that there is a reduction in the density of the VEC matrix and that it is now possible to solve for any of the input combinations using the Direct Solver.

Redundant Equations

There are models in which the techniques outlined here are not applicable. In such cases, we may be able to avoid iterative solving by adding extra equations (also called "redundant equations") to the model. Let's see how this technique works on a simple model.

The ELECMOD Model

Let's consider the first two rules from the ELECMOD model introduced in Chapter 2. They are

$$I = V/R$$
$$P = V\,I$$

The VEC matrix and R-graph for the two equations are shown in Figure 11-2*a*. $NIE=2$, $TNV=4$, and the variables appear only once in each equation. Therefore, given two of the four variables, the Direct Solver should

	1	2
I	x	x
V	x	x
R	x	
P		x

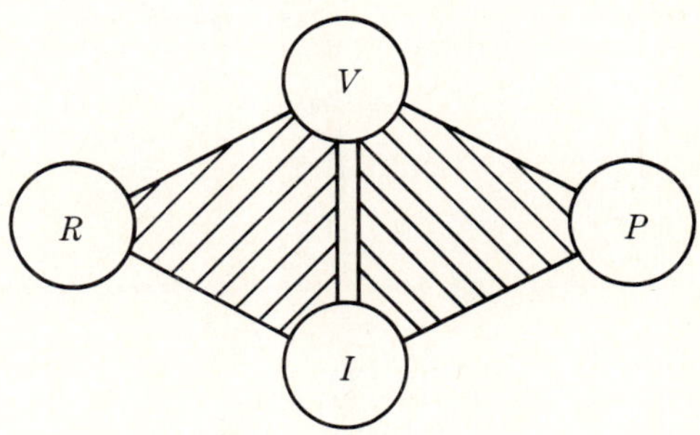

a. VEC matrix and R-graph for the model

```
==================== VARIABLE SHEET ==================...
St Input       Name     Output      Unit       Comment
-- -----       ----     ------      ----       -------
   4           I                    amp        current
   110         V                    volt       voltage
               R        27.5        ohm        resistance
               P        440         W          power

=================== RULE SHEET ======================...
S Rule
- ----
  I = V/R            "    Ohm's Law
  P = V * I          "    Electrical Power
```

b. Rule and Variable Sheets with solution

Figure 11-2.
The ELECMOD model

be able to solve for the other two unless the two unknowns appear simultaneously in both the equations. *NIC* (the number of input combinations)=10. Figure 11-2*b* shows the solution obtained by the Direct Solver for input values $V=110$ and $I=4$.

When $P=440$ and $R=27.5$ are assigned as input, the equations remain unsolved. This implies a set of simultaneous equations as indicated by the loop in the VEC matrix and the ring in the R-graph in Figure 11-2*a*. The variables V and I are unknown and appear simultaneously in both the equations.

An extra equation can be derived if we eliminate one of the two variables V and I from the two equations. Substituting for V from the first rule in the second, we have

$$P = I^2 R$$

When this equation is added to the Rule Sheet and the model is solved, both I and V are evaluated, as shown in Figure 11-3*a*. The derived equation is called a redundant equation because it does not represent any

```
==================== VARIABLE SHEET ===================...
St Input      Name     Output     Unit        Comment
-- -----      ----     ------     ----        -------
              I        4          amp         current
              V        110        volt        voltage
   27.5       R                   ohm         resistance
   440        P                   W           power

==================== RULE SHEET ======================...
S Rule
- ----
  I = V/R               "    Ohm's Law
  P = V * I             "    Electrical Power
  P = I^2 * R           "    Redundant equation
```

a. Rule and Variable Sheets

	1	2	3
I	x	x	x
V	x	x	
R	x		x
P		x	x

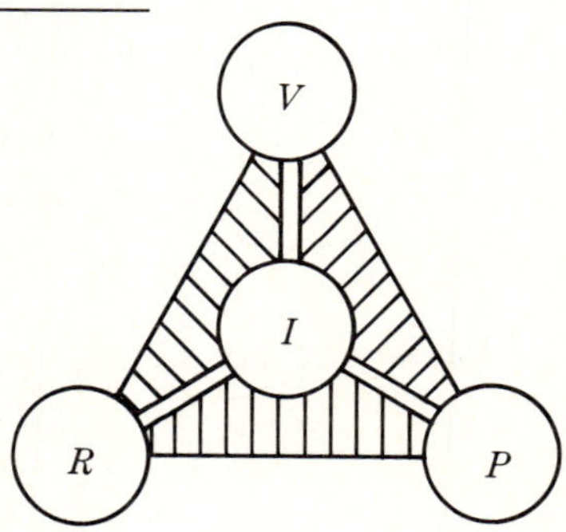

b. The new VEC matrix and R-graph

Figure 11-3.
The ELECMOD model with redundant equation

information in addition to what is known from the original set of independent equations. The VEC matrix and R-graph with the redundant equation are shown in Figure 11-3*b*.

We saw previously that rings in the R-graphs and loops joining the crosses in the VEC matrices indicate simultaneous equations that cannot be accessed and unraveled by the Direct Solver. This is true only for sets of independent equations. It is not valid for Figure 11-3*b* because now only two out of the three equations are independent.

An analysis of the new VEC matrix shows that I is evaluated from the third equation and V from the first. When the Direct Solver looks at the second equation again, there is nothing more to evaluate. So the equation is just checked for consistency; problems of inconsistencies may occur when redundant equations are present in the model (see Chapter 8). In the present example, no inconsistency is detected in this equation, so it is also marked as solved. At this point, since all the equations have been solved or checked, the Direct Solver stops.

Deriving Redundant Equations

When there are n unknown variables appearing simultaneously in n equations, then $n-1$ of these variables have to be eliminated from these n equations. What is left is one equation containing the remaining unknown variable and m other variables that are supposed to be known. The equation must be resolvable with respect to the unknown variable—otherwise, having it in the model would serve no purpose.

It is not always possible to derive a redundant equation. For instance, it is not possible to eliminate x or y from equations like

$$exp(x+y) + x*y = a$$
$$sin(x*y) + x+y = b$$

If a certain combination of input variables is impractical or infrequent, then including a redundant equation to obviate the use of the Iterative Solver may not be worth the effort and the increased solution time.

Balance of Equations and Variables

We modify the formula given in Chapter 7, "General Considerations," to take into account the redundant equations added to a model. The modified formula is as follows:

$$NIE = TNE - NRE = TNV - NIV$$

where

NIE = number of independent equations
TNE = total number of equations
NRE = number of redundant equations
TNV = number of variables
NIV = number of input variables required to solve the model.

In the modified ELECMOD model, $NIE=2$, $TNE=3$, $NRE=1$, $TNV=4$, $NIV=2$; so

$$2 = 3 - 1 = 4 - 2$$

and everything is okay. The integrity of problem-formulation is preserved even after the addition of the redundant equation. Note that the addition of a redundant equation does not reduce the number of input variables required to solve the problem. It only facilitates the solution of the problem with the Direct Solver.

Extraneous Redundant Equations

Sometimes when the Direct Solver cannot solve a problem, we may be tempted to doubt the backsolving power of TK!Solver and add an equation that happens to be merely a rearranged form of an existing one. For example, adding the equation

$$V = I/P$$

which is a "rearranged" form of the second equation, would not help to solve the model for unknowns I and V.

Projectile Model

The projectile model in Figure 11-4*a* and *b* deals with the motion of a projectile (ignoring air resistance). Figure 11-4*a* shows the Rule Sheet containing the equations. Here $TNV=6$, $NIE=3$, $NIV=3$, and $NIC=20$. However, the true number of combinations is 19 because the model cannot be solved when *maxht, time,* and *g* are given. The Calculation Units are as follows: ft/sec for *vel,* rad for *alpha,* sec for *time,* and ft for *maxht* and *range.* The Unit Sheet with the defined conversions is shown in Figure 11-4*b*.

The figure also shows the solution of the following problem: a baseball is thrown with an initial velocity of 100 m/s at an angle of 30 degrees. How far does it travel and how much time does it take? Also calculate the maximum height, given g=32ft/s^2.

```
==================== VARIABLE SHEET ================================...
St Input      Name      Output      Unit       Comment
-- -----      ----      ------      ----       -------
   100        vel                   m/sec  .   initial velocity
   30         alpha                 deg        angle of departure
              range     887.90334  m          horizontal distance
              maxht     128.15781  m          maximum height reached
              time      10.252625  sec        time taken
   32         g                     ft/sec^2   accln. due to gravity

==================== RULE SHEET ====================================...
S Rule
- ----
  maxht = vel^2 * sin(alpha)^2 / (2*g)
  range = vel^2 * sin(2*alpha) / g
  time = sqrt(8*maxht/g)
```

a. Variable and Rule Sheets

```
==================== UNIT SHEET ==============...
From        To          Multiply By   Add Offset
----        --          -----------   ----------
rad         deg         57.29577951
ft          m           .3048
min         sec         60
hour        min         60
ft/sec      m/sec       .3048
ft/sec^2    m/sec^2     .3048
```

b. Unit Sheet

Figure 11-4.
The projectile model

Now let's consider the following modification of the problem: what should be the angle and the velocity with which the ball should be thrown so that it travels 900 meters in 10 seconds? The Direct Solver fails to solve the model with these values as input. The reason is that the first two rules represent a set of two simultaneous equations in the two unknowns *vel* and *alpha*. The loop in the VEC matrix and the ring in the R-graph in Figure 11-5*a* also confirm this. A redundant equation can be derived by eliminating either *vel* or *alpha* from the first two equations.

Substituting for *vel* from the first equation in the second we have

$$range = \frac{maxht * (2*g)}{sin(alpha)\text{^}2} * \frac{sin(2*alpha)}{g}$$

Since $sin(2*alpha) = 2*sin(alpha)*cos(alpha)$, after substitution and simplification we get

$$tan(alpha) = 4 * maxht/range$$

	1	2	3
g	x	x	x
vel	x	x	
alpha	x	x	
range	x		
maxht		x	x
time			x

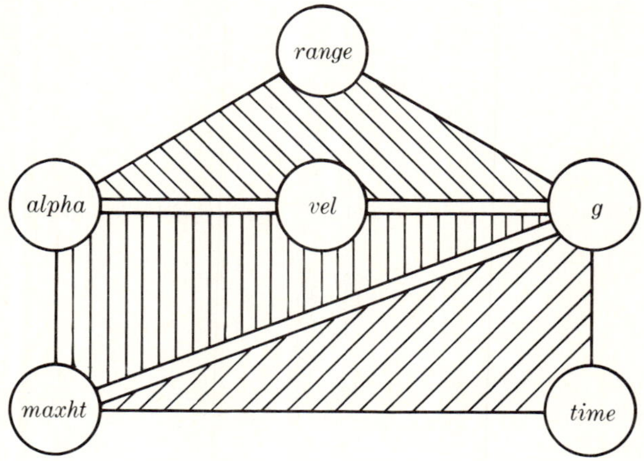

a. For Figure 11-4 rules

	1	2	3	4
g	x	x	x	
vel	x	x		
alpha	x	x		x
range	x			x
maxht		x	x	x
time			x	

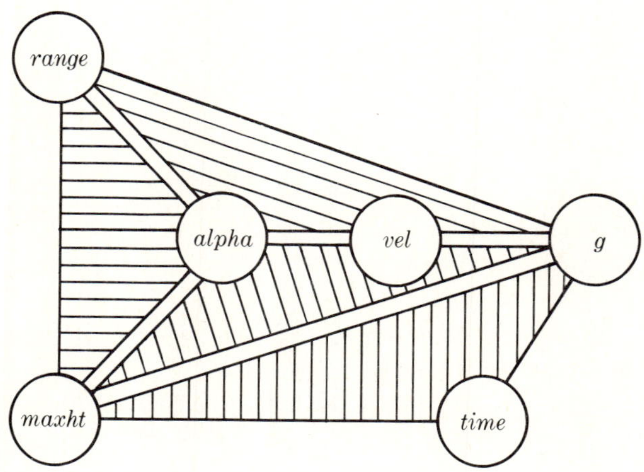

b. For Figure 11-6 rules (includes the redundant equation)

Figure 11-5.
The VEC matrix and R-graph for the projectile model

This is the redundant equation that is resolvable for *alpha* and in which *vel* does not appear. When this equation is entered in the Rule Sheet and the Action key is pressed again, the model is solved. The new VEC matrix and R-graph are shown in Figure 11-5*b*. The solution shown in Figure 11-6 is obtained.

```
==================== VARIABLE SHEET ==============================...
St Input        Name      Output         Unit        Comment
-- -----        ----      ------         ----        -------
                vel       102.36365      m/sec       initial velocity
                alpha     28.451788      deg         angle of departure
   900          range                    m           horizontal distance
                maxht     121.92         m           maximum height reached
   10           time                     sec         time taken
   32           g                        ft/sec^2    accln. due to gravity

==================== RULE SHEET ==================================...
S Rule
- ----
  maxht = vel^2 * sin(alpha)^2 / (2*g)
  range = vel^2 * sin(2*alpha) / g
  time = sqrt(8*maxht/g)
  tan(alpha) = 4 * maxht / range        " redundant equation
```

Figure 11-6.
Variable and Rule Sheets for the projectile model (*vel* and *alpha* evaluated and redundant equation used)

A "Classical" Example*

Consider the following set of equations introduced in Figure 8-4:

$$10*e = b*c*d \tag{11-5}$$

$$f = b/a \tag{11-6}$$

$$a\,\hat{}\,2 = 4E-5/pi()*c*g \tag{11-7}$$

$$d = u*v \tag{11-8}$$

$$w = u/v \tag{11-9}$$

*This example was taken from a set of "classical" models that years ago served to exercise the backsolving technique adopted in TK!Solver. This model deals with the relationships between the characteristics of knitted fabrics. The real meaning of the variables is as follows:

- a = yarn diameter in cm
- b = stitch length in cm
- c = yarn linear density in tex (g/km)
- d = areal stitch density in 1/cm ^ 2
- e = fabric areal density in g/m ^ 2
- f = stitch length/yarn diameter ratio
- g = yarn specific volume in cm ^ 3/g
- u = course (row) density in 1/cm
- v = wale (column) density in 1/cm
- w = wales/courses density ratio.

Another knitting connection: compare the R-graphs in Figures 8-4 and 11-7. In order to accommodate the redundant equations nicely, we must turn the graph from Figure 8-4 inside out (or more precisely, outside in)—like a sock!

The VEC matrix and R-graph are also shown in Figure 8-4. As we mentioned then, the model cannot be solved completely by the Direct Solver when neither a, b, nor c is known and when neither u nor v is known. The two sets of variables and the equations participating in the simultaneity are indicated by two loops in the VEC matrix and the two rings in the R-graph.

We can derive the first redundant equation from the first three equations by eliminating from them b and c. From equation 11-5 we have

$$c = 10 * e \,/\, (b*d)$$

and from equation 11-6, we have

$$b = a * f$$

Substituting for c and b in equation 11-7, we get

$$d * f * a\hat{\ }3 = 4\text{E}{-}4 \,/\, pi() * g * e$$

Similarly, we can derive the second redundant equation from the last two equations by eliminating v from them. Substituting for v from equation 11-9 into equation 11-8, we get

$$d * w = u\hat{\ }2$$

With these two redundant equations added to the model, it can be solved completely by the Direct Solver even for the previously unresolvable combinations. The new R-graph is shown in Figure 11-7.

CONDITIONAL RULES

During problem-solving it very often becomes necessary to use a particular equation only under certain conditions and bypass it at other times. In other words, a "conditional" rule of the form

IF <condition is true> THEN <the rule applies>

is required to use rules selectively. For example, the area of a circle is *pi()/4*diameter^2*, while that of a rectangle is *length*width*. The rule we select depends on the geometric figure being dealt with in the model. Therefore, we would need conditional rules such as

IF figure = *'circle* THEN *area* = *pi()*diameter^2/4*

IF figure = *'rectangle* THEN *area* = *length*width*

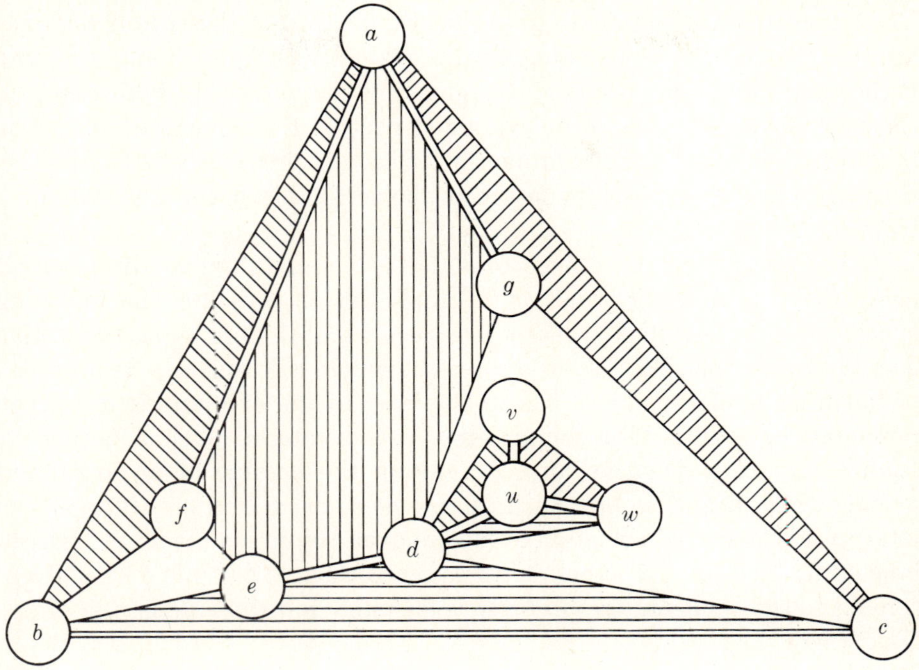

Figure 11-7.
The new R-graph for the model in Figure 8-4 with the addition of the two redundant equations

There is no provision in TK!Solver to formulate conditional rules in this straightforward way. However, we can take advantage of the way TK!Solver treats division of zero by zero and implement such conditional rules.

The 0/0 Bypass

The whole TK!Solver system works on the principle of "always doing everything possible when the ingredients are available," which means always performing all the operations when the operands and function arguments are ready. There is one subtle exception forced on TK!Solver by the laws of mathematics: operations that would lead to indeterminate results are not performed. This is the reason behind bypassing 0/0, 0^0, or *atan2*(0,0), as we discussed in Chapter 5.

There are only two ways in which the rules in the models are used by TK!Solver: (1) to evaluate an unknown variable from the rest of the rule, and (2) to check the rule integrity by evaluating the left-hand side and right-hand side expressions and comparing the values. In both cases all the subexpressions have to be evaluated first. If the solvers encounter on their way one of the indeterminacies mentioned previously, the operation is skipped and the rule is bypassed in the sense that nothing is evaluated from it.

Consequently, what we need to do is to formulate the condition of not using the rule in a way that would imply, let us say, 0/0. The following examples show how to do it. First let's recall that the 0/0 bypass condition does not mean that TK!Solver ignores the whole rule entirely. It may still perform some of the operations in the body of the rule and it may even terminate the solution if a domain error is encountered (such as taking the square root of a negative number, taking the arcsine of an argument greater than 1, and so on). An example of such an occurrence is shown later in this chapter in relation to the quadratic equation model in "Miscellaneous Tricks." It is also possible that, even though the rule does not contribute to the solution, its integrity is checked and the rule is marked as "Satisfied".

Formulating Conditional Rules

Let's consider the following two equations, which are applicable under two different conditions:

$$\text{when } a \neq b, \text{ then } a+b=c*d$$

$$\text{when } a = b, \text{ then } a*(1+b)=c*d$$

Let's suppose the first equation is expressed as

$$\underset{\substack{\uparrow \\ \text{(Conditional part)}}}{0/(a-b)} \quad + \quad \underset{\substack{\uparrow \\ \text{(Original rule)}}}{a+b = c*d}$$

When a is not equal to b, $(a-b)$ is not equal to zero, and the equation becomes

$$0 + a+b = c*d$$

which is the same as $a+b=c*d$, and so this equation is used by the solvers.

On the other hand, when a is equal to b, $(a-b)$ is zero and the equation becomes

$$0/0 + a+b = c*d$$

Because of the 0/0 in the first term, the rule is bypassed by the Solvers.

Formulating the Conditional Part

The $0/(a-b)$ in the rule can be regarded as the "conditional" part that determines the applicability of the equation. When the denominator of the conditional part is zero, the rule is bypassed and when the denominator is non-zero, it is used by the solvers.

The basic principle can be stated as follows: *Express the condition to be tested in the denominator of the conditional part so that the denominator yields a zero when the rule is to be bypassed and a non-zero number when the rule is applicable.*

For the second rule, the expression

$$1-sgn(abs(a-b))$$

can be used in the denominator of the conditional part for making it applicable when a is equal to b. The rule can be written as

$$\underset{\text{(Conditional part)}}{\underset{\uparrow}{0/(1-sgn(abs(a-b)))}} + \underset{\text{(Original rule)}}{\underset{\uparrow}{a*(1+b) = c*d}}$$

When $a=b$, $(a-b)$ is zero, and $sgn(abs(0))=0$, so the denominator of the conditional part is equal to $(1-0)=1$. Thus the equation becomes

$$0 + a*(1+b) = c * d$$

and it is used by the solvers. However, when a is not equal to b, then $sgn(abs(a-b))=1$; the denominator becomes $(1-1)=0$, and the equation is bypassed because of the 0/0. (See Table 5-3 for an explanation of the *sgn* function.)

Thus the 0/0 bypass enables TK!Solver to select the appropriate rule depending on the conditions. The rules entered in the Rule Sheet in Figure 11-8*a* show that the actual equations stand out from the conditional part so that the user doesn't lose track of the original equation. Figure 11-8*b* and *c* shows the Variable Sheets with the solutions for the two different conditions.

```
==================== RULE SHEET ================================...
S Rule
- ----
  0/(a-b)                 +   a+b = c*d         " use when a < > b
  0/(1-sgn(abs(a-b)))  +   a*(1+b) = c*d     " use when a = b
```

a. Rule Sheet (note that the conditional part is distinct from the original equation)

```
==================== VARIABLE SHEET ==========================...
St Input        Name     Output      Unit         Comment
-- -----        ----     ------      ----         -------
   5             a
   8             b
                 c        3.25
   4             d
```

b. Variable Sheet with solution when $a \neq b$

```
==================== VARIABLE SHEET ==========================...
St Input        Name     Output      Unit         Comment
-- -----        ----     ------      ----         -------
   5             a
   5             b
                 c        7.5
   4             d
```

c. Variable Sheet with solution when $a=b$

Figure 11-8.
Example of conditional rules using 0/0 bypass

Expressing Different Conditions

Since TK!Solver rules have only the equal sign to link the left- and right-hand side expressions, relational operators (such as greater than, less than, greater than or equal to, and less than or equal to) may be built into conditional rules as shown in Table 11-1. The first line in each box states the desired result and the second line shows the TK!Solver representation.

Using a User-Defined Function

A user-defined function that would return 0 or 1 depending on the argument can be used in the denominator of the conditional part of the rules. Let's consider the example of the cross-sectional areas of geometric figures

Table 11-1.
Expressing Conditional Rules Using the 0/0 Bypass.

IF expr1 = expr2	THEN	expr3 = expr4
0/(1−sign(abs(expr1−expr2)))	+	expr3 = expr4
IF expr1 <> expr2	THEN	expr3 = expr4
0/(expr1−expr2)	+	expr3 = expr4
IF expr1 > expr2	THEN	expr3 = expr4
0/(1−step(expr2,expr1))	+	expr3 = expr4
IF expr1 < expr2	THEN	expr3 = expr4
0/(1−step(expr1,expr2))	+	expr3 = expr4
IF expr1 ≥ expr2	THEN	expr3 = expr4
0/(step(expr1,expr2)	+	expr3 = expr4
IF expr1 ≤ expr2	THEN	expr3 = expr4
0/(step(expr2,expr1)	+	expr3 = expr4

discussed at the beginning of this section. The User Function Subsheet for the function *choice* is shown in Figure 11-9, while the Rule Sheet with the conditional formulations is shown in Figure 11-10*a*.

When *type* is assigned *'circular* in the Variable Sheet (see Figure 11-10*b*) and the model is solved, the function *choice* returns 1 for *select*. Consequently, the rule for the circular figure is selected (because the denominator is 1), while that for the rectangular figure is bypassed. Similarly, when *type* is assigned *'rectangular* (see Figure 11-10*c*), *select*=0 and so the rule for the rectangular figure is selected, while the one for the circular figure is bypassed.

```
==================== USER FUNCTION: choice =========...
Comment:                          type of cross section
Domain List:                      section
Mapping:                          Table
Range List:                       value
Element Domain         Range
------- ------         -----
1       'circular      1
2       'rectangula    0
```

Figure 11-9.
User Function Subsheet for function *choice*

```
==================== RULE SHEET =====================================...
S Rule
- ----
  select = choice(type)                            " rule selector
  0/select      +   area = pi()/4*dia^2            " circular cr. sect
  0/(1-select) +   area = length*width             " rectangular cr. sect
```

a. Rule Sheet

```
==================== VARIABLE SHEET ================================...
St Input      Name     Output     Unit       Comment
-- -----      ----     ------     ----       -------
   'circular  type                           cross section
   3          dia                 cm         diameter
   4          length              cm         length
   5          width               cm         width
              area     7.0685835  cm^2       cross sectional area
              select   1                     rule selection indicator
```

b. Variable Sheet with solution for circular cross section

```
==================== VARIABLE SHEET ================================...
St Input      Name     Output     Unit       Comment
-- -----      ----     ------     ----       -------
   'rectangu  type                           cross section
   3          dia                 cm         diameter
   4          length              cm         length
   5          width               cm         width
              area     20         cm^2       cross sectional area
              select   0                     rule selection indicator
```

c. Variable Sheet with solution for rectangular cross section

Figure 11-10.
Conditional rules with user-defined function

Given and Element Functions

The *given* function and the *element* function with three arguments have built-in conditional capabilities. In other words, if the variables whose status is being examined have input values, then the *given* function returns the first of the last two arguments; otherwise it returns the last. Similarly, if the element specified in the second argument of the *element* function does not exist in the list, the value specified in the third argument is returned.

This feature of the *given* function was used in the chemical analysis model discussed in Chapter 6. The rule

$$am3 = given('e3,fun(e3),0)$$

works as follows:

IF *e3* has an input value THEN *am3=fun(e3)*
ELSE *am3=0*

Thus a Table Lookup is performed when necessary; otherwise a zero is assigned to *am3*.

Bypassing Rules Using the Given Function

The *given* function can be used to return a "0" or "1" depending on the status of one or more variables. Let's suppose the rule

$$p\hat{}q = r$$

in a model is to be used only when another variable *s* is assigned an input value. We can accomplish this task by using the *given* function in the denominator of the conditional part. The expression (*given's*,1,0) will return 1 when *s* has an input value and 0 otherwise. Thus the formulation

$$0/given('s,1,0) + p\hat{}q = r$$

will activate the rule when *s* has an input value and will bypass it when *s* does not have an input value.

Alternative Ways of Selecting Equations

There are three other ways in which the 0/0 bypass can be used to select equations. The first formulation is as follows:

(*<expression1>* − *<expression2>*) ∗ *<expression3>* = 0

When *<expression3>* is not equal to zero, the rule is used; otherwise it is bypassed. Note that this formulation is a variation of the construct used earlier, but it slightly obscures the original equation.

In the second formulation the expression on either side of the equal sign is multiplied by *<expression3>*:

<expression3> ∗ *<expression1>* = *<expression2>* ∗ *<expression3>*

Here again, if *<expression3>* is equal to zero, the rule is bypassed; otherwise, it is used. In this formulation *<expression3>* occurs twice in a rule, which goes against the spirit of TK!Solver; note also that the solution time is increased, albeit slightly, because of the extra computation.

Switching an equation off and on depending on the status of the variable *xyz* (assigned an input value or not) can also be accomplished directly by one of the following constructs:

$$given('xyz,0/0,1) * <expression1> = <expression2>$$

$$given('xyz,0/0,0) + <expression1> = <expression2>$$

Using the Step Function for Multiple Conditionals

There are problems in science and engineering design in which a particular equation is applicable over a certain range of values and a different one over another range and so on. For example, in the design of columns, the applicable formula for allowable compressive stress depends on the slenderness ratio—the ratio of the height of the column to the diameter. Similarly in the analysis of fluid flow, the equation used for determining the friction factor depends on the Reynolds number.

For example, let's suppose a model contains the equations

$$k = g * h$$

$$t = f * s$$

and the expression for f depends on the value of k, as follows:

When	Then
$k \leq pi()/12$	$f = 3*k/pi()$
$pi()/12 < k \leq pi()/4$	$f = sin(2*k)$
$pi()/4 < k \leq pi()/2$	$f = tan(k)$

Designing the Model

First the value of k has to be checked and then the appropriate expression selected for f. The equation for f can be expressed as

$$f = f1 * A + f2 * B + f3 * C$$

where

$$f1 = 3*k/pi()$$
$$f2 = sin(2*k)$$
$$f3 = tan(k).$$

A,B, and C are expression selectors (at any time only one of them should be 1 and the other two should be 0's).

The *step* function can be used because it compares its two arguments and returns 1 if the first argument is greater than or equal to the second;

otherwise it returns 0. This leads to

$$A = step(pi()/12,k)$$

which will return 1 when k is less than or equal to $pi()/12$ and 0 otherwise. Since trigonometric functions in TK!Solver assume the arguments to be in radians, the Calculation Unit for k is assigned as radians. The rule

$$B = step(pi()/4,k)$$

will return 1 when k is less than or equal to $pi()/4$ and 0 otherwise. But this will not serve the purpose because even when k is less than $pi()/12$, this rule will return 1 for B. Consequently, the values of both $f1$ and $f2$ will be used to evaluate f, which is incorrect. Instead, if we write

$$B = step(pi()/4,k) - A$$

B will be equal to 1 only when k is greater than $pi()/12$ and less than $pi()/4$; B will be equal to 0 when k is less than $pi()/12$ and greater than $pi()/4$. This is what we want.

For C, the equation

$$C = step(pi()/2,k)$$

will not do the job for the same reason that the original equation for B did not. Therefore, C should be set to 0 when either A or B is 1 and should be set to 1 otherwise. We can do this by rewriting the equation for C as

$$C = step(pi()/2,k) - (A+B)$$

With these three equations for A, B, and C, it is possible to select the right expression for calculating f. Figure 11-11*a*, *b*, *c*, and *d* shows the Rule Sheet and Variable Sheet with f evaluated under three different conditions.

Generalizing the Multiple Conditionals

The basic principle used in deriving the three expressions for A, B, and C can be generalized to cover more cases. All we need do is check the condition using the *step* function and subtract from the result the values from the previous checks. Thus if $L1$, $L2$, $L3$,...,Ln are the n limits for the variable x, then the following expressions can be used:

$$\begin{aligned}
A &= step(L1,x) \\
B &= step(L2,x) - A \\
C &= step(L3,x) - (A+B) \\
D &= step(L4,x) - (A+B+C) \\
&\vdots \\
N &= step(Ln,x) - (A+B+C+D+E+...+M)
\end{aligned}$$

to return 1 when appropriate and 0 otherwise.

```
==================== RULE SHEET ==========================================...
S Rule
- ----
  k = g * h
  t = f * s

  f1 = 3*k/pi()               " applicable when k <= pi()/12
  f2 = sin(2*k)               " applicable when pi()/12 < k <= pi()/4
  f3 = tan(k)                 " applicable when pi()/4  < k <= pi()/2

  f = f1*A + f2*B + f3*C

  A = step(pi()/12,k)         " A=1 when k <= pi()/12, else 0
  B = step(pi()/4,k)-A        " B=1 when pi()/12 < k <= pi()/4, else 0
  C = step(pi()/2,k)-(A+B)    " C=1 when pi()/4  < k <= pi()/2, else 0
```

a. Rule Sheet

```
==================== VARIABLE SHEET =====================================...
St Input     Name     Output     Unit       Comment
-- -----     ----     ------     ----       -------
             f        .19098593
   .4        g
   .5        h
             k        11.459156 deg
   1.25      s
             t        .23873241

             A        1
             B        0
             C        0

             f1       .19098593
             f2       .38941834
             f3       .20271004
```

b. Variable Sheet with $A=1$

```
==================== VARIABLE SHEET =====================================...
St Input     Name     Output     Unit       Comment
-- -----     ----     ------     ----       -------
             f        .96355819
   1.3       g
   .5        h
             k        37.242257 deg
   1.25      s
             t        1.2044477

             A        0
             B        1
             C        0

             f1       .62070428
             f2       .96355819
             f3       .76020440
```

c. Variable Sheet with $B=1$

Figure 11-11.
Multiple conditional rules (Calculation Unit for k is radians and a conversion is defined in Unit Sheet)

```
==================== VARIABLE SHEET ===================================...
St Input      Name      Output     Unit       Comment
-- -----      ----      ------     ----       -------
              f         32.461139
   2.2        g
   .7         h
              k         88.235500  deg
   1.25       s
              t         40.576424

              A         0
              B         0
              C         1

              f1        1.4705917
              f2        .06155372
              f3        32.461139
```

d. Variable Sheet with C=1

Figure 11-11.
Continued

MISCELLANEOUS TRICKS

In this section we will take a look at additional tricks in model design that can be directly "imported" into other models.

Index of a Value in a List

Sometimes we are interested in knowing not only the minimum or maximum value in a list, but also the position in which it occurs; that is, we want to know the element number so that this value can be used in further calculations or decision-making. An example of such a situation is given in the case study on capital budgeting in Chapter 15. We will now see how we can find the element number using the *element* function and the 0/0 bypass. Consider the List Subsheet for *profit* shown in Figure 11-12. We are asked to find the highest profit and also the instance in which it occurs.

The *max* function can be used to find the maximum value in the list *profit*, as is shown in the first rule in the Rule Sheet in Figure 11-13. Then this value has to be compared with each of the values in the list, and if the two values are equal, the corresponding instance number has to be returned; otherwise nothing should be done. This sequence suggests that the function *element*( ) has to be used to keep track of the instance number during the scanning of the list, leading to the second rule in the figure.

```
==================== LIST: profit ============...
Comment:                     list of profits
Display Unit:                $
Storage Unit:                $
Element Value
------- -----
1       9000
2       14000
3       21500
4       19000
5       17500
6       14000
```

Figure 11-12.
List Subsheet for *profit*

We have to check if the maximum value *maxval* is equal to the value in the list. We know from Table 11-1 that the expression

$$1 - (sgn(abs(maxval - element('profit,number))))$$

can be used in the denominator of the conditional part. When the expression returns 1, that is, the maximum value is equal to the particular element in the list, the instance number must be returned; this is done by the third rule in the Rule Sheet.

We invoke List Solving by typing /**L**!, and *index* is evaluated as 3. We can use this value to return a message employing a user-defined function to indicate that the third alternative yields the highest profit and should be chosen. The Variable Sheet in Figure 11-13 shows the value for *index*.

```
==================== VARIABLE SHEET ==============================...
St Input      Name      Output     Unit        Comment
-- -----      ----      ------     ----        -------
L  0          profit                           list of profits
              maxval    21500      $           maximum value
              number    6                      instance number
              index     3                      pos of largest element

==================== RULE SHEET ==================================...
S Rule
- ----
* maxval = max('profit)
* number = element()
* 0/(1-sgn(abs(maxval-element('profit,number)))) + index=number
```

Figure 11-13.
Finding the index of the largest element in the list *profit* (Variable Sheet with the position of the largest element in Figure 11-12 and Rule Sheet with the conditional rule)

The same formulation can be used to find the index of the smallest element in a list. However, the *min* function should be used instead of the *max* function in the first rule to pick out the smallest element in the list.

Quadratic Equation Model

TK!Solver deals only with real numbers. However, quadratic equations of the form

$$ax^2 + bx + c = 0$$

may have either real or complex roots. The Iterative Solver, as we discussed in Chapter 9, can only find the real roots one at a time. Suppose we want a generalized quadratic equation solver which, depending on the value of the discriminant

$$d = \sqrt{b^2 - 4ac}$$

would return either both the real roots if $d \geq 0$ or the real and imaginary parts of the complex root if $d < 0$.

The value of the discriminant d has to be used to channel the solution process through the appropriate set of formulas built into the framework of conditional rules with the 0/0 bypass. The conditional part has to distinguish between d less than zero and d greater than or equal to zero. The zero-one valued *step* function used as k=*step*(d,0) is the obvious choice; then k and $(k-1)$ can be used as the denominators in the conditional part.

The formulas for the real roots are

$$x1 = (-b + sqrt(b\,\hat{}\,2 - 4*a*c)) \;/\; (2*a)$$

$$x2 = (-b - sqrt(b\,\hat{}\,2 - 4*a*c)) \;/\; (2*a)$$

Since these should be evaluated only when $k=1$, it suggests the conditional rules

$$0/k + x1 = (-b + sqrt(d)) \;/\; (2*a)$$

$$0/k + x2 = (-b - sqrt(d)) \;/\; (2*a)$$

(Note that here we use d instead of repeating the subexpression for the discriminant; recall Chapter 7.) However, there is a problem with these conditional rules. When k is 0, that is, d is negative, we would expect the rules to be ignored because of the implied 0/0 operation. However, since d is known, TK!Solver makes an attempt to evaluate the expression *sqrt*(d), which results in an error condition (TK!Solver cannot take the square root of negative numbers). We can alleviate this problem by multiplying the discriminant by k as shown on the Rule Sheet in Figure 11-14*a*.

```
==================== RULE SHEET ========================================...
S Rule
- ----
* d = b^2 - 4*a*c                                   " discriminant
* k = step(d,0)                                     " check for complex root
* 0/k       +  x1 = (-b+sqrt(k*d))/(2*a)            " first real root
* 0/k       +  x2 = (-b-sqrt(k*d))/(2*a)            " second real root
* 0/(k-1) +  xr = -b/(2*a)                          " real part of complex root
* 0/(k-1) +  xi = sqrt((k-1)*d)/(2*a)               " imag part of complex root
```

a. Rule Sheet

```
==================== VARIABLE SHEET ====================================...
St Input      Name     Output     Unit         Comment
-- -----      ----     ------     ----         -------
   1          a                                coefficient of x^2
   5          b                                coefficient of x
   4          c                                constant
              d        9                       discriminant
              x1       -1                      first real root
              x2       -4                      second real root
              xr                               real part of complex root
              xi                               imag part of complex root
              k        1                       real = 1, complex = 0
```

b. Variable Sheet with real roots evaluated (note that d is positive and k=1)

```
==================== VARIABLE SHEET ====================================...
St Input      Name     Output     Unit         Comment
-- -----      ----     ------     ----         -------
   1          a                                coefficient of x^2
   -2         b                                coefficient of x
   4          c                                constant
              d        -12                     discriminant
              x1                               first real root
              x2                               second real root
              xr       1                       real part of complex root
              xi       1.7320508               imag part of complex root
              k        0                       real = 1, complex = 0
```

c. Variable Sheet with complex root evaluated (note that d is negative and k=0)

Figure 11-14.
The Quadratic equation model

Likewise, the formulas for the real and imaginary parts of the complex root are built into the next two rules. They are activated only when k is 0. Note that the discriminant in the rule for xi has been multiplied by $(k-1)$. The Variable Sheets (see Figure 11-14*b* and *c*) show the solution of two quadratic equations, one with real roots and the other with complex roots. We could have avoided taking the square roots of negative values in the model by using the *abs* function instead of multiplying d by k or $(k-1)$. However, this would mean limiting the backsolvability, since *abs* is a non-invertible function. (In a case study in Chapter 13, we will expand the model to make it completely backsolvable.)

Formatting Numbers

When we use a model dealing with money, it is convenient to have the values displayed as dollars and cents rather than dollars and as many digits after the decimal place as the Input or Output field can accommodate. Similarly, we may wish to display an integer solution for a particular variable. The built-in functions in TK!Solver provide the necessary building blocks for different kinds of formatters.

To round off a number to its nearest integer, we have to add 0.5 to the number and take the integer part of it using the *int* function. Thus if $T = 5.3$, the nearest integer is given by

$$int(T + 0.5) = int(5.8) = 5$$

If $T = 5.6$, then

$$int(T + 0.5) = int(6.1) = 6$$

Let's assume that the variable T has to be rounded off to one decimal place. Then we should use the following:

$$int(T*10 + 0.5)/10$$

Thus $T = 5.67$ is rounded off to 5.7 while 5.63 is rounded off to 5.6.

Similarly, for rounding off to two decimal places we would use 100 instead of 10 in the rounding-off expression; for three places we would use 1000, and so on (in short, $10^\wedge n$ for n decimal places).

Dollars and Cents Formatter

Displaying numbers in dollars and cents is equivalent to rounding off the values to two decimal places. At the same time we may want to use the full interval value for calculations to maintain accuracy. The equation

$$T\$ = int(T*100 + 0.5)/100$$

will round off the value of T to two decimal places and assign it to $T\$$. (Note that any variable name can be chosen; we just picked $T\$$ for illustration purposes.) Let's consider the simple loan model built in Chapter 2 and shown again here in Figure 11-15.

The value of R, the monthly payment, is displayed in dollars and cents ($R\$$) using the second rule. But if $R\$$ is given as input, the principal P cannot be calculated since *int* is a non-invertible function and R cannot be evaluated from the second rule. To overcome this loss of backsolvability, we can use the *given* function.

```
==================== VARIABLE SHEET ==============================...
St Input      Name     Output      Unit        Comment
-- -----      ----     ------      ----        -------
              R        142.73958 $             payment
   15         I                    %           interest rate
   6000       P                    $           loan amount
   12         N                    1/yr        number of payments
   5          Y                    yr          loan period
              R$       142.74      $           formatted value of R

==================== RULE SHEET ===================================...
S Rule
- ----
  R = I * P/N / (1 - (1 + I/N)^-(N*Y))
  R$ = int(R*100 + .5)/100                      " convert to $ and cents
```

Figure 11-15.
The simple loan analysis model (shows the rule needed for displaying *R* in dollars and cents (*R$*)—precludes backsolving when *R$* is given as input)

A new rule is added so that *R* is assigned the value of *R$* if an input value is specified for *R$*. This is shown in Figure 11-16. The Variable Sheet in the figure shows *P* evaluated for the specified value of *R$*. In fact, a set of equations for *P* can also be used so that it is displayed as dollars and cents.

We may keep only *R$* on the Variable Sheet and delete *R* or move it to the bottom of the sheet as shown in the figure. The last two rules can be used in any model where rounding off is desired and at the same time backsolvability is to be retained. Note that if *R$* is given as input with more than two decimal places and the model is solved, TK!Solver will protest and mark the second rule as inconsistent. Again the *given* function

```
==================== VARIABLE SHEET ===================================...
St Input      Name     Output      Unit        Comment
-- -----      ----     ------      ----        -------
   15         I                    %           interest rate
              P        6315.6974 $             loan amount
   12         N                                number of payments per year
   5          Y                    yr          loan period
   150.25     R$                   $           payment (formatted)

              R        150.25      $           payment (internal)

=================== RULE SHEET ========================================...
S Rule
- ----
  R = I * P/N / (1 - (1 + I/N)^-(N*Y))
  R$ = int(R*100+.5)/100                     " convert R to $ and cents
  R = given('R$,R$,R)                        " if R$ is input R=R$, else R=R
```

Figure 11-16.
Refined loan analysis model (shows backsolvability when *R$* is given as input)

can be used in the second rule so that the value of *R$* is used irrespective of the number of digits specified after the decimal place. The modified rule is as follows:

$$R\$ = given('R\$,R\$,int(R*100 + 0.5)/100)$$

Floor and Ceiling

The floor of a non-integer number is the integer immediately below it. Thus the floor of 9.9 is 9 and that of 9.2 is also 9, while that of −4.5 is −5. The ceiling of a non-integer number is the integer immediately above it.

```
==================== RULE SHEET ===================...
S Rule
- ----
  floor = number - mod(number,1)
  ceiling = floor + sgn(number-floor)
```

a. Rule Sheet

```
==================== VARIABLE SHEET ===============...
St Input      Name     Output     Unit      Comment
-- -----      ----     ------     ----      -------
   9.2        number
              floor    9
              ceiling  10
```

b. Variable Sheet for positive non-integer number

```
==================== VARIABLE SHEET ===============...
St Input      Name     Output     Unit      Comment
-- -----      ----     ------     ----      -------
   45         number
              floor    45
              ceiling  45
```

c. Variable Sheet for positive integer number

```
==================== VARIABLE SHEET ===============...
St Input      Name     Output     Unit      Comment
-- -----      ----     ------     ----      -------
   -3.6       number
              floor    -4
              ceiling  -3
```

d. Variable Sheet for negative non-integer number

Figure 11-17.
Model for floor and ceiling of numbers

Thus the ceiling of 9.9 is 10 and that of 9.2 is also 10, while that of −4.5 is −4. The floor and ceiling of an integer number are the same as the number itself. The built-in functions *mod* and *sgn* can be used to build the floor and ceiling evaluators. This comes in handy in problems dealing with variables that can have only integer values. For example, when the calculation yields 12.4 people for the job, 13 are required, and when the calculation indicates that a bag can hold 98.4 items, only 98 can go into the bag.

Figure 11-17*a* gives the rules for evaluating the floor and ceiling of a number (try to figure out how it works). The Variable Sheets (Figure 11-17*b*, *c*, and *d*) show the results obtained for three numbers.

Making Models More Friendly

Not only can we document a model to make it easily understandable and usable, but we can also build a model so that it traps improper problem formulations and returns diagnostic messages. We will look at these possibilities using the mortgage analysis model shown in Figure 11-18*a*. The Calculation Units are as follows: decimal fraction (1) for *dp*, months (mo) for *n*, and decimal fraction per month (1/mo) for *r*. The Unit Sheet (see Figure 11-18*b*) shows the unit conversions for the model.

The Variable Sheet shows the solution of the following problem: A $10,000 car is purchased with a down payment of $2000 and a 5-year loan. If finance is available at 9.9% APR (annual percentage rate), calculate the monthly payment, the total interest on the loan, and the total payments made on the loan.

What if the buyer wants to pay only $60 per month? How long will it take to pay off the loan? When the model is solved with the value of *A* (the value of *n* is blanked out), the Direct Solver encounters an error and terminates the solution with the message "Exp: Argument error". This happens because the desired payment assigned as the input value of *A* is, in fact, less than the monthly interest on the loan. TK!Solver's argument error message and refusal to come up with an answer are equivalent to a bank's refusing to lose money on the loan. To avoid such follies, we must prevent the third equation from solving for *n*. We accomplish this by multiplying the right-hand side of the rule by *sgn*(*n*). Such multiplication will not affect the equation when *n* is known because the signum of a positive number is 1 and *n* is always positive.

The minimum payment can be found if we assume that only the interest is paid each month (implying an infinite loan term). The rule

$$Amin = Loan * r$$

```
==================== VARIABLE SHEET =====================================...
St Input      Name     Output     Unit       Comment
-- -----      ----     ------     ----       -------
   10000      Price               $          purchase price of asset
   2000       dpaymen             $          down payment
              dp       20         %          down payment percentage
              Loan     8000       $          beginning balance of loan
   5          n                   yr         term of loan
   9.9        r                   %/yr       nominal interest rate on loan
              A        169.58299  $/mo       periodic loan payment amount

==================== RULE SHEET =========================================...
S Rule
- ----
  dpaymen: = Price * dp
  Loan = Price - dpayment
  A = Loan * r/(1-(1+r)^-n)
  T = A * n
  Ti = T - Loan
```

a. Variable and Rule Sheets

```
==================== UNIT SHEET =============...
From        To        Multiply By   Add Offset
----        --        -----------   ----------
yr          mo        12
1           %         100
1/mo        %/mo      100
%/mo        %/yr      12
```

b. Unit Sheet

Figure 11-18.
The mortgage analysis model

calculates the minimum periodic payment *Amin*. If *A* is greater than *Amin*, the loan term *n* is finite. The *sgn* function can be used to evaluate a feasibility indicator, as follows:

$$fin = sgn(A - Amin)$$

Here $fin=1$ means that *A* is greater than *Amin*, so it is okay to evaluate *n* (if it is unknown) from the third rule; therefore we add the following conditional rule:

$$0/max(fin,0) + A = Amin \;/\; (1 - (1+r)\hat{}-n)$$

which is essentially the same as the original third rule with the additional conditional part. Note that *max*(*fin*,0) returns 0 when $fin \leq 0$, that is, $A \leq Amin$ Also the subexpression *Loan***r* is replaced by the equivalent *Amin* to avoid an extra computation. If *fin* is equal to or less than zero, the rule is inapplicable. In the first case ($fin=0$) the term is infinite; in the second case the proposition is infeasible. The user-defined function *prop* shown in the User Function Subsheet in Figure 11-19*a* is used to generate and display the appropriate message. The Rule Sheet with all the rules is shown in Figure 11-19*b*.

Figure 11-20*a-c* shows the Variable Sheets with three different kinds of problems solved. In Figure 11-20*a*, the problem is the same as the one in Figure 11-18, but here the figure shows that the term is finite since A is greater than $Amin$. In Figure 11-20*b*, $Amin$ is assigned to A and the figure shows that the term is infinite. Figure 11-20*c* shows an infeasible proposition since A is less than $Amin$.

Let's consider now what happens if someone is lucky enough to get an interest-free loan. When r is assigned 0 and the model is solved, A cannot be evaluated because a 0/0 bypass occurs in the third rule. This calls for a rule that will be used only when r is zero. The expression $sgn(r)$ will be zero when r is zero and so $(1-sgn(r))$ can be used in the denominator of the conditional part of the rule

$$0/(1-sgn(r)) + A = Loan/n$$

```
==================== USER FUNCTION: prop ================...
Comment:                        feasibility of proposition
Domain List:                    value
Mapping:                        Table
Range List:                     type
Element Domain         Range
------- ------         -----
1       1              'finite
2       0              'infinite
3       -1             'infeasible
```

a. User Function Subsheet for function *prop* to indicate the feasibility of the loan

```
==================== RULE SHEET ==========================================...
S Rule
- ----
  dpayment = Price * dp
  Loan = Price - dpayment
  A = Loan * r/(1-(1+r)^-n) * sgn(n)
  T = A * n
  Ti = T - Loan

  "        * * * *   modification for special cases    * * * *

  Amin = Loan * r                               " minimum monthly payment
  fin = sgn(A-Amin)                             " feasibility indicator
  0/max(fin,0)  + A = Amin / (1-(1+r)^-n)       " evaluates  n  when A>Amin
  term = prop(fin)                            " generates feasibility message
```

b. Rule Sheet with additional rules making the model powerful and friendly

Figure 11-19.
The friendlier mortgage analysis model

```
==================== VARIABLE SHEET ======================================...
St Input      Name     Output      Unit       Comment
-- -----      ----     ------      ----       -------
              term     'finite                solution feasibility
   10000      Price                $          purchase price of asset
   2000       dpaymen              $          down payment
              dp       20          %          down payment percentage
              Loan     8000        $          beginning balance of loan
   5          n                    yr         term of loan
   9.9        r                    %/yr       nominal interest rate on loan
              A        169.58299   $/mo       periodic loan payment amount
              Amin     66          $/mo       minimum periodic payment
              T        10174.980   $          total payments on loan
              Ti       2174.9796   $          total interest on loan
              fin      1                      feasibility indicator
```

a. Finite loan term A > *Amin*

```
==================== VARIABLE SHEET ======================================...
St Input      Name     Output      Unit       Comment
-- -----      ----     ------      ----       -------
              term     'infinite              solution feasibility
   10000      Price                $          purchase price of asset
   2000       dpaymen              $          down payment
              dp       20          %          down payment percentage
              Loan     8000        $          beginning balance of loan
              n                    yr         term of loan
   9.9        r                    %/yr       nominal interest rate on loan
   66         A                    $/mo       periodic loan payment amount
              Amin     66          $/mo       minimum periodic payment
              T                    $          total payments  on loan
              Ti                   $          total interest on loan
              fin      0                      feasibility indicator
```

b. Infinite loan term A = *Amin*

```
==================== VARIABLE SHEET ======================================...
St Input      Name     Output      Unit       Comment
-- -----      ----     ------      ----       -------
              term      infeasib              solution feasibility
   10000      Price                $          purchase price of asset
   2000       dpaymen              $          down payment
              dp       20          %          down payment percentage
              Loan     8000        $          beginning balance of loan
              n                    yr         term of loan
   9.9        r                    %/yr       nominal interest rate on loan
   60         A                    $/mo       periodic loan payment amount
              Amin     66          $/mo       minimum periodic payment
              T                    $          total payments on loan
              Ti                   $          total interest on loan
              fin      -1                     feasibility indicator
```

c. Infeasible loan term A < *Amin*

Figure 11-20.
Variable Sheet with three different solutions

When this rule is added to the Rule Sheet and the model is solved, the results shown in the Variable Sheet in Figure 11-21*a* are obtained. The dollars and cents formatter discussed earlier in the chapter has been added to the rules so that *A* is returned in dollars and cents (*A$*). The Rule Sheet with these additional rules is shown in Figure 11-21*b*.

Thus, using the different features and functions available, we can make models more friendly, versatile, and explicit. It is best to decide how much extra effort to put in this direction on a model-by-model basis. Usually, this effort pays off.

User-Defined Analytical Functions

Sometimes the model designer has a choice between using an analytical or a user-defined function in the model. User-defined functions take time to declare in the User Function Sheet and define in the User Function Subsheet; the data takes up memory too. Therefore, it is best to decide which way to go on a case-by-case basis, depending on the amount of data and complexity of the relationship.

```
==================== VARIABLE SHEET ====================================...
St Input      Name     Output     Unit        Comment
-- -----      ----     ------     ----        -------
              term     'finite                solution feasibility
   10000      Price               $           purchase price of asset
   2000       dpaymen             $           down payment
              dp       20         %           down payment percentage
              Loan     8000       $           beginning balance of loan
   5          n                   yr          term of loan
   0          r                   %/yr        nominal interest rate on loan
              A        133.33333 $/mo         periodic loan payment amount
              Amin     0          $/mo        minimum periodic payment
              T        8000       $           total payments  on loan
              Ti       -.0000002 $            total interest on loan
              fin      1                      feasibility indicator
              A$       133.33     $/mo        payment in $ and cents
```

a. Variable Sheet with solution for interest-free loan

```
==================== RULE SHEET ==========================================...
S Rule
- ----
  0/(1-sgn(r))  + A = Loan/n        " for interest free loan
  A$ = int(A*100+.5)/100            "  dollars and cents
  A = given('A$,A$,A)               "      formatting
```

b. Rule part of the sheet with the newly added rules

Figure 11-21.
Extended mortgage model with rule for interest-free loan and dollars and cents formatting

Let's consider the information from the tax table shown in Table 11-2. An immediate thought that comes to mind is to use two user-defined functions, one relating the filing status and pre-move expenses and the other the filing status and moving expenses with Table Lookup Mapping. If *fun1* and *fun2* are the two functions, then the following rules can be used:

$$Ded1 = fun1(status)$$
$$Ded2 = fun2(status)$$

One Function Only

An examination of the data shows that the moving expenses are twice the pre-move expenses. So instead of two functions, one function, say *fun1*, can be used and the two rules will be

$$Ded1 = fun1(status)$$
$$Ded2 = 2 * Ded1$$

No Function Necessary

In each of the deduction columns all values are the same except for the middle ones, which are half of the rest; that is, in both columns the proportion of values is 2,2,1,2,2. A fitting function that will map the *status* 1,2,3,4,5 into the proportion values (or deduction coefficients *DC*) is

$$DC = abs(sgn(status - 3)) + 1$$

For instance, when $status = 2$, $abs(sgn(2-3)) = 1$, so $DC = 1 + 1 = 2$. When $status = 3$, then $DC = 1$. The rules using the deduction coefficient *DC* to calculate *Ded1* and *Ded2* will be simply

$$Ded1 = 750 * DC$$
$$Ded2 = 1500 * DC$$

Table 11-2.
Filing Status and Deductible Pre-move and Moving Expenses.

Filing Status	Deductible pre-move expenses	Deductible moving expenses
1	1500	3000
2	1500	3000
3	750	1500
4	1500	3000
5	1500	3000

Building and Using the Random Number Generator

TK!Solver was designed to behave in a predictable or deterministic manner. Given a set of equations and a set of input values, TK!Solver will obtain the same solution time and again. However, TK!Solver models can be built to behave randomly if this is required.

A drill exercise is an example of a model in which we require random behavior. In such an exercise, TK!Solver generates a question at random and the student types in an answer. TK!Solver then checks to see if the answer is correct and returns an appropriate message. This sequence may be applied to multiplication tables, names and symbols of elements in chemistry, names of capitals and countries—just about anything that TK!Solver can do by itself so that it can verify the answers. Here we look at the technique required to set up a multiplication table drill.

Generating Random Numbers

We can use the following recursive formula for generating a sequence of pseudo-random numbers:

$$x_i = Ax_{i-1} \text{ modulo } B$$

In order to take advantage of this or other recursive relations, we have to use List Solving because

- Only List Solving provides for storing the results in the lists (instance-by-instance).
- The whole list is available for retrieval at each instance of the List Solving process, regardless of the status of a particular variable (input or not).

We already used these attributes of lists and List Solving to generate a series of Fibonacci numbers in Chapter 6 and to illustrate the iteration process in Chapter 9. Now we will use these attributes to build a generator of N random numbers x, valued between 1 and B, by Block Solving the rule

$$x = mod(element('x,element()-1)*A,B)$$

from 2 to $N+1$ (provided there is a non-zero seed in the first element of list x). Using $A=4676$, $B=414971$, and a seed value of the first element $x=123456$, and then Block Solving from 2 to 41, we obtain the following sequence of 40 random numbers.

55595	325887	159085	144905	95122
190374	74100	253428	343108	356531
76029	405786	287123	178941	200449
296428	207924	155963	146580	295006
94188	390542	383250	290959	84452
138857	301992	232222	249346	260131
280688	370554	305936	288357	92555
358786	206579	151699	116553	387398

However, for drill exercise and for many other applications, we need to generate random numbers piecemeal every time a solution is initiated rather than generating a table of random numbers. We can accomplish this by taking advantage of yet another feature of List Solving: an element from a list can be retrieved and used in calculations, and the result can be stored again in the same position in the list, all during the same instance. In the present example, List Solving for just one instance will suffice. The seed from the first element of the list x is used to generate the new random number, which in turn is stored back in the same position of the same list x so that it is available as a seed for the next List Solving. The modified rule is as follows:

$$x = mod(element('x,1)*A,B)$$

As was explained in Chapter 10, in order to List Solve for N instances, TK!Solver must have a list that contains N elements and is associated with an input variable. Since the list x has to accept the resulting value, x cannot be declared as an input variable. Consequently, in order to make the rule work as required, TK!Solver needs an input list, say, z with one element in it. This list need not have anything in common with the rules in the model—it can be a dummy list. If we need integer random numbers valued between 1 and n, we need to include another rule as shown in Figure 11-22*a* and assign the value of n on the Variable Sheet as shown in Figure 11-22*b*. When List Solving is invoked, *rnd* is generated and displayed as shown in the figure.

Multiplication Table Drill

For the multiplication table, we will need to generate and use two random numbers. The exercise is a two-step process. In the first, the random numbers within a chosen range have to be generated by List Solving (/L!) and displayed. The second process begins when the student enters a plausible answer and presses the Action key ! to invoke answer-checking by the Direct Solver. While the Direct Solver is checking the answer, the rules

```
==================== RULE SHEET ======================================...
S Rule
- ----
* x = mod(element('x,1)*16807,2147483647)
* rnd = int(n*x*4.6566128752E-10) + 1
```

a. Rule Sheet(first rule retrieves seed and stores back new value of x for next number)

```
==================== VARIABLE SHEET ==================================...
St Input      Name     Output    Unit      Comment
-- -----      ----     ------    ----      -------
   20         n                            upper limit for rnd
L             x                            seed and repository for x
              rnd      11                  random number
L  0          z                            dummy input list
```

b. Variable Sheet with random number (the list z is used as a dummy input list so that List Solving can be invoked)

Figure 11-22.
A random number generator

generating the random numbers need to be turned off. The student should see a message stating whether the answer is correct and be given the opportunity to answer the same question again, if desired. Until the student asks for a new question by typing /L!, the generated random numbers should not change. This means that conditional rules are required. Figure 11-23*a* shows the Rule Sheet for the model.

The first two rules and the fourth and fifth rules are the random number generators with the additional conditional part added so that they can be bypassed when necessary. The dummy list k with 1 as the first element is useful here: during List Solving this value is assigned to k, so the random numbers are generated. The variable k also has an input value of zero assigned in the Variable Sheet. When the Direct Solver is used, that is, when the answer is being checked, $k=0$, so the rules for random number generation are bypassed.

However, the values of a and b would disappear after a student enters an answer and presses the Action key. Therefore, the generated numbers have to be stored in lists during List Solving so that they can be used for checking the answers. The lists y and q in the third and sixth rules serve this purpose.

For retrieving these values when the Direct Solver is invoked, the *element* function can be used as shown in the figure. These rules are bypassed

```
==================== RULE SHEET ======================================...
S Rule
- ----
* 0/k      +   x = mod(element('x,1)*16807,2147483647)    " seed for a
* 0/k      +   a = int(n*x*4.6566128752E-10) + 1           " generate a
* 0/k      +   y = a                                    " store a in list y

* 0/k      +   p = mod(element('p,1)*16807,2147483647)    " seed for b
* 0/k      +   b = int(n*p*4.6566128752E-10) + 1           " generate b
* 0/k      +   q = b                                    " store b in list q

* 0/(k-1) +    a = element('y,1)     " get a from list y and display
* 0/(k-1) +    b = element('q,1)     " get b from list q and display
* 0/k      -    state  =  1                           " answer expected
* 0/(k-1) +    state = sgn(abs(a*b - a_x_b))          " answer check
* you_are  =    fun(state)                            " display message
```

a. Rule Sheet

```
==================== USER FUNCTION: fun ==========...
Comment:                          checks the solution
Domain List:                      value
Mapping:                          Table
Range List:                       message
Element Domain        Range
------- ------        -----
1        -1           'on
2        0            'correct
3        1            'wrong
```

b. User Function Subsheet for *fun*

Figure 11-23.
Drill exercise in multiplication table

during List Solving. Finally, for checking if the answer is correct or not, the expression

$$sgn(abs(a*b - a\_x\_b))$$

can be used. This expression returns 0 if the answer is correct and 1 otherwise. The expression is used as part of a conditional rule so that the answer is checked only when the Action key ! is pressed. Then a user-defined function can be employed to give the student a message that TK!Solver is ready for input and subsequently about the correctness of the answer. The User Function Subsheet for the function *fun* is shown in Figure 11-23*b*. The last rule in Figure 11-23*a* returns the appropriate message. During List Solving the rule

$$0/k - state = 1$$

is used and *state* is set to −1. So the last rule returns *'on* for the variable *you_are* at the end of List Solving.

Using the Model

Different seed values have to be used for x and p. They are entered in their respective List Subsheets. The extent of the multiplication table (that is, the upper limit for a and b) has to be specified as an input value for the variable n. When List Solving is invoked, the values of a and b are displayed as shown in Figure 11-24*a*. The value in the Output field of *you_are* tells the student that he or she is "on" and that TK!Solver is ready for input.

```
==================== VARIABLE SHEET ===================================...
St Input      Name      Output     Unit       Comment
-- -----      ----      ------     ----       -------
   20         n                               select times table
L             x                               seed for a, store back new x
L             y                               store a in list y

L             p                               seed for b, store back new p
L             q                               store b in list q

L  0          k                               switch for generating a,b

              you_are   'on                   * * *  The Slateboard  * * *

              a         11                    a times
              b         12                    b is
              a_x_b                           equal to what?
```

a. Values for a and b generated by List Solving, and the message *'on*

```
==================== VARIABLE SHEET ===================================...
St Input      Name      Output     Unit       Comment
-- -----      ----      ------     ----       -------
              you_are   'wrong                * * *  The Slateboard  * * *

              a         11                    a times
              b         12                    b is
   121        a_x_b                           equal to what?
```

b. Incorrect answer pointed out

```
==================== VARIABLE SHEET ===================================...
St Input      Name      Output     Unit       Comment
-- -----      ----      ------     ----       -------
              you_are   'correct              * * *  The Slateboard  * * *

              a         11                    a times
              b         12                    b is
   132        a_x_b                           equal to what?
```

c. Correct answer—message displayed

Figure 11-24.
Drill exercise in multiplication table, Variable Sheets

The Variable Sheet in Figure 11-24*b* also shows that in this instance when a value is entered for *a_x_b* and the Action key is pressed, TK!Solver finds the answer to be incorrect and displays the message '*wrong* in the Output field of *you_are*. When the correct value is entered and the Action key is pressed, the message becomes '*correct* as shown in Figure 11-24*c*. By initiating List Solving again, we can generate the next set of values for a and b.

TK!Solver and Logical Inference

TK!Solver is primarily a numerical problem-solving tool and contains no special facilities for performing logical or Boolean operations. However, these operations can be realized through combinations of arithmetic operations. For example, the Boolean values "true" and "false" can be represented by 1 and 0 respectively. In keeping with the spirit of backsolving, a hallmark of TK!Solver, the Boolean operations can also be made invertible where appropriate. For example, if $z = a.\mathrm{AND}.b$, then $z=1$ implies that both a and b must be 1. In the following discussion a, b, and z play the role of logical variables and thus have values of either 0 or 1.

The NOT. Operation

The operation

$$z = \mathrm{NOT}.a$$

is represented in TK!Solver by

$$z = 1 - a$$

Thus when $a=1$, $z=0$, and when $a=0$, $z=1$. Note that the equation is backsolvable.

The .AND. Operation

The operation

$$z = a.\mathrm{AND}.b$$

is represented in TK!Solver by

$$z = a * b$$

In addition, $z=1$ implies that both $a=1$ and $b=1$. This can be expressed by the following two rules:

$$z * a = z$$
$$z * b = z$$

Similarly, $a=0$ or $b=0$ implies that $z=0$. This may be expressed by another two rules:

$$z * (1-a) = 0$$

$$z * (1-b) = 0$$

These four rules along with the basic equation make .AND. invertible where appropriate. When $z=0$, it is not possible to conclude anything about the values of a or b, since both could be zero or only one of them could be zero. In such cases the additional equations are bypassed because of the 0/0 division.

The .OR. Operation

The operation

$$z = a.\text{OR}.b = \text{NOT}.(\text{NOT}.a.\text{AND}.\text{NOT}.b)$$

is equivalent to

$$\text{NOT}.z = \text{NOT}.a.\text{AND}.\text{NOT}.b$$

and is represented in TK!Solver by

$$1-z = (1-a) * (1-b)$$

We used the so-called de Morgan's law to transform the operation into a combination of NOT. and .AND. operations and treat it as shown. In order to secure backsolvability where appropriate, we again add the following four rules:

$$z * a = a$$

$$z * b = b$$

$$a * (1-z) = 0$$

$$b * (1-z) = 0$$

With these building blocks, we can build models to make logical inferences.

The Automobile Model

Let's consider the following statements:

1. If any assembly in an automobile is faulty, the automobile is faulty.
2. The wheels and the carburetor are assemblies in an automobile.
3. The carburetor is considered fit if it is clean or faulty if it is dirty.
4. The wheel assembly consists of four mounted wheels and a spare.

5. Each of the four mounted wheels is considered fit if it is intact or faulty if it is punctured.

6. The spare is considered fit if it is available or faulty if it is missing.

7. The wheel assembly is considered fit if either all the four mounted wheels are intact or three of the mounted wheels are intact and a spare is available.

We may regard "fit" and "faulty" to be equivalent to the logical values "true" and "false" respectively. The TK!Solver representation will, of course, be 1 and 0. There will be two sets of variables in the model, as shown in Figure 11-25: symbolic variables denoting the state of the automobile, assemblies, and parts, and logical variables serving for setting up the logical relationships.

The model contains two groups of rules: one expresses the logical relationships, and the other maps the symbolic values onto the logical values

```
...======== VARIABLE SHEET =============================================
    Name     Output    Unit        Comment
    ----     ------    ----        -------
                                     *** Symbolic Variables ***

    automob                        status of automobile (fit or faulty)
    carbure                        status of carburetor (dirty or clean)
    wheels                         wheel assembly (fit or faulty)
    lfwheel                        left front wheel (intact or punctured)
    rfwheel                        right front wheel (intact or punctured)
    lrwheel                        left rear wheel (intact or punctured)
    rrwheel                        right front wheel (intact or punctured)
    spare                          spare wheel (available or missing)

                                     *** Logical Variables ***

    a                              automobile
    c                              carburetor
    w                              wheel assembly
    lf                             left front wheel
    rf                             right front wheel
    lr                             left rear wheel
    rr                             right rear wheel
    s                              spare wheel

    fw                             four wheels intact
    tw                             three wheels intact
    tws                            three wheels intact and spare availabl

    w1                             if rf=lr=rr=1 then w1=1, else w1=0
    w2                             if lf=lr=rr=1 then w2=1, else w2=0
    w3                             if lf=rf=rr=1 then w3=1, else w3=0
    w4                             if lf=rf=lr=1 then w4=1, else w4=0
```

Figure 11-25.
Partial Variable Sheet of the automobile model (note two sets of variables—symbolic and logical)

(see Figure 11-26). The latter group consists of eight rules supported by the user-defined functions shown in Figure 11-27*a*, *b*, *c* and *d*. These rules take care of points 3, 5, and 6.

Points 1 and 2 may be expressed as

$$a = w.\text{AND}.c$$

For expressing conditions 4 and 7, we make use of two auxiliary logical variables *fw* and *tw* representing "all four mounted wheels are fit" and "three out of the four mounted wheels are fit," respectively. These variables are defined as follows:

$$fw = lf.\text{AND}.rf.\text{AND}.lr.\text{AND}.rr$$
$$tw = w1.\text{OR}.w2.\text{OR}.w3.\text{OR}.w4$$

where

$$w1 = rf.\text{AND}.lr.\text{AND}.rr$$
$$w2 = lf.\text{AND}.lr.\text{AND}.rr$$
$$w3 = lf.\text{AND}.rf.\text{AND}.rr$$
$$w4 = lf.\text{AND}.rf.\text{AND}.lr.$$

```
==================== RULE SHEET ==========================================...
S Rule
- ----
  "      * * * Mapping of Symbolic to Boolean Variables * * *

  automobile = fun(a)
  carburetor = fnc(c)
  wheels = fun(w)
  lf = fnw(lfwheel)
  rf = fnw(rfwheel)
  lr = fnw(lrwheel)
  rr = fnw(rrwheel)
  spare = fns(s)

  "                 * * * Logical Relationships * * *

  a = w * c                                   " a = w.AND.c
  (1-w) = (1-fw) * (1-tws)                    " w = fw.OR.tws
  fw = lf * rf * lr * rr                      " fw = lf.AND.rf.AND.lr.AND.rr
  tws = tw * s                                " tws = tw.AND.s
  (1-tw) = (1-w1)*(1-w2)*(1-w3)*(1-w4)        " tw = w1.OR.w2.OR.w3.OR.w4
  w1 = rf * lr * rr                           " w1 = rf.AND.lr.AND.rr
  w2 = lf * lr * rr                           " w2 = lf.AND.lr.AND.rr
  w3 = lf * rf * rr                           " w3 = lf.AND.rf.AND.rr
  w4 = lf * rf * lr                           " w4 = lf.AND.rf.AND.lr
```

Figure 11-26.
Rule Sheet for the automobile model (note the two groups of rules)

```
==================== USER FUNCTION: fun ====================...
Comment:                              automobile and wheel assembly
Domain List:                          bool
Mapping:                              Table
Range List:                           cond
Element Domain       Range
------- ------       -----
1       1            'fit
2       0            'faulty
```

a. fun — condition of car and wheel assembly

```
==================== USER FUNCTION: fnc ====================...
Comment:                              condition of carburetor
Domain List:                          bool
Mapping:                              Table
Range List:                           carb
Element Domain       Range
------- ------       -----
1       1            'clean
2       0            'dirty
```

b. fnc — condition of carburetor

```
==================== USER FUNCTION: fnw ====================...
Comment:                              condition of wheels
Domain List:                          bool
Mapping:                              Table
Range List:                           wheels
Element Domain       Range
------- ------       -----
1       1            'intact
2       0            'punctured
```

c. fnw — condition of wheels

```
==================== USER FUNCTION: fsw ====================...
Comment:                              availability of spare
Domain List:                          bool
Mapping:                              Table
Range List:                           spwhl
Element Domain       Range
------- ------       -----
1       1            'available
2       0            'missing
```

d. fsw — availability of spare wheel

Figure 11-27.
User Function Subsheets for the automobile model

Condition 7 is then expressed as

$$w = fw.\text{OR}.tws$$

where

$tws = tw.\text{AND}.s$

The four backsolvability rules for each of the .AND. and .OR. operations are then added to the model. However, only the basic logic equations without these complementary rules are shown in Figure 11-27. The model is ready for making logical deductions.

When we assign inputs to the effect that "the left rear wheel is punctured but the automobile is fit for use," TK!Solver deduces that the other three wheels are intact, the spare is available, and the carburetor is clean. This is shown in the Variable Sheet in Figure 11-28*a*.

Suppose we know that the carburetor is clean, the front wheels are intact, and the spare is available, but we find that the car does not run. The TK!Solver model deduces that the wheel assembly must be faulty and that the two rear wheels are punctured. See the Variable Sheet in Figure 11-28*b*.

On the other hand, if we state that the wheels are fit but the spare is missing and the carburetor is dirty, TK!Solver concludes that all the four wheels are intact but the car is faulty and cannot be used. This is shown in Figure 11-28*c*.

Let's suppose we insist that the automobile is fit to run although both rear wheels are punctured. This is a false statement according to the premises on which the model is based. TK!Solver detects the breach in logic and points out the inconsistency as shown in Figure 11-29, where *tw* and *tws* are marked "Overdefined".

It is interesting to trace the chain of reasoning behind this message and behind the displayed values of other output variables. Along one path of the solution propagation, TK!Solver deduced that once the automobile is fit, both the carburetor and wheel assembly must be okay. On the other hand, since at least one of the wheels is punctured, $fw=0$. This and $w=1$ imply that $tws=1$. In the meantime, TK!Solver finds that none of the combinations of three wheels is fit, that is, $w1=w2=w3=w4=0$, and consequently, $tw=0$. Of course, this conclusion clashes with the already evaluated $tws=1$, regardless of the availability of the spare. The termination of the solution due to the error renders all the output values ineffective as in the case of numerical calculations. In the spirit of TK!Solver, we have to suspect the input information and remove the unsound part of it. When any of the input values is blanked, TK!Solver returns a valid solution. In

```
==================== VARIABLE SHEET ===...
St Input      Name     Output     Unit
-- -----      ----     ------     ----


   'fit       automob
              carbure  'clean
              wheels   'fit
              lfwheel  'intact
              rfwheel  'intact
   'puncture  lrwheel
              rrwheel  'intact
              spare    'availabl
```

a. One wheel *'punctured*, automobile *'fit*

```
==================== VARIABLE SHEET ===...
St Input      Name     Output     Unit
-- -----      ----     ------     ----


   'faulty    automob
   'clean     carbure
              wheels   'faulty
   'intact    lfwheel
   'intact    rfwheel
              lrwheel  'puncture
              rrwheel  'puncture
   'availabl  spare
```

b. TK!Solver showing what could be wrong

```
==================== VARIABLE SHEET ===...
St Input      Name     Output     Unit
-- -----      ----     ------     ----


              automob  'faulty
   'dirty     carbure
   'fit       wheels
              lfwheel  'intact
              rfwheel  'intact
              lrwheel  'intact
              rrwheel  'intact
   'missing   spare
```

c. Car faulty because of carburetor

Figure 11-28.
TK!Solver making logical deductions

fact, if we "fix" the right rear wheel by dropping the *'punctured* status, TK!Solver brings back the solution shown in Figure 11-28.

```
(25s) Status: > Overdefined

=================== VARIABLE SHEET ===...
St Input      Name     Output     Unit
-- -----      ----     ------     ----


   'fit       automob
              carbure  'clean
              wheels   'fit
              lfwheel
              rfwheel
   'puncture  lrwheel
   'puncture  rrwheel
              spare


              a        1
              c        1
              w        1
              lf
              rf
              lr       0
              rr       0
              s

              fw       0
>             tw       0
>             tws      1

              w1       0
              w2       0
              w3       0
              w4       0
```

Figure 11-29.
Variable Sheet after termination of solution due to contradictory input information

Thus TK!Solver can be used for modeling of logical inference and reasoning. Here again, this goes beyond what TK!Solver was originally designed for. This is but one example of many innovative applications to come when TK!Solver is s-t-r-e-t-c-h-e-d in the desired direction.

12

TK!Solver and Other Programs and Languages

TK!Solver is a world in itself, but it is also part of a large family of software products and problem-solving tools available to the users of personal computers. Many of TK!Solver's features are unique and allow the user to control the problem-solving process better than any other tool available. Yet TK!Solver is not equally good for all classes of problems, and there are some problems that it is not designed to handle at all. Hence we need

- To compare TK!Solver with other computing techniques in order to choose the correct one for the problem at hand.
- To mutually augment the capabilities of TK!Solver and other computer programs and languages through interfacing.

TK!SOLVER VS. BASIC AND SPREADSHEETS

The *TK!SATN* journal published by Software Arts Products Corp. for TK!Solver users contained in its premier issue (Spring 1983) an article entitled "What's the Difference?" which addressed the question of the competitive standing of BASIC (representing procedural languages), VisiCalc (representing spreadsheets), and TK!Solver. The authors showed that each of these three approaches has strong points and weaknesses which come out differently depending on the nature of the problem. The authors of the article used a car loan payment problem and they did a convincing job of comparing the three programs. The conclusion states that "The TK!Solver program, a spreadsheet program, and BASIC are each useful tools for solving the original loan example" and it mentions notable differences that show up when the original problem is to be modified. The article goes on to state:

> Because of their tabular input/output format, spreadsheet programs are good for problems that are best structured as, well, spreadsheets. If you have columns of values, each column related to others in your problem, a spreadsheet may be your best bet. If you can set up your problem comfortably in one or two columns, however, a spreadsheet is probably not the most appropriate tool.
>
> If the problem you want to solve typically involves the same input variables and you usually want to solve for the same unknown variables (say, profits given sales and costs, or tax given filing status and income), a spreadsheet may be the most efficient way to go. But if you then want to look at your problem from a different perspective (say find sales necessary to produce a given profit given certain costs), you have to begin redesigning and editing your spreadsheet model. With TK!Solver you can solve for any variable you choose.

Comparing BASIC with TK!Solver or with a spreadsheet program, we should note that using a procedural programming language like BASIC requires that a significant amount of time be invested in learning syntax and usage technicalities. Writing a BASIC program takes longer than setting up a VisiCalc template or a TK!Solver model. However, a BASIC program can perform calculations very quickly, especially when it is compiled into object code. Therefore a BASIC program may be the most useful approach if the same problem is to be solved over and over again. With BASIC, most of the programming effort usually goes into the design of the user-computer dialogue and input/output segments. With a spreadsheet program or with TK!Solver, this is taken care of automatically and these programs also have the additional advantages of professionally designed scrolling and other useful features and a command structure common for a variety of applications. These advantages, in turn, imply limited flexibility, whereas in BASIC we can tailor the input/output and the solving process according to the peculiarities of a particular application.

The *TK!SATN* article points out that TK!Solver lets us focus on the problem itself—not on how the problem is going to be solved. Solving the problem with TK!Solver is straightforward: it takes little time to set up the model and to formulate the problem. It will solve for multiple values or use iteration effortlessly. We can easily alter our perspective on the problem and proceed smoothly when the solution of one problem triggers a new one with different assumptions.

As we have seen, TK!Solver offers a fairly comprehensive problem-solving environment with a rich collection of tools and utilities including total care of input/output operations, formats, and file management in a standard way. This alone may justify using TK!Solver for tasks for which only a few of its other features are utilized. The previous chapters explained, summarized, and exemplified many good reasons and many good ways of using TK!Solver as a viable and advantageous alternative to other problem-solving techniques.

The authors of this book had many opportunities to compare BASIC with TK!Solver during their own use of TK!Solver and during the writing of this book. More often than not a whole book of BASIC programs, formulas, and empirical data or a substantial part of it could be covered by a few TK!Solver models.

In the next two sections we will share the experience of building a single TK!Solver model in place of one or more programs in BASIC. BASIC was chosen for the comparison as it is the most popular language in the world of personal computers. However, the same could be done with FORTRAN, Pascal, and others.

This TK!Solver versus BASIC discussion would not be complete without mentioning the potential role of TK!Solver in the development of dedicated programs and packages written in BASIC or other procedural languages. These programs are frequently based on mathematical models and assumptions that are quite costly to develop, test, and debug because of the rigors of these languages, their I/O conventions, and so on. We have seen several times how TK!Solver stepped in as a testing bed or prototyping board, serving to sort out the mathematics and to test the model prior to coding. In this way TK!Solver saves the programmer a considerable amount of time and effort.

The comparison of TK!Solver with spreadsheets or newer integrated software systems like 1-2-3, VisiOn, or Apple's Lisa is problematic. Spreadsheets concentrate on the information formatting and perception aspects of the human-computer interface. When it comes to the problem-solving process, however, spreadsheets have to be told the exact and rigid sequence of operations, not unlike programming in BASIC or other procedural programming languages. In fact, in some cases using a spreadsheet may present more problems than programming in BASIC.

Suppose we are interested in investment analysis based on the formula linking the total value *T* after *Y* years, initial investment *P*, and the nominal interest *i*. This could be expressed by the formula

$$T = P\ (1+i)^N$$

and we would like to be able to input any three of these four variables and let the computer calculate and display the value of the fourth. Using TK!Solver, we just type in the rule **T=P*(1+i)^N** and the computer is ready to solve problems for any unknown. Using BASIC, we would first have to express each of the four variables explicitly in terms of the other three (a trivial process in this particular case). We then would have to sandwich the four essential assignment statements between dozens of other statements that read in different sets of input data and that transfer control to the appropriate assignment statement for the evaluation of the answer. This is possible but not easy. It may be even harder to build this kind of "universal problem solver" within the framework of current spreadsheet programs: we would have to devise a rather elaborate and hard-to-use scheme, and the reason for using a spreadsheet would be lost.

It should be possible to devise a spreadsheet with Direct and Iterative Solvers and with other TK!Solver features or to include a spreadsheet feature in TK!Solver (although this evolutionary step has not yet been taken). Later in this chapter we will see how TK!Solver and spreadsheet programs can interface via the Data Interchange Format (DIF).

Eight in One

If you have a copy of the book *Some Common BASIC Programs* by Lon Poole and Mary Borchers (Osborne/McGraw-Hill, 3rd edition, 1979), try and decide as an exercise which problems in the book can easily be formulated in terms of TK!Solver models, which can be formulated with a bit of thought, and which cannot be formulated at all. Don't try linear programming since that definitely belongs to the "cannot" group. The Multiple Linear Regression program is an example from the middle group. We will look in detail at the following eight programs in the easy-to-convert group:

1. Future Value of Regular Deposits (Annuity)
2. Regular Deposits
3. Regular Withdrawals From an Investment
4. Minimum Investment for Withdrawals

5. Principal on a Loan
6. Regular Payment on a Loan
7. Term of Loan
8. Annual Interest Rate on a Loan

Future Value of Regular Deposits (Annuity)

The first of these programs calculates the future value when equal deposits of a known amount are made regularly over a period of time. The program is based on the following formula:

$$T = R\,\frac{(1 + i/N)^{NY} - 1}{i/N} \tag{12-1}$$

where

T = total value after Y years
R = amount of regular deposits
N = number of deposits per year
Y = number of years
i = nominal interest rate.

The BASIC program with a sample run is shown in Figure 12-1. (The program extends the formula by allowing the input of the time period as years and months.)

Figure 12-2 shows the equivalent TK!Solver model. The problem solved in the Variable Sheet is the same as the one in the sample run. Only a single rule is necessary, as the Rule Sheet shows. In addition to the *years* and *months* in the BASIC program, we also incorporated *days* and used the sum $Y+M+D$ in place of "number of years" Y. The Calculation Units for all three time variables had to be specified as years. Then the conversion factors for years to months and years to days were established in the Unit Sheet and the Display Units for M and D changed to months and days, respectively.

Also defined in the Unit Sheet is the conversion from decimal fraction to percent (%). In conformity with the formula (and the rule in Figure 12-2), the Calculation Unit for the interest rate i had to be specified as a decimal fraction first and then changed to the more commonly used percent (%) for the Display Unit. Strictly speaking, ratios defined in terms of decimal fractions or percentages are dimensionless, so considering "percent" to be a unit of measurement is questionable. However, there is no reason why the TK!Solver's Unit Conversion feature should not be used for

```
 10 PRINT "FUTURE VALUE OF REGULAR DEPOSITS (ANNUITY)"
 20 PRINT
 30 REM - STATEMENTS 30 TO 100 REQUEST USER INPUT
 40 INPUT R
 50 PRINT "NOMINAL INTEREST RATE";
 60 INPUT I
 70 PRINT "NUMBER OF DEPOSITS PER YEAR";
 80 INPUT N
 90 PRINT "NUMBER OF YEARS, MONTHS";
100 INPUT YO,M
104 REM - CALCULATE YEARS FROM YEARS AND MONTHS
105 Y=(12*YO+M)/12
108 REM - CALCULATE INTEREST RATE PER DEPOSIT
109 REM - CONVERT FROM PERCENT TO DECIMAL
110 I=I/N/100
119 REM - CALCULATE FUTURE VALUE BY FORMULA
120 T=R*((1+I)^(N*Y)-1)/I
129 REM - ROUND OFF TO NEAREST CENT, PRINT
130 PRINT "FUTURE VALLE = $"; INT(T*100+.5)/100
139 REM - PRINT BLANK LINE TO SEPARATE DATA FROM QUESTION
140 PRINT
149 REM - RESTART OR END PROGRAM? USER INPUT REQUESTED
150 PRINT "MORE DATA? (1=YES, 0=NO)";
160 INPUT X
170 IF X=1 THEN 20
180 END

:RUN
FUTURE VALUE OF REGULAR DEPOSITS ANNUITY

AMOUNT OF REGULAR DEPOS:T?  50
NOMINAL INTEREST RATE?  5
NUMBER OF DEPOSITS PER YEAR?  12
NUMBER OF YEARS, MONTHS?  10,5
FUTURE VALUE = $ 8179.31

MORE DATA?  (1=YES, 0=NC)?  0

END PROGRAM
```

Figure 12-1.
BASIC program for evaluation of annuities (from Poole and Borchers, *Some Common BASIC Programs*)

conversions between percent and decimal fraction. As for the unit name of the latter, the TK!Solver literature and TK!SolverPacks flourish with a wide variety of names (including a cumbersome construct %_as_decimal). We will use (see the Unit Sheet in Figure 12-2) the unit name "1" for "unity" which is the simplest and most fitting choice. (We are saying, in essence, that 30 months is equivalent to 2.5 years and 14% is equivalent to 0.14 1's.)

Regular Deposits

Next is a program that calculates the amount required as a regular deposit in order to accrue a certain amount in a specified time period. The

```
==================== VARIABLE SHEET ==================================...
St Input     Name     Output      Unit        Comment
-- -----     ----     ------      ----        -------
             T        8179.3120 $             future value
   50        R                  $             amount of regular deposit
   5         i                  %             nominal interest rate
   12        N                                number of deposits/year
   10        Y                  years         number of years
   5         M                  months        number of months
   0         D                  days          number of days

==================== RULE SHEET ======================================...
S Rule
- ----
* T = R*((1+i/N)^(N*(Y+M+D))-1)/(i/N)

==================== UNIT SHEET ======================================...
From       To        Multiply By  Add Offset
----       --        -----------  ----------
1          %         100
years      months    12
years      days      365
```

Figure 12-2.
TK!Solver model supplanting the modified BASIC program

formula is as follows:

$$R = T\frac{i/N}{(1 + i/N)^{NY} - 1} \tag{12-2}$$

To deal with the problem, Poole and Borchers introduce a separate BASIC program of about the same length and structure as the one shown in Figure 12-1. This second program accepts input values for future value, interest rate, number of deposits per year, and number of years (and months), and calculates the amount of regular deposits. With TK!Solver, we can use the same model as we used in Figure 12-2 to calculate the amount of the deposit: we need only reset the variable values by typing /**RVY**, type in the input values of *T,i,N,Y,M,D,* press the Action key !, and read the resulting output value of *R*.

Regular Withdrawals From an Investment

The third BASIC program calculates the maximum amount that may be withdrawn regularly from an investment over a period of time, according to the following formula:

$$R = P\left(\frac{i/N}{(1 + i/N)^{NY} - 1} + \frac{i}{N}\right) \tag{12-3}$$

where

R = amount of regular withdrawal
P = initial investment
i = nominal rate of interest
N = number of withdrawals per year
Y = number of years.

When looking at this formula, we discover that there is only a small difference between this formula and the previous one for calculating the regular deposit (just an added expression i/N in the right-hand side). A simple modification of the original model in Figure 12-2 yields the new model in Figure 12-3, which covers the first two programs as well as this one. The modification consists of taking i/N out of the brackets, introducing the case key K, replacing variables T (the first two programs) and P (the last program) by a single variable V, and rearranging the Variable Sheet. We have to assign the case key K "0" for solving problems of the first two types and "1" for problems of the last type.

Minimum Investment for Withdrawals

The fourth program of Poole and Borchers calculates the minimum investment required to allow regular withdrawals over a specified time period according to the following formula:

$$P = \frac{RN}{i}\left(1 - \frac{i/N}{(1 + i/N)^{NY}}\right) \tag{12-4}$$

```
==================== VARIABLE SHEET ==========================================
St Input      Name    Output     Unit       Comment
-- -----      ----    ------     ----       -------
   9.5        i                  %          nominal interest rate
   4          N                             number of deposits or
                                            withdrawals per year
   10         Y                  years      number of years
   6          M                  months     number of months
   0          D                  days       number of days

   1          K                                       c a s e   k e y
                                                 K = 0             K = 1
                                            ----------------------------------
              R       303.09124  $          regular deposit ! regular withdrawal
   8000       V                  $          future value    ! initial investment

=================== RULE SHEET ===============================================
S Rule
- ----
* R = V * (1/((1+i/N)^(N*(Y+M+D))-1) + K) * (i/N)
```

Figure 12-3.
TK!Solver model in Figure 12-2 generalized to include regular withdrawals from an investment

Principal on a Loan

The fifth program calculates the initial amount borrowed (which depends on the interest rate), the amount of regular payments, the number of payments per year, and the term of the loan. The formula to be used is equivalent to formula 12-4, but P stands for the principal instead of the initial investment, and R and N apply to payments rather than withdrawals.

Regular Payment on a Loan

Similarly, the formula

$$R = \frac{i\ P/N}{1 - (i/N + 1)^{-NY}} \qquad (12\text{-}5)$$

used by the sixth program to calculate the amount required as regular payments in order to repay a loan over a specified time period is equivalent to formula 12-3, which is used to calculate regular withdrawals from an investment.

Needless to say, all the problems that can be solved using formulas 12-4, 12-5, and 12-6 are automatically included in the TK!Solver model in Figure 12-3.

Term of Loan

The TK!Solver model in Figure 12-3 can also be used to calculate the period of time needed to repay the loan. For this calculation, Poole and Borchers introduced their seventh program, which is based on the following formula:

$$Y = -\frac{\log\,(1 - (Pi/NR))}{\log\,(1 + (i/N))}\ \frac{1}{\mathrm{N}} \qquad (12\text{-}6)$$

Figure 12-4 shows the solution of the model for the term of payment Y (note the amended Comment field in the figure reflecting the variety of situations and variables the model can be used for).

TK!Solver returns the unknown term in years. The rule in Figure 12-3 cannot split the term automatically into years, months, and days (although it is possible to assign $Y=11$ to input, solve for M, assign its rounded-off value as input, and solve for D). This chore and also the inconvenience of having to assign zeros to M and D when only years are given may be alleviated by modifying the model as shown in the Rule Sheet in Figure 12-5.

```
==================== VARIABLE SHEET ============================================
St Input       Name     Output      Unit       Comment
-- -----       ----     ------      ----       -------
   14          i                    %          nominal interest rate
   12          N                               number of deposits, withdrawals
                                               or payments per year
               Y        11.416088 years        number of years
   0           M                    months     number of months
   0           D                    days       number of days

                                                        c a s e   k e y
   1           K                                    K = 0            K = 1
                                               ----------------------------------
   146.59      R                    $          regular deposit | regular withdrawal
                                                               | or regular payment
   10000       V                    $          future value    | initial investment
                                                               | or loan principal
```

Figure 12-4.
TK!Solver model in Figure 12-3 used for calculation of the term of loan (modified comments reflect its usage in place of all eight BASIC programs)

```
==================== VARIABLE SHEET ============================================
St Input       Name     Output      Unit       Comment
-- -----       ----     ------      ----       -------
   14          i                    %          nominal interest rate
   12          N                               number of deposits, withdrawals
                                               or payments per year
               Y        11          years      number of years
               M        4           months     number of months
               D        30.205319   days       number of days

                                                        c a s e   k e y
   1           K                                    K = 0            K = 1
                                               ----------------------------------
   146.59      R                    $          regular deposit | regular withdrawal
                                                               | or regular payment
   10000       V                    $          future value    | initial investment
                                                               | or loan principal

               t        11.416088              term
               u        0                      problem set-up indicator

==================== RULE SHEET ================================================
S Rule
- ----
* R = V * (1/((1+i/N)^(N*t)-1) + K) * (i/N)

* t = Y + M + D
* Y = int(t)
* M = int((t-Y)*12)/12

* u = given('R,'V,'N,'i,0,1)
* 0/u+     Y = given('Y,Y,0)
* 0/u+     M = given('M,M,0)
* 0/u+     D = given('D,D,0)
```

Figure 12-5.
TK!Solver model in Figure 12-4 modified for calculation of the term in *Y,M,D* components and for assigning default values of zero, if necessary

First, the $Y+M+D$ expression in the first rule is replaced by an auxiliary variable t, which is defined in the second rule. The next two rules truncate Y and M down to whole numbers.

Second, the right-hand side expressions of the last three rules assign default values of zero to Y,M,and D if they are not assigned input values. However, such an assignment would preclude the evaluation of the unknown term of loan, investment, or annuity.

In order to reconcile this contradiction, we introduce another auxiliary variable u and define it using the *given* function so that $u=0$ when all the other variables have input values (that is, when the term is unknown) and $u=1$ otherwise. The "if" construct is then used in the last three rules so that they are in operation and assign default zeros only when the term is known.

The difference between the Y, M, and D values in Figure 12-4 and in the Variable Sheet in Figure 12-5 shows the effect of the model modification. The auxiliary variables t and u may be deleted from the Variable Sheet.

Annual Interest Rate on a Loan

Poole's and Borchers' eighth BASIC program calculates the rate of interest when the following are given: the amount of the loan, the amount of the regular payments, the number of payments per year, and the term of the loan. This program is longer and more complicated than the previous programs. The reason is that the structure of the mathematical relationship does not allow the interest rate i to be expressed explicitly in terms of the other variables. So Poole and Borchers take an initial guess for the interest rate $i=10\%$. Their program evaluates an approximate value of R using formula 12-5 and compares it with the given one. If the difference is bigger than one cent, the program modifies the value of i and repeats the cycle until eventually there is a match, at which point the program prints the resulting i. Sound familiar? It is an iteration process, which in TK!Solver is taken care of by the Iterative Solver.

With TK!Solver, we can invoke iteration for unknown i simply by assigning i a guess value (provided the rest of the variables have input values) and pressing the Action key !. Alternatively (and appropriate to this application), we can use the Automatic Iteration feature. For this purpose, we check the Global Sheet to make sure that the Automatic Iteration option is set to YES and we assign, let us say, **10** as the First Guess value on the Variable Subsheet for i. Once this is done, whenever all variables but i are assigned input values, TK!Solver automatically picks up

```
==================== VARIABLE SHEET ==========================================
St Input      Name    Output      Unit      Comment
-- -----      ----    ------      ----      -------
              i       14.000486 %           nominal interest rate
   12         N                             number of deposits, withdrawals
                                            or payments per year
   11         Y                   years     number of years
   5          M                   months    number of months
              D       0           days      number of days

                                                  c a s e    k e y
   1          K                                K = 0          K = 1
                                            ----------------------------------
   146.59     R                   $         regular deposit ! regular withdrawal
                                                            ! or regular payment
   10000      V                   $         future value    ! initial investment
                                                            ! or loan principal
```

Figure 12-6.
The result of iterating for unknown rate of interest i

the guess $i=10$ and iterates for the correct value of i. Figure 12-6 shows the solution of a problem for data similar to those in Figures 12-4 and 12-5.

It would not be difficult to amend the TK!Solver model further and to make it a substitute for two more of the BASIC programs as well. They are the Last Payment on a Loan and the Remaining Balance on a Loan, and this would make our exercise "Ten in One"—ten different programs in BASIC covered by a single TK!Solver model.

INTERFACING THROUGH DIF

DIF is a Data Interchange Format created by Software Arts that allows data transfer between programs using a particular data storage format. When the same data has to be used in different programs or the data generated by one program is to be used in another, this format presents an ideal alternative to reentering the entire data. Using DIF can save a lot of time, labor, and frustration.

As mentioned previously, TK!Solver, VisiCalc, and BASIC each have their own merits and limitations. The DIF format is a vehicle for moving data from one program to the other in order to get the best of all three worlds. The data generated by List Solving in TK!Solver may be used by a graphics program written in BASIC. Or it can be used in an application program like VisiPlot to generate graphs for presentation purposes. The cash flow data from a VisiCalc template can be used in TK!Solver for calculating the Internal Rate of Return (IRR) using the Iterative Solver.

Using DIF in TK!Solver

We create DIF files using the DIF (#) option of the Storage command /S. It is possible to save more than one list in a DIF file. The cursor should be positioned in the row containing the name of the first list to be saved when the Storage command is invoked. Figure 12-7 shows the List Sheet with the names of the lists used in Chapter 6 in the section "User-Defined Functions," where Linear Interpolation was discussed. These lists can be saved as a DIF file and then plotted with VisiPlot.

With the cursor highlighting the list name *xsin*, we invoke the Storage command by typing /S. In response to the Storage command prompt, we then choose the DIF option by typing #. A new prompt "DIF Storage: S L" is displayed in the Prompt/Error line. Since the lists have to be stored, we choose the Save option by typing **S**. This brings up the prompt "DIF Save: Point to last list (1n)" shown in the figure. The "1n", as you may recall, is the Pointer Indicator. We can specify the destination row using any of the Cursor Movement commands or their combinations. Note that when the DIF option is used, the destination row has to be below the initial cursor position. This is unlike other commands such as Blank, where pointing can be done in any direction.

The Down Arrow key is used to move the cursor to the last row and then the Enter key is pressed. A prompt for the filename "DIF Save: Filename' appears. We enter the filename **example** and press the Enter key. TK!Solver appends the extension ".DIF" to the specified filename when a DIF file is being stored.

Units in a DIF File

As seen in Figure 12-7, the Storage Unit for x and *xsin* in the lists is *rad*, while the Display Unit is *deg*. In the saved DIF file, the values of x

```
(1n) Name:xsin
DIF Save: Point to last list (1n)
=================== LIST SHEET ================================...
Name        Elements   Unit       Comment
----        --------   ----       -------
xsin        5          deg        arguments (storage unit is rad)
ysin        5                     function value
x           21         deg        x values (storage unit is rad)
y           21                    y = sin(x)
yfun        21                    interpolated y values
yerr        21                    y - yfun  (interpolation error)
```

Figure 12-7.
List Sheet with prompt for last list to be saved in DIF file

and *xsin* are stored in the Storage Unit *rad*. Other programs reading or writing DIF files have to treat the data accordingly. The Storage and Display Unit names are also stored in the file. When we use the DIF Load Option /S#L to load this file back into TK!Solver, the values of *x* and *xsin* will be displayed in the Display Unit provided a conversion between *rad* and *deg* exists in the Unit Sheet. If a conversion has not been specified, the values displayed will be incorrect.

Generating a Plot Using VisiPlot

We will take the *x* and *yerr* lists from the DIF file *example* and use VisiPlot to produce a graph of *x* versus *yerr*. VisiPlot treats each of the lists in the file as a "series." The data points in a series are assumed to have a "periodicity," that is, they are assumed to occur at a certain frequency. Thus, if a series contains monthly sales data beginning from January 1982, the periodicity is said to be 12 (for monthly), the "major start" is 1982, and the "minor start" is 1 (since January is the first month). VisiPlot terminology reflects the fact that VisiPlot is well oriented for business graphics. It can be used for drawing different kinds of graphs: line, bar, hi-lo, pie, area, and xy.

When the VisiPlot program is up and running, we choose the Load option from the VisiPlot menu and select the file *example* for loading. The name of the first list *xsin* is displayed and the prompt for the periodicity appears. Since we are only interested in displaying an xy plot, we just press the Enter key in response to this prompt and to the prompts for the major and minor starts for all the lists. Since the TK!Solver Storage Unit of *x* is radians, the values of *x* in VisiPlot are in radians.

Once the file is loaded, we choose the Plot option from the VisiPlot main menu. This displays the Plot menu. For drawing the xy graph, we select the xy option and specify the *x* list as the X-axis values and *yerr* as the Y-axis values. We display the plot using the Plot command (see Figure 12-8). The Options command can be used to display a title at the top of the graph. The screen image can be printed or it can also be saved as a file and used later.

The graph in Figure 12-8 gives a better picture of the "interpolation error" as a function of *x* than the graph in Figure 6-29. Note that here the Y-axis also has a label.

VisiPlot can use the data generated by List Solving in TK!Solver to display bar graphs, pie charts, and so forth for presentation purposes. Users can also take advantage of the color graphics capabilities of VisiPlot.

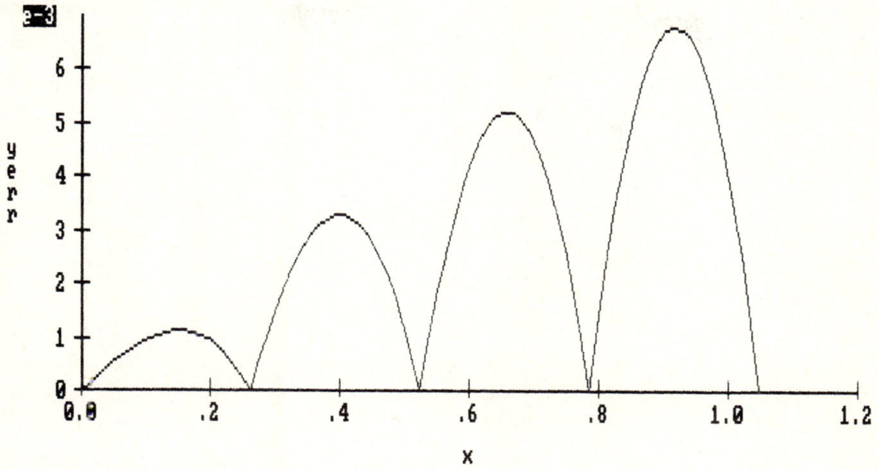

Figure 12-8.
Plot generated by VisiPlot using the lists in the DIF file *example* (note that the lists *x*, *y*, *yfun*, and *yerr* each contain 81 points)

Using DIF for Data Entry

When a large amount of data is to be used in a BASIC program, the program should permit the user to correct entries, to make additions and modifications of the data easily, and to store the data in a file so that the necessity of reentering the same data will be avoided. This means that a part of the programmer's time and effort has to be diverted to these I/O aspects of the program. TK!Solver's ability to save data in the DIF format provides a simple alternative.

In TK!Solver the data can be entered in a List Subsheet and saved as a DIF file. This provides the ease of editing, adding, deleting, and storing data that goes with TK!Solver. A BASIC program to read the values in the DIF file can be used as a subroutine in the main program. Also the data generated by the BASIC program can be saved in the DIF format so that it can be used by TK!Solver, VisiCalc, or other programs. Thus the DIF option serves as an excellent data-entry interface to programs in BASIC and other languages.

Using Data From Experiments

User-defined functions in TK!Solver can be used to express empiric relationships between variables, as was described in Chapter 6. If the acquired data is stored in the DIF format, you can load it directly into TK!Solver and avoid manual entry of the data when you are defining the argument and function values. For example, the load and extension data obtained from a testing instrument may be stored by the data acquisition program in DIF format, loaded directly in TK!Solver, and used as a data base for calculations involving load-deformation characteristics.

Using the Data From TK!Solver In a BASIC Program

Data generated by List Solving in TK!Solver (for example, profit figures from the sale of various products or production figures over a certain period) may require sorting before the information can be appreciated. There is no sort function in TK!Solver. However, the data can be stored in a DIF file and processed by a sorting program written in BASIC or other languages, and then, if necessary, returned to TK!Solver through another DIF file.

INTERFACING WITH WORD PROCESSING

After developing and using a model for solving problems, we often need to write a report explaining the model and the calculation results. The report generally includes the model and the results in the form of different TK!Solver sheets, tables, and plots. One way to produce such a report is to print the different sheets on the printer using the TK!Solver Print command (/P) and to insert the different pages at the appropriate places or to cut and paste the information in the text. However, when a word processing program is used to generate a report, the print file feature in TK!Solver can be employed advantageously to incorporate the necessary information automatically in the right places in the text.

We examine how this process works using WordStar, the word processing program from MicroPro International. The discussion is based on the WordStar program which runs on the IBM PC under MS-DOS. TK!Solver runs under this operating system and produces DOS files. The authors used the print file feature extensively when writing this book using WordStar.

Generating a Print File in TK!Solver

The Printer Device or Filename field in the Global Sheet is used for generating the print file. The default setting in this field is PRN (for Printer), and when the Print command (/P) is used to print the contents of any sheet, the output goes to the printer. This default setting should be changed to the name of the print file to be written. If the destination diskette is not in the default drive, the drive designator must precede the filename. When the Print command is issued, the output is automatically sent to the diskette. TK!Solver appends an extension to the filename. This extension is computer-specific and for the IBM PC it is ".prf." However, it is not possible to load a print file back into TK!Solver. When an attempt is made, TK!Solver beeps, displays the message "Invalid storage file", and terminates the command.

Let's consider the Rule Sheet shown in Figure 12-9. To save this as a print file under the name *test* on drive *B*, we must change the default entry in the Printer Device or Filename field on the Global Sheet to **B:test**. The cursor is moved back to the first rule field in the Rule Sheet. We then invoke the Print command by typing **/P**. After we point to the last line and press the Enter key, the disk drive turns and the specified lines are written on the diskette under the name *test.prf*. As the file is being written, the contents are displayed on the screen.

Whenever information is to be stored as a new print file, a new name has to be specified in the Global Sheet. Otherwise, the contents of the file whose name appears in this field are overwritten by the new one. Unlike the Storage command, TK!Solver does not seek confirmation before overwriting an existing file.

```
==================== RULE SHEET ==============================================
S Rule
- ----
  " To generate a Print File do the following:

  "    Enter the filename in Printer Device or Filename field on Global Sheet
  "    Change the settings in Page Breaks ON and Page Numbers ON fields to NO
  "    With the cursor in the first row to be printed type /P
  "    Point to the last line using the Cursor Movement Commands
  "    When the cursor is in the destination row press the Enter Key

  " The Print File has the extension .PRF appended to it.

  "       In fact, this is how this figure was generated  !!!
```

Figure 12-9.
Rule Sheet to be written to a print file

Normally, when we are using the printer, the Page Breaks On and Page Number On fields are set to YES so that after the contents are printed, the paper is advanced until the end of the page. If these two fields are set to YES and the Print command is used to generate a print file, blank lines are stored on the diskette until the end of the page is reached. To avoid this, the Page Breaks On field should be set to NO. (When Page Breaks On is set to NO, the setting in the Page Number On field is ignored.)

Using the Print File in WordStar

We bring the report into which the TK!Solver print file is to be incorporated into the WordStar editor by pressing **D** (for Document). Then we move the cursor to the position where the print file is to be inserted. The WordStar command Control-KR is used to insert a file from the disk into the file being edited. When the filename is specified in response to the WordStar prompt, the file is read into the report. We must also specify the extension added by TK!Solver while specifying the filename. Thus to load the print file *test* created earlier, we would type **test.prf** in response to the file-name prompt.

A line of carets (^) and at-signs (@) appears as the last line of the inserted file. This line is an end-of-file mark in TK!Solver. We can delete it by moving the cursor to that line and pressing Control-Y, the line delete command in WordStar. In a similar manner, we can incorporate the different print files that go into the report in their appropriate places. The complete report can then be saved with any of the WordStar Save commands Control-KS, Control-KD, or Control-KX.

Sometimes when a file is inserted on a page containing text, the file may be too long to fit the available line space and it will be split. To avoid this, we can use the WordStar conditional page command, .CP <number>. The <number> is an integer specifying the number of lines that should remain on the page. If there is no room on the page for the specified number of lines, a new page is started. The command is useful to avoid breaking up tables and graphs.

Using WordStar to Edit a TK!Solver Sheet

We may want to include in the report just the rules without the Status fields or just the variable names and their values (input and output) instead of the entire sheet. Since we cannot choose the required fields when using the Print command in TK!Solver, the editing commands in

WordStar can be used to delete the unwanted information. The block column feature in WordStar is especially useful for deleting rectangular blocks of information. For example, we can delete with one command the Status fields of all the rules or the Comment fields of all the variables. We turn on this mode by typing Control-KN; this is a toggle command, so executing the command again turns the mode off (the default). To specify the beginning of the block we type Control-KB and the end by typing Control-KK. The marked block is then deleted by typing Control-KY.

If we want to edit the print file we can bring it by itself into the WordStar editor by typing the D (for document) or the N (for non-document) command.

TK!SOLVER MODELS AND BASIC

The DIF format allows us to transfer data between TK!Solver and other programs. However, this data transfer is limited to values stored as lists. It is not possible to store the contents of other sheets such as the Variable Sheet in DIF format for use in other programs. Likewise, the DIF format cannot be used to load data into the Variable Sheet.

But there may be occasions when you need to do just that—to use the information from different sheets in other programs or vice versa. (The previous section showed how to use TK!Solver print files with word-processing programs.) In order to use the TK!Solver model for purposes outside TK!Solver, you have to save the model using the /SS command. TK!Solver writes the contents into the so-called storage file. TK!Solver storage files are standard ASCII text files and so can be read as text by other programs.

Likewise, information from other sources can be brought into TK!Solver in the form of ASCII text files that conform to the TK!Solver storage format. Thus, you could create TK!Solver models without having TK!Solver! In this section, we will look at two BASIC programs—one for reading TK!Solver models and the other for creating them. Note that these programs have been included specifically for illustration purposes and have no error checks built into them.

Reading a TK!Solver Model

Figure 12-10 shows the BASIC program for reading a TK!Solver model file. The program prompts for the filename and adds the ".tk" extension, if

```
10 REM  ***  Program to read and display the
20 REM  ***   contents of a TK!Solver file
30 CLS
40 DIM A$(1000)
50 REM  *** Get the nane of the TK file to be read
60 INPUT "Name of file to be read"; F$
70 REM  *** Add the extension .tk if necessary
80 IF RIGHT$(F$,3) <> ".tk" THEN F$ = F$ + ".tk"
90 N=1
100 OPEN F$ FOR INPUT AS #1
110 REM  *** If end of file is reached then exit
120 IF EOF(1) THEN GOTO 170
130 REM  *** Read the file and echo on screen
140 INPUT #1, A$(N)
150 PRINT A$(N)
160 N = N + 1 : GOTO 120
170 CLOSE #1: END
```

Figure 12-10.
BASIC program for reading TK!Solver storage files

necessary. The contents are read and stored in the array A$ so that they can be used for specific purposes. The contents are also echoed on the screen. To print it on a printer, you would have to modify line 150. If the printer were attached to an IBM PC, you would change the PRINT command in line 150 to LPRINT.

Model Listing

Figure 12-11 shows a partial listing of the model ELECMOD generated by the BASIC program (recall Chapter 2, Figures 2-14 through 2-19). The listing has been annotated. The first line in the figure identifies the file as a TK!Solver storage file. The second line is the familiar "=v" (Select the Variable Sheet command) and signifies that the lines that follow belong to the Variable Sheet. The "#1" in the next line refers to the first row of the Variable Sheet. The colon (:) in ":n" is the Goto command, while the letter n stands for the Name field. This is followed by the variable name *I* and then ":v" which means go to the Value field, and so on.

As you examine the figure, you will realize that it is made up of a sequence of instructions that TK!Solver uses to recreate the model when you use the /SL command to load the model. Of course, this sequence was created when you saved the model in the first place.

The figure shows that the Variable Sheet is followed by the Unit Sheet. You can use the program to print out the entire contents. You can also modify the program to select information from specific portions of the model, depending on your needs.

```
TK!1                    * TK!Solver file identifier
=v                      * Select Variable Sheet
#1                      * First row of Variable Sheet
:n                      * Goto Name field
I                       *   Name of first variable
:v                      * Goto Value field
167.36401674            *   Value of first variable
:s                      * Goto Status field
o                       *   Variable is an Output variable
:u                      * Goto Unit field
amp                     *   Calculation Unit is amp
:d                      * Assign Display Unit
amp                     *   Display unit is amp
:c                      * Goto Comment field
current                 *   Comment for first variable
#2                      * Second row of Variable Sheet
:n                      * Goto Name field
V                       *   Name of second variable
:v                      * Goto Value field
20                      *   Value of second variable
:s                      * Goto Status field
i                       *   Variable is an Input variable
.                       .
.                       .
.                       .
.                       .
#11                     * Eleventh row of Variable Sheet
:n                      * Goto Name field
d                       *   Name of eleventh variable
:v                      * Goto Value field
.001                    *   Value of eleventh variable
:s                      * Goto Status field
i                       *   Variable is an Input variable
:u                      * Goto Unit field
m                       *   Calculation unit is m
:d                      * Assign Display Unit
cm                      *   Display Unit is cm
.                       .
.                       .
.                       .
=u                      * Select Unit Sheet
#1                      * First row of Unit Sheet
:f                      * Goto From field
hour                    *   Unit name in From field
:m                      * Goto Multiply By field
60                      *   Conversion factor is 60
:t                      * Goto To field
min                     *   Unit name in To field
#2                      * Second row of Unit Sheet
.                       .
.                       .
.                       .
.                       .
```

Figure 12-11.
Partial annotated listing of the model ELECMOD generated by the BASIC program in Figure 12-10

Creating Models

In order to create a model outside TK!Solver, you will have to establish a sequence of instructions that TK!Solver can follow to load the contents.

```
10 REM  *** Program to create a TK!Solver Variable Sheet
20 REM  ***        from the information provided
30 CLS
40 DIM N$(50),NA$(50),VA(50),ST$(50),CU$(50),DU$(50),CO$(50),LI$(50)
50 INPUT "Name of file to be written: "; F$
60 IF RIGHT$(F$,3) <> ".tk" THEN F$ = F$ + ".tk"
70 INPUT "Number of variables = "; N
80 REM  *** Get the information for each of the variables
90 FOR I = 1 TO N
100 N$(I)=RIGHT$(STR$(I),LEN(STR$(I))-1)
110 PRINT
120 PRINT "Enter the following for variable #" I
130 INPUT "Name: "; NA$(I)
140 INPUT "Value: "; VA(I)
150 INPUT "Status (i, o, g): "; ST$(I)
160 INPUT "Calculation Unit: "; CU$(I)
170 INPUT "Display Unit: "; DU$(I)
180 INPUT "Comment: "; CO$(I)
190 INPUT "Associated Listname: "; LI$(I)
200 PRINT
210 NEXT I
220 REM  *** Write the info into a file
230 OPEN F$ FOR APPEND AS #1
240 PRINT#1,"TK!1"
250 PRINT#1,"=v"
260 FOR I = 1 TO N
270 PRINT#1, CHR$(35)+N$(I)
280 PRINT#1,":n" : PRINT#1,NA$(I)
290 PRINT#1,":v" : PRINT#1,VA(I)
300 PRINT#1,":s" : PRINT#1,ST$(I)
310 IF CU$(I) = "" GOTO 340
320 PRINT#1,":u" : PRINT#1,CU$(I)
330 PRINT#1,":d" : PRINT#1,DU$(I)
340 PRINT#1,":c" : PRINT#1,CO$(I)
350 IF LI$(I) = "" GOTO 370
360 PRINT#1,":a" : PRINT#1, LI$(I)
370 NEXT I
380 CLOSE #1:END
```

Figure 12-12.
BASIC program for creating a TK!Solver Variable Sheet

Figure 12-12 shows the listing of a BASIC program for creating a Variable Sheet.

Line 40 declares arrays to store the information associated with the variables. The array size 50 is chosen arbitrarily. Line 50 prompts for the filename, while 70 gets the number of variables. In the FOR/NEXT loop in lines 90-210, information about each variable is obtained and stored in the appropriate array.

Line 240 is for the TK!Solver file identifier, while line 250 specifies a Variable Sheet. The FOR/NEXT loop in lines 250-360 writes the given information into the file. The Enter key should be pressed if there is no information for a particular prompt. For example, if no list is associated with a variable, then in response to the "Associated Listname:" prompt, you should press the Enter key.

In this manner, you can write similar programs to create other sheets and entire models that you can subsequently load into TK!Solver.

13

Case Studies: Mathematics

In TK!Solver applications, the mathematical, computational, and subject-matter aspects are intertwined. The problems discussed in this chapter represent a selection of mathematical building blocks that can be used alone or as parts of other models. Some of the topics like quadratic equations and elements of a triangle emphasize the flexibility of problem formulations typical of TK!Solver. Other topics (definite integrals and linear differential equations) extend TK!Solver's mathematical capabilities. Still others (kissing circles and optimization) take advantage of the ease with which TK!Solver solves sets of simultaneous non-linear equations.

QUADRATIC EQUATION (GENERALIZED MODEL)

Usually the coefficients a, b, and c of a quadratic equation are given and we want to find the roots (we have to evaluate the discriminant first in order to proceed with the evaluation of real or complex roots). This is how the model "Miscellaneous Tricks" built in Chapter 11 works (see Figure 11-14).

The quadratic equation and its solution may also be looked at as a relationship between six variables, $a,b,c,d,x1,x2$ in the case of real roots and

a,b,c,d,xi,xr in the case of complex roots. Looking at the model this TK!Solver-way, we may want to have the model resolvable for any combination of values of three input variables out of the six. However, the Direct Solver cannot solve the model in Figure 11-14 for certain input combinations. In the case of real roots, all three coefficients, or at least a and b, have to be known in order for the Direct Solver to do anything; if only a and b are known, the root indicator k=1 has to be input as well.

Clearly we need some redundant equations. Adding the equations for the real roots $x1$ and $x2$ yields

$$x1 + x2 = -b/a$$

Similarly, by multiplying the equations for the real roots and simplifying, we obtain another equation:

$$x1*x2 = c/a$$

Dividing the first equation by the second, we get

$$1/x1 + 1/x2 = -b/c$$

In fact, when these three equations are added to the model, the rule for $x2$ in Figure 11-14a can be deleted. We don't need to make these rules conditional in order to make them applicable to real cases only. Unless $x1$ or $x2$ is known, they will remain untouched anyway.

The backsolvability of the original model when there are complex roots is also limited. A redundant equation can be derived from the equations for d, xr, and xi. Substituting for d from the first rule in the equation for xi, we have

$$xi = sqrt((k-1) * (b\hat{}2 - 4*a*c))/(2*a)$$

Substituting for a in this equation from xr=$-b/(2*a)$ we get

$$xi\hat{}2/xr = (k-1) * (xr + 2*c/b)$$

The new Rule Sheet and the Variable Sheets with two sample solutions are shown in Figure 13-1a-c. Using the Generalized Quadratic Equation model, the Direct Solver can now handle any of the 39 combinations of three input variables out of $a,b,c,x1,x2$ or a,b,c,xr,xi.

The last rule on the Rule Sheet automatically evaluates the root indicator k whenever $x1$, $x2$, xr, or xi is assigned input values. This is important because if any of these is given, then less than the full contingent of the coefficients a, b, and c is available to evaluate the discriminant d from the first rule; this, in turn, blocks the evaluation of k from the second rule (unless d happens to be assigned an input value), and without k the solution cannot move ahead. A flowchart representation of the work of the "multiple given" rule for k is shown in Figure 13-2.

```
=================== RULE SHEET ==============================================
S Rule
- ----
*               d = b^2 - 4*a*c                   " discriminant
*               k = step(d,0)                     " check for complex root

* 0/k +        x1 = (-b + sqrt(k*d)) / (2*a)      " first real root
*         x1 + x2 = -b/a                          " second real root
*         x1 * x2 = c/a                           " redundant equation
*     1/x1 + 1/x2 = -b/c                          " redundant equation

* 0/(k-1) +    xr = -b / (2*a)                    " real part of complex root
* 0/(k-1) +    xi = sqrt((k-1)*d) / (2*a)         " imag part of complex root
*            xi^2 = (k-1) * xr * (xr + 2*c/b)     " redundant equation

* k = given('x1,1,given('x2,1,given('xr,0,given('xi,0,k))))
```

a. Rule Sheet

```
=================== VARIABLE SHEET ==========================================
St Input    Name    Output     Unit    Comment
-- -----    ----    ------     ----    -------
   1        a                          )  parameters of quadratic
            b       5                  )  equation in general form
   4        c                          )  a*x^2 + b*x + c = 0
            d       9                  discriminant
            x1      -1                 first real root
   -4       x2                         second real root
            xr                         real part of complex root
            xi                         imag part of complex root
            k       1                  root indicator
```

b. Variable Sheet with solution for real roots

```
=================== VARIABLE SHEET ==========================================
St Input    Name    Output     Unit    Comment
-- -----    ----    ------     ----    -------
   1        a                          )  parameters of quadratic
            b       -2                 )  equation in general form
            c       4                  )  a*x^2 + b*x + c = 0
   -12      d                          discriminant
            x1                         first real root
            x2                         second real root
   1        xr                         real part of complex root
            xi      1.7320508          imag part of complex root
            k       0                  root indicator
```

c. Variable Sheet with solution for complex roots

Figure 13-1.
Generalized Quadratic Equation Model

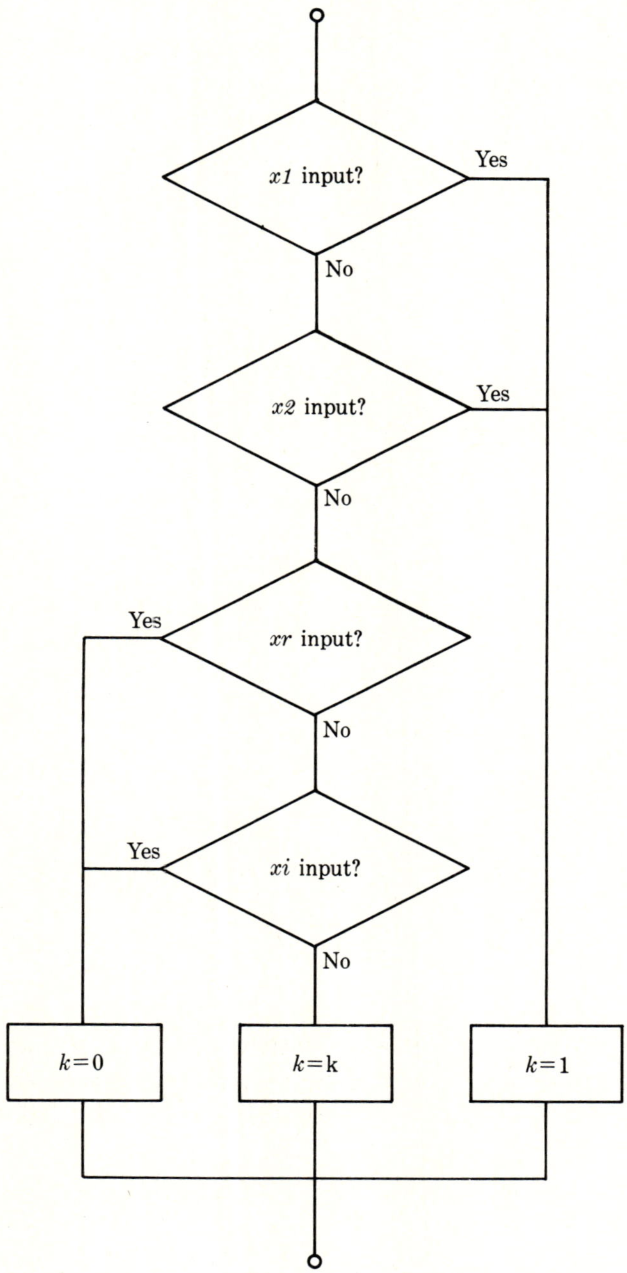

Figure 13-2.
Flowchart for the multiple use of the *given* function in the last rule in Figure 13-1

CUBIC EQUATION

The cubic equation $x\wedge 3-9*x+4=0$ served us well in Chapter 9 to introduce and demonstrate the Iterative Solver. Iteration is the usual way of solving cubic and higher order polynomial equations. However, sometimes we want to find out whether a cubic equation has three real roots or one real and two imaginary roots and get their solution at once. Fortunately, there are explicit formulas for solving cubic equations, and we can build a model that will use the Direct Solver to solve these equations—at the expense of increasing the model complexity.

The Rule Sheet and Variable Sheet of a "cubic equation solver" are shown in Figure 13-3*a* and *b*. The first group of rules evaluates the auxiliary variables—the parameters r, s, and t of an equivalent cubic equation in the so-called normal form and the parameters p and q of a cubic equation in the so-called reduced form. This first group also includes formulas for the radicand R and the root indicator k. If $R \leq 0$, then $k=0$ and there are three real solutions, two of which may be equal. If $R>0$, then $k=1$, and there are one real and two complex roots. The next two groups of rules apply to either of these two situations depending on the value of the root indicator k. Vieta's trigonometric substitutions are used for evaluating three real roots. Cardano's formulas are used for the evaluation of one real root and the real and imaginary parts of the complex roots:

$$x2 = re + i.im \quad \text{and} \quad x3 = re - i.im$$

where $i=\sqrt{-1}$.

The last rule on the Rule Sheet assigns a default value $r=0$ when parameters p and q are assigned input values, that is, when we want to solve a cubic equation given in reduced form.

The model may be used for solving for all roots of cubic equations with the Direct Solver when the parameters of general form, normal form, or reduced form are known. However, the backsolvability is limited. It is possible to build a generalized cubic equation solver that would accept any combination of four independent parameters and roots and solve for the rest of the model—not unlike the previously discussed generalized quadratic equation solver (this modification is left to you).

ELEMENTS OF A TRIANGLE

In science and engineering we frequently encounter problems involving the evaluation of unknown elements of a triangle. There are three independent equations relating six elements or variables (three sides and three

```
==================== RULE SHEET ===========================================
S Rule
- ----
* r = b/a
* s = c/a
* t = d/a
* p = s - r^2/3
* q = 2*r^3/27 - r*s/3 + t
* R = (p/3)^3 + (q/2)^2
* k = step(R,0)

* 0/(k-1)+    w^2 = abs(p/3)                  "
*        cos(phi) = (q/2)/w^3                 "     three
*       x1 + r/3 = -2*w*cos(phi/3)            "     real
*       x2 + r/3 = 2*w*cos((pi()-phi)/3)      "     roots
*       x3 + r/3 = 2*w*cos((pi()+phi)/3)      "

* 0/k+         u^3 = -q/2 + sqrt(abs(R))      "
* 0/k+         v^3 = -q/2 - sqrt(abs(R))      "     one real
*       x1 + r/3 = u + v                      "     and two
* 0/k+          re = -(x1+r)/2                "     complex
*               im = (u-v)*sqrt(3/4)          "     roots

* r = given('p,'q,0,r)      "default r=0 when p or q is given
```

a. Rule Sheet

```
==================== VARIABLE SHEET =======================================
St Input      Name    Output     Unit      Comment
-- -----      ----    ------     ----      -------
              x1      -3.201472            1st real root
              x2      2.7465682            2nd real root
              x3      .45490409            3rd real root
              re                           real part of complex root
              im                           imag part of complex root

              a                            parameters of general form
              b                            of the cubic equation
              c                            a*x^3 + b*x^2 + c*x + d = 0
              d

              r       0                    parameters of
              s       -9                   normal form
              t       4                    x^3 + r*x^2 + s*x + t = 0

   -9         p                            parameters of reduced form
   4          q                            y^3 + p*y + q = 0 ,  y=x-r/3

              R       -23                  radicand
              w       1.7320508            Vieta     )
              phi     1.1756967             -"-      )  auxiliary
              u                            Cardano   )  parameters
              v                             - " -    )

              k       0                    Solution indicator:
                                           k=0 for 3 real roots,
                                           k=1 for 1 real and 2 complex
```

b. Variable Sheet with three real roots evaluated

Figure 13-3.
The Cubic Equation Solver

angles; see Figure 13-4). This means that given the values of three elements out of six, we should be able to evaluate the remaining three.

The Rule Sheet in Figure 13-5 shows one possible choice of three independent equations. The fact that the variables b and c appear twice in the second equation (cosine theorem) means that it cannot be solved directly for unknowns b or c. An unpleasant consequence of the distribution of the variables in the rules is that the Direct Solver may yield a full solution for only two sets of input variables (a,b,c and $b,c,[\alpha]$) out of 19, as follows:

$a\ b\ c$ $\quad$ $a\ c\ \alpha$ $\quad$ $a\ \alpha\ \gamma$ $\quad$ $b\ c\ \gamma$ $\quad$ $c\ \alpha\ \beta$
$a\ b\ \alpha$ $\quad$ $a\ c\ \beta$ $\quad$ $a\ \beta\ \gamma$ $\quad$ $b\ \alpha\ \beta$ $\quad$ $c\ \alpha\ \gamma$
$a\ b\ \beta$ $\quad$ $a\ c\ \gamma$ $\quad$ $b\ c\ \alpha$ $\quad$ $b\ \alpha\ \gamma$ $\quad$ $c\ \beta\ \gamma$
$a\ b\ \gamma$ $\quad$ $a\ \alpha\ \beta$ $\quad$ $b\ c\ \beta$ $\quad$ $b\ \beta\ \gamma$

(There are actually 20 combinations of three elements out of six; one combination—$\alpha\ \beta\ \gamma$—is missing from this list because the values of

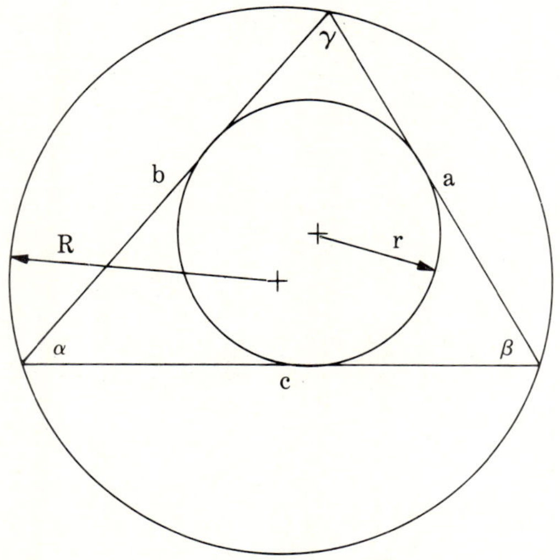

Figure 13-4.
Elements of triangle

three angles are related by the first rule and would not constitute a set of independent input values.)

For 11 combinations, the Direct Solver yields partial solutions (for instance, if *a*, *b*, and α are given, only β and γ can be evaluated). To get the complete solution for all three variables in all cases except the two previously mentioned, we must use the Iterative Solver.

The inconvenience of using the Iterative Solver may be avoided if we add three redundant equations: two other versions of the cosine theorem and an additional relationship following from the sine theorem as shown on the Rule Sheet in Figure 13-6. TK!Solver, working with this model, finds a complete solution for any of the 19 combinations of input variables using the Direct Solver.

The model shown in Figure 13-6 may have problems with ambiguous input information. For instance, there are two possible solutions for given

```
==================== RULE SHEET ================================...
S Rule
- ----
* alpha + beta + gamma = pi()              " sum of angles = pi
* a^2 = b^2 + c^2 - 2*b*c*cos(alpha)       " cosine theorem
* a/sin(alpha) = b/sin(beta)               " sine theorem
```

Figure 13-5.
Three-rule triangle model

```
==================== VARIABLE SHEET ================================...
St Input      Name      Output      Unit       Comment
-- -----      ----      ------      ----       -------
   3          a                                length of side a
   4          b                                length of side b
              c         3.8284271              length of side c
   45         alpha                 deg        angle opposite to side a
              beta      70.528779   deg        angle opposite to side b
              gamma     64.471221   deg        angle opposite to side c

==================== RULE SHEET ====================================...
S Rule
- ----
* alpha + beta + gamma = pi()
* a^2 = b^2 + c^2 - 2*b*c*cos(alpha)
* b^2 = c^2 + a^2 - 2*c*a*cos(beta)
* c^2 = a^2 + b^2 - 2*a*b*cos(gamma)
* a/sin(alpha) = b/sin(beta)
* b/sin(beta) = c/sin(gamma)
```

Figure 13-6.
Six-rule triangle model

$a=3$, $b=4$, and $\alpha=45$: one for an acute triangle with $c=3.83$, $\beta=70.53$, and $\gamma=64.47$ (see the Variable Sheet in Figure 13-6), and another for an obtuse triangle with $c=1.83$, $\beta=109.5$, and $\gamma=25.5$ (see Figure 13-7).

TK!Solver routinely returns the value for an acute triangle because when it evaluates β from the sine theorem, it takes the principal value of the arcsin of $sin(\alpha)*b/a$ (or 0.9428), which is 70.53 degrees, and it ignores the fact that arcsin(0.9428)=109.5 degrees is also true. Curiously, TK!Solver may obtain the latter solution from the simple three-rule model shown in Figure 13-5 by iterating from guesses, say, $c=2$ and $\gamma=20$. In the six-rule model, the redundant equations prevent the iteration and the only way to obtain the alternative solution with $\gamma=109.5$ is to modify the right-hand side expression in the fifth rule to read $b/sin(pi()-beta)$.

We may further enhance the triangle model by incorporating into it the triangle perimeter P and area A and radii r and R of the inscribed and circumscribed circles. The Rule Sheet of the complete model is shown in Figure 13-8; seven out of the 14 rules are independent and seven are

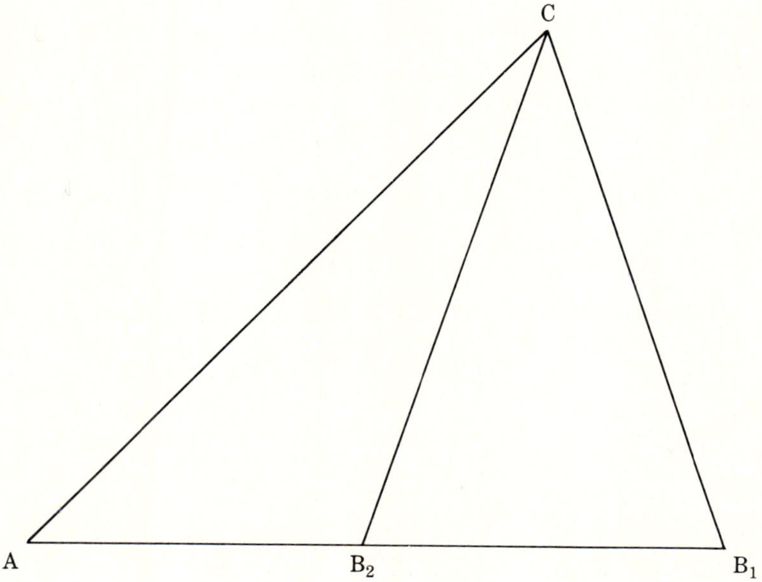

Figure 13-7.
Acute (AB_1C) and obtuse (AB_2C) triangles

```
=================== RULE SHEET =======...
S Rule
- ----
* alpha + beta + gamma = pi()
* a^2 = b^2 + c^2 - 2*b*c*cos(alpha)
* b^2 = c^2 + a^2 - 2*c*a*cos(beta)
* c^2 = a^2 + b^2 - 2*a*b*cos(gamma)
* a/sin(alpha) = b/sin(beta)
* b/sin(beta) = c/sin(gamma)
* P = a + b + c
* 2*A = a*b*sin(gamma)
* 2*A = b*c*sin(alpha)
* 2*A = c*a*sin(beta)
* 2*A = P*r
* 2*R = a/sin(alpha)
* 2*R = b/sin(beta)
* 2*R = c/sin(gamma)
```

Figure 13-8.
Enhanced triangle model Rule Sheet

redundant. The Variable Sheet is seen in Figure 13-9. It shows the solution of the triangle in Figure 13-4. The Unit Conversion feature is applied only to the angles because the arguments of the trigonometric functions have to be defined in radians (hence the Calculation Units are radians), but the degrees as Display Units are more convenient to work with.

There are 120 different combinations of three elements out of seven, but a triangle may be defined only in 115 different ways (in addition to the previously mentioned three angles, there are other variable triplets that are not independent, such as A,P,r or R,a,A, and so on). In addition to the

```
=================== VARIABLE SHEET ==================================...
St Input      Name     Output      Unit        Comment
-- -----      ----     ------      ----        -------
              a        14.908327               length of side a
              b        17.320508               length of side b
   19         c                                length of side c
              alpha    48.194872   deg         angle opposite to side a
   60         beta                 deg         angle opposite to side b
              gamma    71.805128   deg         angle opposite to side c
              P        51.228835               perimeter
              A        122.6544C               area
   10         R                                radius of escribed circle
              r        4.7884908               radius of inscribed circle
```

Figure 13-9.
Enhanced triangle model Variable Sheet (the solution represents the triangle in Figure 13-4)

19 combinations mentioned, the following 24 combinations of input variables lead to complete solution by the Direct Solver:

1. Any two sides and R or A or P (9 cases).
2. Any side and adjacent angle and R or A (12 cases).
3. Any two angles and R (3 cases).

The remaining 72 require the use of the Iterative Solver.

The model shown in Figure 13-8 works without a hitch for acute triangles; it works fine for obtuse triangles too, but only if an obtuse angle is defined as an input value or evaluated from one of the first four rules (for instance, when all the sides a,b,c or two of the angles α,β,γ are given). If the input information implies an obtuse triangle and an obtuse angle is supposed to be evaluated from the value of its sine, TK!Solver returns an incorrect value for the acute angle and detects an inconsistency in one of the first four rules. We can see this happen, for instance, if we try to solve the model with input values $a=5$, $b=2$, and $\gamma=50$. The Direct Solver "blows up." If we try again with input value $\alpha=107.58532018$ instead of γ, the Direct Solver solves the problem and returns $\gamma=50$ (we calculated α for the original problem using the six-rule model, which evaluated correct α from the cosine theorem).

Solving fancy triangle problems with the Iterative Solver may also not always be a straightforward procedure. The arguments of an implied arcsin function may easily slip beyond 1 during the iteration process, and in that case, the solution is terminated due to argument error. As an example let's find the elements of a triangle with angle $\gamma=75$ degrees and radii of described and inscribed circles 10 and 4. In order to identify feasible guesses, we try the Direct Solver with input values $a=17$, $b=13$, and $\gamma=75$. The solution shows $R=9.6$ and $r=4.4$, which are not far from the required 10 and 4. So we make $a=17$ a guess, remove b from input, assign to input $R=10$ and $r=4$, and attempt an iteration. TK!Solver makes one iteration step and stops during the second indicating "ASIN: argument error" in the rule $2*R=a/sin(alpha)$.

One way to solve the problem at hand is to introduce a new variable and rule $Rr=R/r$, assign input value $Rr=2.5$, remove R and r from input, keep inputs $b=13$ and $\gamma=75$, and start iterating from guess $a=17$ as before. We obtain a solution in three iteration steps with $R=12.23$ and $r=4.892$. These values differ from the original assignment, but they are in correct proportion. In order to get "our" triangle, we just scale down the solution by doing the following: we move one of the calculated angles to input, remove b from input, assign to input $R=10$, delete Rr (which we

```
==================== VARIABLE SHEET ===================================...
St Input      Name     Output     Unit        Comment
-- -----      ----     ------     ----        -------
              a        19.115601              length of side a
              b        10.628718              length of side b
              c        19.318517              length of side c
   72.897474  alpha               deg         angle opposite to side a
              beta     32.102526  deg         angle opposite to side b
   75         gamma               deg         angle opposite to side c
              P        49.062836              perimeter
              A        98.125672              area
   10         R                               radius of escribed circle
              r        4                      radius of inscribed circle
```

Figure 13-10.
TK!Solver feat: solution of triangle for given *gamma*=75, *R*=10, *r*=4

don't need anymore), and solve again. Figure 13-10 shows the final solution of the problem.

We may easily modify the triangle models to include isosceles triangles by adding the rules $a=b$, or for equilateral triangles by adding $a=b$ and $b=c$. The number of required input variables reduces to 2 and 1 respectively.

THE CIRCLE

The circle is a beautiful figure and easy to work with if we stay in the domain of geometry and use compasses, rulers, and sharp pencils for solving such problems as constructing tangents, packing circles, dividing them, and so on. Unfortunately, this is not always possible, convenient, or accurate enough, in which case we must work with numbers. Let's examine two problems that are far from trivial when it comes to that.

Tangents to a Circle

Given a circle of radius r with center at $x0$, $y0$, we want to find the coordinates x, y of the touching point of a tangent to the circle from the point xp, yp outside the circle. A "quick and dirty" way of doing it is shown in Figure 13-11. We type into the Rule Sheet the equation of a circle, the equation of the normal passing through the desired point (here the gradient or slope m comes into the game), and the equation of the tangent that must be perpendicular to the normal (hence the slope $-1/m$) and pass through xp, yp and x, y.

```
==================== VARIABLE SHEET =====================
St Input      Name     Output      Unit
-- -----      ----     ------      ----
              x        2.7637079
   2          x0
              y        3.6455619
   3          y0
   1          r
              m        .84529946
   1          yp
   5          xp
```

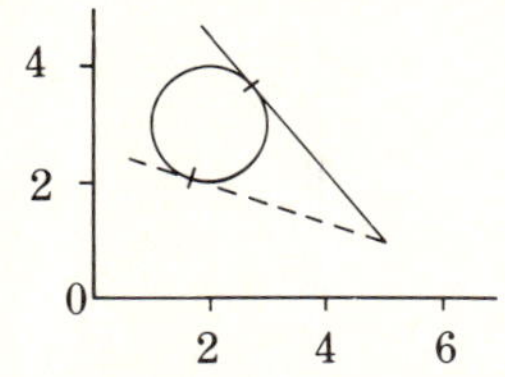


```
==================== RULE SHEET =========================
S Rule
- ----
* (x-x0)^2 + (y-y0)^2 = r^2       " equation of circle with center at x0,y0
* m = (y-y0)/(x-x0)               " gradient of normal at  contact point
* (y-yp)/(x-xp) = -1/m            " gradient of tangent from point xp,yp
```

Figure 13-11.
Fast solution for tangent to a circle

We end up with three simultaneous equations for three unknowns x, y, and m that can only be solved by the Iterative Solver after we make either x or y a guess and assign an initial guess value. One such solution is shown in the Variable Sheet in Figure 13-11. Curiously, it was not possible to obtain the other tangent (see the sketch) regardless of the guess value of x or y. The reason is that the *sqrt* function always returns a positive value; consequently, when the first rule is approached with a guessed value of x or y, it returns y or x from the upper half or the right half of the circle respectively. The Iterative Solver solved for the lower tangent only when both x and y were assigned as guesses with the values 1.5 and 2.1 respectively.

Another problem with this model is that we may guess the x or y from outside their domain. If we guess such x or y that

$$abs(x-x0) > r \quad \text{or} \quad abs(y-y0) > r$$

TK!Solver will attempt to evaluate the square root of a negative argument with a consequent termination of the solution and an error message. Even if the initial guess is satisfactory, the iteration process may slip outside of the domain of x or y, in which case the Iterative Solver dies.

As is often the case, generalizing the problem to take into account all the available knowledge (in this instance the theorems on tangents to a circle) yields models that are more reliable and easier to use. The model in Figure 13-12a and b is a typical example of this approach. Here we generalize the problem to cover common tangents to two circles (a tangent from a point to a circle will then represent a particular case with a radius of one of the circles equal to zero).

In the first part of the model, we define the coordinates of the touching points with respect to the local system of coordinates with axis *x0* passing through the centers of both circles. In the second part of the model, we

```
=================== RULE SHEET ==========================================
S Rule
- ----
* L = sqrt((xc2-xc1)^2 + (yc2-yc1)^2)
* sin(alpha) = (r2 - r1*t)/L
* x10 = -r1*sin(alpha)*t
* y10 = -r1*cos(alpha)*p
* x20 = -r2*sin(alpha) + L
* y20 = -r2*cos(alpha)*p*t

* sinphi = (yc2-yc1)/L
* cosphi = (xc2-xc1)/L
* x1 = xc1 + x10*cosphi - y10*sinphi
* y1 = yc1 + x10*sinphi + y10*cosphi
* x2 = xc1 + x20*cosphi - y20*sinphi
* y2 = yc1 + x20*sinphi + y20*cosphi

* t = ft(type)
* p = fp(place)
```

a. Rule Sheet

```
=================== VARIABLE SHEET =========================================
St Input      Name      Output      Unit      Comment
-- -----      ----      ------      ----      -------
   'ext       type                            type of common tangent ('ext or 'int)
   'high      place                           location  of common tangent with
                                              respect to xc1,yc1 ('low or 'high)
   1          r1                              radius of circle 1
   2          xc1                             x-coord. of center of circle 1
   3          yc1                             y-coord. of center of circle 1

   0          r2                              radius of circle 2
   5          xc2                             x-coord. of center of circle 2
   1          yc2                             y-coord. of center of circle 2

              x1        2.7637079             x-coord. of point on circle 1
              y1        3.6455619             y-coord. of point on circle 1
              x2        5                     x-coord. of point on circle 2
              y2        1                     y-coord. of point on circle 2

              L         3.6055513             distance between xc1,yc1 and xc2,yc2
              alpha     -2810349              angle between  x0-axis and tangent
              x10       .27735010             local x-coordinate of x1,y1
              y10       .96076892             local y-coordinate of x1,y1
              x20       3.6055513             local x-coordinate of x2,y2
              y20       0                     local y-coordinate of x2,y2
              sinphi    -.5547002             sine of coord. transform. angle
              cosphi    .83205029             cosine of coord. transform. angle

              t         1
              p         -1
```

b. Variable Sheet showing the solution of the problem in Figure 13-11

Figure 13-12.
Common tangents to two circles

transform these coordinates into the original global coordinates in which the centers of the circles were defined. The coefficients *t* and *p* determine whether we want an internal or an external tangent and whether the contact point on the first circle should be above or below the center point of that circle. There are a total of four possibilities. The Table Lookup user-defined functions *ft* and *fp* are used to make the choice in "almost" plain English (see the comments for the variables *type* and *place*).

Most important, we do not need to guess and iterate when solving for the unknown coordinates of the contact points; the Direct Solver does the job. The Variable Sheet in Figure 13-12*b* shows the solution of the same problem as in Figure 13-11. In order to obtain a solution for the other tangent, which was hard to get from the simple model, we must change either the *type* from *'ext* to *'int* or the *place* from *'high* to *'low*. Finally, in Figure 13-13*a* and *b* we show an example of all four common tangents to two circles and all four quadruplets of the coordinates of the contact points generated by List Solving (over all combinations of *type* and *place*) and the Table feature.

Kissing Circles

Martin Gardner's *Mathematical Circus* (New York: Alfred A. Knopf, 1979, pp. 32-34) describes the following problem: how can four circles be placed so that each circle touches all the others, with every pair touching at a different point? There are two possible situations: either three circles surround the smallest one, or three circles are inside the largest one. The radii and the coordinates of the centers of the circles and the contact points are naturally interrelated. If we know what the relationships are, we can build a TK!Solver model and then use it to calculate the missing elements.

There is a curious relationship between the four radii which inspired British chemist Frederick Soddy to write a poem quoted by Gardner. We include the second stanza that reveals the relationship together with the relevant rule in the model in Figure 13-14. The term "bend" in the poem stands for "curvature," which is the reciprocal value of the radius. The largest circle, which surrounds the three smaller ones, is considered to be concave with respect to them and to have a negative curvature and radius. The solution in the Variable Sheet gives the radius of a circle embracing a nickel, a dime, and a quarter. Since every variable appears twice in the rule, the Iterative Solver has to be used. The solution to this problem, as well as the solution when the small circle (radius 0.161 cm) is embraced by

Tangent to the circle: coordinates of contact points

case	1	2	3	4
type	ext	int	ext	int
place	low	low	high	high
x1	6.189553528	7.550416027	2.370956026	4.373150852
y1	.6524851983	2.157570617	7.653247286	7.982556772
x2	16.64216515	12.33718798	13.77821702	14.72013686
y2	7.489363899	11.38182204	12.73993546	7.013082421

a. Coordinates of contact points

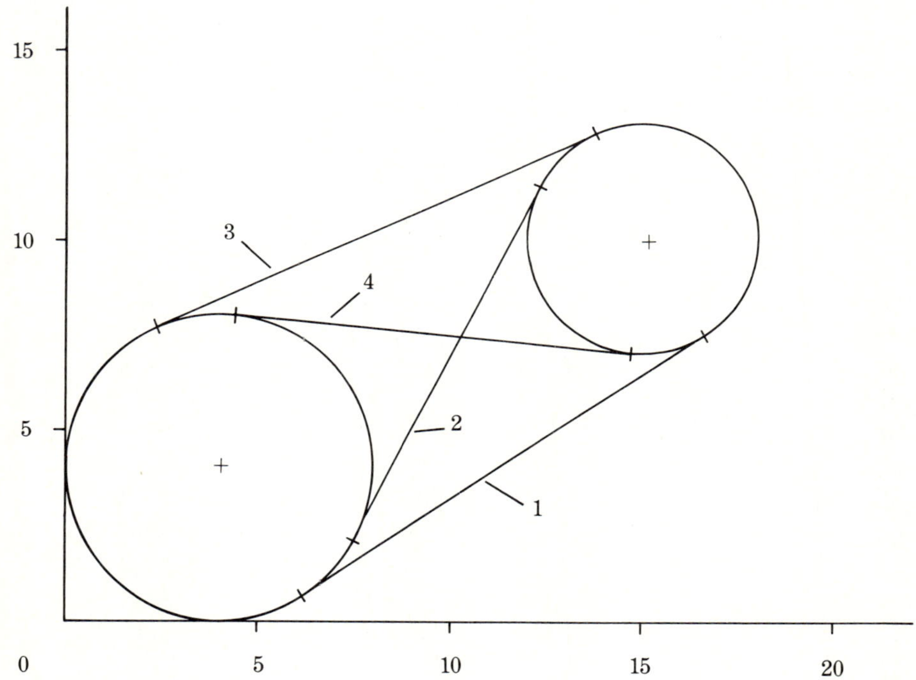

b. Graphical representation

Figure 13-13.
Four cases of common tangents to a circle

the nickel, dime, and quarter, is shown in Figure 13-15.

The condition of two circles that touch each other, with radii r_i and r_j and coordinates of center points x_i, y_i and x_j, y_j, may be written as follows:

$$(x_i - x_j)^2 + (y_i - y_j)^2 = (r_i + r_j)^2$$

```
==================== VARIABLE SHEET =========================================
St Input       Name     Output       Unit       Comment
-- -----       ----     ------       ----       -------
   1.21        r1                    cm         Four circles to the kissing come.
   .89         r2                    cm         The smaller are the benter.
   1.065       r3                    cm         The bend is just the inverse of
               r4       -2.307285    cm         The distance from the center.
                                                Though their intrigue left Euclid dumb
                                                There's now no need for rule of thumb.

==================== RULE SHEET =============================================
S Rule
- ----
  "   Since zero bend's a dead straight line
  "   And concave bends have minus sign,
  "   >>> The sum of the squares of all four bends <<<
  "   >>> Is half the square of their sum.         <<<

* 2*(1/r1^2 + 1/r2^2 + 1/r3^2 + 1/r4^2) = (1/r1 + 1/r2 + 1/r3 +1/r4)^2

  " (From "The Kiss Precise" by Frederick Soddy, Nature, Vol. 137, p.1021)
```

Figure 13-14.
Four kissing circles, model with Soddy's Formula

The Rule Sheet of a model for four touching circles, based on this condition, is shown in Figure 13-16. The first three rules establish the mutual position of the first three circles. The last three rules determine the position of the fourth embracing or embraced circle. All the equations are independent (the relationship between the circle radii from Figure 13-14 could be added as a redundant rule). Six out of twelve variables have to be known in order to solve for the remaining six. We must use the Iterative Solver because of the simultaneity of the equations. Typically, we have to guess the values of three variables in order to obtain a complete solution. The model works reasonably well for a variety of combinations of input variables. However, we must be careful to avoid attempting to take a square root of a negative argument at the beginning or in the process of iteration (this is not unlike the problems with the first model of tangents to a circle in Figure 13-11).

Figure 13-17 shows the Variable Sheet with a solution of the "nickel-dime-quarter" problem when the smaller fourth circle is inside the three. The solution looks odd with only three values in the Output field. Here is how to arrive at it: we assign the radii and choose the origin of the coordinates to go through the center of the quarter by assigning $x1=y1=0$. Then we place the dime on the X-axis next to the quarter by assigning $y2=0$; when we press the Action key !, the Direct Solver returns $x2=2.1$. Next we place the nickel so that it touches both the quarter and the dime; we have to guess $x3$ ($r1=1.21$ is a good starting point) and the Iterative Solver returns the final values of $x3$ and $y3$.

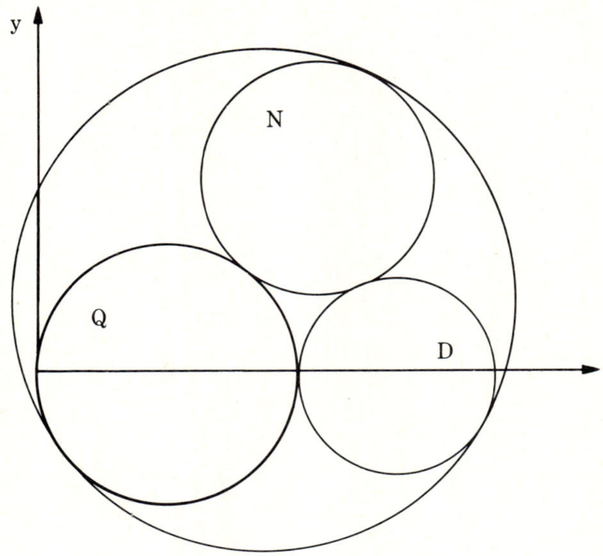

a. Large circle embracing nickel, dime, and quarter

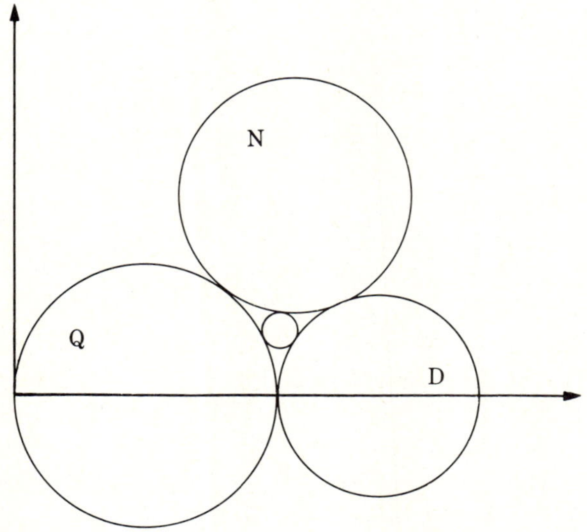

b. Small circle embraced by nickel dime, and quarter

Figure 13-15.
Two arrangements for kissing circles

```
==================== RULE SHEET ======...
S Rule
- ----
* (x2-x1)^2 + (y2-y1)^2 = (r1+r2)^2
* (x3-x2)^2 + (y3-y2)^2 = (r2+r3)^2
* (x1-x3)^2 + (y1-y3)^2 = (r1+r3)^2

* (x4-x1)^2 + (y4-y1)^2 = (r4+r1)^2
* (x4-x2)^2 + (y4-y2)^2 = (r4+r2)^2
* (x4-x3)^2 + (y4-y3)^2 = (r4+r3)^2
```

Figure 13-16.
Rule Sheet for kissing circles

```
==================== VARIABLE SHEET ====================================...
St Input     Name   Output      Unit    Comment
-- -----     ----   ------      ----    -------
   1.21      r1                         radius          FIRST
   0         x1                         ) center        CIRCLE
   0         y1                         ) coordinates

   .89       r2                         radius          SECOND
   2.1       x2                         ) center        CIRCLE
   0         y2                         ) coordinates

   1.065     r3                         radius          THIRD
   1.3722857 x3                         ) center        CIRCLE
   1.8145129 y3                         ) coordinates

             r4     .16099359           radius          CIRCLE
             x4     1.2345324           ) center        TOUCHING
             y4     .59628288           ) coordinates   ALL THREE
```

Figure 13-17.
Variable Sheet with solution for Figure 13-15*b*

In order to speed up the complete solution including the elements of the fourth circle, we transfer the evaluated *x2*, *x3*, and *y3* from the Output to the Input field, that is, we fix the position of the dime and the nickel. It is then sufficient to assign only two guesses, *r4*=0.1 and *x4*=1.21(=*r1*). This secures a quick convergence to the final solution shown in Figure 13-17. (Some early versions of TK!Solver converge to the correct final solution in this case and then display an "Inconsistency" message; the cancellation of the guess status of *r4* and *x4*, the transfer of the value of *y4* from output to input, and an error-free solving with the Direct Solver prove the correctness of the results.)

The model in Figures 13-16 and 13-17 does not cover the coordinates x_{ij}, y_{ij} of the touching points of circles i and j. There are several ways to formulate relevant equations, some of which fit the TK!Solver environment better than others. The following ones should work well:

$$\frac{x_j - x_i}{x_{ij} - x_i} = 1 + \frac{r_j}{r_i}$$

and

$$\frac{y_j - y_i}{y_{ij} - y_i} = 1 + \frac{r_j}{r_i}$$

Now you try these yourself.

DIFFERENTIATION

We touched upon the subject of differentiation when we looked at the Newton-Raphson iterative procedure in Chapter 9. There we saw that the Iterative Solver uses approximate values of the derivatives of error terms with respect to guess variables in order to assess the slopes of the error functions around the guess point and to calculate the direction and the size of the next iteration step. With the Iterative Solver, differentiation is performed internally and the differentiation mechanism and results are not directly available to the user.

Sometimes we have a need to characterize the slopes of the functions and to know the values of the first or higher order derivatives of one variable with respect to another (later we will need this in connection with optimization). It is always possible, given the analytical description of the function, to find its derivatives in closed form (unlike integration when some integrals do not exist). Although the rules for differentiation are well-defined, following them in the case of complicated functions may be annoyingly laborious and error-prone.

TK!Solver is not capable of symbolic differentiation in closed form. However, it can not only evaluate the derivatives when their closed form is defined, but it can also be used to approximate numerical differentiation, thus sparing us from the difficulties encountered with symbolic differentiation and from having to type in the derivatives of complicated functions. Suppose we have the following function:

$$y = e^{\tan\sqrt{x}}(3x^2 - 5) \ / \ (x^4 + 2)$$

The rule for evaluating this function is given in Figure 13-18a followed by another five rules expressing the derivative dy/dx, which we arrived at using standard differentiation techniques. The next group of three rules

```
==================== RULE SHEET ====================================================
S Rule
- ----
* y = exp(tan(sqrt(x)))*(3*x^2-5)/(x^4+2)                        " y = f(x)

* u = exp(tan(sqrt(x)))                                          " Symbolic
* v = (3*x^2-5)/(x^4+2)                                          " differentiation
* du%dx = exp(tan(sqrt(x)))/(2*sqrt(x)*cos(sqrt(x))^2)           " using product, chain
* dv%dx = (6*x*(x^4+2)-4*x^3*(3*x^2-5))/(x^4+2)^2                " and quotient rules
* dy%dxS = v*du%dx + u*dv%dx                                     " 1st derivative

* y1 = exp(tan(sqrt(x-dx)))*(3*(x-dx)^2-5)/((x-dx)^4+2)           " Numerical diffe-
* y2 = exp(tan(sqrt(x+dx)))*(3*(x+dx)^2-5)/((x+dx)^4+2)           " rentiation
* dy%dxN = (y2-y1)/(2*dx)                                         " 1st derivative

* d2y%dx2 = (y2-2*y+y1)/dx^2                                      " 2nd derivative
```

a. Rule Sheet

```
===================== VARIABLE SHEET ===============================================
St Input    Name     Output     Unit      Comment
-- -----    ----     ------     ----      -------
L           y        -1.164892
L   1.2     x
L           v        -.1669285
L           u        6.9783873
            dv%dx    2.0507192
            du%dx    15.207790
            dy%dxS   11.772099
    .0001   dx
            dy%dx
            y2       -1.163715
            y1       -1.166069
            dy%dxN   11.772100
            d2y%dx2  20.05
            exper    20.05
```

b. Variable Sheet

Figure 13-18.
Example of symbolic and numerical differentiation

serves to evaluate the derivative based on the following linear approximation formula:

$$f'(x_0) = [f(x_0+h) - f(x_0-h)] / (2h)$$

Generating the necessary rules in TK!Solver is extremely simple: we copy the original rule *y=exp...*, go into the Editor, and modify it by changing *y* to *y1* and subtracting *dx* from *x* wherever the latter appears. Then we copy this rule and edit it again by changing *y1* to *y2* and replacing the minus signs in front of *dx* with plus signs. The third rule is trivial. The approximation is usually very good. For instance, in our case, at x=1.2

and with dx=0.0001 we receive the following:

$$dy/dx_S = 11.77200994264$$
$$dy/dx_N = 11.77200995$$

The value of the increment dx has to be chosen carefully. If it is too small (let's say, equal to or less than the default Comparison Tolerance 1E−6), the effect of the increment on the function value may be lost or distorted and the approximation of dy/dx may go haywire. If the increment is too large, the approximate derivative may no longer represent a tangent to the curve at the point, as it is supposed to, but instead some broadly based secant.

The numerical differentiation technique described here may easily be extended to partial differentiation for functions of two or more independent variables and also to higher order derivatives. The last rule in Figure 13-18*a* serves to approximate the second derivative of our sample function. The Variable Sheet with the results is shown in Figure 13-18*b*.

Differentiation of Polynomials

If we are given the polynomial function

$$y = poly(x,'a)$$

then the symbolic derivative may be represented in TK!Solver as

$$dy\%dx = poly(x,'b)$$

provided that the list *'b* was generated by List Solving using the rule

$$b = a*(count('a)-element())/sgn(count('a)-element())$$

The last rule indeed transforms each coefficient a associated with the ith power term of the polynomial to $i*a$. In order to make the list *'b* one element shorter than the list *'a*, we use the 0/0 bypass to skip the last instance. As a result, we have a true replication of the differentiation formula for polynomials. Once the list *'b* is generated, the last rule may be commented out.

If, for example, we assign the list of coefficients *'a* for a given fourth order polynomial, then TK!Solver generates the list *'b* displayed using the Horizontal Table option as follows:

a	0.15	−0.3	−1.8	1.2	1.5
b	0.6	−0.9	−3.6	1.2	

The graph of the function and its derivative, plotted by the TK!Solver Plot facility, is shown in Figure 13-19.

DEFINITE INTEGRALS

If we are interested in knowing the area under the graph of a parabola $y=a*x\wedge 2+b*x+c$ in the interval between $x1$ and $x2$, we can express this area in terms of a definite integral and write down a rule

$$area = poly(x2,a/3,b/2,c,0) - poly(x1,a/3,b/2,c,0)$$

However, there is a class of functions whose integrals cannot be expressed in closed form in terms of elementary functions and that can only be evaluated numerically. An efficient numerical method for evaluating definite integrals is the so-called Simpson's rule:

$$\int_{x_1}^{x_2} f(x)\,dx \approx \frac{h}{3}\ \{f(x_1) + 4f(x_1 + h) + 2f(x_2 + 2h) + \cdots + 2f[x_1 + (n-2)h] + 4f[x_1 + (n-1)h] + f(x_2)\}$$

where $h=(x2-x1)/n$ and n is the number of intervals (it must be even).

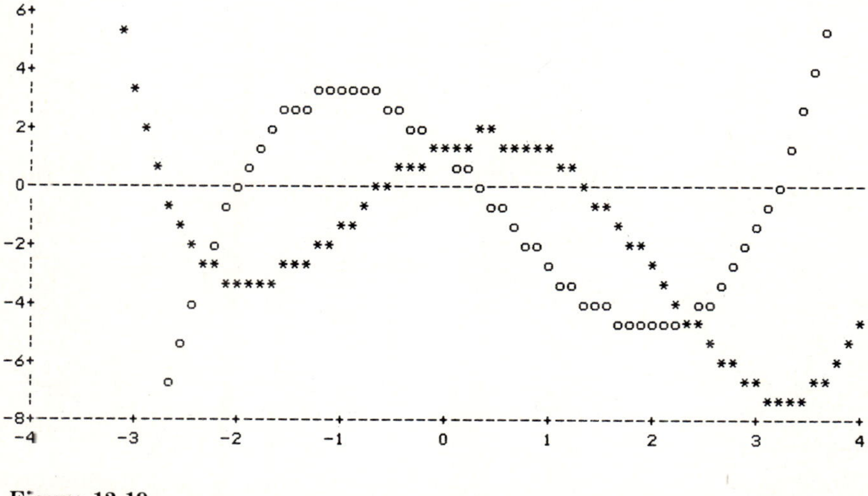

Figure 13-19.
Graph of the function $y=.15*x\wedge 4-.3*x\wedge 3-1.8*x\wedge 2+1.2*x+1.5$ and its derivative $y'=.6*x\wedge 3-.9*x\wedge 2-3.6*x+1.2$ ($*=y$ and $o=y'$)

A "Simpson integrator" may be easily built in the form of a TK!Solver rule as

$$S = (x2-x1)/(3*n)*dot('c,'f)$$

where $'c$ refers to a list of $n+1$ Simpson's coefficients

1 4 2 4 2 .... 2 4 2 4 1

and $'f$ is a list of $n+1$ operands $f(x)$ for x equally spaced between $x1$ and $x2$.

The procedure for evaluating a definite integral is as follows:

1. Select the number of intervals n (the larger the number n, the lesser the difference between the true and approximate values of the integral; $n=10$ usually gives sufficient accuracy).
2. Type in the rule defining the approximate value of the definite integral S.
3. Declare c, x, and f as lists and make the first two inputs.
4. Type in the values of c.
5. Type in or edit a rule defining the integrand in the form of f equals function of x.
6. Assign lower and upper limits $x1$ and $x2$ as input values.
7. Generate a list of x values by diving into the List Subsheet and typing **x1\:11\x2\!y** (\ stands for the Enter key).
8. Generate a list of f by typing **/L!** to List Solve.
9. Solve again by pressing **!**.

The last step may be eliminated if an extra element equal to 0 is added at the end of the list c. This extra element will compensate for the one-instance delay that occurs in evaluating list functions during List Solving (see Chapter 10). Consequently, the final value of the definite integral S will be displayed after Step 8. If you repeat the procedure for different integrands, you may skip the first four steps.

The authors experimented with the evaluation of the definite integral of $sin(x)$ from $x1=0$ through $x2=pi()/2$ with $n=10$. The result of $S=1.0000034$ differed very little from the known correct value 1.

Evaluating the circumference of an ellipse is only one of numerous problems requiring numerical approximations of definite integrals. The equation of an ellipse in parametric form (provided the semi-axes with lengths of a and b lie along the coordinate axes X and Y respectively) are as follows:

$$x = a\ \cos(t) \quad \text{and} \quad y = b\ \sin(t)$$

The length of a quarter-circumference of an ellipse can be expressed with the following formula:

$$\int_{t_1}^{t_2} \sqrt{x'^2 + y'^2}\ dt = \int_0^{\pi/2} \sqrt{a^2\ \sin^2 t + b^2 \cos^2 t}\ dt$$

This integral cannot be taken in closed form. The TK!Solver model for evaluation of the ellipse circumference with the solution for a=2 and b=1 is shown in Figure 13-20. The approximation is very good judging from comparative experiments with n=20 and 50:

n	**S (full precision)**
10	2.4221122897
20	2.4221120552
50	2.4221120553

These results show that the value of S evaluated when n=10 may be considered very close to the true value. It is definitely much better than another approximation rule that produces

$$Length = pi()/4*(3/2*(a+b) - sqrt(a*b)) = 2.423746$$

```
==================== VARIABLE SHEET ========================================
St Input        Name   Output      Unit       Comment
-- -----        ----   ------      ----       -------
   0            x1                            lower limit
   1.5707963    x2                            upper limit
L  0            c                             coefficients in Simpson's formula
L  0            x                             values of independent variable
L               f      1                      function values
                S      2.4221123              approximate value of integral
   2            a
   1            b

==================== RULE SHEET ============================================
S Rule
- ----
   f = sqrt((a*sin(x))^2+(b*cos(x))^2)
   S = (x2-x1)/(3*10)*dot('c,'f)
```

Figure 13-20.
Evaluation of quarter-circumference of an ellipse using Simpson's rule

LINEAR DIFFERENTIAL EQUATIONS

TK!Solver does not solve differential equations either analytically or numerically. However, it can help us obtain and use differential equations. We saw this in Chapter 7 in an example of a non-linear, second-order differential equation of a cable curve. Two types of ordinary linear differential equations are discussed here.

First-Order Inhomogeneous Equations

First-order inhomogeneous equations of the following general form:

$$y' + p(x) + q(x) = 0$$

have the following general solution:

$$y = e^{-P}\,[C - \int q(x)\, e^{P}\, dx]$$

where C is a constant depending on the conditions of a particular problem, and

$$P = \int p(x)\, dx$$

Success in solving differential equations of this type depends on the possibility of taking the indicated integrals. Let's consider a population dynamics problem where the growth y' of the population $y(t)$ is affected not only by the difference between the birth and death rate k, but also by the immigration or emigration rate $r(t)$—the rate at which members of the population are being added or subtracted from the system, that is

$$y' = ky + r(t)$$

If the immigration law is the periodic function

$$r(t) = a\ (1 + sin\ t)$$

we end up with an inhomogeneous differential equation, the solution of which is as follows:

$$y = C\ e^{kt} - \frac{a}{k} - \frac{a\ b}{k^2 + 1}(k\ sin\ t + cos\ t)$$

where C is a constant that can be evaluated after substituting a known population y at a given time t in this equation.

The Rule Sheet with the final equation is shown in Figure 13-21. The Variable Sheet in this figure shows the evaluation of the integration con-

```
==================== VARIABLE SHEET ==========================================
St Input      Name     Output      Unit        Comment
-- -----      ----     ------      ----        -------
   1200       y                                population
   0          t                                time

   -3         k                                diff bet. birth and death rate
   1000       a                                )  constants of immigration law
   1.5        b                                )  r(t) = a*(1+b*sin(t))
              C        1016.6667               integration constant

==================== RULE SHEET ==============================================
S Rule
- ----
  y = C*exp(k*t) - a/k - a*b/(1+k^2)*(k*sin(t)+cos(t))
```

Figure 13-21.
Solution of population dynamics problem

stant C for a particular set of parameters k, a, and b and for the known population $y=1200$ at time $t=0$. Once the value of the integration constant is evaluated, it may be transferred to input; now the model is ready to solve for y given t or vice versa.

Second-Order Homogeneous Equations

Oscillatory phenomena in mechanical, electrical, biological, economic, and other systems may be described by second-order homogeneous equations with constant coefficients:

$$y'' + ay' + by = 0$$

which, in mechanical terms, determine the linear relationship between the acceleration y'', the velocity y', and the displacement y, regardless of the values of the independent variable x. The solution of this equation depends on the roots of the characteristic equation

$$r^2 + ar + b = 0$$

The solution of the differential equation depends on the sign of the discriminant of the characteristic equation. The three different general solutions are given in the Rule Sheet in Figure 13-22. The list of variables with additional explanatory comments is shown in Figure 13-23.

As may be seen from the Rule Sheet, the evaluation of the function $y=f(x)$ and its derivative dy/dx (named $dy\%dx$) is performed by one of three groups of rules depending on the sign of the discriminant d. You may notice that only some of the discriminant-dependent rules were made

```
==================== RULE SHEET ==============================================
S Rule
- ----
  "     *** Second Order Homogeneous Equation  y" + a*y' + b*y = 0 ***

* d = a^2 - 4*b                    " Discriminant of the characteristic equation

* 0/(1-abs(sgn(d))) +        y = (C1+C2*x)/exp(a*x/2)          " Critical
* 0/(1-abs(sgn(d))) +  dy%dx = (C1+C2*(x-a/2))/exp(a*x/2)    " damping, d=0

* 0/max(d,0)     - r1 = (a-sqrt(abs(d)))/2                     " Overdamping,
* 0/max(d,0)     - r2 = (a+sqrt(abs(d)))/2                     " d > 0
*                   y = C1*exp(r1*x) + C2*exp(r2*x)
*               dy%dx = r1*C1*exp(r1*x) + r2*C2*exp(r2*x)

* 0/min(d,0) +      w = sqrt(abs(d))/2                         " Underdamping,
*                   y = A*cos(w*x-phi)/exp(a*x/2)              " d < 0
*               dy%dx = - a*y/2 - A*w*sin(w*x-phi)/exp(a*x/2)
*                ampl = A/exp(a*x/2)
*                   P = 2*pi()/w
```

Figure 13-22.
Linear Differential Equation Solver

```
==================== VARIABLE SHEET ==========================================
St Input      Name     Output      Unit      Comment
-- -----      ----     ------      ----      -------
   .1         y                              function, y = f(x)
   0          x                              independent variable
   0          dy%dx                          derivative of y with respect to x

   3          a                              coefficient      )
   65.4       b                              coefficient      )   characteristic
              d        -252.6                discriminant     )
              r1                             1st root         )   equation
              r2                             2nd root         )

              C1                             constant         )   d = 0  or
              C2                             constant         )     d > 0

              A        .10176588             constant                )
              phi      .18656262             constant, phase angle   )
              ampl     .10176588             amplitude               )   d < 0
              w        7.9466974             circular frequency      )
              P        .79066623             period                  )
```

Figure 13-23.
Variable Sheet for Linear Differential Equation Solver

conditional; the use of the remaining rules is controlled by the availability of the real roots of the characteristic equations ($d>0$ case) or the circular frequency ($d<0$ case). The formulas for the derivatives $dy\%dx$ were included in order to facilitate evaluation of the integration constants in the case of initial or boundary conditions related to velocity.

Let's see how this model is used on an example of the damped motion of a mass attached to a spring. The process is governed by Hooke's law

$$Force = spring\ constant \times stretch$$

or

$$F = k\ s$$

and Newton's second law

$$Mass \times Acceleration = Force$$

or

$$m\ y'' = F$$

Here y stands for displacement and the independent variable x for time.

Let us suppose in the equilibrium position $y=0$, the force $F=m*g=49.05$ N, generated by a mass m of 5 kg under the acceleration of gravity $g=9.81$ m/s^2, stretches the spring for $s_0=0.15$ m. According to Hooke's law, the spring constant $k=F/s_0=327$ N/m. In addition to this data, we need two initial conditions. Suppose the displacement and the acceleration at time $x=0$ are equal to $y(0)=0.1$m and $y'(0)=0$ respectively (that is, the mass was lifted 10 cm and released).

We could have built a model that would deal exclusively with mechanical systems such as springs with attached masses. The model would probably be equipped with additional relationships and a Unit Conversion Table related to the subject. However, in order to use the generalized equation solver in Figure 13-22, we have to analyze the conditions of the particular problem and translate them to the generalized language of the model.

The force acting on the mass consists of the force of gravity

$$F1 = m\ g$$

and the spring force acting in the opposite direction

$$F2 = -\ k\ s_0 - k\ y$$

(The first part holds the mass in the equilibrium position and the second is responsible for the displacement y from the equilibrium position.) In the resulting force $F1+F2$, the force of gravity and the first part of the spring force cancel each other. Newton's law after substitution for the resulting force is as follows:

$$m\ y'' = -\ k\ y$$

Consequently, $b=k/m=327/5=65.4$ is to be assigned as an input value. If $a=0$, there would be no damping and the mass would oscillate with a constant amplitude equal, according to the initial conditions, to 0.1 m (see Figure 13-24).

Suppose there is a damping force, proportional to the velocity, that slows down the motion. Damping is characterized by the damping factor *c;* if we assume the damping factor $c=15$ kg−s/m, then our coefficient $a=c/m=3$. We assign this value to input in addition to the already assigned $b=65.4$ and solve in order to evaluate the discriminant. Once we find out that it is negative, we look for the solution in the "underdamped" region. We assign the initial values $y=0.1$, $x=0$, and $dy\%dx=0$, assign guesses for the constants A and *phi,* and solve again. The results are shown in Figure 13-23. Next we can move the integration constants A and *phi* to input, blank the y and $dy\%dx$, and investigate the obtained solution of the differential equation by solving for different values of x. The graph of the oscillation of the system during the first 1.8 seconds generated from the List Solving results is shown in Figure 13-25.

Next we can look at the problem of critical damping. We assign $d=0$ and solve for a (it is equal to 16.174, implying that the damping factor $c=80.87$). At the same time we may assign the initial values and use the Iterative Solver to solve for the unknown integration constants—this time *C1* and *C2* (equal to 0.1 and 0.0124 respectively). Then the inputs and outputs have to be turned around again to obtain the motion diagram (curve "c" in Figure 13-26).

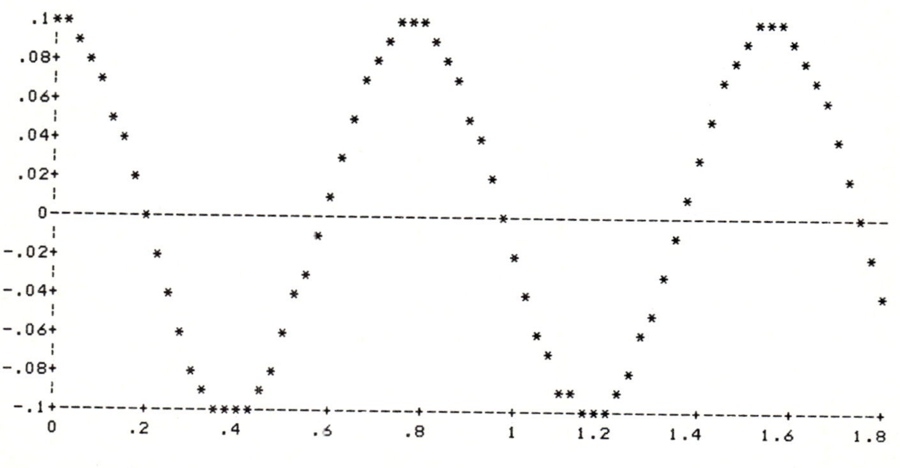

Figure 13-24.
Graphical representation of Figure 13-23; equation is $m\ y'' = k\ y$ ($a=0$, harmonic motion)

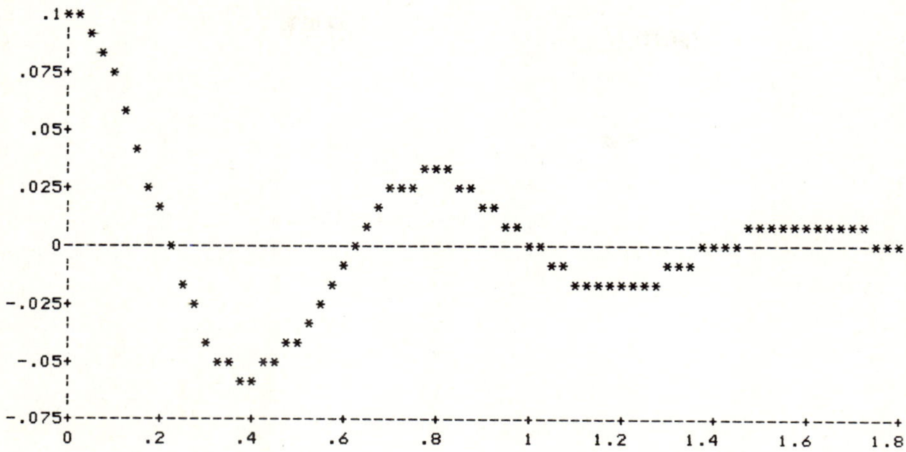

Figure 13-25.
Graphical representation of the solution of second-order equation by model in Figure 13-22 ($d < 0$, underdamping)

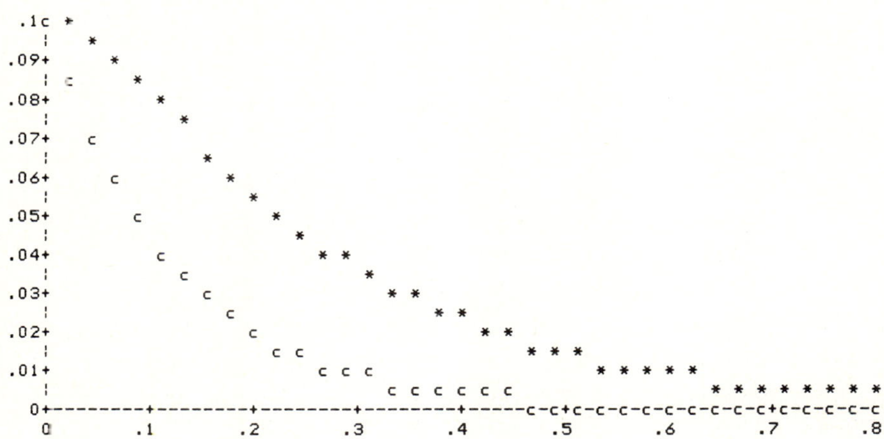

Figure 13-26.
Graphical representation of the solution of second-order equation by model in Figure 13-22 (with c=critical damping, $d=0$, and *=overdamping, $d > 0$)

Finally, we increase the damping factor by 15% (that is, $c=93$) and go through the solution process again. The integration constants this time are $C1=0.15125$ and $C2=-0.05125$. The response curve, designated by the symbol "*", is also shown in Figure 13-26. Once the solution of the differential equation has been found, there are many aspects we can investigate. For instance, we may want to know what damping factor is necessary to reach $y=0.001$ at the end of the first second. In this case the unknown a and the integration constants *C1* and *C2* have to be looked for simultaneously. For that purpose we copy the rules for y and $dy\%dx$ and include in them explicitly the initial conditions $y(0)=0.1$ and $y'(0)=0$. According to the conditions of the problem, we assign $y=0.001$ as input and also guess values for unknown a and *C1*. The Iterative Solver returns $a=17.9$, meaning that the damping factor should be $c=89.5$.

The model presented in Figure 13-22 may be easily generalized to cover second-order inhomogeneous equations with constant coefficients in which the zero in the right-hand side is replaced by a function of the independent variable. Applications include important issues of forced oscillation and resonance. The solution of an inhomogeneous equation may be obtained in the form of a sum of the general solution of the homogeneous equation and the particular solution of the inhomogeneous equations. The generalized forms of the latter are known for many common functions. These solutions can be used for building a model that would help with solving many inhomogeneous equations.

OPTIMIZATION

The quest for doing things the best possible way and securing optimum results is behind most of our activities. However, not all optimization problems can be described mathematically. And many of those that can are too complicated to be solved by computers—even the most powerful ones. Many of the "computable" optimization problems may not fit your personal computer and some of those that do are beyond the capabilities of TK!Solver (most notable in this category are linear programming problems).

Yet there are many optimization problems that can be efficiently attacked by TK!Solver either directly (by letting us formulate the problem and returning its solution) or indirectly (by providing us with a fast tool for examining our options under changing circumstances). Almost any TK!Solver application fits the second group. Here we concentrate on the first category and explore optimization techniques that require solving sets of non-linear equations—a task in which TK!Solver is at its best.

Extreme Values of Functions

If the objective function is expressed in terms of a non-linear equation of one or more independent variables, and if there are no additional constraints attached, the optimization problem becomes equivalent to the problem of finding an extremum (that is, minimum or maximum) of the function. We take advantage of the fact that the derivatives of the objective function with respect to independent variables (or free parameters in the optimization setting) are equal to zero at the extremum points: we simply type in the rules expressing these conditions and solve.

Earlier in this chapter, we saw various ways of evaluating the derivatives. We can put these techniques to use now. As a simple exercise, you may want to try the numerical differentiation to find a maximum of the function $y=sin(x)$ (the obvious result is $y=1$ at $x=\pi()/2$). You type in the following rule expressing the equality of the derivative to zero:

$$(sin(x+dx)-sin(x-dx))/dx = 0$$

assign $dx=0.0001$ as an input and $x=0.7$ as a guess, and solve. You can observe x creeping up and the iteration process terminates at true $y=1$ and $x=1.5707963$ (in fact a check with the Calculator mode reveals that $x-pi()/2=-1.8e-9$).

You also may try to find the maximum and minimum of the polynomial function in Figure 13-19. Create the model (assigning list $'a$ and generating list $'b$ as explained before), assign zero to dy/dx, guess x, and solve. The authors tried guess values $x=0$ and $x=3$. In the first case the Iterative Solver returned maximum $y=1.6915$ at $x=0.31386$, and in the second case minimum $y=-7.1946$ at $x=3.1861$—both after four iteration steps. These results are in agreement with the graph of the function and its derivative in Figure 13-19.

We can better deal with optimization problems with more than ten parameters by using special optimization algorithms and programs based on repeated evaluation of the objective function, analyzing the terrain, and moving gradually toward the target. However, searching for the points with zero values of the derivative is different. This technique may be preferable when the derivatives are easy to obtain and when we have a multitude of local optima to choose from after further analysis.

As an example, we consider an objective function

$$f(x,y) = z = 2\,x^3 - x^2\,y + y^3 + y^2 - 2\,y$$

The Rule Sheet with the function and its first and second derivatives is shown in Figure 13-27*a* and the Variable Sheet with a solution in Figure

13-27*b*. In order to find an extremum, we assign input values $fx=fy=0$, assign a value to x, and solve. When guess $x=1$, the solution converges to the maximum (because both fxx and fyy are negative), as shown in Figure 13-27*b*. Iterating from guess $x=-1$ yields minimum $z=-0.6369$ at $x=0.1808$ and $y=0.5424$.

An interesting solution results from the guesses $x=-1$ and $y=1$: $z=-0.6311$ at $x=0$ and $y=0.5486$. The second derivatives fxx and fyy show different signs and the extremum indicator $detH<0$. This means that the solution converged to the so-called saddle point, that is, neither minimum nor maximum.

Constrained Optimization With Lagrange Multipliers

Most of the real-world optimization problems have the feasible solution space constrained by various conditions. These conditions are expressed by equalities or inequalities with the functions of the parameters or constants on either side. Equality-constrained optimization problems may be easily handled by TK!Solver when we use the so-called Lagrange multipliers.

The essence of this method is as follows: we introduce the so-called Lagrangian function which is a sum of the original objective function and the non-zero sides of the equality constraints, each multiplied by its own new variable called the Lagrange multiplier. We take the derivatives of this function with respect to all free parameters and multipliers and set them equal to zero. This yields as many equations as there are parameters and multipliers (or constraints). The solution of this set of equations represents the optimum point.

As an example we will consider the following problem: find the maximum and minimum volumes of a rectangular solid block whose total edge length is 24 m and whose surface area is 22 m^2.

First we define the volume V, the sum of edges E, and the total surface area A (see the first three rules in the Rule Sheet in Figure 13-28). Then we create the following Lagrangian function:

$$LF = x*y*z + L1*(E - 4*(x+y+z)) + L2*(A - 2*(x*y + y*z + z*x))$$

The next step is to take the derivatives of LF with respect to all the unknown variables x, y, and z, as well as to the Lagrange multipliers $L1$ and $L2$, and equate these derivatives to zero. We don't need to worry about the $\partial LF/\partial L1$ and $\partial LF/\partial L2$ being made equal to zero; these conditions are already stated by the second and third rules. We take $\partial LF/\partial x$, type it in as

```
=================== RULE SHEET ===============================================
S Rule
- ----
* z = 2*x^3 - x^2*y + y^3 + y^2 - 2*y

* fx = 6*x^2 - 2*x*y
* fy = -x^2 + 3*y^2 + 2*y - 2

* fxx = 12*x - 2*y
* fyy = 6*y + 2
* fxy = -2*y

* detH = fxx*fyy - fxy^2
```

a. Rule Sheet

```
==================== VARIABLE SHEET ==========================================
St Input      Name      Output       Unit      Comment
-- -----      ----      ------       ----      -------
              z         2.1719239              function z = f(x,y)
              x         -.3950806              independent variable
              y         -1.185242              independent variable

   0          fx                               dz/dx
   0          fy                               dz/dy
              fxx       -2.370484              d2z/dx2
              fyy       -5.111451              d2z/dy2
              fxy       2.3704838              d2dz/dxdy

              detH      6.4974193              determinant of Hessian matrix
                                               (local extremum when detH > 0)
```

b. Variable Sheet with solution for the maximum value

Figure 13-27.
Finding maximum and minimum of two unknowns

the fourth rule, and make it equal to zero. Because the other two derivatives are similar, we just copy the fourth rule and edit it to make it appropriate for these two derivatives.

Thus we end up with five simultaneous equations for unknowns $x,y,z,L1$, and $L2$ (we don't count the first equation, which will automatically evaluate V after finding out x,y,z). We assign given $E=24$ and $A=22$ as input, guess $x=y=L1=1$, and after five iteration steps, get the solution shown in the Variable Sheet in Figure 13-28. Peeking around this solution (that is, solving with assumed $x=1.4$ and again with $z=3.1$) shows that the result obtained represents the maximum. (There are more rigorous methods to establish this, but our check is as good and faster.)

Then we try for the minimum volume with the guesses $x=y=10$ and $L1=1$. The Iterative Solver converges to the minimum $V=5.615$ at $x=y=2.577$ and $z=0.845$.

```
==================== VARIABLE SHEET ===========================...
St Input      Name     Output      Unit        Comment
-- -----      ----     ------      ----        -------
              V        6.3849002               volume
   24         E                                sum of edges
   22         A                                surface area
              x        1.4226497               width
              y        1.4226497               depth
              z        3.1547005               height
              L1       -.5059831               Lagrange multiplier
              L2       .71132487               Lagrange multiplier

==================== RULE SHEET ===============================...
S Rule
- ----
  V = x*y*z
  E = 4*(x + y + z)
  A = 2*(x*y + y*z + z*x)

  y*z - 4*L1 - 2*L2*(y+z) = 0
  x*z - 4*L1 - 2*L2*(x+z) = 0
  x*y - 4*L1 - 2*L2*(x+y) = 0
```

Figure 13-28.
Constrained optimization with Lagrange multipliers

CURVE FITTING

The simplest way of generating a description of the relation between two sets of experimental data—the so-called linear regression—was discussed in Chapter 10. There are two conditions that must be met before the resulting regression lines can be used reliably:

1. The scattering effect of extraneous factors must be low; that is, the related quantities must depend primarily on each other.

2. The true relationship between the quantities must be close to linear; that is, the rate of change of one quantity with respect to the other must be constant or the changes in both quantities must be proportional.

In many situations the underlying dependency mechanism is far from linear, and fitting a straight line to the data does not make sense. This brings up the issue of curve fitting or curvilinear regression. Sometimes the nature of the relationship is known (for instance, exponential growth or decay), and we want to know the extent and the parameters of the fit. Sometimes we want to find by trial and error what type of mathematical relationship fits our data best.

Prominent among the myriads of non-linear relationships are those that can be reduced to linear by a simple transformation of one or both

```
==================== RULE SHEET ================...
S Rule
- ----
* xvariance=(n*dot('x,'x)-(sum('x))^2)/n
* yvariance=(n*dot('y,'y)-(sum('y))^2)/n
* xyvariance=(n*dot('x,'y)-sum('x)*sum('y))/n
* n=count('x0)
* xmean=sum('x)/n
* ymean=sum('y)/n
* b1 = xyvariance/xvariance
* b2 = xyvariance/yvariance
* ymean = a1 + b1*xmean
* xmean = a2 + b2*ymean
* correlation = sqrt(b1*b2)

* x = x0
  "x = 1/x0
  "x = ln(x0)
  "y = y0
  "y = 1/y0
* y = ln(y0)
```

Figure 13-29.
Curvilinear regression model Rule Sheet (see Figure 13-32 for Variable Sheet)

variables. An example of such a relationship would include exponentiation, taking the square root, or reciprocal value. The processing of the data is thus performed in two stages: transformation of the data and linear regression itself. TK!Solver may be used efficiently for both. The Rule Sheet in Figure 13-29 shows one way of taking advantage of TK!Solver's flexibility.

The first block of rules represents ordinary linear regression. It differs from the model in Figure 10-13 only in naming the variables and providing the values of slope and intercept for both $y=f1(x)$ and $x=f2(y)$. The second block serves for the transformation of the data $x0$, $y0$ into linear regression variables x,y. There are three transformation rules for both x and y. This represents 9 combinations altogether or 9+9 types of functional relationships, including two linear ones (see Figure 13-30). More function types can be added if needed.

To use the model we do the following:

1. Type the data into lists $x0$ and $y0$.
2. Select the type of function by making one rule for x operational and one rule for y. The rest of the rules must be commented out (as in Figure 13-29).
3. Generate the transformed lists x and y by List Solving /**L**!.
4. The linear regression parameters are calculated by simple solving !.

For example, Figure 13-31 shows the weights of chick embryos from ages 6 to 16 days (from *Statistical Methods* by G.W. Snedecor and W.G. Cochran, Iowa State University Press, 1979). True linear regression when $x=x0$ and $y=y0$ shows a rather poor correlation coefficient of 0.8627. This is not surprising because the chick embryos grow exponentially since the rate of increase at any stage is proportional to the size already attained. So we keep the rule $x=x0$ and activate $y=ln(y0)$, List Solve to generate x and y, solve again, and find that for

$$y = ln(-6.1921)\ e^{0.451\ x}$$

or

$$y_0 = 0.00205\ e^{0.451\ x0}$$

Transformation		Y = f1(X)	X = f2(X)
x=x0	y=y0	Y = a1 + b1*X	X = a2 + b2*X
x=x0	y=ln(y0)	Y = c1*exp(b1*X)	X = a2 + b2*ln(Y)
x=ln(x0)	y=y0	Y = a1 + b1*ln(X)	X = c2*exp(b2*Y)
x=ln(x0)	y=ln(y0)	Y = c1*X^b1	X = c2*Y^b2
x=1/x0	y=y0	Y = a1 + b1/X	X = 1/(a2 + b2*Y)
x=x0	y=1/y0	Y = 1/(a1 + b1*X)	X = a2 + b2/Y
x=/x0	y=1/y0	Y = 1/(a1 + b1/X)	X = 1/(a2 + b2/Y)
x/x0	y=ln(y0)	Y = c1*exp(b1/X)	X = 1/(a2 + ln(Y))
x=ln(x0)	y=1/y0	Y = 1/(a1 + ln(X))	X = c2*exp(b2/Y)

Note: c1=exp(a1), c2=exp(a2)

Figure 13-30.
Function types attainable by the model in Figure 13-29

x0	y0	y
6	.029	-3.5404594
7	.052	-2.9565116
8	.079	-2.5383074
9	.125	-2.0794415
10	.181	-1.7092582
11	.261	-1.3432349
12	.425	-.85566611
13	.738	-.30381145
14	1.13	.122217633
15	1.882	.632335041
16	2.812	1.03389597

Figure 13-31.
Table showing the dry weights $y0$ of chick embryos at age $x0$ days; $y=ln(y0)$

```
==================== VARIABLE SHEET ==========================================
St Input      Name     Output     Unit        Comment
-- -----      ----     ------     ----        -------
                                              ** CURVILINEAR REGRESSION **

L  1          x0                              Data: variable x
L  1          y0                              Data: variable y
L             x        1                      Variable x, transformed
L             y        0                      Variable y, transformed
              n        11                     Number of observations
              xmean    11                     Mean of the x list
              ymean    -1.230749              Mean of the y list
              xvarian  110                    Variance of the x list
              yvarian  22.414749              Variance of the y list
              xyvaria  49.613591              Covariance of the two lists
              correla  .99916538              Correlation coefficient
              a1       -6.192108              Intercept in  y = ax + bx*x
              b1       .45103265              Slope in        -   "   -
              a2       13.724184              Intercept in  x = ay + by*y
              b2       2.2134350              Slope in        -   "   -
```

Figure 13-32.
Curvilinear regression model: Variable Sheet with solution for chick embryo problem

there indeed is a very good fit as indicated by the correlation coefficient equal to 0.9992. This means that the chick embryos already know how to obey the laws of nature! Figures 13-29 and 13-32 show the relevant contents of the Rule and Variable Sheets.

Regression analysis, curve fitting, and other mathematical statistics techniques do not always go hand in hand with TK!Solver features and capabilities. There are computational needs in statistics that are not easily met by TK!Solver. On the other hand, there are features in TK!Solver that are not needed in statistical calculations (for instance backsolving—unless we want to calculate what the data should be in order to arrive at a particular mean value and variation coefficient). However, the affinity of TK!Solver and statistical methods is considerable, especially at the stage of data conversion and method selection and while utilizing the results of statistical analysis in the problem-solving and decision-making process. This affinity may justify, as in the previous example, using TK!Solver to perform the statistical calculations as well.

14

Case Studies: Science and Engineering

The fields of science and engineering are probably the most fertile grounds for TK!Solver applications. Selecting representative topics for this chapter was harder than for any other chapter. The final choice represents a wide cross section ranging from the mathematically trivial (lenses) to involved (eigenvalues and eigenvectors) and from typical TK!Solver treatment of quantitative relationships (AC circuits and shaft design) to unusual treatment (stoichiometry and color coding of resistors).

LENSES

Lenses are used to concentrate or disperse light and to generate images. They are an essential component of eyeglasses, cameras, microscopes, and other optical instruments. There are two main types of lenses—converging and diverging—as shown in Figure 14-1*a* and *b*.

The size and location of an image can be found with the following lens equation:

$$1/p + 1/q = 1/f$$

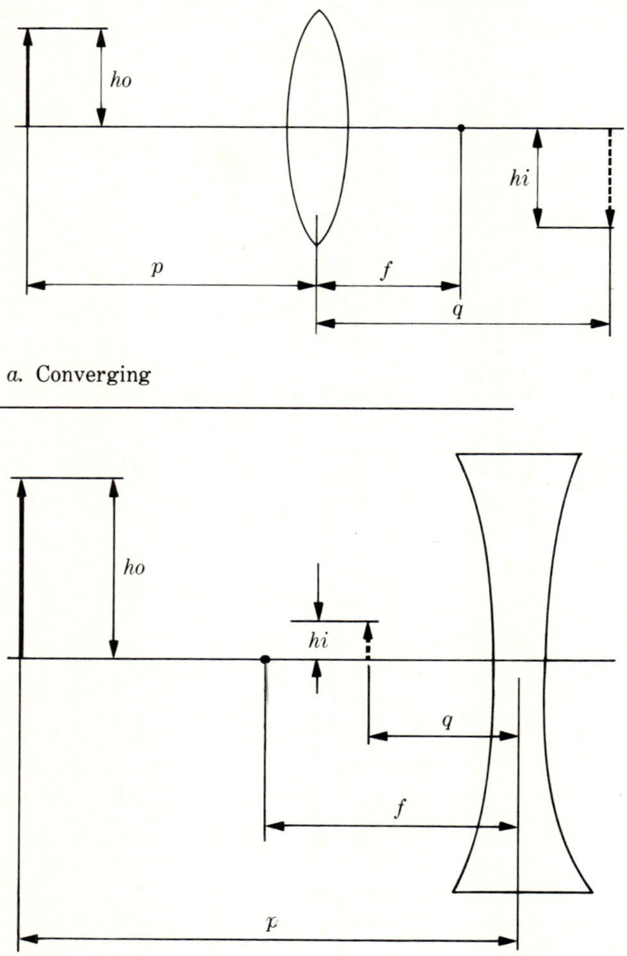

Legend:
p = object distance
q = image distance
f = focal length
ho = object height
hi = image height

a. Converging

b. Diverging

Figure 14-1.
Types of lenses

The linear magnification produced by a lens is given by the formula

$$m = hi/ho = -q/p$$

The sign conventions normally adopted for lenses are shown in the following chart.

Variable	Positive Value	Negative Value
f	Converging lens	Diverging lens
p	Real object	Virtual object
q	Real image	Virtual image
m	Erect image	Inverted image
hi	Erect image	Inverted image

Figure 14-2 shows the Rule Sheet with the lens equation and the equations for magnification.

Example 1

A key 5 cm long is placed 45 cm from a converging lens whose focal length is 30 cm. Find the location, size, and nature of the image.

Since the lens is converging, the focal length is positive, so f is assigned 30. The values of p=45 and ho=5 are also assigned and the model is solved as shown in the figure. The image is real since q is positive, and it is at a distance of 90 cm from the lens. Since m=−2, the image is inverted and is 10 cm long—twice the original 5 cm.

We may see from the equations that for a real, inverted image (that is, q>0 and hi<0) the following apply:

Object Distance	Image Size	Image Distance
$f < p < 2f$	Larger than object	$q > 2f$
$p = 2f$	Same size as object	$q = 2f$
$p > 2f$	Smaller than object	$f < q \leq 2f$

```
==================== VARIABLE SHEET ==============================...
St Input      Name      Output     Unit       Comment
-- -----      ----      ------     ----       -------
   45         p                    cm         object distance
              q         90         cm         image distance
   5          ho                   cm         height of object
              hi        -10        cm         height of image
              m         -2                    linear magnification
   30         f                    cm         focal length of lens

==================== RULE SHEET ===================================...
S Rule
- ----
  1/p + 1/q = 1/f                      " lens equation
  m = -q/p                             " magnification and distances
  m = hi/ho                            " magnification and heights
```

Figure 14-2.
Variable and Rule Sheets for simple lens model

We may verify this by List Solving for varying values of p, as shown in Figure 14-3, which displays the results in TK!Solver table format.

Example 2

What are the values of p and q when m=3 and f=60? The Direct Solver fails to solve this problem. The loop in the VEC matrix and the ring in the R-graph indicate the reason for the failure—the set of simultaneous equations in p and q. We need a redundant equation so that we can avoid using the Iterative Solver. From the second equation, we have $p=-q/m$. Substituting this for p in the first equation and simplifying, we get the redundant equation

$$1-m = q/f$$

When this equation is added to the Rule Sheet and the model is solved, p is found to be 40 cm and q=−120 cm.

The Lensmaker's Equation

The focal length f of a thin lens is given by the following so-called lensmaker's equation, which takes into account the radii of curvature of the two surfaces and the refractive index of the lens material relative to the medium it is in:

$$1/f = (n-1) * (1/R1 + 1/R2)$$

where

n is the refractive index of the material relative to the medium it is in.

p	q	hi
35	210	-30
40	120	-15
45	90	-10
50	75	-7.5
55	66	-6
60	60	-5
65	55.71428572	-4.285714286
70	52.5	-3.75
75	50	-3.333333333
80	48	-3

Figure 14-3.
Table showing the effect of object distance on image distance and image size

R1 is the radius of curvature of one surface
R2 is the radius of curvature of the second surface.

We add this equation to the Rule Sheet and solve the following problem.

Example

A meniscus lens has one concave and one convex surface. The concave surface of the lens has a radius of curvature of 25 cm, and the convex surface has a radius of curvature of 30 cm. If the refractive index of the glass used is 1.60, find the focal length of the lens. Is the lens converging or diverging?

Since the first surface is concave, *R1* is negative, and since the second surface is convex, *R2* is positive. The values of *R1* and *R2* are assigned with the appropriate signs. The Direct Solver solves the problem and the solution is shown in Figure 14-4. Based on the sign convention given earlier, we find that the lens is diverging since *f* is negative.

Adding Subject-Specific Terminology

We can make the model more informative by relating the values of the variables to the types of lenses. Employing a user-defined function, we can relate the sign of *f* to the type of lens—converging or diverging. A Table

```
==================== VARIABLE SHEET ====================================...
St Input      Name     Output    Unit       Comment
-- -----      ----     ------    ----       -------
              f        -250      cm         focal length of lens

   1.6        n                             refractive index of material
   -25        R1                 cm         radius of curv. 1-st surface
   30         R2                 cm         radius of curv. 2-nd surface

==================== RULE SHEET ========================================...
S Rule
- ----
* 1/p + 1/q = 1/f                        " lens equation
* m = -q/p                               " magnification and distances
* m = hi/ho                              " magnification and heights

* 1-m = q/f                              " redundant equation

* 1/f = (n-1)*(1/R1 + 1/R2)              " lensmaker's equation
```

Figure 14-4.
Variable Sheet with solution for meniscus lens and Rule Sheet with redundant equation and lensmaker's equation

Lookup Mapping is used for the function *lenfun*, which is defined as follows:

Domain	Range
1	*'converging*
−1	*'diverging*

Thus if f is negative, $sgn(f) = -1$, and the message *'diverging* is returned by the function.

A plane surface has an infinite radius of curvature; since it is not possible to specify infinity during problem-solving, we use the concept of curvature in the model. Curvature is the reciprocal of the radius of curvature. If we denote the curvatures of the two surfaces as *k1* and *k2*, then these curvatures can be calculated from the following equations:

$$k1 = 1/R1$$
$$k2 = 1/R2$$

The lensmaker's equation is modified to use the curvatures instead of $1/R1$ and $1/R2$. Problems involving plane surfaces can now be solved.

However, we will encounter a problem if we use these two equations "as is" in the model; for example, if the first surface is plane and we assign 0 to *k1*, a division by zero will be attempted in the first of the two equations and the solution will be terminated with a "Division by zero" message. To prevent this, we can rewrite the equation for *k1* as

$$k1 = sgn(R1)/abs(R1)$$

Similarly, the equation for *k2* can be rewritten as

$$k2 = sgn(R2)/abs(R2)$$

These two rules are now added to the Rule Sheet. But this new formulation precludes solving for *R1* (and similarly for *R2*) from the new rule since this variable appears twice in the rule.

To make up for the loss of backsolvability and to avoid the "Division by zero" error we can use the 0/0 bypass and add two more equations:

$$0/k1 + k1 = 1/R1$$
$$0/k2 + k2 = 1/R2$$

With these four equations added to the model plus the modified lensmaker's equation, it is possible to solve problems involving all three types of surfaces. These rules are shown in Figure 14-5*a*.

A user-defined function can be used to return a message about the surface type—plane, concave, or convex—depending on the signum of *k1* and

```
==================== RULE SHEET ===============================================
S Rule
- ----
* 1/f = (n-1)*(k1 + k2)             " modified lensmaker's equation

* k1 = sgn(R1)/abs(R1)              " calculate k1
* 0/k1 +   k1 = 1/R1                " if k1=0, bypass the rule

* k2 = sgn(R2)/abs(R2)              " calculate k2
* 0/k2 +   k2 = 1/R2                " if k2=0, bypass the rule

* lenstype = lenfun(sgn(f))         " returns type of lens
* surf1 = surfun(sgn(k1))           " returns type of first surface
* surf2 = surfun(sgn(k2))           " returns type of second surface
```

a. Partial Rule Sheet

```
===================== VARIABLE SHEET ==========================================
St Input     Name      Output     Unit      Comment
-- -----     ----      ------     ----      -------
   50        f                    cm        focal length of lens

   1.6       n                              refractive index of material
             R1                   cm        radius of curv. 1-st surface
             R2        30         cm        radius of curv. 2-nd surface

             surf1     'plane               1-st surface: concave or convex
             surf2     'convex              2-nd surface: concave or convex
             lenstyp   'convergi            lens: converging or diverging

   0         k1                   1/cm      curvature of first surface
             k2        .03333333  1/cm      curvature of second surface
```

b. Partial Variable Sheet

Figure 14-5.
Modified lens model

k2. The Domain and Range values of the function *surfun* are given here:

Domain	Range
−1	*'concave*
0	*'plane*
1	*'convex*

Example

A converging lens of focal length 50 cm is to be made from glass of refractive index 1.6. If one of the surfaces is plane, what should be the radius of curvature of the other?

The value $k1 = 0$ is assigned since one of the surfaces is plane, while the value for f is entered as given (50) since the lens is a converging lens. Then

n=1.6 is assigned and the model is solved. The solution shown in the Variable Sheet in Figure 14-5*b* is obtained. The radius of curvature of the other surface is found to be 30 cm and the surface is convex.

ALTERNATING CURRENT CIRCUITS

This study illustrates how a model can be built from fundamental textbook definitions and expanded along the way as the problems being solved warrant. With the model in its final form, we will be able to solve a wide class of problems in AC circuits. Figure 14-6*a* shows the Rule Sheet with the common definitions of some properties of AC circuits. The Unit Sheet with the conversions in the model is shown in Figure 14-6*b*. We can see

```
==================== RULE SHEET ============================...
S Rule
- ----
* I = V/Z                             " Ohm's law for ac
* Xl = 2*pi()*f*L                     " inductive reactance
* Xc = 1/(2*pi()*f*C)                 " capacitive reactance
* Z = sqrt(R^2 + (Xl-Xc)^2)           " impedance of the circuit
* tan(phi) = (Xl-Xc)/R                " phase angle
* pf = cos(phi)                       " power factor
* P = I*V*pf                          " power in circuit
* AP = V*I                            " apparent power

* Vr = I*R                            " PD across resistor
* Vl = I*Xl                           " PD across inductor
* Vc = I*Xc                           " PD across capacitor
* V = sqrt(Vr^2 + (Vl-Vc)^2)          " PD across entire circuit

* f0 = 1/(2*pi()*sqrt(L*C))           " resonant frequency
```

a. Rule Sheet (the sets of rules are separated by blank rows)

```
==================== UNIT SHEET ==============...
From       To        Multiply By    Add Offset
----       --        -----------    ----------
1          %         100
rad        deg       57.29577951
uF         F         .000001
mH         H         .001
Hz         c/s       1
kHz        Hz        1000
kW         W         1000
```

b. Unit Sheet

Figure 14-6.
The AC circuits model

three sets of rules in the Rule Sheet. Initially, only the first set is entered; then the second and finally the third set are added to solve the subsequent examples.

Example 1

A 60-ohm resistor, a 75-μF capacitor, and a 0.25-H inductor are connected in series with a 120-V, 60-Hz power source, as shown in Figure 14-7. Calculate the following: (a) the current through the circuit, (b) the impedance of the circuit, (c) the power factor, and (d) the power dissipated by the circuit. What should be the minimum rating in volt-amperes of the power source?

The Calculation Unit for C is Farads (F), while that for pf is the decimal fraction. The given values are assigned and the model is solved. The first group of variables in the Variable Sheet in Figure 14-8 displays the solution. Note that only this set is present when the problem is solved. The apparent power AP is also the minimum rating of the power source and is found to be 171.30 VA.

Example 2

Find the potential difference across the resistor, inductor, and capacitor of the earlier problem. Are these values in accord with the applied potential difference of 120 V?

In order to solve this problem, we must add to the Rule Sheet the formulas for the potential difference across each of the elements. These rules comprise the second group in the Rule Sheet in Figure 14-6*a*. We cannot

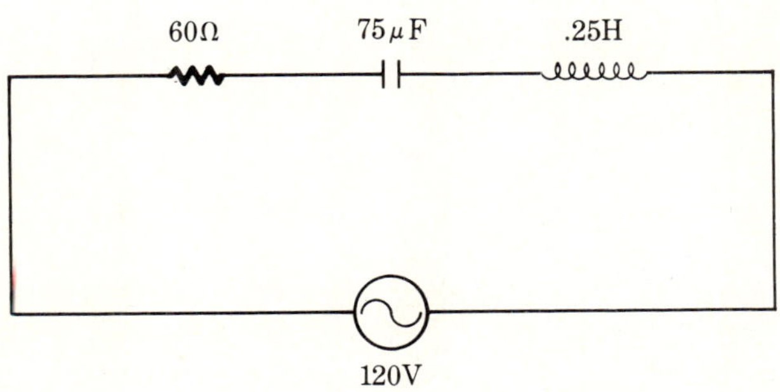

Figure 14-7.
The AC circuit to be analyzed

St	Input	Name	Output	Unit	Comment
	60	f		Hz	frequency
	.25	L		H	inductance
	75	C		uF	capacitance
	60	R		ohm	resistance
		Xc	35.367765	ohm	capacitive reactance
		Xl	94.247780	ohm	inductive reactance
	120	V		volt	source voltage
		I	1.4274737	amp	current
		Z	84.064595	ohm	impedance
		phi	44.460224	deg	phase angle
		pf	71.373686	%	power factor
		P	122.26087	W	power dissipated
		AP	171.29685	volt*amp	apparent power
		Vr	85.648423	volt	voltage drop across resistor
		Vc	50.486555	volt	voltage drop across capacitor
		Vl	134.53623	volt	voltage drop across inductor
		f0	36.75526	Hz	resonant frequency

Figure 14-8.
Complete Variable Sheet for the AC circuits model showing the solutions for all three examples (a blank line separates each solution)

simply sum up the individual potential differences to verify if they are in accordance with the applied potential difference because *Vl* is 90 degrees ahead of *Vr* and *Vc* is 90 degrees behind *Vr*. The applied potential difference *V* is given by the rule

$$V = sqrt(Vr\char`^2 + (Vl - Vc)\char`^2)$$

Upon solving the model with these new rules, if we find out that the equality in the added equation for *V* doesn't hold, then the answer to the question is "no;" the individual potential differences are not in accordance with the applied potential difference. Otherwise, the answer is "yes."

When the problem is solved, we get the results shown in the second group in the Variable Sheet. No inconsistency is detected in the added rule for *V*, so the individual potential differences are in agreement with the applied potential difference of 120 V.

Example 3

Find the resonant frequency *f0* of the circuit in the previous problem. The resonant frequency of an AC circuit is the frequency at which the capacitive reactance *Xc* is equal to the inductive reactance *Xl;* this is given by the equation

$$f0 = 1/(2*pi()*sqrt(L*C))$$

This rule is added to the Rule Sheet and the problem is solved. The resonant frequency, *f0*, is found to be 36.755 Hz, as shown in the Variable Sheet in Figure 14-8.

STOICHIOMETRY

The analysis and synthesis of chemical compounds involves chemical reactions—a process during which one or more substances called reactants are changed into one or more new substances called products. Stoichiometry is the quantitative study of chemical reactions. A chemical equation, showing the relative amounts of the different elements and compounds involved, is used to represent the reaction. The equation is used in the study of the so-called "mass-mass" relationships. Typical applications include finding out what mass of a product can be expected from a specific mass of a reactant, estimating how much of a particular reactant is needed to react with a specific amount of another reactant, and so on.

A typical sequence of steps involved in solving mass-mass problems is as follows:

1. Write the chemical equation and balance it.
2. Find the number of moles of the given substance; a *mole* is defined as the ratio of the mass of the substance to the formula mass of the substance.
3. Determine the mole ratio of the required substance to the given substance using the balanced equation.
4. Express the moles of the required substance in grams.

Reaction of Cuprous Chloride With Hydrogen Sulfide

How many grams of cuprous sulfide could be produced from 9.90 grams of CuCl reacting with an excess of H_2S gas?

Building the Model

The chemical equation for this reaction is

$$a*\mathrm{CuCl} + b*\mathrm{H_2S} = c*\mathrm{Cu_2S} + d*\mathrm{HCl}$$

where a, b, c, and d are the unknown coefficients of the different compounds that balance the equation. This equation can be entered in the Rule

```
==================== RULE SHEET ==============================================
S Rule
- ----
* a*CuCl + b*H2S = c*Cu2S + d*HCl        " chemical equation

* CuCl = Cu + Cl
* H2S = H*2 + S
* Cu2S = Cu*2 + S
* HCl = H + Cl

* (mCuCl)/(CuCl)/a = (mCu2S)/(Cu2S)/c   " a moles CuCl yield c moles Cu2S
```

Figure 14-9.
Rule Sheet for cuprous chloride problem (note the similarity between variable names and element names)

Sheet, as shown in Figure 14-9. Note the choice of variable names in the rule; they serve a dual purpose. First, they are similar or identical to the chemical formulas of the compounds. Second, they represent the formula masses of the different compounds. In order to calculate the required formula mass, we can, in turn, express each of these compounds in terms of its component elements using the element symbols as the variable names. This is seen in the next four rules in Figure 14-9.

This choice of variable names has yet another advantage. The symbols of the common elements (if not all the elements) and their corresponding atomic masses can be entered in the Variable Sheet, as shown in Figure 14-10*a*. We can then save this sheet using the Variable Save (/SV) option and load it whenever required. The Variable Sheet with this information serves as a template for solving different problems without our having to remember or look up the periodic table and enter the values of the atomic masses. This part of the Variable Sheet can also be "hidden" from the user. However, we must be careful not to reset the variable values using the /RV option or all the values for the atomic masses will be lost.

The last rule in Figure 14-9 represents steps 2 to 4 of the earlier sequence for solving mass-mass problems. The rule implies that a moles of CuCl yield c moles of Cu_2S.

Solving the Problem

The first step in solving the problem is to balance the equation. Since there are two Cu atoms on the right-hand side, there should be two on the left-hand side. So a is assigned 2; it follows that c should be assigned 1. Since $a=2$, there are two Cl atoms on the left-hand side, so d is assigned 2. The given mass of CuCl is assigned to $mCuCl$. The model is solved and the

```
===================== VARIABLE SHEET ============================================
St Input      Name    Output     Unit       Comment
-- -----      ----    ------     ----       -------
                                            **INTERNATIONAL ATOMIC MASSES**
   227.02777 Ac
   26.98154  Al
   243.06139 Am
   121.75    Sb
   39.948    Ar
   74.9216   As
   209.98704 At
   137.33    Ba
   247.07032 Bk
   9.01218   Be
   208.9804  Bi
   10.81     B
   79.904    Br
   112.41    Cd
```

a. The element symbols and atomic masses

```
==================== VARIABLE SHEET =============================================
St Input      Name    Output     Unit       Comment
-- -----      ----    ------     ----       -------
                                            ** S O L U T I O N **

              CuCl    98.999                mol. mass of cuprous chloride
              H2S     34.0758               mol. mass of hydrogen sulfide
              Cu2S    159.152               mol. mass of cuprous sulfide
              HCl     36.4609               mol. mass of hydrogen chloride

   2          a                             coeff. in chemical formula
              b       1                            - " -
   1          c                                    - " -
   2          d                                    - " -

   9.9        mCuCl              g          mass of cuprous chloride
              mCu2S   7.9576804  g          same of cuprous sulfide
```

b. Solution of the given problem

Figure 14-10.
The Variable Sheet

solution is shown in Figure 14-10*b*. Thus 7.96 grams of Cu_2S can be produced from 9.9 grams of CuCl. The gram molecular masses of the different compounds are also shown in the figure.

What if 10 grams of Cu_2S are required to be produced? In that case, all that we must do is assign the specified value to *mCu2S*, blank out the value of *mCuCl*, and solve. TK!Solver comes up with the answer that 12.44 grams of CuCl are required for the chemical reaction.

Reaction of Calcium Hydroxide With Phosphoric Acid

Consider the following reaction:

$$a*\mathrm{Ca(OH)_2} + b*\mathrm{H_3PO_4} = c*\mathrm{Ca_3(PO_4)_2} + d*\mathrm{H_2O}$$

How many grams of calcium hydroxide will be needed to react completely with 10 grams of phosphoric acid?

Note that instead of the parentheses in the formulas of some of the compounds, the percent symbol (%) is used in the variable names because

```
==================== RULE SHEET =============================...
S Rule
- ----
  "** P R O B L E M **
  "  How many grams of calcium hydroxide will be needed
  "  to react completely with 10 grams of phosphoric acid?

* a*Ca%OH%2 + b*H3PO4 = c*Ca3%PO4%2 + d*H2O

* Ca%OH%2 = Ca + (O + H)*2
* H3PO4 = H*3 + P + O*4
* Ca3%PO4%2 = Ca*3 + (P + O*4)*2
* H2O = H*2 + O

* (mCa%OH%2)/(Ca%OH%2)/a = (mH3PO4)/(H3PO4)/b
```

Figure 14-11.
Rule Sheet with the rules and the problem (note the use of % instead of the parentheses in the chemical formula)

```
==================== VARIABLE SHEET ======================================...
St Input      Name      Output      Unit      Comment
-- -----      ----      ------      ----      -------
                                              ** S O L U T I O N **

              Ca%OH%2   74.0946               mol. mass of calcium hydroxide
              H3PO4     97.99506              mol. mass of phosphoric acid
              Ca3%PO4   310.18272             mol. mass of calcium phosphate
              H2O       18.0152               mol. mass of water

   3          a                               coeff. in chemical formula
   2          b                                          - " -
   1          c                                          - " -
              d         6                                - " -

   10         mH3PO4                g         mass of phosphoric acid
              mCa%OH%   11.341582   g         same of calcium hydroxide
```

Figure 14-12.
Variable Sheet with the solution of the problem in Figure 14-11

parentheses are used in TK!Solver rules for enclosing arguments of functions or for controlling the precedence of operations. Thus in the first rule in Figure 14-11, $Ca(OH)_2$ is represented as Ca%OH%2. The next four rules specify the composition of each of the compounds. The last rule expresses the fact that b moles of H_3PO_4 are required to react with a moles of $Ca(OH)_2$. The Variable Sheet with the solution is shown in Figure 14-12.

SHAFT DESIGN

Shaft design involves the determination of the correct shaft diameter to ensure satisfactory strength and rigidity when the shaft is transmitting power under various operating and loading conditions. Shafts are usually circular in cross section and may be either hollow or solid. The design of shafts of ductile materials is based on strength and is governed by the maximum shear theory, while the design of shafts of brittle materials is based on the normal stress theory.

This model deals with circular shafts—both hollow and solid—of ductile materials. The essential difference between the sets of equations applicable to hollow shafts and solid shafts is that in the former both the inner and outer diameters are taken into account, while in the latter there is only one diameter involved. For example, the equations for areas of cross sections are

$$\text{area of hollow shaft} = pi()*(D\hat{}2-d\hat{}2)/4$$

$$\text{area of solid shaft} = pi()/4*D\hat{}2$$

where

D = the diameter of the solid shaft or outer diameter of the hollow shaft

d = the inner diameter of the hollow shaft.

When $d=0$, the equations become identical. We take advantage of this in the model design and use only the equations applicable for hollow shaft setting $d=0$ when dealing with solid shafts. A user-defined function *fun* with Table Lookup Mapping is used for this purpose. The Domain and Range values of the function are given here:

Domain	**Range**
'hollow	0
'solid	1

```
=================== RULE SHEET ==========================================
S Rule
- ----
* 0/fun(type) + d = 0                  " set d=0 for solid shaft
* K = d/D                              " diameter ratio

* A = pi()*(D^2-d^2)/4                 " cross sectional area
* I = pi()*(D^4-d^4)/64                " moment of inertia
* k = sqrt(I/A)                        " radius of gyration
* Lok = L/k                            " the L/k ratio
* n = nvalue(state)                    " assign n based on state

* Mt = 63000*P/N                       " torsional moment
* Mb = W*L/8                           " bending moment
* Sb = Mb*D/(2*I)                      " bending stress
* Sa = 4*Fa/(pi()*(D^2-d^2))           " axial stress
* Txy = Mt*D/(4*I)                     " torsional shear stress
* theta = 584*Mt*L/(G*(D^4-d^4))       " angle of twist

* indic = min(loadfun(load),0)         " no load, tensile load: indic=0
* 0/(1-sgn(abs(loadfun(load)))) + Fa = 0      "set Fa=0 for no load
* 0/(1+loadfun(load))+alpha = loadfun(load)  "set alpha: no or tens load

* 0/(step(Lok,115)*indic)  + alpha = Sy/(pi()^2*n*E)*Lok^2  " L/k=>115
* 0/((1-step(Lok,115))*indic)  + alpha = 1/(1-.0044*Lok)    " L/k <115

  "              ASME  Code equation

* Ss = D/(4*I)*sqrt((Kb*Mb+alpha*Fa*D*(1+K^2)/8)^2 + (Kt*Mt)^2)
```

Figure 14-13.
Rule Sheet for design of power transmission shafts

The first rule in the Rule Sheet in Figure 14-13 sets d to 0 if the shaft is solid. The rules in this model are based on the equations given in Chapter 9 of Schaum's Outline Series book *Machine Design* by A.F. Hall, A.R. Holowenko, and H.G. Laughlin (New York: McGraw-Hill, 1961). The sample problems are also taken from that chapter. The model design techniques discussed in Chapters 7 and 11 of our book were used to simplify the equations before entering them in the Rule Sheet. For example, the original equation for the torsional stress was

$$Txy = 16*Mt*D/(pi(D\wedge 4-d\wedge 4))$$

By substituting for the denominator in this equation from the rule for I (the fifth rule), we obtain the rule for Txy shown in the figure.

Another user-defined function *nvalue* with Table Lookup Mapping is used to relate the state of the shaft—hinged, fixed, or partially restrained as in a bearing—to the value of n. The Domain and Range values of the function are as follows:

Domain	Range
'hinged	1
'fixed	2.25
'bearing	1.6

The column-action factor, *alpha*, is unity for a tensile load, zero for no load, and for a compression load it depends on the L/k ratio. The user-defined function *loadfun* with Table Lookup Mapping is used to distinguish between the three types of loading. The Domain and Range values of the function are as follows:

Domain	Range
'none	0
'compress	−1
'tensile	1

The 0/0 bypass can be used to set *alpha* to 0 or 1 for no load or tensile load respectively. This is accomplished by the rule

$$0/(1+loadfun(load)) + alpha = loadfun(load)$$

shown in the Rule Sheet. This rule is bypassed when the load is a compression load. We now need a rule that will set the axial load Fa to zero when there is no load and be bypassed at other times. Using the 0/0 bypass and the *sgn* and *abs* functions, we come up with the following rule:

$$0/(1-sgn(abs(loadfun(load)))) + Fa = 0$$

In the case of a compression load, the value of *alpha*, as mentioned earlier, depends on the L/k ratio. The applicable equations are as follows:

$$alpha = 1/(1-0.0044(L/k)) \qquad \text{for } L/k < 115$$
$$alpha = Sy/(pi()\hat{}2*n*E) * (L/k)\hat{}2 \qquad \text{for } L/k \geq 115$$

where Sy is the yield stress in compression and E is the modulus of elasticity.

We can formulate these equations as conditional rules using the *step* function in the denominator of the conditional part in order to check the value of L/k and turn on the appropriate equation. At the same time, either of these rules should be used only for a compression load, and both should be bypassed for no load and tensile load conditions. To accomplish this, we use the following rule to set an indicator *indic* to zero for no load and tensile load conditions:

$$indic = min(loadfun(load),0)$$

As seen in the Rule Sheet in Figure 14-13, *indic* is used along with the *step* function in the denominator of the conditional part of the rules for *alpha*. Note that a rule $Lok=L/k$ is used in the model so that the actual value of the ratio can be displayed.

Hollow Shaft Example

A hollow shaft of 20-inch outside diameter is supported by two bearings 20 feet apart. The shaft is driven by a flexible coupling at one end and drives a ship's propeller at 100 rpm. The maximum thrust on the propeller is 120,000 lb when the shaft is transmitting 8000 hp. The shaft weighs 15,000 lb. Determine the maximum shear stress in the shaft by means of the ASME code equation, taking into account the weight of the shaft and the column effect. Assume that $Kb = 1.5$ and $Kt = 1.0$.

The given input values are assigned and the model is solved. Figure 14-14 shows the Variable Sheet with the solution obtained by the Direct Solver. The Calculation Unit for *L* is inches. The maximum shear stress *Ss* is found to be 3686.31 psi.

Solid Shaft Example

A section of commercial shafting 5 ft long between bearings carries a 200-lb pulley at its midpoint, as indicated in Figure 14-15. The pulley is

```
=================== VARIABLE SHEET ========================================
St Input      Name     Output     Unit      Comment
-- -----      ----     ------     ----      -------
   'hollow    type                          shaft: solid or hollow
   'bearing   state                         hinged, fixed, bearing
   'compress  load                          tensile, compress, none
   120000     Fa                  lb        axial load
   15000      W                   lb        shaft weight
   8000       P                   hp        power transmitted
   100        N                   rpm       shaft speed
   20         D                   in        outer diameter
   12         d                   in        inner diameter
   20         L                   ft        length of shaft
              E                   lb/in^2   modulus of elasticity
              G                   lb/in^2   torsional modulus of elasticity
   1.5        Kb                            shock & fatigue factor, bending
   1          Kt                            shock & fatigue factor, torsion

              K        .6                   ratio of inner to outer dia
              k        5.8309519  in        radius of gyration
              n        1.6                  n value based on shaft state
              alpha    1.2211541            column-action factor
              A        201.06193  in^2      cross sectional area of shaft
              I        6836.1056  in^4      rectangular moment of inertia
              Mb       450000     in*lb     bending moment
              Mt       5040000    in*lb     torsional moment
              Sa       596.83104  lb/in^2   axial stress (tens. or comp.)
              Sb       658.26953  lb/in^2   bending stress (tens. or comp.)
              Ss       3784.8693  lb/in^2   allowable stress
              Sy                  lb/in^2   yield stress in compression
              Txy      3686.3093  lb/in^2   torsional shear stress
              theta               deg       angle of twist
              Lok      41.159660            the L/K ratio
              indic    -1                   0 for no load and tensile loads
```

Figure 14-14.
Variable Sheet with solution of the hollow shaft example

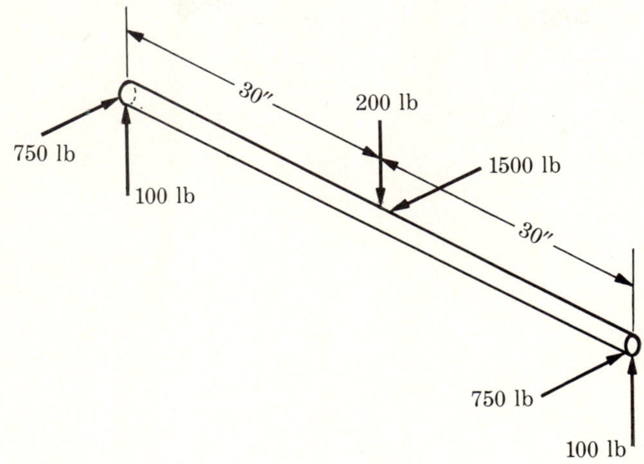

Figure 14-15.
Solid shaft example: vertical and horizontal loads acting on the pulley shaft

keyed to the shaft and receives 20 hp at 150 rpm, which is transmitted to a flexible coupling just outside the right bearing. The belt drive is horizontal and the sum of the belt tensions is 1500 lb. Assume $Kt = Kb = 1.5$. Calculate the necessary shaft diameter and determine the angle of twist between bearings, with $G = 12 * 10\hat{}6$ psi.

The vertical and horizontal loading are shown in Figure 14-15. Since the arrangement of the elements on the shaft will vary from one example to another, it is better to draw the moment diagrams and calculate the maximum bending moment from them. Once this is done, the model can be used to solve the rest of the problem. It follows from the figure that the maximum bending moment is

$$Mb = sqrt(3000\hat{}2 + 22500\hat{}2) = 22700 \text{ in}*\text{lb}$$

According to the ASME code for a shaft with keyway, the maximum allowable stress is 6000 lb/in^2; so *Ss* is assigned an input value of 6000. Since there is no axial loading, *load* is assigned *'none;* when the other input values and the calculated value of *Mb* are also assigned and the Action key is pressed, the Direct Solver fails to solve the problem. The reason is that since *D* is unknown, *I* cannot be evaluated, and the rules for *Sb*, *Ss*, and *Txy* remain unsolved. Therefore, the Iterative Solver has to be used. Since we are interested in evaluating *D*, we make *D* a guess with an initial guess value of 4. The solution shown in Figure 14-16 is obtained in

```
==================== VARIABLE SHEET ============================================
St Input      Name     Output     Unit       Comment
-- -----      ----     ------     ----       -------
   'solid     type                           shaft: solid or hollow
   'bearing   state                          hinged, fixed, bearing
   'none      load                           tensile, compres, none
              Fa       0          lb         axial load
              W        3026.6667  lb         shaft weight
   20         P                   hp         power transmitted
   150        N                   rpm        shaft speed
              D        3.1352183  in         outer diameter
              d        0          in         inner diameter
   5          L                   ft         length of shaft
              E                   lb/in^2    modulus of elasticity
   12000000   G                   lb/in^2    torsional modulus of elasticity
   1.5        Kb                             shock & fatigue factor, bending
   1.5        Kt                             shock & fatigue factor, torsion

              K        0                     ratio of inner to outer dia
              k        .78380456  in         radius of gyration
              n        1.6                   n value based on shaft state
              alpha    0                     column-action factor
              A        7.7201447  in^2       cross sectional area of shaft
              I        4.7428677  in^4       rectangular moment of inertia
   22700      Mb                  in*lb      bending moment
              Mt       8400       in*lb      torsional moment
              Sa       0          lb/in^2    axial stress (tens. or comp.)
              Sb       7502.7872  lb/in^2    bending stress (tens. or comp.)
   6000       Ss                  lb/in^2    allowable stress
              Sy                  lb/in^2    yield stress in compression
              Txy      1388.1809  lb/in^2    torsional shear stress
              theta    .25385810  deg        angle of twist
              LoK      76.549695             the L/K ratio
              indic    0                     0 for no load and tensile loads
```

Figure 14-16.
Variable Sheet with solution for the solid shaft problem (note that the value of *Mb* was calculated from the moment diagram and assigned as input)

seven iterations. Note that both *alpha* and *Fa* are evaluated as zero since there is no load. The angle of twist is evaluated as 0.2539 degrees. However, since the pulley is located in the center of the shaft, the actual angle of twist is 0.2539/2=0.12695 degrees.

The diameter *D* is evaluated as 3.14 in. However, shafts come in standard sizes and the next standard size has a 3 1/4-in. diameter. To see if the allowable stress *Ss* is exceeded when a 3 1/4-in. shaft is chosen, we assign the value of *D*=3.25 to input and solve again. *Ss* is evaluated as 5386.47, which is below the allowable 6000.

Expanding the Model

The model can be expanded to include a user-defined function that would return the nearest standard shaft diameter. A rule to check if the allowable stress has been exceeded can be added and a message returned accordingly.

HELICAL SPRING ANALYSIS

Mechanical springs are used in machines to exert force, to provide flexibility, and to store or absorb energy. Essentially there are two types—flat springs and wire springs. Helical springs are classified as wire springs and are usually made of wire with a circular cross section. These springs are subjected to a torsional shear stress and to a transverse shear stress. In addition, there is the stress effect due to the helix curvature. A correction factor K is used to take into account the effects of transverse shear and curvature. The equations, based on S. Timoshenko's treatment of the action of axial forces on open-coiled helical springs, are given in the Rule Sheet in Figure 14-17*a* (S. Timoshenko, *Strength of Materials, Part II*, 3rd ed. Princeton: Van Nostrand, 1956, p. 292).

```
==================== RULE SHEET ==================================...
S Rule
- ----
* EI = pi()*wdia^4*E/64
* GJ = pi()*wdia^4*G/32
* spl_def = spl0 + disp
* spl0/wlen = sin(alpha)
* 2*pi()*sprad*nc/wlen = cos(alpha)
* disp = P*sprad^2*wlen*(sin(alpha)^2/EI + K*cos(alpha)^2/GJ)
* 16/3*(K-1) = 1/(.25/(wdia/sprad)^2-1)
```

a. Rule Sheet

```
==================== VARIABLE SHEET ==========================================
St Input      Name      Output      Unit       Comment
-- -----      ----      ------      ----       -------
   2          P                     lb         applied load
   .05        wdia                  in         diameter of wire
              wlen      26.182492   in         length of wire
   .2         sprad                 in         spring radius
              spl0      4.5465420   in         original spring length
              spl_def   4.8465420   in         spring length - deformed
   .3         disp                  in         displacement
   10         alpha                 deg        helical angle
              nc        20.518829              number of coils
   12000000   G                     lb/in^2    shear modulus
   30000000   E                     lb/in^2    tensile modulus
              EI        9.2038847   lb*in^2    bending rigidity
              GJ        7.3631078   lb*in^2    torsional rigidity
              K         1.0625                 corr factor: finite wdia/sprad
```

b. Variable Sheet with solution of a problem

Figure 14-17.
Helical spring analysis

Example 1

A helical spring with a helix angle of 10 degrees and a radius of 0.2 in. is made from steel wire of 0.05-in. diameter. If the spring deforms 0.3 in. under a load of 2 lb, find the length of wire, the original length of the spring, the number of coils, and the correction factor K. Assume G=12E6 psi and E=30E6 psi.

The Calculation Unit for *alpha* is radians and a conversion between radians and the Display Unit degrees is defined in the Unit Sheet. The solution obtained by the Direct Solver is also shown in Figure 14-17*b*. The number of coils *nc* has been returned as 20.518829. In practice this means that 21 coils are required, that is, the ceiling of the number has to be returned. This can be done if we add the rule

$$nc\_req = int(nc) + sgn(mod(nc,1))$$

and to ensure backsolvability, the rule

$$nc = given('nc\_req,nc\_req,nc)$$

is also added to the model. Note that the rule for the ceiling is different from that given in Figure 11-17*a*. Since the number of coils can only be a positive number, the present rule will suffice (it does not handle negative non-integer numbers correctly). When we solve the model after adding these two rules, *nc_req* is evaluated as 21.

```
==================== VARIABLE SHEET ==========================================
St Input      Name     Output     Unit       Comment
-- -----      ----     ------     ----       -------
   2          P                   lb         applied load
   .05        wdia                in         diameter of wire
              wlen     26.138669  in         length of wire
   .2         sprad               in         spring radius
   4          spl0                in         original spring length
              spl_def  4.3        in         spring length - deformed
   .3         disp                in         displacement
              alpha    8.8025594  deg        helical angle
              nc       20.555494             number of coils
   12000000   G                   lb/in^2    shear modulus
   30000000   E                   lb/in^2    tensile modulus
              EI       9.2038847  lb*in^2    bending rigidity
              GJ       7.3631078  lb*in^2    torsional rigidity
              K        1.0625                corr factor: finite wdia/sprad
              nc_req   21                    actual number of coils
```

Figure 14-18.
Variable Sheet with solution obtained by Iterative Solver

Example 2

What will be the helical angle if a spring 4 in. long is required and the other given values are the same? Is there a change in the number of coils?

Since both *wlen* and *alpha* are unknown, the Direct Solver cannot evaluate either of them from the fourth, fifth, or sixth rules. Also, *nc* is unknown so a redundant equation does not help either. Therefore, the Iterative Solver has to be used. Since *alpha* is to be calculated, it is made a guess variable with an initial guess value of 10. After four iterations, the solution shown in Figure 14-18 is obtained. The required number of coils remains the same as before.

COLOR CODING OF RESISTORS

An eight-unit color code is used to identify the resistance characteristics of fixed non-metallic resistors. The values of individual resistors are represented by bands of three of the eight available colors at one end of the resistor body. To determine the value of a resistor, we must decode these color-band markings into resistance values using the standard color-number coding list. Figure 14-19 shows a resistor with the bands and

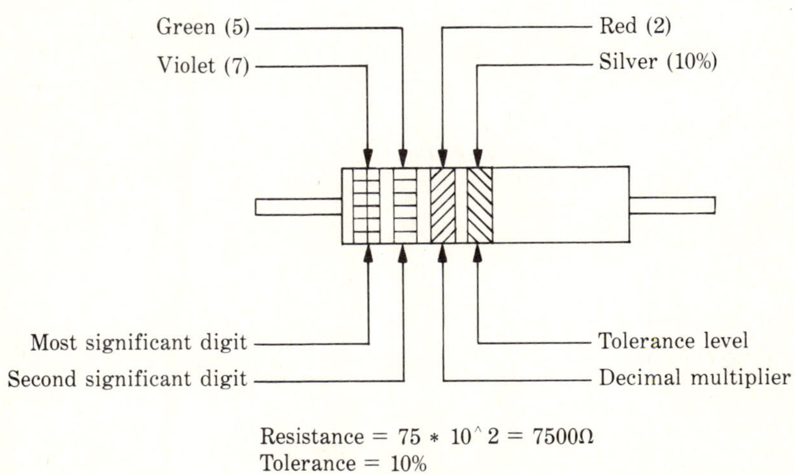

Figure 14-19.
Resistor with color markings and decoding scheme

decoding scheme. The first two colors represent the first two significant digits of the resistance value. The third color represents the decimal-multiplier factor, or the number of zeroes to the right or decimal places to the left of the first two digits. A fourth color band is used to denote the resistor tolerance; a gold band indicates a 5% tolerance, a silver indicates a 10% tolerance, and absence of a band implies 20% tolerance.

A user-defined function can be used to convert the color codes into the corresponding numeric values and vice versa. The User Function Subsheet for function *rescol* is shown in Figure 14-20.

The first three rules in the Rule Sheet in Figure 14-21 take care of this conversion. The fourth rule calculates the value of the resistance *R_mnf* according to the scheme given in Figure 14-19. The fifth rule uses the user-defined function *toltab* with Table Lookup Mapping to convert the color of the tolerance band into the tolerance %. The Domain and Range values of the funciton are as follows:

Domain	**Range**
0	*'cantget*
5	*'gold*
10	*'silver*
10	*'none*

The Variable Sheet in Figure 14-21 shows the resistance calculated for the resistor shown in Figure 14-19.

```
==================== USER FUNCTION: rescol ========...
Comment:                          Resistor color codes
Domain List:                      color
Mapping:                          Table
Range List:                       number
Element Domain      Range
------- ------      -----
1        'black     0
2        'brown     1
3        'red       2
4        'orange    3
5        'yellow    4
6        'green     5
7        'blue      6
8        'violet    7
9        'gray      8
10       'grey      8
11       'white     9
```

Figure 14-20.
User Function Subsheet for function *rescol*

```
==================== VARIABLE SHEET ==================================...
St Input      Name      Output     Unit       Comment
-- -----      ----      ------     ----       -------
   'violet    first                           color of first band
   'green     second                          color of second band
   'red       third                           color of third band
   'silver    fourth                          color of fourth band

              d1        7                     value of first color
              d2        5                     value of second color
              d3        2                     value of third color

              R_mnf     7500       ohm        resistance manufactured
              tol_mnf   10         %          manufacturer's tolerance

==================== RULE SHEET ======================================...
S Rule
- ----
  d1 = rescol(first)               " map first color to d1
  d2 = rescol(second)              " map second color to d2
  d3 = rescol(third)               " map third color to d3
  R_mnf = (10*d1+d2) * 10^d3       " resistance value
  fourth = toltab(tol_mnf)         " find tol_mnf for fourth color
```

Figure 14-21.
Variable and Rule Sheets with value of resistance for resistor in Figure 14-20

Reverse Decoding

What if we want to select a resistor to meet our particular requirements? What should the color bands be if we want a resistor of 46380 ohms with a tolerance of 7%?

This problem implies a reverse decoding, and we need to add a few more rules to take care of this inverse operation. The first step is to determine the magnitude *mag* of the required resistance *R_req*. The rule for this is shown in the partial Rule Sheet in Figure 14-22*a*. The next rule calculates the nearest manufactured resistance, *R_mnf* corresponding to *R_req*. The values of *d3* and *d2* can be calculated with the next two rules in the figure. There is no need to add a separate rule for *d1* since the rule

$$R\_mnf = (10*d1+d2) * 10\wedge d3$$

shown in the Rule Sheet in Figure 14-21 can do the job. In fact, the new rules for *d3* and *d2* are based on this rule. Once the values of the three digits are known, TK!Solver can find the colors using the first three rules in Figure 14-21.

```
==================== RULE SHEET =======================================...
S Rule
- ----
* mag = 10^int(log(R_req) - 1)              " determine magnitude
* R_mnf = int((R_req/mag+.5)) * mag         " calculate R_mnf from R_req

* d3 = int(log(R_mnf) - 1)                  " calculate d3
* d2 = mod(R_mnf/10^d3,10)                  " calculate d2
* fourth = tolstep(abs(tol_all))            " find fourth color for tol_all
```

a. Partial Rule Sheet with the additional rules needed for reverse decoding

```
==================== VARIABLE SHEET ====================================...
St Input     Name      Output     Unit      Comment
-- -----     ----      ------     ----      -------
             first     'yellow              color of first band
             second    'blue                color of second band
             third     'orange              color of third band
             fourth    'gold                color of fourth band

             d1        4                    value of first color
             d2        6                    value of second color
             d3        3                    value of third color

             R_mnf     46000      ohm       resistance manufactured
             tol_mnf   5          %         manufacturer's tolerance

   46380     R_req                ohm       required resistance
   7         tol_all              %         allowable tolerance

             mag       1000                 magnitude of R_req
```

b. Variable Sheet with the color bands determined for the specified resistance

Figure 14-22.
Enhanced resistor color coding model

For finding the color corresponding to the value of the allowable tolerance *tol_all*, we cannot use the function *toltab*. This is because the specified value of *tol_all* may not be a standard one and may not be defined in the function. When the given value (7% in this case) is used as the argument, a "User Function: argument error" message will occur when TK!Solver tries to do a Table Lookup. So a function *tolstep* with Step Mapping between the same Domain and Range values as *toltab* for finding the tolerance percent corresponding to a given color because the Step Mapping is non-invertible (recall from Chapter 6 the section "User-Defined Functions"). In addition, we take the absolute value of *tol_all* in the last rule to ensure absolute tolerance.

The Variable Sheet with the color bands for the required resistor is shown in Figure 14-22*b*.

EIGENVALUES AND EIGENVECTORS

The mathematical concepts of eigenvalue (or characteristic value) and eigenvector can be applied to the analysis of many engineering problems. These concepts are helpful in identifying principal normal stresses, natural frequencies of vibration of mechanical and electrical systems, modes of deflection in which an equilibrium of a structure may be achieved, and so forth.

The eigenvalues and eigenmatrices are not easy to understand or compute. Before we show how to use TK!Solver for their computation, let's do some explanation. Suppose we have an $n \times n$ matrix A which relates all inputs *x1,x2,...,xn* to all outputs *y1,y2,...,yn*. Is it possible to find n coefficients *L1,L2,...,Ln*, each *Li* of which would represent the dependence of just *yi* on *xi* only? The answer is "yes," and the L's are the eigenvalues. In order to have such a transformation, the n-dimensional system of coordinates, in which the inputs x are given, has to be transformed; the n-dimensional eigenvectors associated with each eigenvalue *Li* serve the purpose of this transformation.

Let's consider the equation of a conic section (ellipse or hyperbola)

$$a\, x^2 + 2\, b\, x\, y + c\, y^2 = 1$$

and find out how the system of coordinates would have to be transformed so that the coordinates would coincide with the figure's axes of symmetry and the *xy* term would vanish.

The coefficients on the left-hand side of the equation may be arranged in the form of a symmetrical matrix

$$\begin{matrix} a & b \\ b & c \end{matrix}$$

and our task may be considered as one of replacing this matrix by another one containing only diagonal elements. These elements will be the eigenvalues and they may be found by solving the first two equations in the Rule Sheet in Figure 14-23 for L. The other unknowns are the components of the eigenvector *C1* and *C2*. That makes it two equations for three unknowns. The third equation was added to make *C1* and *C2* fit as the coordinate transformation coefficients *sin*(*phi*) and *cos*(*phi*), where *phi* would be the angle of the desired rotation of the coordinates.

Suppose we have an ellipse with $a=4$, $c=7$, and $b=-1$. We assign these as input values, guess *C1*=0.9, and solve. The solution is shown in the Variable Sheet in Figure 14-23. This is just one eigenvalue and associated eigenvectors. There should be another one because of the size of the

```
==================== VARIABLE SHEET ==========================================
St Input        Name        Output        Unit        Comment
-- -----        ----        ------        ----        -------
   3            a
   -2.5         b
   10           c
                C1          .95229551
                C2          .30517743
                L           2.1988374

==================== RULE SHEET ===...
S Rule
- ----
  a*C1 + b*C2 = L*C1
  b*C1 + c*C2 = L*C2

  C1^2 + C2^2 = 1
```

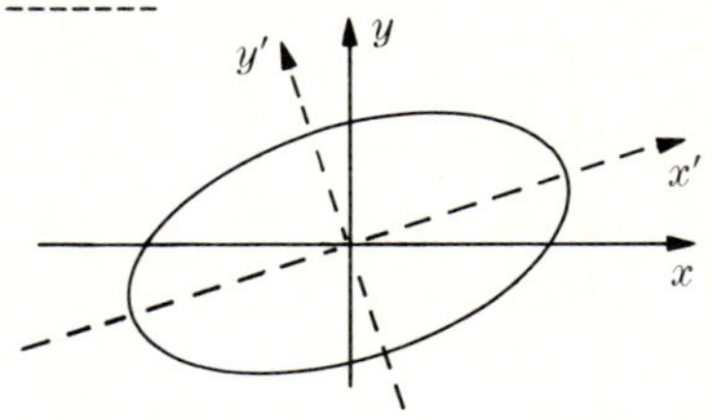

Figure 14-23.
Transformation of coordinates via eigenvalues

matrix, 2×2. We get it by iterating from a guess $C2$=0.9 (the results are L= 10.801, $C1$=0.305, and $C2$=−0.952). Thus the equation of our ellipse in the transformed system of coordinates will be

$$2.199\,x'^2 + 10.801\,y'^2 = 1$$

if we want the large diameter along the x' axis. The eigenvectors arranged as the coordinate transformation coefficients are

0.952	0.305
−0.305	0.952

and the angle of rotation from the old system to the new one is phi= $asin$(0.2898)=17.8 degrees.

The next example deals with the evaluation of the largest normal stress when the triaxial state of stress is defined by a stress matrix:

$$\begin{matrix} \sigma_{xx} & \sigma_{xy} & \sigma_{xz} \\ \sigma_{yx} & \sigma_{yy} & \sigma_{yz} \\ \sigma_{zx} & \sigma_{zy} & \sigma_{zz} \end{matrix} \quad = \quad \begin{matrix} 12 & 5 & 6.3 \\ 5 & 20 & 4 \\ 6.3 & 4 & 30 \end{matrix}$$

(Stresses are expressed in millions of N/m ^ 2.) We should look for a transformation to coordinates in which all the off-diagonal shear stresses would vanish and only the principal stresses along the diagonal would remain. In other words, we have to find the eigenvalues of the matrix. The largest of them will represent the magnitude of the largest normal stress, and the associated eigenvector will indicate the direction in which this stress occurs.

We will use the model in Figure 14-24*a* for evaluation of the eigen-

```
==================== RULE SHEET ======================================...
S Rule
- ----
* (a11-L)*x1 +      a12*x2 +      a13*x3 = 0
*      a21*x1 + (a22-L)*x2 +      a23*x3 = 0
*      a31*x1 +      a32*x2 + (a33-L)*x3 = 0

* (a11-L)*(a22-L)*(a33-L) + a12*a23*a31 + a13*a21*a32 = part
* part + (a11-L)*a23*a32 + (a22-L)*a31*a13 + (a33-L)*a12*a21 = det
```

a. Rule Sheet

```
==================== VARIABLE SHEET ==================================...
St Input      Name      Output      Unit       Comment
-- -----      ----      ------      ----       -------
   12         a11                              )
   5          a12                              )
   6.3        a13                              )
   5          a21                              ) Cofficients
   20         a22                              )
   4          a23                              ) of matrix A
   6.3        a31                              )
   4          a32                              )
   30         a33                              )

              L         34.073904              Eigenvalue

              x1        .38039387              ) Eigenvector
              x2        .41935554              ) components
   1          x3                               )

              det       -2027.247              Determinant of (A - LI)
```

b. Variable Sheet

Figure 14-24.
Eigenvalue/eigenvector solver for 3 × 3 matrix

values and eigenvectors of 3×3 matrices. The first three rules represent the standard definition of eigenvalues. It is clear from this definition that a trivial (and also useless) solution of the system is $x1=x2=x3=0$ regardless of L. A useful consequence of this fact is that the determinant of the matrix A (with L subtracted from the diagonal elements) must be equal to zero too. This condition is expressed in the last two rules in Figure 14-24*a*. (They are, in fact, only one rule which had to be split in order to be fully visible.) This rule is referred to as a "characteristic equation" and represents a cubic equation in L. We may use it only to evaluate the eigenvalues or also to look for them by examining the function $det=f(L)$ (the roots of the characteristic equation are the eigenvalues).

The solution of our problem is shown in Figure 14-24*b*. In order to obtain it, we assign the values of matrix coefficients as input. We also assign one of the eigenvector components $x3=1$. Then we assign $L=30$ and *x2*=0.5 as guesses and solve (the iteration takes five steps). The results show that the maximum normal stress is 34.07E6 N/m^2 and that the *x*,*y*,*z* components of its vector are in the proportion of 0.38:0.42:1. This is the maximum eigenvalue as we verified beforehand by examining the *det*=*f*(*L*) function (the other eigenvalues and principal stresses are 8.75E6 and 19.18E6 N/m^2).

15

Case Studies: Finance and Management

The recent emphasis on quantitative techniques in financial analysis and management provides ample scope for TK!Solver applications. In this chapter we will see how TK!Solver can help the financial analyst choose the correct investment alternative and analyze a firm's operating characteristics. The examples in Inventory Management and Waiting Line theory demonstrate how TK!Solver can help management make decisions.

CAPITAL BUDGETING

Capital budgeting is an important process that helps the investor select those capital investment projects that provide the highest return on investment under the conditions of acceptable risks. The two commonly used techniques for capital budgeting are the Net Present Value (NPV) and Internal Rate of Return (IRR).

Since money in hand today can be invested to grow to some larger amount in the future, it follows that money received at some future date is worth less than money received today. For example, let's say we are promised \$100 at the end of a year. But if the same amount were available today, we could deposit it in a bank and earn 5.5% interest on it so that at the end of the year we would have $105.50. Similarly, to receive $100 at the end of a year, we would have to invest only $94.79. This $94.79 is known as the *present value* of the future amount of $100. The 5.5% interest we receive is known as the *rate of return* on the investment.

In a capital investment, money is received periodically, typically at the end of each year. The present value of a capital investment project is the stream of cash inflows from the project, discounted to the present using the cost of capital. The main factors affecting the cost of capital (discount rate) are the returns available on alternative investment opportunities, the degree of risk, and inflation. The net present value (NPV) is the present value of the cash inflows minus the present value of the cash outflows. If the NPV is positive, the project is expected to yield a return in excess of the cost of capital. If the NPV is zero, the yield is expected to equal the exact cost of capital. If the NPV is negative, the yield is expected to be less than the cost of capital, and the investment is not profitable.

The first rule in the Rule Sheet in Figure 15-1 uses the built-in *npv* function and returns the net present value *netpv,* of a stream of cash flows defined in the list *cashflow,* at the discount rate *drate.* Recall that a similar rule was used in Chapter 6 in the section "List Functions" to illustrate the working of the *npv* function. The user-defined function *fun* is used to return a message based on the sign of *netpv,* indicating whether the

```
=================== VARIABLE SHEET =====================================...
St Input      Name      Output     Unit      Comment
-- -----      ----      ------     ----      -------
   12         drate                %         discount rate
              netpv$    280.77     $         net present value (formatted)
              message   'yes                 investment indicator

              futval    441.80480 $          future value
              netpv     280.77494 $          net present value (internal)

=================== RULE SHEET ========================================...
S Rule
- ----
* netpv = npv(drate,'cashflow)              " net present value
* message = fun(sgn(netpv$))                " message about investment

* netpv$ = int(100*netpv + .5)/100          " dollars and cents
* netpv = given('netpv$,netpv$,netpv)       "    formatting

* futval = netpv*(1+drate)^(count('cashflow)-1)    " future value
```

Figure 15-1.
Variable and Rule Sheets for the capital budgeting model; note the dollars and cents formatter in the Rule Sheet

investment is profitable or not or whether it breaks even. The Domain and Range values of the function are as follows:

Domain	Range
−1	*'no*
0	*'ok*
1	*'yes*

Thus in the second rule, if *netpv* is positive, *sgn*(*netpv*) is 1, and the function returns the message *'yes*. In order to display the value of the NPV in the dollars and cents format, we add the formatter, given in Chapter 11 in the section "Miscellaneous Tricks," to the rules. The future value *futval* of the cash flow series is given by the formula

$$futval = netpv * (1 + drate)\wedge(n-1)$$

where n is the number of values in the stream of cash flows (in the list *cashflow*). The *count* function can be used in the rule to return the value of n; this leads to the last rule in the Rule Sheet.

Example

Consider the following investment proposal: a proposed investment of $10,000 is expected to produce cash inflows of $2,800, $3,000, $4,000, and $4,000 respectively at the end of each succeeding year. If the cost of capital (discount rate) is 12%, is the investment worthwhile?

In order to create the list *cashflow*, we must declare the listname on the List Sheet and enter the values in the List Subsheet. Note that the initial investment is entered as a negative value since it is a cash outflow. The List Subsheet is shown in Figure 15-2.

```
==================== LIST: cashflow ===========...
Comment:                      cash flow values
Display Unit:                 $
Storage Unit:                 $
Element Value
------- -----
1       -10000
2       2800
3       3000
4       4000
5       4000
```

Figure 15-2.
List Subsheet for *cashflow* with the stream of cash flow values

The Calculation Unit for the discount rate in the *npv* function is assumed to be a decimal fraction, so a conversion is defined in the Unit Sheet to make the Display Unit the more convenient percent (%). The discount rate of 12% is assigned to *drate* and the model is solved. We can see from the Variable Sheet in Figure 15-1 that the investment is profitable since the message *'yes* is displayed.

Internal Rate of Return

The NPV method does not indicate the actual rate of return that a project is expected to yield. We must use the *internal rate of return* (IRR) criterion to get the actual rate of return for a particular capital investment. Using the IRR, we can evaluate projects with the cost of capital as the benchmark for acceptance. The project with the highest IRR is considered the best.

The IRR is the discount rate at which the present value of the cash flow is equal to the initial investment. Alternately, it is the discount rate at which the net present value of an investment is zero. IRR can be found with the Iterative Solver. There can be more than one IRR for an investment, and the particular value returned by the Iterative Solver depends on the initial guess value. We may use List Solving to generate the net present values for a series of discount rates; the plot of NPV versus discount rate crosses the zero NPV line at points corresponding to the IRR values.

Example

The ABC Manufacturing Company is considering the installation of machinery requiring an initial investment of $100,000. If returns of

```
==================== VARIABLE SHEET ===================================...
St Input       Name     Output     Unit        Comment
-- -----       ----     ------     ----        -------
               drate    15.435647  %           discount rate
   0           netpv$              $           net present value (formatted)
               message  'ok                    investment indicator

               futval   2.0497E-6  $           future value
               netpv    .000001    $           net present value (internal)
```

Figure 15-3.
Variable Sheet with calculated IRR; note the message *'ok*

$20,000, $40,000, $40,000, $30,000, and $20,000 are expected at the end of succeeding years, what is the internal rate of return on the investment?

The cash outflow and inflows are defined in the List Subsheet of *cashflow*. Since IRR has to be calculated, *netpv$* is assigned zero, and *drate* is assigned a guess value of 12. After five iterations, the solution shown in Figure 15-3 is obtained. The message is *'ok* since *netpu$* is zero.

Profitability Index

The profitability index provides a measure of the profitability of an investment on a per dollar basis. With this index, it is possible to compare projects requiring significantly different cash outflows. The profitability index is expressed in the following formula as the ratio between the present value of cash inflows and the present value of cash outflows:

$$\textit{prof index} = \frac{\textit{net present value} + \textit{cash outflows}}{\textit{cash outflows}}$$

Example

The XYZ Company is considering investment projects A, B, and C. Project A requires an initial investment of $10,000, B requires $30,000, and C requires $18,000. The cash flows at the end of each year for the three projects are as follows:

Year	Project A	Project B	Project C
1	2,500	6,000	6,000
2	3,000	10,000	6,500
3	4,000	12,000	6,500
4	4,000	16,000	7,000

Using the profitability index criterion, which option should XYZ Company choose, assuming that the cost of capital is 13%?

Since three projects have to be compared, List Solving can be used. The initial investment and the cash flows from the three projects are entered in the three lists *projA*, *projB*, and *projC* respectively. In order to use these lists in successive instances of List Solving, we must modify the first rule as shown in Figure 15-4. The variable *option* is declared as a list with *'projA*, *'projB*, and *'projC* as its elements. It is also made an input.

In this example, there is only one cash outflow in each project, the initial investment, that has to be taken into account to calculate the profitability index. The *element* function can be used to access this value from

```
==================== VARIABLE SHEET ====================================...
St Input      Name     Output     Unit      Comment
-- -----      ----     ------     ----      -------
   13         drate               %         discount rate
L             netpv$   1198.25    $         net present value (formatted)
              message  'yes                 investment indicator

              futval              $         future value
L             netpv    1198.2451 $          net present value (internal)

L  projC      option                        list of project options
L             Pindex   1.0665692            profitability index

==================== RULE SHEET ========================================...
S Rule
- ----
  netpv = npv(drate,option)                 " net present value
  message = fun(sgn(netpv$))                " message about investment

  netpv$ = int(100*netpv + .5)/100          " dollars and cents
  netpv = given('netpv$,netpv$,netpv)       "    formatting

  "futval = netpv*(1+drate)^(count('cashflow)-1)    " future value

  Pindex = 1-netpv/element(element('option,element()),1) " profit index
```

Figure 15-4.
Rule Sheet with the modified rule for *netpv*, the rule for *Pindex*, and the Variable Sheet with the *Pindex* and *netpv$* for projC

option	netpv$	profitable	prof index
projA	-212.69	no	.978730499
projB	1270.9	yes	1.042363431
projC	1198.25	yes	1.066569172

Figure 15-5.
Table showing the relative merits of the three options

the corresponding list. This leads to the last rule shown in the Rule Sheet in Figure 15-4. The innermost *element*() function returns the instance number. The next *element* function returns the name of the list for the project, while the outermost one returns the first value in that list. *Pindex* is declared as a list and List Solving is initiated.

Figure 15-5 shows the results displayed with the table-generating feature. We can see that Project A yields a negative NPV and therefore is not profitable. Project B has a higher NPV than Project C, but the profitability index of C is higher than that of B. Hence, Project C is the option to be chosen.

Getting More From the Model

Instead of us looking at the generated table and deciding which of the projects is the best, TK!Solver can be made to choose the best option and display it. The basic idea is as follows: we make the list *Pindex* the Domain list of a user-defined function *maxfun* so that the Domain values are generated during List Solving. The values in the Range list, *inst*, of the function are also generated simultaneously and correspond to the instance numbers. Then, when we use the Direct Solver, the *max* function can pick out the maximum value from the list *Pindex* and the element number can be returned by the function *maxfun*. The element in the list *option* corresponding to this position can then be displayed on the Variable Sheet.

To accomplish this, we need rules that will be activated only when the Direct Solver is used after List Solving. Since the *element*( ) function returns zero during Direct Solving, this function can be used in the denominator of the conditional part of a rule so that the rule is bypassed at other times. The rule to return the element number *elem* corresponding to the maximum value is as follows:

$$0/(1-sgn(element())) + elem = maxfun(max('Pindex))$$

The rule

$$choice = element('option,elem)$$

returns the project name corresponding to *elem* from the list *option*. Note that this need not be a conditional rule because unless *elem* is known, this rule will not be solved and *elem* is evaluated only when the Direct Solver is used.

```
==================== VARIABLE SHEET ====================================...
St Input      Name     Output      Unit       Comment
-- -----      ----     ------      ----       -------
   13         drate                %          discount rate
L             netpv$   1198.25     $          net present value (formatted)
              message  'yes                   investment indicator

              futval               $          future value
L             netpv    1198.2451   $          net present value (internal)

L  'projC     option                          list of project options
L             Pindex                          profitability index

              elem     3                      element number of max Pindex
              choice   'projC                 project to be chosen
```

Figure 15-6.
Variable Sheet showing *choice* made by the Direct Solver

These rules are now added to the Rule Sheet. When the Action key is pressed, TK!Solver beeps, and the rule used for calculating *Pindex* is marked "Element: argument error" because there is no element in the list *option* corresponding to the 0th position. Since this rule is not required now it is commented out. When the Action key is pressed again, "'projC" appears in the Output field of *choice*, as shown in Figure 15-6.

Thus using this two-stage process, TK!Solver can display the best option. Earlier the values of *Pindex* were first generated and then we "looked" at them (see Figure 15-5). Now TK!Solver does the looking as well.

BREAKEVEN AND LEVERAGE ANALYSIS

Over the short run, the operating costs of a firm can be broadly divided into two categories—variable costs and fixed costs. Variable costs include such things as the raw materials, labor, and energy used in the production processes; these costs vary with output. On the other hand, fixed costs vary little with output; they include administrative expenses, depreciation on plant and equipment, and rent.

Breakeven analysis is a valuable management tool for studying the relationships between fixed costs, variable costs, and profits. This type of analysis is used to determine the breakeven point (the point at which total revenues will just cover total costs and the profit is zero). Breakeven analysis is especially useful when considering new products and plant expansion. The number of units to be produced at the breakeven point is given by the first rule in the Rule Sheet in Figure 15-7. The operating earnings of a firm, also known as EBIT (for earnings before interest and taxes) is given by the fourth rule in the figure.

Example

ABC Industries has fixed costs of $300,000 per year. The variable cost per unit of product is $6. If the company sells its product at $10 a piece, how much should it produce and sell in order to have an EBIT of $100,000 per year? Find also the breakeven production.

The given values are entered and the model is solved. From the Variable Sheet in Figure 15-7, we can see that the company has to produce and sell 100,000 units per year to achieve the desired EBIT. The number of units that must be produced at the breakeven point is 75,000.

```
==================== VARIABLE SHEET ====================================...
St Input     Name     Output    Unit      Comment
-- -----     ----     ------    ----      -------
   10        price              $         price per unit
   6         vcpu               $         variable cost per unit
             totvarc  600000    $         total variable cost
   300000    fixcost            $         fixed operating cost
             be_unit  75000               breakeven units
             unitsol  100000              number of units sold
             sales    1000000   $         total sales
   100000    ebit               $         earnings before int. & taxes

==================== RULE SHEET =========================================...
S Rule
- ----
  be_unit = fixcost/(price-vcpu)              " breakeven quantity
  totvarc = vcpu * unitsold                   " total variable cost
  sales = price * unitsold                    " sales
  ebit = unitsold*(price-vcpu) - fixcost      " EBIT
```

Figure 15-7.
Variable and Rule Sheets for breakeven analysis

Net Income

The net income is calculated after the company takes into account the interest paid, the dividend on the preferred stock, and the taxes. Net income is given by the rule

$$netincome = (ebit - fixcharge) * (1 - taxrate)$$

where

$$fixcharge = intexp + prefdiv/(1 - taxrate)$$

as shown in the Rule Sheet in Figure 15-8*a*.

Leverage

Financial analysts use the concept of *leverage* to examine the risk-return tradeoffs of different types of financial decisions. This concept permits an analyst to quantify the change in earnings caused by a change in the level of sales. The higher the leverage, the higher will be the increase in earnings for a given increase in sales, and also the greater the risk. The breakeven point is also higher for a higher leverage. Essentially there are two distinct types of leverages—operating leverage and financial leverage.

```
==================== RULE SHEET ========================================...
S Rule
- ----
* be_unit = fixcost/(price-vcpu)                  " breakeven quantity
* totvarc = vcpu * unitsold                       " total variable cost
* sales = price * unitsold                        " sales
* ebit = unitsold*(price-vcpu) - fixcost          " EBIT
* fixcharge = intexp + prefdiv/(1-taxrate)        " fixed charges
* netincome = (ebit-fixcharge) * (1-taxrate)      " net income

* dol = 1 + fixcost/ebit              " degree of operating leverage
* dfl = 1/(1-fixcharge/ebit)          " degree of financial leverage
* eps = netincome/comstock            " earnings per share
* dcl = dol*dfl                       " degree of combined leverage
```

a. Rule Sheet

```
==================== VARIABLE SHEET ===================================...
St Input      Name     Output     Unit       Comment
-- -----      ----     ------     ----       -------
   25         price               $          price per unit
              vcpu     10         $          variable cost per unit
   750000     totvarc             $          total variable cost
   400000     fixcost             $          fixed operating cost
              be_unit  26666.667             breakeven units
   75000      unitsol                        number of units sold
              sales    1875000    $          total sales
              ebit     725000     $          earnings before int. & taxes

   40         taxrate             %          tax rate
   200000     intexp              $          interest expenses
   175000     comstoc                        outstanding common stock shares
   0          prefdiv             $          preferred dividend payments
              fixchar  200000     $          fixed charges
              netinco  315000     $          net income
              eps      1.8        $          earnings per share
              dol      155.17241  %          degree of operating leverage
              dfl      138.09524  %          degree of financial leverage
              dcl      214.28571  %          degree of combined leverage
```

b. Variable Sheet with solution of a problem

Figure 15-8.
Breakeven and Leverage Analysis model

The *degree of operating leverage* (DOL) is defined as the percentage change in a firm's EBIT resulting from a given percentage change in output or sales. The DOL at a given output or sales is

$$DOL = \frac{EBIT + fixed\ cost}{EBIT}$$

This can be simplified so that EBIT appears only once. The equation is entered in the Rule Sheet as

$$dol = 1 + fixcost/ebit$$

The *degree of financial leverage* (DFL) is defined as the percentage change in the *earnings per share* (EPS) available to common stockholders resulting from a given percentage change in EBIT. The DFL at a given output or sales is

$$DFL = \frac{EBIT}{EBIT - fixcharge}$$

This formula is also simplified when it is entered in the Rule Sheet in Figure 15-8*a* so that EBIT appears only once. The earnings per share is given by the next rule in the Rule Sheet in which the net income is what is available for the common stockholders. The *degree of combined leverage* is a measure of the combined effects of *operating* and *financial leverage* and is given by their product, as shown in the final rule in the Rule Sheet.

Example

XYZ Manufacturing Company sold 75,000 units of the only product it produces at $25 per unit. The fixed costs per year are $400,000, and the total variable cost per year is $750,000. The company has 175,000 shares of common stock outstanding, and the annual interest payments on debts total $200,000. If the tax rate is 40%, calculate the earnings per share and the three leverages—combined, operating, and financial.

The Calculation Unit for *taxrate, dol, dfl,* and *dcl* is the decimal fraction (1), while the Display Unit is percent (%). The given values are assigned (since there are no preferred stocks, *prefdiv* is assigned zero), and the Action key is pressed. The solution obtained by the Direct Solver is shown in the Variable Sheet in Figure 15-8*b*. The earnings per share *eps* is $1.8. Note also that the variable cost per unit *vcpu* is evaluated as $10.

Modernizing the Plant

The company is considering a change to a highly automated process that would bring down the variable cost per unit to $6, while the fixed costs would increase to $600,000 per year. There are two ways in which it could raise the $800,000 required for the purpose: selling common stock at $50 per share or selling preferred stock with an 8.5% dividend. Assuming that the sales remain constant, we are asked to find which alternative is preferable if we take into account only the earnings per share and the leverages.

The given value of *vcpu* is assigned, the value of *fixcost* is changed to 600,000, and the value in the Input field of *totvarc* is blanked out. Let's consider the first alternative: since the $800,000 is raised by selling common stock, at $50 per share the number of shares sold is 800,000/50, so the number of outstanding common stock shares *comstock* increases by this amount. We can use the Calculator mode to add the new value to the present value in *comstock* by typing **comstock + 800000/50** in its Input field and pressing the Enter key. The new total 191,000 is displayed in the Input field. Alternately, we could invoke the Editor and type **800000/50 +** and press the Enter key. When the model is solved, we obtain the results shown in Figure 15-9*a*.

```
==================== VARIABLE SHEET =======================================...
St Input     Name     Output     Unit      Comment
-- -----     ----     ------     ----      -------
   25        price               $         price per unit
   6         vcpu                $         variable cost per unit
             totvarc  450000     $         total variable cost
   600000    fixcost             $         fixed operating cost
             be_unit  31578.947            breakeven units
   75000     unitsol                       number of units sold
             sales    1875000    $         total sales
             ebit     825000     $         earnings before int. & taxes

   40        taxrate             %         tax rate
   200000    intexp              $         interest expenses
   191000    comstoc                       outstanding common stock shares
   0         prefdiv             $         preferred dividend payments
             fixchar  200000     $         fixed charges
             netinco  375000     $         net income
             eps      1.9633508  $         earnings per share
             dol      172.72727  %         degree of operating leverage
             dfl      132        %         degree of financial leverage
             dcl      228        %         degree of combined leverage
```

a. Solution for common stock alternative

```
==================== VARIABLE SHEET =======================================...
St Input     Name     Output     Unit      Comment
-- -----     ----     ------     ----      -------
   25        price               $         price per unit
   6         vcpu                $         variable cost per unit
             totvarc  450000     $         total variable cost
   600000    fixcost             $         fixed operating cost
             be_unit  31578.947            breakeven units
   75000     unitsol                       number of units sold
             sales    1875000    $         total sales
             ebit     825000     $         earnings before int. & taxes

   40        taxrate             %         tax rate
   200000    intexp              $         interest expenses
   175000    comstoc                       outstanding common stock shares
   68000     prefdiv             $         preferred dividend payments
             fixchar  313333.33  $         fixed charges
             netinco  307000     $         net income
             eps      1.7542857  $         earnings per share
             dol      172.72727  %         degree of operating leverage
             dfl      161.23779  %         degree of financial leverage
             dcl      278.50163  %         degree of combined leverage
```

b. Solution for preferred stock alternative

Figure 15-9.
Variable Sheets (note that *eps* is higher in *a.* than in *b.*)

Let's look at the second alternative: the value of *comstock* is changed back to the original 175,000. Since a dividend of 8.5% is paid on the amount raised, the total dividend payment is 8.5%*800000; again, the Calculator mode is used to assign this value to *prefdiv*. With the cursor in its Input field, we type **8.5/100*800000** and press the Enter key. We see 68000 displayed in the Input field. Now when the Action key is pressed, the solution shown in Figure 15-9*b* is obtained.

We can see from the figure that the combined leverage *dcl* is higher for the preferred stock financing than for the common stock alternative. However, the earnings per share *eps* of the common stock alternative is higher than that of the preferred stock. Also the *eps* of the preferred stock alternative is lower than the *eps* obtained with the common stock alternative shown in Figure 15-8*b*. So the common stock alternative is preferable.

INVENTORY MANAGEMENT— ECONOMIC ORDER QUANTITY MODEL

A routinely encountered task in inventory management is that of balancing the cost of managing the inventory against the cost of placing inventory replenishment orders. The two basic questions to be answered are

1. How much to buy (or make)?
2. When to buy (or make)?

The right quantity to order is the quantity that best balances the costs incurred in placing orders against the cost of holding the inventory. When the right quantity is determined, the total cost is minimum; the resulting order quantity is called the *economic order quantity* (EOQ). Figure 15-10 gives a graphical representation of the cost relationships. The rules for the EOQ model are shown in the Rule Sheet in Figure 15-11*a*.

Example

The ABC company uses 1000 units of part #R345 per year. Each part costs $12.50 and the holding cost is $1.25 per unit per year. If the ordering cost is $5 per order, find the economic order quantity. Also if the company works 365 days per year and the lead time is 5 days, what is the reorder point?

The Variable Sheet with the given data and the solution of the problem is shown in Figure 15-11*b*. *TOC* and *THC* are the same, indicating that the solution is optimal.

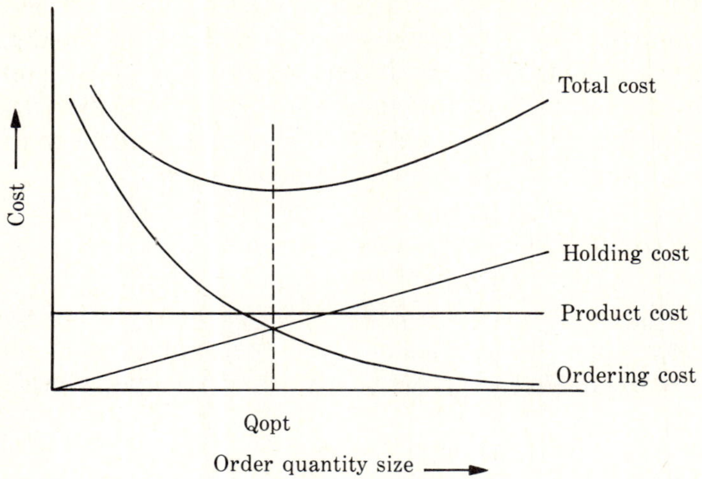

Figure 15-10.
Graphical representation of the cost relationships in inventory management

```
==================== RULE SHEET ========================================...
S Rule
- ----
* TC = TPC + THC + TOC              " total annual cost
* TPC = AD*CPU                      " annual product cost
* THC = Q/2*HC                      " annual holding cost
* TOC = AD/Q*OC                     " annual ordering cost
* Q = sqrt(2*AD*OC/HC)              " optimal order quantity
* RP = DD*L                         " reorder point
* DD = AD/WD                        " daily demand
```

a. Rule Sheet

```
==================== VARIABLE SHEET ====================================...
St Input      Name    Output      Unit     Comment
-- -----      ----    ------      ----     -------
   12.5       CPU                 $        cost per unit
   1000       AD                           annual demand
   365        WD                           working days per year
   5          OC                  $        ordering cost (per order)
   1.25       HC                  $        holding cost per unit
   5          L                   days     lead time

              Q       89.442719            calculated order quantity
              RP      13.698630            reorder point
              TC      12611.803   $        annual total cost of inventory
              TPC     12500       $        actual cost of product
              THC     55.901699   $        annual holding cost
              TOC     55.901699   $        annual ordering cost
              DD      2.7397260            daily demand
```

b. Variable Sheet with optimal order quantity evaluated

Figure 15-11.
The EOQ model

Getting an Integer Solution

Looking at the Variable Sheet in Figure 15-11*b*, we see that Q is found to be 89.442719. However, it is not possible to order fractions of a part. Assuming that the company policy is to round off the values to the nearest integer, we can add the following rules to the model:

$$Qorder = int(Q+.5)$$
$$Q = given('Qorder, Qorder, Q)$$

These rules round off the value of Q to *Qorder*, the nearest integer, and also maintain backsolvability if *Qorder* is given as input (recall in Chapter 6 the section "TK-Specific Functions"). Once the order quantity is rounded off, *THC* and *TOC* change, so *TC* also changes. We have to modify the equations involving Q by replacing Q with *Qorder* as shown in Figure 15-12*a*. A similar set of rules may be added for *RP*. The new solution is also shown in Figure 15-12*b*.

```
==================== RULE SHEET ==========================================...
S Rule
- ----
* TC = TPC + THC + TOC                   " total annual cost
* TPC = AD*CPU                           " annual product cost
* THC = Qorder/2*HC                      " annual holding cost
* TOC = AD/Qorder*OC                     " annual ordering cost
* Q = sqrt(2*AD*OC/HC)                   " optimal order quantity
* RP = DD*L                              " reorder point
* DD = AD/WD                             " daily demand

* Qorder = int(Q+.5)                     " return nearest integer value
* Q = given('Qorder,Qorder,Q)            " if Qorder is input, Q=Qorder
```

a. Rule Sheet with additional and modified rules

```
==================== VARIABLE SHEET ======================================...
St Input      Name     Output      Unit     Comment
-- -----      ----     ------      ----     -------
   12.5       CPU                  $        cost per unit
   1000       AD                            annual demand
   365        WD                            working days per year
   5          OC                   $        ordering cost (per order)
   1.25       HC                   $        holding cost per unit
   5          L                    days     lead time

              Q        89.442719            calculated order quantity
              RP       13.698630            reorder point
              TC       12611.805 $          annual total cost of inventory
              TPC      12500     $          actual cost of product
              THC      55.625    $          annual holding cost
              TOC      56.179775 $          annual ordering cost
              DD       2.7397260            daily demand

              Qorder   89                   quantity to be ordered
```

b. Variable Sheet with integer solution for order quantity *Qorder*

Figure 15-12.
Modified EOQ model

Expanding the Scope of the Model

XYZ Company, the seller of the part, offers a 2% discount on order quantities of 100 or more. If the holding cost *HC* is the same as before, is this a good offer?

The rule for calculating *Q* (the fifth rule) is not required to solve this problem. So we comment it out by typing " in front of the rule. The order quantity 100 is assigned to *Qorder*. The Calculator mode can be used to enter the discounted cost per unit. In the Input field of *CPU*, we enter **12.50*(100−2)/100**; CPU is evaluated and displayed as 12.25. (Note that a rule *NCPU=CPU*DR* could have been added for the same purpose; in that case *NCPU* would be the new cost per unit and *DR* the discount rate. The *CPU* in the second rule would have to be modified to *NCPU*.)

Figure 15-13 shows the solution. The total cost *TC* is found to be 12362.5, which is lower than the cost obtained in Figure 15-12. So it is profitable to take advantage of the 2% discount and order in quantities of 100. Note that the *THC* is higher and *TOC* is lower than in the previous solution.

Shortage Costs

The EOQ formula assumes that there is no delay in the replenishment of the inventory. However, in practice delays do occur and management

```
==================== VARIABLE SHEET ======================================...
St Input        Name       Output       Unit        Comment
-- -----        ----       ------       ----        -------
   12.25        CPU                     $           cost per unit
   1000         AD                                  annual demand
   365          WD                                  working days per year
   5            OC                      $           ordering cost (per order)
   1.25         HC                      $           holding cost per unit
   5            L                       days        lead time

                Q          100                      calculated order quantity
                RP         13.698630                reorder point
                TC         12362.5      $           annual total cost of inventory
                TPC        12250        $           actual cost of product
                THC        62.5         $           annual holding cost
                TOC        50           $           annual ordering cost
                DD         2.7397260                daily demand

   100          Qorder                              quantity to be ordered
```

Figure 15-13.
Variable Sheet with *TC* calculated taking the discount rate for bulk orders into account (note that *TC* is less than that in Figure 15-12)

has to take shortage costs into account. The optimal order quantity with shortages *Qs* is given by the following equation:

$$Qs = Q * sqrt(1+HC/SC)$$

where *SC* is the shortage cost per unit per year. When this rule is added to the Rule Sheet, *Qs* (or its nearest integer value) should be used instead of *Q* (or *Qorder*) in the rules for calculating *THC* and *TOC*. The fifth rule in Figure 15-11*a* should be reinstated. If *SC*=$19 and the other input data is as appears in Figure 15-11*b*, then *Qs* is found to be 92.34, that is, 92 parts need to be ordered instead of 89.

Continuous Process

The basic EOQ equation can be modified to include the case in which one part of a production system acts as a supplier to another part. If *DD* is the daily demand rate for an item going into a process whose production rate is *PP* units per day, then the total holding cost is given by the equation

$$THC = (PP-DD)*Q*HC/(2*PP)$$

and the EOQ formula is

$$Q = sqrt(2*AD*OC/HC * PP/(PP-DD))$$

The model can also be extended to take into account the seasonal demands for goods, inflation effects, and so on.

QUEUING PROBLEMS

Queuing or "waiting line" theory is a standard operations-management tool that is used extensively to determine optimum service facilities and work load allocations. A waiting line situation develops whenever arrivals at a service facility desire similar service (an example is the supermarket checkout counter). Waiting line theory provides a means for estimating the probable length of the waiting line, the probable waiting time, as well as other characteristics of queues. With this information, managers can answer questions such as the following: "Is it worthwhile to add one more teller in the bank?" or "How many machines should be allocated to each operator?"

Different waiting line models can be used. The selection depends on factors such as arrival pattern, service pattern, the layout of the service area, the number of stages (phases) involved, and the queue discipline. In this model, a random (Poisson distribution) arrival pattern with exponential service is considered. It is a single-channel, single-phase structure. Figure 15-14*a* shows the Rule Sheet with the rules in the model.

Example

The Getrich Bank is considering opening a drive-in window for customer service. Management estimates that customers will arrive at the rate of 15 per hour. The teller can service customers at the rate of one every

```
==================== RULE SHEET ========================================= ...
S Rule
- ----
* atime = 1/arate                              " time between arrivals
* stime = 1/srate                              " service time
* nwl = arate^2/(srate*(srate-arate))          " number in waiting line
* ns = 1/(srate/arate - 1)                     " number in system
* wtl = ns/srate                               " waiting time in line
* wts = 1/(srate-arate)                        " waiting time in system
* utiln = arate/srate                          " utilization of teller
```

a. Rule Sheet

```
==================== UNIT SHEET ==============================================
From         To          Multiply By   Add Offset
----         --          -----------   ----------
hr           min         60
1            %           100
```

b. Unit Sheet

```
==================== VARIABLE SHEET ===================================== ...
St Input     Name      Output     Unit       Comment
-- -----     ----      ------     ----       -------
   15        arate                1/hr       customer arrival rate
   3         stime                min        avg. serving time per customer
             atime     4          min        average time between arrivals
             srate     20         1/hr       serving rate

             nwl       2.25                  average number in waiting line
             ns        3                     average number in system
             wtl       9.0000000  min        average waiting time in line
             wts       12         min        average waiting time in system
             utiln     75         %          teller utilization
```

c. Variable Sheet with solution of the problem

Figure 15-14.
The Teller model

three minutes. Assuming Poisson arrivals and exponential service, find

1. The average number in the waiting line.
2. The average number in the system.
3. The average waiting time in line.
4. The average waiting time in the system.
5. The utilization of the teller (the percentage of time the teller is occupied).

The Calculation Unit for *stime* (service time), *atime* (time between arrivals), *wts* (waiting time in system), and *wtl* (waiting time in line) is hours. The necessary conversions are defined in the Unit Sheet as shown in Figure 15-14*b*. The Variable Sheet with the solution of the problem is shown in Figure 15-14*c*.

Further Analysis

Because of the limited space available and the manager's desire to provide an acceptable level of service, the bank manager would like to ensure, with 95% confidence, that not more than three cars will be in the system at any one time. What is the present level of service for the three-car limit? What level of utilization of the teller must be attained, and what must be the service rate of the teller to assure the 95% level of service?

The probability *Pn* that there are exactly *n* units in a system is

$$Pn = (1-arate/srate) * (arate/srate) \hat{\ } n$$

The present level of service for three cars or less is the probability that there are 0, 1, 2, or 3 cars in the system. Based on the formula, it follows that

$$P3 = \sum_{n=0}^{3}(1-arate/srate)*(arate/srate) \hat{\ } n$$

This can be entered in the Rule Sheet as

$$P3 = (1-arate/srate)*(1+arate/srate+(arate/srate) \hat{\ } 2 + (arate/srate) \hat{\ } 3)$$

The probability of having more than three cars in the system *Pmo3* is given by

$$Pmo3 = 1 - P3$$

Both these rules are entered in the Rule Sheet and the model is solved again. The Calculation Unit for *P3* and *Pmo3* is the decimal fraction 1,

```
=================== VARIABLE SHEET ==========================================
St Input        Name      Output      Unit        Comment
-- -----        ----      ------      ----        -------
   15           arate                 1/hr        customer arrival rate
                stime     1.8914832   min         avg. serving time per customer
                atime     4           min         average time between arrivals
                srate     31.721138   1/hr        serving rate

                nwl       .42419733               average number in waiting line
                ns        .89706814               average number in system
                wtl       1.6967893   min         average waiting time in line
                wts       3.5882725   min         average waiting time in system
                utiln     47.287080   %           teller utilization
   95           P3                    %           prob. of <= 3 cars in system
                Pmo3      5           %           prob. of >  3 cars in system
```

Figure 15-15.
Variable Sheet after Iterative Solving

while the Display Unit is percent (%); *P3* is evaluated as 68.4%, while *Pmo3*=31.6%. Thus at the present level of service, there is only 68.4% probability that there will be three or fewer cars in the system at any time.

To determine the teller utilization at a 95% probability that there are three or fewer cars in the system at any one time, we assign 95 as input to *P3* and blank out the input value of *stime*. The Iterative Solver has to be used to solve this problem because *srate* is unknown, and it occurs more than once in the rule for **P3**. A guess value of 2.5 is assigned to *stime*, the reciprocal of *srate*, and the model is solved (the value 2.5 is chosen because the new *stime* has to be lower than the previous one since the desired probability is higher). After five iterations, the solution shown in Figure 15-15 is obtained. The teller utilization is 47.29%; the serving time decreases to 1.89 minutes, and the teller serves about 32 customers per hour, which is significantly higher than the 20 obtained in Figure 15-14*c*. However, the teller is idle for about 53% of the time.

The service could be speeded up if the manager added another teller or restricted the type of transactions at the drive-in window. The model can be expanded to examine these different possibilities.

16

Case Studies: Home Applications

This chapter contains three TK!Solver case studies: determining heating costs, figuring income tax, and calculating blood alcohol concentration. These applications show the wide variety of home-related mathematical problems that can be analyzed with the help of TK!Solver. Missing from this chapter are the notorious mathematical problems dealing with mortgages and loan repayments; these models have already found their way into Chapters 2, 9, 11, and 12.

Another home application area conspicuously missing from this chapter is TK!Solver's help with homework assignments and with the study of quantitative subjects for students of all ages; however, examples of these applications are spread all over the book.

In the home, programming in BASIC, Pascal, or other languages is useful for learning more about computers, programming, and computer science. However, such programming knowledge will not significantly help a student with course work in physics, chemistry, math, engineering, and other quantitative disciplines. TK!Solver remedies this situation by providing a direct link between specialized disciplines and a personal computer and by letting the student experiment with the relationships and laws of nature using mathematical language so that concepts are not obscured by programming technicalities.

HOME ENERGY CALCULATIONS

Insulation reduces the heat loss from our homes and saves us money. The heat loss depends on the resistance to heat flow of the materials used in the construction, the area to be insulated, and the place (city) where the house is located. The resistance to heat flow of a material is given by the "R-value" which, in general, varies with the thickness of the material layer. Heating degree-days are the number of degrees the daily average temperature is below 65 degrees Fahrenheit. Obviously this varies from place to place. Once the heat loss is calculated, the amount of fuel used can be determined based on the heat content of the fuel. Then the potential savings with the addition of insulation can be estimated.

Building the Model

The user-defined function *fun1* is used to relate the annual degree-days to the place. Figure 16-1*a* shows the User Function Subsheet.

Another user-defined function *fun2* is used to relate the fuel and its heat content. The heat content is expressed in terms of Btu/unit of fuel, where the unit is gallon for oil, cubic foot for natural gas, ton for coal, and kWh for electricity. The typical values used for the definition of *fun2* are as follows:

Domain	**Range**
'oil	91000
'natl_gas	750
'electricity	3410
'coal	18750000

A third user-defined function *funR* expresses the relationship between the material type and its R-value. The R-values shown in the User Function Subsheet in Figure 16-1*b* correspond to the unit thickness of the material. The R-value is constant for the following: *'ext_airfilm, 'int_airfilm, 'bldg_paper, 'single_window, 'double_window,* and *'ext_door.* In the figure, the R-value is given for 3/4 inch of *'air_space* and is the same for higher thicknesses. For the other types of materials, the R-value is given for a thickness of one inch and varies directly as the thickness. Thus for a piece of 1/2-inch plywood, the R-value is 1.25/2=0.625. The Storage and Display Units for the R-value are ft^2*hr*oF/Btu. Note that the Calculation Unit for the variable using the R-value should be the same as the Display Unit on the User Function Subsheet. (Recall in Chapter 6 the section "User-Defined Functions.")

```
==================== USER FUNCTION: fun1 =======================...
Comment:                        Normal total heating degree-days
Domain List:                    cityname
Mapping:                        Table
Range List:                     dday
Element Domain       Range
------- ------       -----
1       'Anchorage   10864
2       'Boston      5634
3       'Chicago     6155
4       'Denver      6283
5       'Hartford    6172
6       'Houston     1396
7       'Miami       141
8       'NY_Buffalo  6875
9       'Raleigh     3393
10      'San_Franci  3015
11      'Seattle     4424
12      'Tucson      1800
```

a. fun1: place and degree days

```
==================== USER FUNCTION: funR ===========...
Comment:                        R-values of materials
Domain List:                    matlname
Mapping:                        Table
Range List:                     Rvalue
Element Domain       Range
------- ------       -----
1       'plywood     1.25
2       'gypsum      .9
3       'air_space   .91
4       'ext_airfil  .17
5       'int_airfil  .68
6       'bldg_paper  .06
7       'bevel_sidi  .81
8       'mineral_wo  3.7
9       'glass_wool  3.7
10      'blanket     3.7
11      'batts       3.7
12      'loose_fill  3.33
13      'ins_board   2.8
14      'single_win  1
15      'double_win  2
16      'ext_door    2
17      'dummy       0
```

b. funR: R-values of different materials

Figure 16-1.
User Function Subsheets

Since the actual R-value for a material layer depends on the thickness of the layer, the R-value is calculated as a product of the thickness and the R-value for unit thickness as defined in the function *funR*. This calculation is done by the third rule in the Rule Sheet in Figure 16-2. All the three variables *material, thickness,* and *Rlist* are declared as lists. The total resistance to heat flow is the sum of the R-values of each of the materials used. The built-in *sum* function is used in the fourth rule for this calculation.

```
==================== RULE SHEET =====================================...
S Rule
- ----
* degday = fun1(place)                    " number of degree days
* htcont = fun2(fuel)                     " heat content of fuel
* Rlist = thickness*funR(material)        " compute actual R-values
* Rtotal = sum('Rlist)                    " R-values: total
* htloss = 1/Rtotal*24*area*degday        " annual heat loss
* fl_used = htloss/htcont                 " fuel used per year
* $spent = fl_used*costpu                 " annual $ spent
```

Figure 16-2.
The Rule Sheet for home energy calculations

Using the Model

Let's say we live in Denver, Colorado, and would like to find out how much we can save by insulating the walls of the house. Oil is used for heating and costs $1.25 per gallon. The area of the walls under consideration is 800 ft^2 and a section of the wall consists of the following components:

Material	**Thickness**
Gypsum board	3/8″
Air space	3.5″
Plywood board	3/8″
Bevel-lapped siding	1/2″ × 8″

We need to find out how much we can save by filling the air space with mineral wool.

The problem has to be solved in two steps. In the first step, the money spent for heating without the insulation has to be calculated, and in the second step, the money spent for heating with the proposed amount of insulation needs to be determined. List Solving has to be used because this is the way to fill the list *Rlist* with the actual R-values for the different materials based on their thicknesses.

This represents a unique application of List Solving. Generally List Solving is used to solve a model repeatedly for multiple instances (values) of input variables. Since the section of the wall has different components, the R-values corresponding to each of the sections based on the thickness have to be calculated first so that the sum of these R-values can be taken to find the total resistance *Rtotal*. List Solving is used here for this purpose.

The wall has to be "built" in the List Subsheets for *material* and *thickness*. The List Subsheet for *material* is accessed and the different component names are entered. Note that *'int_airfilm* and *'ext_airfilm* are entered in the list *material* to take into account the air films on either side of the wall. As we saw in Chapter 10, the List function *sum* does not take into account the last instance evaluated during List Solving. Instead of solving again (as we did then), we can introduce a dummy element at the end of the list and solve an extra instance. The sum obtained will include the "true" last instance. So we add an element *'dummy* at the bottom of the list. Note that *'dummy* is defined in the domain of the function *funR* as shown in Figure 16-1*a*. Otherwise a "User Function: argument error" will occur. The List Subsheet for *material* is shown in Figure 16-3*a*.

The thicknesses of the different components are entered in the corresponding positions in the List Subsheet of *thickness*. Note that for *ext_airfilm* and *int_airfilm* we enter 1 because the R-value is constant; and for *air_space* we also enter 1 because the R-value is the same for any thickness equal to or above 3/4 inch. We also have to fill the last element corresponding to the dummy wall component so we enter 0. The List Subsheet for *thickness* is shown in Figure 16-3*b*.

```
==================== LIST: material ===...
Element Value
------- -----
1       'int_airfilm
2       'gypsum
3       'air_space
4       'plywood
5       'bevel_siding
6       'ext_airfilm
7       'dummy
```

a. material showing the components in the section of the wall

```
==================== LIST: thickness ===...
Element Value
------- -----
1       1
2       .375
3       1
4       .375
5       1
6       1
7       0
```

b. thickness showing the thickness of each component

Figure 16-3.
List Subsheets

The known values are assigned. We declare *material* and *thickness* as input and and initiate List Solving by typing /L!. The Variable Sheet with the solution is shown in Figure 16-4*a*. So we will spend $490.80 without insulation.

Now let's look at the situation if we do insulate. The mineral wool fibers will take the place of the air space in the present construction. We replace *'air_space* in the List Subsheet of *material* by *'mineral_wool.* Since the thickness of the proposed insulation is 3.5 inches, we change the third value in the list *thickness* to 3.5 because this value corresponds to the third element in the list *material—'mineral_wool.* The elements in the two lists

```
==================== VARIABLE SHEET ======================================...
St Input      Name     Output      Unit        Comment
-- -----      ----     ------      ----        -------
   'Denver    place                            name of city
   800        area                 ft^2        area of home being considered
   'oil       fuel                             fuel used
   1.25       costpu               $/unit      cost per unit of fuel
L  'specify   materia                          list of different materials
L  0          thickne                          thickness: each material layer

              $spent   490.79747 $             money spent per year

L             Rlist                hr*ft^2*o list with individual R-values
              degday   6283                    annual degree-days for city
              Rtotal   3.37625     hr*ft^2*o sum of R-values
              htcont   91000       Btu/unit    heat content per unit of fuel
              htloss   35730056.  Btu          annual heat loss
              fl_used  392.63797  unit         fuel used per year
```

a. Money spent without insulation

```
==================== VARIABLE SHEET ======================================...
St Input      Name     Output      Unit        Comment
-- -----      ----     ------      ----        -------
   'Denver    place                            name of city
   800        area                 ft^2        area of home being considered
   'oil       fuel                             fuel used
   1.25       costpu               $/unit      cost per unit of fuel
L  'specify   materia                          list of different materials
L  0          thickne                          thickness: each material layer

              $spent   107.48755 $             money spent per year

L             Rlist                hr*ft^2*o list with individual R-values
              degday   6283                    annual degree-days for city
              Rtotal   15.41625    hr*ft^2*o sum of R-values
              htcont   91000       Btu/unit    heat content per unit of fuel
              htloss   7825093.7  Btu          annual heat loss
              fl_used  85.990040  unit         fuel used per year
```

b. Money spent with insulation

Figure 16-4.
Variable Sheet

must correspond for us to obtain correct results. This correspondence may be checked with the Table feature.

List Solving is initiated once again. The Variable Sheet with the new solution is shown in Figure 16-4*b*. We spend less money and stand to save \$490.80−\$107.49=\$382.31 per year by insulating.

The model can be expanded to calculate the cost of insulation and the payback period on the investment.

INCOME TAX RETURN

You can use TK!Solver to build your own customized tax calculation system. It will differ in several respects from other programs and packages available for the same purpose.

First, you can take advantage of the ease of building and modifying TK!Solver models and tailor your system by using only those schedules and forms or their parts that are applicable to your situation. If the situation changes, you can easily include additional variable names and lines any place in the Variable Sheet. The same applies to the rules, which can be easily added to, removed, or modified. The models reflecting various schedules and forms may be built, filled, and played with separately and then merged. It may take only an hour or two to set up all the necessary models, during which time you are gaining a better understanding of the underlying logic of the tax system and the interconnections of various items and components.

Second, having built the model or models you become very much a master of your destiny (within the constraints of the tax law) rather than a filer of forms and reporter of facts. TK!Solver's backsolving capability and Iterative Solver features enable you to pose and answer questions such as what should a certain deduction or composition of deductions be if you are not prepared to pay more than a certain amount. TK!Solver can also keep an eye on various ratios and percentages for "sensitive" items such as charitable contributions and business expenses. TK!Solver's flexibility should enhance your insight and help you to optimize your financial planning decisions well in advance of filing your tax return.

Third, TK!Solver will not fill in the forms for you as some other programs do or claim to do. Theoretically, at least, the possibility exists that a program, let us say in BASIC, would accept information from TK!Solver and fill in the forms. Practically, unless you have an inexpensive commercially available program for this purpose, it may not be worth your spending hours of programming effort to save minutes on printing the forms instead of filling in the final version manually after the numbers have been worked out in TK!Solver. You may need hard copies of one or more draft versions, but you don't need a formatter for that; screen dumps and hard copies of sheets and tables may be easier to work with.

Here we will look at some partial models and a few model-design peculiarities. We start with Frank B. and Evelyn H. Jones' Form 1040, which is included in the booklet *Your Federal Income Tax,* IRS publication 17 (Rev. Nov. 82). The Rule Sheet is shown in Figure 16-5, and the Variable Sheet with the solution is shown in Figure 16-6. The "*tf*" in the variable names stands for form "*t*en *f*orty," and the end part of the variable name corresponds to a line number on the form.

It is simple. The only aspect worth discussing is the tax computation itself. If you want to make your model universally applicable you can use the *apply* function to select the correct Tax Rate Schedule depending on your Filing Status. The Tax Rate Schedules as user-defined functions with linear interpolation are definitely easier to input than the whole Tax Tables. Using the schedules may give a slightly different tax than using the tables (the difference is only a few dollars). This difference may be taken care of at the time of filing the final return when most of us use the Tax Tables. Alternatively, if the status is fixed and if you play within a

```
==================== RULE SHEET ==============================...
S Rule
- ----
  "Exemptions
*    tf6e = tf6a + tf6b + tf6c + tf6d
  "Income
*    tf9c = tf9a - tf9b
*    tf22 = tf7 + tf8 + tf9c + tf13 + tf17b + tf18 + tf21
*    tf31 = tf23 + tf29
*    tf32 = tf22 - tf31
  "Tax Computation
*    tf33 = tf32
*    tf35 = tf33 - tf34a
*    tf36 = 1000*tf6e
*    tf37 = tf35 - tf36
*    schedule = fun(Box)
*    tf38 = apply(schedule,tf37)
*    tf40 = tf38
*    tf49 = tf41 + tf44
*    tf50 = tf40 - tf49
*    tf59 = tf50 + tf51
  "payments
*    tf67 = tf60 + tf61 + tf66
*    tf59m67 = tf59 - tf67
*    tf68 = -min(tf59m67,0)
*    tf68 = tf69 + tf70
*    tf71 = max(tf59m67,0)
```

Figure 16-5.
Rule Sheet for Form 1040

Input	Name	Output	Comment
2	Box		Filing Status
2	tf6a		Exemptions - yourself
1	tf6b		Exemptions - spouse
2	tf6c		Number of children
2	tf6d		Number of other dependents
	tf6e	7	Total number of exemptions
20939.65	tf7		Wages, salaries, tips etc.
427.5	tf8		Interest income
562.5	tf9a		Dividends
200	tf9b		Dividends exclusion
	tf9c	362.5	Dividends income
1392	tf13		Capital gain
2075	tf17b		Taxable part of pensions
11354.85	tf18		Rents, royalties etc.
50	tf21		Other income
	tf22	36601.5	Total income
3498.44	tf23		Moving expenses
70	tf29		Deduct.for mar.couples, both working
	tf31	3568.44	Total adjustments
	tf32	33033.06	Adjusted gross income
	tf33	33033.06	Amount from tf32
2243.67	tf34a		Itemized deductions
	tf35	30789.39	Adjust. gross income minus deductions
	tf36	7000	Exemptions x $1000
	tf37	23789.39	Taxable income
	tf38	3834.3475	Taxes from Tax Table or Rate Schedule
	tf40	3834.3475	Total taxes
300	tf41		Credit for the elderly
12.5	tf44		Part. credit for polit. contributions
	tf49	312.5	Total credits
	tf50	3521.8475	Balance
564.97	tf51		Selfemployment tax
	tf59	4086.8175	Total tax
2200.8	tf60		Total Federal income tax withheld
2000	tf61		1982 estimated tax payments
27.55	tf66		Regulated Investment Company credit
	tf67	4228.35	Payments
	tf59m67	-141.5325	Total tax minus payments
	tf68	141.5325	Overpaid
	tf69	141.5325	Amount to be refunded
0	tf70		Amount to be applied to 1983 tax
	tf71	0	Amount you owe
	schedul	'yj	Tax Rate Schedule

Figure 16-6.
Variable Sheet for Form 1040 (Status and Unit fields are left out; *tf*7 through *tf*71 are in $)

fairly narrow margin of taxable income, you can use only a small part of the Tax Table as a user-defined function with Step Mapping.

The model for "Schedule A—Itemized Deductions" is shown in Figures 16-7 and 16-8. You may look at the first seven rules in Figure 16-8, which reflect the curious way of deducting on medical expenses. Also worth noting is the double *apply* function in Figure 16-8 for evaluating state sales taxes—if the different states and family sizes are to be covered. The inner *apply* selects the user-defined function name according to the state and family size. The outer one uses this name for the Table Lookup of the amount depending on income.

```
Input      Name       Output      Comment
-----      ----       ------      -------
400        A1                     Medicines and drugs
           A2         330.3286    1% of Form 1040, line 33
           A3         69.6714     Deductible medicine expenses
276        A4                     Total insurance premiums
826.86     A5a                    Doctors, dentists, nurses, hospitals
22.5       A5b                    Transportation
           A6         1195.0314   Total expenses
           A7         990.9858    3% of Form 1040, line 33
           A8         204.0456    Deductible expenses
           A9         138         Half Insurance premiums
           A10        204.0456    Medical deductions
1291.48    A11                    State and local income taxes
529.66     A12                    Real estate taxes
           A13a       325         General sales taxes
           A15        2146.14     Taxes deductions
1556.59    A16a                   Home mortgage interest
74.9       A18                    Other interest expenses
           A19        1631.49     Interest expense deductions
529.5      A20a                   Cash contributions
           A23        529.5       Contribution deductions
900        A24                    Total casualty or theft
150        A25a                   Union and professional dues
82.5       A26                    Other misc. deductions
           A27        1132.5      Losses and miscel. deductions
           A28        5643.6756   Sum of itemized deductions
           A29        3400        Reduction
           A30        2243.6756   Total itemized deductions

33032.86   tf33                   Adjusted gross income
'NY        state                  State
6          fam_siz                Family size
           income     34182.86    "Available" income
200        tf9b                   Dividends exclusion
70         tf29                   Deduction for married couples
725        B6                     ASC exclusion
155        B12                    Nontaxable distribution
2          Box                    Filing Status
```

Figure 16-7.
Variable Sheet for itemized deductions on Schedule A (Status and Unit fields are left out; most variables are in $)

```
==================== RULE SHEET ===================================...
S Rule
- ----
* A2 = .01*tf33
* A3 = max(A1-A2,0)
* A6 = A3 + A4 + A5a + A5b
* A7 = .03*tf33
* A8 = max(A6-A7,0)
* A9 = min(A4/2,150)
* A10 = max(A8,A9)
* income = tf33 + tf9b + tf29 + B6 + B12
* A13a = apply(apply(state,min(fam_size,6)),min(income,95000))
* A15 = A11 + A12 + A13a
* A19 = A16a + A18
* A23 = A20a
* A27 = A24 + A25a + A26
* A28 = A10 + A15 + A19 + A23 + A27
* A29 = rd(Box)
* A30 = A28 - A29
* tf34a = A30
```

Figure 16-8.
Rule Sheet for itemized deductions on Schedule A

As the third and last example, we examine the model for "Deduction for a married couple when both work" in Figure 16-9*a*. The size and complexity of the Rule Sheet in Figure 16-9*b* are typical of most of the remaining models. What is interesting here is the check of the contents of Form 1040 against Schedule E. This is performed automatically when the models are merged.

Input	Name	Output	Comment
20939.65	W1a		Your part of Wages etc. in tf7
0	W1b		Spouse'e part of Wages etc. in tf7
4642.5	W2a		Your other taxable income
1400	W2b		Spouse's other taxable income
	W3a	25582.15	Your total earned income
	W3b	1400	Spouse's total earned income
0	W4a		Your part of adjustments, tf24,25,26
0	W4b		Spouse's part of adjust., tf 24,25,26
	W5a	25582.15	Your qualified earned income
	W5b	1400	Spouse's qualified earned income
	W6	1400	Deduction base
	W8	70	Deduction
20939.65	tf7		Wages, salaries, tips etc.
0	tf12		Business income
6042.5	E27		Supplemental income
0	tf24		Employee business expenses
0	tf25		Payments to an IRA
0	tf26		Payments to a Keogh retirement plan

a. Variable Sheet (Status and Unit fields are left out; all variables are in $)

```
==================== RULE SHEET ==...
S Rule
- ----
* W3a = W1a + W2a
* W3b = W1b + W2b
* W5a = W3a - W4a
* W5b = W3b - W4b
* W6 = min(W5a,W5b,30000)
* W8 = .05*W6
* tf29 = W8

  "Check:
* W1a + W1b = tf7
* W2a + W2b = tf12 + E27
* W4a + W4b = tf24 + tf25 + tf26
```

b. Rule Sheet

Figure 16-9.
Deduction for a married couple when both work

HOW MUCH CAN A PERSON DRINK AND STILL DRIVE?

"Driving under the influence" concerns everyone—law enforcers, party-goers, and potential victims. There are statutes in all states prohibiting the operation of a vehicle under the influence of alcohol. The penalties for such an offense include revocation or suspension of a driver's license, fines, and imprisonment.

The measure used to determine a person's state of influence is the blood alcohol concentration (BAC) in percent (%). A person with an alcohol concentration of 0.05% or less by weight in his or her blood or breath is regarded as not being under the influence. A person with a BAC greater than 0.05% but less than 0.10% may or may not be under the influence, so other sobriety tests are required to determine that person's state. However, a person with a BAC of 0.10% or more is regarded as being under the influence. The BAC depends, among other things, on the body weight, the percentage of alcohol in the liquor, and the time elapsed after drinking. Beer contains about 4% alcohol while whiskey contains alcohol equal to half of the "proof" marked on the label. Thus, an 86 proof whiskey has 43% alcohol in it.

As liquor is being consumed, the alcohol is absorbed into the blood stream and is eliminated by the body through metabolism and direct excretion. The rate of alcohol elimination depends on an individual's constitution—0.015% for slow dissipators, 0.018% for average dissipators, and 0.02% for high dissipators. Neither drugs nor coffee affect the rate of elimination. Only time or a drastic measure such as hemodialysis will reduce the blood alcohol level.

We can build a model based on the BAC calculations to find out how much a person can drink and still be able to drive safely, or how long a person has to wait before driving back from a party, and so on. Figure 16-10*a* shows the Rule Sheet with the equations for the BAC model.

The user-defined function *drfun* relates the dissipation rate and the level of dissipation. A Table Lookup Mapping is chosen for this function whose Domain and Range values are as follows:

Domain	**Range**
'low	0.015
'average	0.018
'high	0.02

The *given* function is used in the fourth rule to check whether an input value is specified for *dr;* if so, the Table Lookup is not performed. Other-

```
==================== RULE SHEET ===============================================
S Rule
- ----
* BACb = (150/weight)*(pab/50)*bottles*size*.025    " BAC from beer
* BACw = (150/weight)*(paw/50)*shots*.025           " BAC from whiskey
* BAC = BACb+BACw                                   " total BAC
* dr = given('dr,dr,drfun(level))   " if dr is not input, do table lookup
* aBAC = BAC - dr*t                 " BAC after time t
* state = stfun(aBAC)               " state of the person after time t
```

a. Rule Sheet

```
==================== VARIABLE SHEET ===========================================
St Input     Name      Output    Unit      Comment
-- -----     ----      ------    ----      -------
   6         bottles                       number of bottles of beer
   12        size                oz        size of a beer bottle
   6         shots                         whiskey: number of 1 oz shots
   200       weight              lb        body weight
   4         pab                 %         percent of alcohol in beer
   43        paw                 %         percent of alcohol in whiskey
   5         t                   hr        hours after first drink
   'average  level                         diss level (low, average,high)

             BACb      .108      %         BAC from beer
             BACw      .09675    %         BAC from whiskey
             BAC       .20475    %         total BAC

             dr        .018      1/hr      dissipation rate
             aBAC      .11475    %         actual BAC after time t
             state     'drunk              status of person after time t
```

b. Variable Sheet with solution of a drinking problem

Figure 16-10.
The BAC model

wise it is performed provided *level* has been assigned an input value. The reason for this formulation is that if there is a separate rule

$$dr = drfun(level)$$

and if the specified value of *dr* is different from that in the function, a "User Function: argument error" will occur in this rule. The formulation in the fourth rule prevents this error.

The user-defined function *stfun* is used to return a message about the sobriety of the person based on the BAC. The function uses Step Mapping and the Domain and Range values are as follows:

Domain	**Range**
0	*'sober*
0.05	*'may_be*
0.1	*'drunk*
100	*'drunk*

The last line in the function definition specifies the upper bound. It does not mean that there will be pure alcohol in someone's veins. Its inclusion prevents a user-function argument error in the last rule when *aBAC* is greater than 0.1%.

Needless to say, the authors and the publisher disclaim any responsibility for consequences resulting from the use of any of the models in the book and the "Driving Under the Influence" model in particular.

Is It Safe to Drive?

At a party, a person weighing 200 pounds started drinking at 6 P.M. and continued drinking until 10 P.M. During the course of the evening, the person consumed six 12-ounce bottles of beer and six one-ounce shots of whiskey (86 proof). If the level of dissipation was *'average*, what was the person's BAC at 11 P.M.? Can the person drive safely?

Here *pab* (the percent of alcohol in beer) is assigned 4 as input while *paw* (the percent of alcohol in whiskey) is assigned 43 since the whiskey is 86 proof. Then *t* (the hours after the first drink) is assigned 5 since five hours have elapsed between the first drink at 6 P.M. and 11 P.M. The Variable Sheet in Figure 16-10*b* shows that the BAC at 11 P.M. (given by *aBAC*) is 0.115%. This means that the person is still drunk, as indicated by *state*, and cannot drive safely. Note that the Calculation Unit for the different variables is the same as the Display Unit.

When Does the Person Become Sober?

List Solving can be used to determine when a person becomes sober. A list of values is defined for *t* from 5 to 10 in steps of 0.5. Then *aBAC* and *state* are declared as lists and List Solving is initiated. The table-generating feature is used to produce the table shown in Figure 16-11. We

time (hr)	aBAC (%)	status
5	.11475	drunk
5.5	.10575	drunk
6	.09675	may_be
6.5	.08775	may_be
7	.07875	may_be
7.5	.06975	may_be
8	.06075	may_be
8.5	.05175	may_be
9	.04275	sober
9.5	.03375	sober
10	.02475	sober

Figure 16-11.
Table showing change in *aBAC* and status of person with time

can see that it takes nine hours from the time of the first drink (that is, at 2 A.M.) for the BAC of the person with average dissipation to come down to an acceptable level ($aBAC = 0.04275\%$).

The model can be expanded to include a variety of alcoholic beverages.

17

Case Studies: Word Problems

TK!Solver does not understand natural language. Consequently, it cannot accept and solve word problems formulated in plain English. However, TK!Solver can solve word problems if they are expressed in an algebraic form. Sometimes the algebraic reformulation is harder to work than solving the original problem by straightforward reasoning. At other times, however, the algebraic formulation is simple and TK!Solver may be used without a hitch. TK!Solver is able to accept even a sketchy formulation and work from there, or it can help a user develop a more precise one.

PAINTERS

Let's start with a classic "painting" problem.* If George can paint a room in four hours and Lenny can paint the same room in two hours, how long will it take them to paint the room together?

*This and the next two problems ("Currents and Speeds" and "Amy Lowell Goes Out to Buy Cigars") are taken, with slight modification, from the book by Sheila Tobias, *Overcoming Math Anxiety* (Boston: Houghton Mifflin, 1978).

We can see that in one hour Lenny will paint one-half of the room and George will paint one-quarter of the room. Thus, at the end of one hour of painting together, they will have covered three-quarters of the room. If three-quarters of the room is done in one hour, the remaining one-quarter will be done in an additional one-third of an hour, and the whole room will be painted in 1 1/3 hours.

In the TK!Solver model we let t be the time it takes George and Lenny to paint the room together. In t hours George paints $t/4$ of the room and Lenny paints $t/2$. The sum of $t/4$ and $t/2$ must equal one room, and so we have the rule

$$t/4 + t/2 = 1$$

The Direct Solver is helpless with this equation because t appears twice. However, if we assign t any guess value, for instance 0, the Iterative Solver immediately returns the correct answer $t = 1.333333$. We can use the Direct Solver as well if we factorize the equation so that it reads

$$t*(1/4 + 1/2) = 1$$

Generalizing the Problem

It is also possible to generalize the problem with the following equation to yield the time that either George or Lenny spends painting:

$$tG/4 + tL/2 = 1$$

where tG and tL are the times spent by George and Lenny respectively. This single equation will yield either tG or tL, provided the other one is known (for instance, if $tL=0$, that is, if George works on his own, it will indeed take him $tG=4$ hours to paint the room). If both tG and tL are unknown, we need an additional rule to find these values. If we state $tG=tL$ and make either of them a guess, we get $tG=tL=1.333333$ as before. If George spends three times as much time painting as Lenny, the second rule would be $tG=3*tL$ and the Iterative Solver would yield the solution $tG=2.4$ and $tL=0.8$.

CURRENTS AND SPEEDS

Another classic problem is that of a ship that travels directly west to Hawaii at 20 nautical miles per hour and, because of the wind, makes the return trip at 30 nautical miles per hour. We want to find its average speed.

Speed is defined as distance divided by time; if we use variable names v, d, and t for speed, distance, and time, respectively, and if we indicate the westward and eastward journeys by suffixes 1 and 2, we can define two rules, one for each of the journeys, as follows:

$$v1 = d1/t1$$
$$v2 = d2/t2$$

The average speed is equal to

$$va = (d1+d2)/(t1+t2)$$

Altogether we have three equations with seven variables, five of which are unknown (only two, $v1=20$ and $v2=30$, are given). The fact that the distance in both journeys is the same yields another equation, $d1=d2$. We are still short one equation or additional information.

The distance really doesn't matter as far as the average speed is concerned. Indeed, regardless of the value of $d1$ or $d2$ that we assign (50 miles or 5000 or anything else), the Direct Solver always returns the average speed va as 24. In fact, we don't need the distances $d1$ and $d2$ (nor the times $t1$ and $t2$) in the first place. From the first and second equations we can substitute for $t1$ and $t2$ in the third to get

$$va = \frac{d1 + d2}{d1/v1 + d2/v2}$$

Since $d1$ and $d2$ are equal, they cancel out, and we end up with the following single rule linking the speeds:

$$va = 2/(1/v1 + 1/v2)$$

When designing large and complicated models for repetitive use, it is advisable to apply whatever mathematical skills we can muster in order to simplify the model, cut out unnecessary rules and variables, and avoid, if possible, the use of the Iterative Solver. This is not so crucial when we are modeling simple word problems; here we simply put in (in the form of rules or values of input variables) all the information we have (or we think we have) and let TK!Solver solve the problem or help us sort out the inconsistencies or deficiencies in our reasoning.

AMY LOWELL GOES OUT TO BUY CIGARS

Using TK!Solver to solve word problems may be illustrated with another simple example: Amy Lowell goes out to buy cigars. She has 25 coins in her pocket worth $3.45 in all. She has seven more dimes than nickels, and she has quarters too. How many dimes, nickels, and quarters does she have?

As shown in Figure 17-1, we choose variable names *q*, *d*, and *n* to denote the quantities of quarters, dimes, and nickels; then we simply enter into the Rule Sheet, one after another, the rules reflecting the assignment. The only "vague" phrase we cannot express explicitly by a separate rule is "and she has quarters too"; actually, we take this fact into account by including quarters (but not pennies) in rules 1 and 2.

So we end up with three equations for three unknowns *q*, *n*, and *d*. Unfortunately, there is no point of departure for the Direct Solver, that is, there is no equation with one unknown variable only, so we have to resort to the Iterative Solver. Assigning *q* a guess value doesn't help because there are still two unknowns, *d* and *n*, in each of the three equations. However, assigning *d* or *n* a guess value will do the trick; another unknown can be evaluated from the third equation and the solution can propagate without trouble. The solution is shown in the Variable Sheet in Figure 17-1.

It is not hard to change the parameters of the problem—as long as the changes make sense. The original formulation quoted in Tobias' book assumed that the sum of money in Amy's pocket was equal to $7.15. Using this figure, we edit the second equation and solve again; we get $q=29.14$, $d=1.43$, and $n=-5.57$. Here the TK!Solver solution with the fractional number of coins and the negative number of nickels does not make sense.

Let's generate a whole set of feasible problems, keeping the first and the third rules as they are. Consequently, the only varying parameter

```
==================== RULE SHEET ========================================...
S Rule
- ----
  "          *** AMY LOWELL GOES OUT TO BUY CIGARS ***

  q + d + n = 25                  " She has 25 coins in her pocket
  25*q + 10*d + 5*n = 345         " $3.45 in all
  d = n + 7                       " She has seven more dimes than nickels

==================== VARIABLE SHEET ====================================...
St Input     Name     Output     Unit       Comment
-- -----     ----     ------     ----       -------
             q        8                     quarters
             d        12                    dimes
             n        5                     nickels
```

Figure 17-1.
Amy Lowell model with the solution; the standard positions of Variable Sheet and Rule Sheet are swapped

would be the sum of money in the second rule (denoted by *sum*); the rule has to be modified as follows:

$$25*q + 10*d + 5*n = sum$$

The best way to explore all the possibilities without missing any and without having to use the Iterative Solver is to make n a list and assign it a sequence of natural numbers from 0 through 25 (as many coins as were in Amy's pocket). List Solving then yields the set of values, displayed using the table-generating feature as shown in Figure 17-2. Only the solutions on the first ten lines make sense because starting from $n=10$ the number of quarters becomes negative, and starting from $n=15$ the sum of money becomes negative as well. The first ten lines represent the complete set of solutions of the problem constrained by the first and third equations.

As we noticed when trying to solve the problem for $7.15, we must not only exclude solutions with negative values, but we must also ensure that all the results are integers. If we try to force a solution for a sum of, let us say, exactly four dollars, the Iterative Solver responds with $q=11.143$, $d=10.429$, and $n=3.429$. Again this does not make sense because Amy can

Money in Amy's pocket

q	d	n	sum
18	7	0	520
16	8	1	485
14	9	2	450
12	10	3	415
10	11	4	380
8	12	5	345
6	13	6	310
4	14	7	275
2	15	8	240
0	16	9	205
-2	17	10	170
-4	18	11	135
-6	19	12	100
-8	20	13	65
-10	21	14	30
-12	22	15	-5
-14	23	16	-40
-16	24	17	-75
-18	25	18	-110
-20	26	19	-145
-22	27	20	-180
-24	28	21	-215
-26	29	22	-250
-28	30	23	-285
-30	31	24	-320
-32	32	25	-355

Figure 17-2.
Solution of the Amy Lowell model for different numbers of nickels

have only whole coins in her pocket. TK!Solver does not hesitate to return a nonsensical solution because it is not particularly well equipped to solve the so-called Diophantine equations which imply solutions in whole numbers or integers. However, TK!Solver can assist us in solving such equations if we formulate the problems thoughtfully and interpret the results. For instance, the first ten lines in Figure 17-2 may be looked upon as the complete set of whole number solutions of our three equations in four unknowns *q*, *d*, *n*, and *sum*.

DOUGHNUTS AND DOUGHNUT HOLES

Here is another classic problem that illustrates the use of TK!Solver for solving Diophantine equations and a few other things: Jack bought an equal number of doughnuts and doughnut holes (the edible ones, not the empty spaces in the center of doughnuts). He brought them to his office and was glad to find that they could be arranged in a rectangular array with all the doughnuts forming the inside array and all the doughnut holes forming the border (see Figure 17-3*a*). He was sure that he didn't need to remember the exact number because if he stepped out, his friend Jill would not be able to eat any without destroying the array and thus giving herself away in the process. Jill, however, was able to eat an equal number of doughnuts and doughnut holes and rearrange what was left so that

a. Jack's arrangement

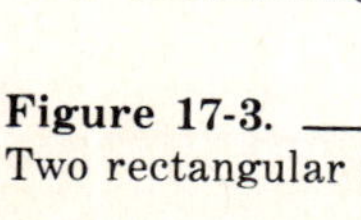

b. Jill's arrangement

Figure 17-3.
Two rectangular arrangements of equal number of doughnuts and doughnut holes

there was again a doughnut array in the middle and a doughnut hole border (see Figure 17-3*b*). How many doughnuts and doughnut holes were there originally, and how many was Jill able to eat without being found out? How many were left?

A TK!Solver model in Figure 17-4 shows the expressions for the numbers of doughnuts and doughnut holes expressed in terms of the size of the doughnut array and also the condition that the numbers of doughnuts and of doughnut holes are equal. There are three equations, four unknowns, and a tacit and obvious condition that all the resulting values be whole numbers. Without this constraining condition, an infinite number of sets of values of the four unknowns would fit the three equations, but only a few of these will come out as integer numbers. In order to find out which ones, we can create a list of assumed values for *rows* and let TK!Solver solve the three equations for the remaining three unknowns (*columns*, *doughnuts*, and *doughnut holes*); then we can select those solutions that come out as integers.

We should decide what number of rows to try. It should not be less than three. We can easily see that for two rows of doughnuts, regardless of the number of doughnut columns, we will always need a larger number of encircling doughnut holes. We can say that 3 is the lower bound for the number of rows. We will see later that the upper bound, that is, the maximum number of rows to be examined, can be estimated as well. At this point, we could try to go up to 15. However, there is another problem: the Direct Solver cannot solve our three equations for the unknown variables

```
==================== VARIABLE SHEET ==========================================
St Input      Name     Output     Unit        Comment
-- -----      ----     ------     ----        -------
   4          rows                            # of rows in doughnut array
              columns 6                       # of columns in doughnut array
              dough    24                     # of doughnuts
              dholes   24                     # of doughnut holes

==================== RULE SHEET ==============================================
S Rule
- ----
  "    ***   D O U G H N U T S   &   D O U G H N U T   H O L E S    ***
  "The doughnuts form a rectangular matrix:
        dough = rows*columns
  "The doughnut holes form a border, i.e. their number equals
  "the perimeter of doughnut matrix plus four in the corners:
        dholes = 2*(rows + columns) + 4
  "The number of doughnuts and doughnut holes is the same:
        dough = dholes
```

Figure 17-4.
Doughnuts and Doughnut Holes model. The solution applies to Jill's arrangement in Figure 17-3*b*.

columns, dough, and *dholes,* so we have to guess, let us say, *columns* and let TK!Solver iterate. An input value for *rows* will turn the rules into a set of three simultaneous linear equations. Consequently, it should be okay to fill the list of guesses for *columns* with zeros.

We declare all the variables as lists, make *rows* the input and *columns* the guess, enter the values as stated, and List Solve by typing **/L!**. The results displayed in tabular form look as follows:

rows	columns	dough	dholes
3	10	30	30
4	6	24	24
5	4.666666667	23.33333333	23.33333333
6	4	24	24
7	3.6	25.2	25.2
8	3.333333333	26.66666667	26.66666667
9	3.142857143	28.28571429	28.28571429
10	3	30	30
11	2.888888889	31.77777778	31.77777778
12	2.8	33.6	33.6
13	2.727272727	35.45454545	35.45454545
14	2.666666667	37.33333333	37.33333333
15	2.615384615	39.23076923	39.23076923

We can easily see that the first two instances represent integer solutions and thus the solution to our problem: Jack bought 30 doughnuts and 30 doughnut holes; he arranged them as shown in Figure 17-3*a*. Jill ate 6 of each and rearranged the rest as shown in Figure 17-3*b*.

The table also reveals solutions for the number of rows equal to 6 and 10 that are equivalent to the solutions in the second and first lines of the table respectively. It is obvious that if 3 rows and 10 columns satisfy the conditions, so do 10 rows and 3 columns (the same applies to the numbers 4 and 6). The first instance (3 rows and 10 columns) represents the minimum number of rows (our lower bound) and maximum number of columns. Because of the interchangeability of rows and columns, the maximum number of columns also represents the maximum number of rows in any integer solution. This number (10 in our case) could have been used as an upper bound for the rows in the list, saving us and TK!Solver the trouble of examining the cases with 11 through 15 rows (or more—we really were not sure how far to go in order not to miss any integer solution). If we went only from *rows*=3 through *rows*=10, we still would have covered all the integer solutions.

We could have saved even more time if we had taken full advantage of the fact that for every solution with fewer rows than columns there is an equivalent solution with as many columns and rows. The great divide between the group of "lying" and "standing" arrays is the point when *rows*= *columns*. We enter this condition as an additional rule, remove *rows* from input, define *columns* as guess, solve again, and get *rows*=*columns*= −0.828 and *dough*=*dholes*=0.686. With the value of *rows* unknown, the Iterative Solver had to deal with a quadratic equation, and from the guess *columns*=0, it converged to a wrong root. If the guess is 2 or higher, the iteration yields *rows*=*columns*=4.828. Since this is a non-integer, it does not belong to the class of feasible solutions. To find the largest candidate, we round this number down to 4, which is the true upper bound of our search space. Consequently, even if we had not gone beyond *rows*=4 in our search, we would still have examined all the cases necessary to find all the integer solutions. Incidentally, both instances of this reduced search space, *rows*=3 and *rows*=4, yield integer solutions.

Doubleframing the Doughnuts

What about keeping the number of doughnuts equal to the number of doughnut holes but having the array of doughnuts "doubleframed" by the doughnut holes, as shown in Figure 17-5? The second rule in Figure 17-4 has to be modified as follows to take into account pairs of rows and columns of doughnut holes around the doughnuts and the four quadruplets of doughnut holes in the corners:

$$dholes = 4*(rows + columns) + 16$$

The lower bound of the number of rows to be examined for integrality is 2∗2+1=5. The upper bound, found when *rows*=*columns*, is 9.657 rounded

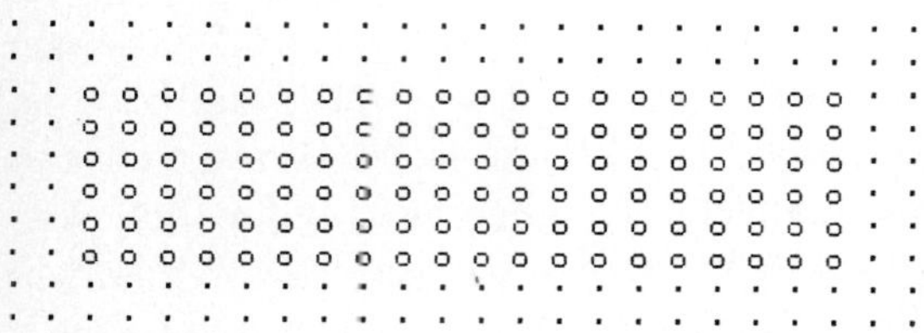

Figure 17-5.
Rectangular arrangement of equal number of doughnuts and doughnut holes with the former "doubleframed" by the latter

down to 9. List Solving for *rows*=5 through 9 yields the following results in table format (the column with the numbers of doughnut holes is omitted because these numbers are obviously equal to the numbers of doughnuts):

rows	**columns**	**dough**
5	36	180
6	20	120
7	14.66666667	102.6666667
8	12	96
9	10.4	93.6

Excluding the non-integer solutions, we see that there are six different arrangements, three of which are shown here and three others which may be obtained by interchanging *rows* and *columns*. We can go further and expand our investigation to cover situations with 3, 4, 5, or any number of rows and columns of doughnut holes surrounding arrays of doughnuts.

Getting More Serious

Up until now our casual approach was good enough to yield quick solutions to these puzzles. More involved problems, however, require closer attention to the model design and efficiency of the solution process.

We denote twice the thickness of the doughnut hole frame by n and express the equality of doughnuts and doughnut holes by equating the right-hand sides of the first and second equations from the original model in Figure 17-4 as follows:

$$r*c = n*(r+c) + n\text{^}2$$

(Here r and c denote number of rows and columns respectively.) We rewrite this equation so that c appears only once, as follows:

$$c*(r-n) = n*(r+n)$$

Thanks to this modification, we will not need to use the Iterative Solver when calculating number of columns c and number of doughnuts or doughnut holes $m=r*c$ for any given values of n and r. We also include the rules $r=n+1$ and $r=c$, applicable, respectively, when looking for the lower and upper bound values of r (we still will have to use the Iterative Solver for this purpose). When not in use, these rules have to be commented out. This new model is shown in Figure 17-6; the displayed solution applies to the arrangement in Figure 17-5.

Playing with the model reveals that for 3, 4, 5, and 6 rows (or columns)

```
=================== VARIABLE SHEET ======================================
St Input      Name     Output     Unit        Comment
-- -----      ----     ------     ----        -------
              m        120                    # of doughnuts or doughnut holes
   4          n                               twice the frame thickness
   6          r                               rows of doughnuts
              c        20                     columns of doughnuts
```

```
=================== RULE SHEET =======================================...
S Rule
- ----
  "        *** Doughnuts & doughnut holes: serious model ***

  c*(r-n) = n*(r+n)     "equality of doughnuts and doughnut holes
  m = c*r               "number of doughnuts or doughnut holes

  "r = n + 1            " lower bound
  "r = c                " upper bound
```

Figure 17-6.
Generalized Doughnuts and Doughnut Holes model

surrounding the arrays of the doughnuts, there are 12, 8, 12, and 18 ways respectively to arrange them. The number of doughnuts and doughnut holes increases rapidly with increasing thickness of the frame. For a 50-fold frame there are 32 possible arrangements ranging from 225×260 (or 260×225) with 58,500 dots and circles to 101×20,100 (or 20,100×101) with 2,030,100 dots and circles (it does not make sense to refer to doughnuts and doughnut holes any more).

It was interesting to find out how far one could go with TK!Solver. The largest integer number available is 999,999,999,999. From previous experience it was known that the lower bound r yields a solution with the highest aspect ratio of the array (that is, the least square-like array) and with the highest number of dots and circles. Therefore, the lower bound rule was activated, 999,999,999,999 was assigned to m, a guess value of $r=10000$ was assigned, and the model was solved for unknown n. The result was $n=7936.5053$, which was not good because the value of n had to be an integer. So it was rounded down to 7936, which is equivalent to 7936/2=3968 rows or columns of dots surrounding a rectangular array of the same number of circles. Then $r=7936$ was assigned as input, c was removed from input, the equation for lower bound was brought in, and the model was solved again. It was found that the lower bound $r=7937$, the maximum number of dots and circles that can be handled by TK!Solver; $m=999,809,031,936$; and the related number of columns $c=125,968,128$ (see Figure 17-7).

The next step was to find the upper bound of the range of r to be examined for feasible integer solutions. The lower bound equation was com-

```
==================== VARIABLE SHEET ======================================
St Input      Name    Output     Unit      Comment
-- -----      ----    ------     ----      -------
              m       9.9981E11            # of doughnuts or doughnut holes
   7936       n                            twice the frame thickness
              r       7937                 rows of doughnuts
              c       125968128            columns of doughnuts

==================== RULE SHEET ==========================================...
S Rule
- ----
  "        *** Doughnuts & doughnut holes: serious model ***

  c*(r-n) = n*(r+n)     "equality of doughnuts and doughnut holes
  m = c*r               "number of doughnuts or doughnut holes

  r = n + 1             " lower bound
  "r = c                " upper bound
```

Figure 17-7.
Generalized Doughnuts and Doughnut Holes model with lower bound number of doughnut rows for the maximum number of doughnuts or doughnut holes which can be handled by TK!Solver

mented out, the one for upper bound was brought in, $r=7937$ was assigned as a guess value, the model solved, and the solution in Figure 17-8 obtained. The true upper bound value of r is the rounded-down integer $r=19{,}159$. Instead of using TK!Solver as we did before to examine all solutions between $r=7937$ and $r=19159$ for integer solutions, we can take advantage of the grasp of the problem acquired during this exercise and

```
==================== VARIABLE SHEET ======================================
St Input      Name    Output     Unit      Comment
-- -----      ----    ------     ----      -------
              m       367074900            # of doughnuts or doughnut holes
   7936       n                            twice the frame thickness
              r       19159.199            rows of doughnuts
              c       19159.199            columns of doughnuts

==================== RULE SHEET ==========================================...
S Rule
- ----
  "        *** Doughnuts & doughnut holes: serious model ***

  c*(r-n) = n*(r+n)     "equality of doughnuts and doughnut holes
  m = c*r               "number of doughnuts or doughnut holes

  "r = n + 1            " lower bound
  r = c                 " upper bound
```

Figure 17-8.
Generalized Doughnuts and Doughnut Holes model with upper bound number of doughnut rows for $n=7936$

write the following simple dedicated BASIC program for this examination:

```
10 DEFDBL C,M,N:N=7936
20 FOR R=7937 TO 19159
30 C=N*(R+N)/(R-N)
40 IF C=INT(C) THEN M=R*C:PRINT R,C,M
50 NEXT R:END
```

(DEFDBL declares 17 digits double-precision in IBM PC BASIC; the program may become more complicated if written in a BASIC without the double-precision feature.)

Incidentally, there are only 27 integer solutions out of the range of 19,159−7,937+1=11,223 values of r. In other words, there are 27 ways of arranging an array of circles surrounded by 3968 rows and columns of an equal number of dots. The most square-like arrangement (that is, the arrangement with the largest of the smaller sides of the arrays) was detected at $r=16{,}128$. The corresponding $c=23{,}312$, and the number of dots or circles $m=375{,}975{,}936$.

MONKEY AND BANANA

The following problem comes from Jim Fixx's *Games for the Super-Intelligent* (Doubleday: Garden City, NY, 1972): A rope lying over the top of a fence is the same length on one side of the fence as it is on the other. It weighs one third of a pound per foot. On one end hangs a monkey holding a banana, and on the other end a weight equal to the weight of the monkey. The banana weighs two ounces per inch. The rope is as long (in feet) as the age of the monkey (in years), and the weight of the monkey (in ounces) is the same as the age of the monkey's mother. The combined age of the monkey and its mother is thirty years. One half of the weight of the monkey, plus the weight of the banana, is one fourth as much as the weight of the weight and the weight of the rope. The monkey's mother is half as old as the monkey will be when it is three times as old as its mother was when she was half as old as the monkey will be when it is as old as its mother will be when she is four times as old as the monkey was when it was twice as old as its mother was when she was one third as old as the monkey was when it was as old as its mother was when she was three times as old as the monkey was when it was one fourth as old as it is now. How long is the banana?

The problem looks somewhat more complicated than the one about Amy Lowell's money. Yet a human aided by TK!Solver, without either of

```
=================== VARIABLE SHEET ===========================...
St Input       Name    Output     Unit       Comment
-- -----       ----    ------     ----       -------
   .33333333   rld                lb/ft      rope linear density
               ww      18         oz         weight of weight
               mw      18         oz         weight of monkey
   2           bld                oz/in      banana linear density
               rl      12         ft         rope length
               ma      12         year       monkey's  age
               Ma      18         year       monkey's mother's age
               bw      11.5       oz         banana weight
               rw      64         oz         rope weight
               ma1     36         year
               Ma2     12         year
               ma3     24         year
               Ma4     24         year
               ma5     6          year
               Ma6     3          year
               ma7     9          year
               Ma8     9          year
               ma9     3          year
               bl      5.75       in         banana length
```

Figure 17-9.
Variable Sheet for Monkey and Banana model with the solution

them being super-intelligent, may successfully attack this problem along a similar route: by meticulously registering every bit of information contained in the problem-formulation and making out of it either a rule or an input value for some variable. The variables may be introduced along the way and named according to the following convention:

Prefix		**Suffix**	
b-	banana	*-a*	age
m-	monkey	*-l*	length
M-	mother monkey	*-w*	weight
w-	weight	*-ld*	linear density
r-	rope		

(The concept of linear density—see the last suffix—is borrowed from the field of textile science; it defines the ratio of the weight to the length of linear bodies. This concept naturally applies to the rope and it also may be used with the banana.)

The first entry will go into the Variable Sheet (Figure 17-9) as the input value for rope linear density $rld=1/3$ lb/ft. The next useful piece of information is the equality of the weights of the weight ww and the monkey mw—hence the first rule (see Figure 17-10). The next is the input value for the banana linear density $bld=2$ oz/in. Then the equalities of the rope length to the monkey age and the monkey weight to its mother's age are reflected in the second and third rules respectively. The combined

```
==================== RULE SHEET ==============================================
S Rule
- ----
* ww = mw           " the weight of the weight is equal to the weight of the monkey
* rl = ma           " the rope is as long in ft as the age of the monkey in years
* mw = Ma           " the weight of the monkey is the same as the age of its mother
* ma + Ma = 30       " the combined ages of the monkey and its mother are thirty
* mw/2 + bw = (ww + rw)/4  " one half the weight of the monkey plus the weight
                           " of the banana is one fourth as much as the weight
                           " of the weight and the weight of the rope
* Ma = ma1/2         " monkey's mother is half as old as the monkey will be
* ma1 = 3*Ma2        " when it is three times old as its mother
* Ma2 = ma3/2        " when she was half as old as the monkey will be
* ma3 = Ma4          " when it is as old as its mother will be
* Ma4 = 4*ma5        " when she is four times as old as the monkey was
* ma5 = 2*Ma6        " when it was twice as old as its mother was
* Ma6 = ma7/3        " when she was one third as old as the monkey was
* ma7 = Ma8          " when it was as old as its mother was
* Ma8 = 3*ma9        " when she was three times as old as the monkey was
* ma9 = ma/4         " when it was one fourth as old as it is now
* bw = bld*bl        " definition of banana linear density
* rw = rld*rl        " definition of rope linear density
```

Figure 17-10.
Rule Sheet for Monkey and Banana model

ages of the monkeys goes into rule 4. The fifth rule is more elaborate, but again, it just follows the wording of the problem (note the explanatory comments next to each rule in Figure 17-10). The next ten rules are simple; the tricky part is to build them following the hundred-word long sentence in the problem formulation. We build them up in a domino-like fashion using nine additional auxiliary variables denoted by suffixes 1 through 9.

At this point 15 rules have been generated (from $ww=mw$ through $ma9=ma/4$) with 18 variables (*rld* through *ma9*), two of which are given. But the banana length *bl* (the quantity for which the problem is supposed to be solved) has not yet appeared in the Variable Sheet in Figure 17-9; this variable must be added to the Variable Sheet, meaning that the number of unknown variables exceeds the number of rules by two, and we have to look for two more rules. A clue: the given linear densities *bld* and *rld* have not yet appeared in any of the rules. An obvious remedy is to add the definitions of *bld* and *rld* to the Rule Sheet (see the last two rules in Figure 17-10). Now we have the correct number—17 rules or equations in 17 unknowns.

An attempt to use the Direct Solver leads nowhere, indicating the presence of a set of simultaneous equations, and linear ones for that matter, because none of the variables appears in a non-linear term in any of the equations. Strictly speaking, the last two equations are non-linear, but the known *bld* and *rld* reduce them to linear ones for our purposes.

The most natural approach is to make the variable we are solving for, the banana length *bl*, the guess and to use the Iterative Solver. We assign a guess value of 6 inches (which, by the way, is almost everybody's first guess after listening to the problem). TK!Solver responds with nothing but *bw*=12, which was evaluated by solving the second to the last equation (since *bld* is given and *bl* is guessed).

Without analyzing the problem further, the next obvious step would be

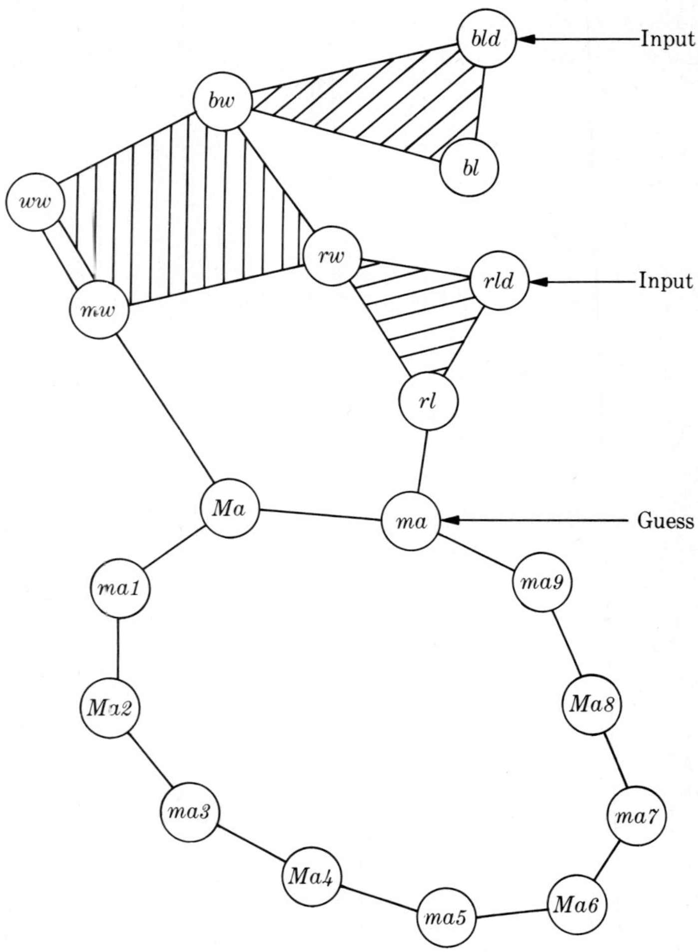

Figure 17-11.
R-graph for Monkey and Banana model

to try adding one more guess and solving again. Assigning almost any guess value to any other variable would work and yield the solution shown in Figure 17-9. A look at the R-graph in Figure 17-11 shows why. The only set of simultaneous equations we need be concerned with is represented by the *ma*'s and *Ma*'s ring. We may "break" it by assigning a guess value to any variable except *bw* and *bl*. This means that we don't need *bl* as a guess and that any other single guess value (for instance $ma=0$) will trigger the solution of the problem.

This analysis also shows how this and other weird-looking word problems are set up. In fact, all the nine auxiliary *ma* and *Ma* variables may be eliminated and the ten "ring" equations reduced to one, $3*ma=2*Ma$. This and the $ma+Ma=30$ equation solved together yield $ma=12$ and $Ma=18$. From here solving for *bl* is a matter of a simple substitution, which can be handled by the Direct Solver.

Index